ENNIS AND NANCY HAM LIBRARY
ROCHESTER COLLEGE
800 WEST AVON ROAD
ROCHESTER HILLS, MI 48307

Suburban Sprawl

MAXINE GOODMAN LEVIN
COLLEGE OF URBAN AFFAIRS

Cleveland State University

Cities and Contemporary Society

Series Editors: Richard D. Bingham and Larry C. Ledebur,
Cleveland State University

Sponsored by
The Urban Center, Levin College of Urban Affairs
Cleveland State University

This new series focuses on key topics and emerging trends in urban policy. Each volume is specially prepared for academic use, as well as for specialists in the field. The next title in the series is an edited volume by Dennis R. Judd, *The Infrastructure of Play: Building the Tourist City in North America*, a work about how tourism has transformed North American cities and the role of tourism in urban planning.

Suburban Sprawl

Private Decisions and Public Policy

Wim Wiewel and Joseph J. Persky
editors

CITIES AND
CONTEMPORARY
SOCIETY

M.E. Sharpe
Armonk, New York
London, England

Copyright © 2002 by M. E. Sharpe, Inc.

All rights reserved. No part of this book may be reproduced in any form
without written permission from the publisher, M. E. Sharpe, Inc.,
80 Business Park Drive, Armonk, New York 10504.

Library of Congress Cataloging-in-Publication Data

Suburban sprawl : private decisions and public policy / edited by Wim Wiewel and
Joseph J. Persky.
   p. cm. — (Cities and contemporary society)
   Includes bibliographical references and index.
   ISBN 0-7656-0967-3 (cloth: alk. paper) — ISBN 0-7656-0968-1 (paper: alk. paper)
   1. Suburbs—Illinois—Chicago Metropolitan Area. 2. Population density—Illinois—
Chicago Metropolitan Area. I. Wiewel, Wim. II. Persky, Joseph. III. Series.

HT352.U62 C47 2002
307.74'09773'11—dc21   2002066975

Printed in the United States of America

The paper used in this publication meets the minimum requirements of
American National Standard for Information Sciences
Permanence of Paper for Printed Library Materials,
ANSI Z 39.48-1984.

BM (c) 10 9 8 7 6 5 4 3 2 1
BM (p) 10 9 8 7 6 5 4 3 2 1

Contents

List of Tables, Figures, and Maps	vii
Acknowledgments	xi
Introduction	
Joseph J. Persky and Wim Wiewel	xiii

1. Public Works and Land Use: The Importance of Public Infrastructure in Chicago's Metropolitan Development, 1830–1970
   Bonnie Lindstrom   3

2. Urban Land Cover Change in Northeastern Illinois: A Landsat View from 1972 to 1997
   Y.Q. Wang   25

3. Property Taxes, Schools, and Sprawl
   Richard F. Dye and Therese J. McGuire   42

4. Land Use Planning Tools in Illinois: Preventing or Promoting Sprawl?
   Jean M. Templeton   62

5. Transportation in the Chicago Metropolitan Region Since 1970
   Joseph DiJohn   88

6. Commercial Motor Carrier Operations in the Northeast Illinois Region: Impacts on Land Use Trends Since 1970
   Piyushimita Thakuriah   115

7. The Role of Regional Planning Agencies in Suburban
   Deconcentration
   Bonnie Lindstrom   135

8. Housing Policy and Urban Sprawl in the Chicago
   Metropolitan Region
   Charles J. Orlebeke   157

9. Employment Subcenters and Subsequent Real Estate
   Development in Suburban Chicago
   John F. McDonald and Daniel P. McMillen   182

10. High Technology Employment Concentration and
    Urban Sprawl in the Chicago Metropolitan Area
    Daniel Felsenstein   207

11. The Impact of Federal and State Expenditures on
    Residential Land Absorption: A Quantitative Case
    Study—Chicago
    Joseph J. Persky, Haydar Kurban, and Thomas W. Lester   228

12. New Federal and State Policies for Metropolitan Equity
    Wim Wiewel and Kimberly Schaffer   256

About the Authors   309

Index   311

List of Tables and Figures

Tables

2.1	Land Cover Change in Metropolitan Chicago Region Between 1972 and 1997	30
2.2	Urban Land Cover Change Between 1985 and 1997 in Northeastern Illinois Counties	31
2.3	Urban Land Cover Change by Distance from Downtown Chicago	33
2.4	Selected Municipalities That Changed the Most in Area Between 1980 and 1990	38
2.5	Selected Municipalities That Changed the Most in Area Between 1990 and 1997	39
2.6	Selected Municipalities That Changed the Most in Area Between 1980 and 1997	40
3.1	Variables Used in the Analysis	46
3.2	Regression Results for Three Measures of "Sprawl"	50
3.3	Variable Values for Selected Metropolitan Areas	52
5.1	Regional Transportation Authority Annual Ridership	96
5.2	Six-County Employment and Population Decentralization Between 1970 and 1990	98
5.3	Completion Dates of Major Chicago-Area Expressways	100
5.4	Population Densities and per Capita GDPs of Selected Urban Clusters	102
5.5	Year of Maximum Population with Different Hypothetical City Limits	103
5.6	Percentage Change in Vehicle Registrations and Vehicle Miles Traveled	104

5.7	Percentage Change in Vehicle Miles Traveled and Highway Lane Miles, 1985–1995	105
5.8	Number of Lane Miles per Four Measures of Traffic Generation	107
5.9	Chicago-Area Automobile Work-Trip Lengths, 1970 and 1990	107
5.10	Chicago-Area Automobile Work-Trip Durations, 1970 and 1990	108
5.11	Complexity of Trips in DuPage County, 1970 and 1990	109
6.1	Six-County Employment Decentralization Trends and Trends in Trucking and Courier Firms Between 1970 and 1990	118
6.2	Number of Trucking and Courier Establishments in the Six Counties from 1970 to 1996 and the Percentage Change in the Number of Large Establishments	126
6.3	Average Number of Trucks and Number of Drivers Employed with Commercial Driver's License (CDL) in Companies Located in the Counties in Northeast Illinois	127
6.4	Differences in Distances Traveled by Trucks Between 1970 and 1986	129
9.1	Suburban Developments	186
9.2	Average Effective Property Tax Rates in 1988	189
9.3	Industrial Development	192
9.4	Commercial Development	194
9.5	Residential Development	198
10.1	High Technology Indicators for Metropolitan Areas	211
10.2	Estimated Employment Effects (Direct and Indirect): I-88 and I-94 High Technology Agglomeration	217
10.3	Distribution of Workers by Place of Residence and Income Group	218
10.4	Estimates of Residential and Nonresidential Land Consumption in the Outer Suburbs	220
10.5	Summary of Sprawl Effects of I-88 and I-94 Agglomerations Versus Two Alternative Scenarios	222
11.1	Population and Area by Ring, 1990	234
11.2	Change in Area by Ring, 1970–1990	235
11.3	Federal Program Groupings	236
11.4	Average Annual per Capita Federal Expenditures, 1989–1996	238

11.5	Average Annual per Capita Spatially Related Programs—Cost Reducing, 1989–1996	239
11.6	Per Capita State Expenditures by Geography, 1989–1996	244
11.7	Per Capita Spatially Related State Expenditures by Geography, 1989–1996	246
12.1	Explanations of Policy Recommendation Evaluations	293

Figures

1.1	Growth of Chicago by Annexations to 1899	8
1.2	Northeastern Illinois Expressways	18
2.1	Land Cover Change of Metropolitan Chicago Region Between 1972 and 1997 Derived by Classification of Landsat Remote Sensing Data	33
2.2	County Index and Distance Zones from Downtown Chicago	34
2.3	Urban Land Cover Change in a Subset Area of Naperville, West Suburb of Chicago	35
2.4	Urban Land Cover Change of a Subset Area of I-355 Corridor in West Suburb of Chicago	36
3.1	Aggregate Effective Property Tax Rates with Respect to Equalized Assessed Value. Municipalities in the Chicago Metropolitan Area, 1996	56
5.1	Lane Miles per 1,000 Population in McHenry County, 1983–1995	106
6.1	Wage per Unit of Population in the Six Counties in Northeast Illinois from 1983 to 1995	120
6.2	Road Capacity Relative to Population, Number of Employed Persons, Number of Vehicles Registered, and Wages Earned in Six Counties in Northeast Illinois: Trends from 1983 to 1995	121
6.3	Major Contributors to Percentage Increase in VMT in the Chicago Area from 1973 to 1993	123
7.1	*2020 RTP* Highway and Transit Projects	143
9.1	Post-1990 Commercial Development	191
9.2	Post-1990 Industrial Development	195
9.3	Post-1990 Residential Development	197
10.1	Analytic Framework for Estimating the Suburban Sprawl Impacts Arising from High Technology Employment Agglomeration	214

Acknowledgments

The Brookings Institution's Center for Urban and Metropolitan Policy took the initiative for a nationwide set of case studies, of which this book represents the Chicago case. We thank Bruce Katz for his leadership role. We also thank Amy Liu for her consistent support and Janet Pack for her substantive comments. Researchers from other cities in the project also offered helpful insights. The John D. and Catherine T. MacArthur Foundation provided major funding; we are particularly grateful to Rebecca Riley, who has single-handedly done more to promote attention to these issues in Chicago than anyone else. At the University of Illinois at Chicago, the Great Cities Institute housed the project; David Perry, Lauri Alpern, and Denita Johnson all helped. All of the authors of the various chapters contributed ideas and comments on the work each of us was doing; thus, while the chapters have individual authors, they also represent a significant amount of collective work. Tingwei Zhang, whose project report was published elsewhere, provided invaluable assistance on Geographic Information Systems (GIS). Robert Bruegman continually challenged our assumptions and biases in a productive and collegial way; the result is better for his input.

The project's advisory committee similarly helped us stay on course; we thank Jerry Adelman, Rita Athas, Mary Sue Barrett, Scott Bernstein, Larry Christmas, Joanne Eckman, Jim Ford, Scott Goldstein, Jacques Gordon, Julie Hamos, Jesse Jackson Jr., Elmer Johnson, Rob Krebs, Howard Learner, Lynn Montei, Barack Obama, Aurie Pennick, Phil Peters, George Ranney, Rebecca Riley, Bill Syversen, and William Testa for their contributions. Doug Timmer and Kristen Kepnick each provided important assistance. Finally, in addition to being a coauthor on one of the chapters, Kimberly Schaffer played an invaluable role in keeping the entire project on track.

JOSEPH J. PERSKY AND WIM WIEWEL

Introduction

Sprawl, or metropolitan deconcentration, has characterized Chicago's development virtually from the earliest days of the city's existence. While the term "sprawl" has only become popular in recent years, people and firms have long been moving out of the city to greener pastures (or cornfields) in search of more space, a healthier environment, or to get away from undesirable aspects of urban life. Indeed, the rate at which the urban land area expanded compared to the increase in population was probably greater in the 1920s than at any time before or since. Much of the public concern with sprawl seems to be with growth in general, not just with land consumption that is high relative to population growth. But growth does not automatically equal sprawl, or the antisprawl movement would simply be a no-growth movement. While we do not attempt here to define sprawl definitively or quantitatively, we use the term in this paper to describe the deconcentration of the urban region. That deconcentration could be characterized by a decrease in population density or by an increase in land consumption at a rate faster than population growth or both. Other identifying regional characteristics associated with deconcentration include large-scale separation of land uses, fragmented units of local government, and the decline of the central city in relative importance to the region as a whole.

The purpose of this book is to examine this process of sprawl, especially in the last thirty years, and in particular to answer the question: What has been the role in this process of federal and state programs and policies? Have they had a clear causal role? Or have they critically aided and abetted a largely market-driven historical trend? Or have they mostly been minor components of a long-standing process of urban growth?

Discussions of sprawl in Chicago usually start with the statement that from 1970 to 1990 the amount of urbanized land grew by 46 percent, while the population increased by only 4 percent. As we shall see later, the precise meaning of this fact is subject to considerable debate. Nevertheless, it sets the stage for a daunting array of facts about urban growth in Chicago:

- In 1950 the city of Chicago had 3.6 million people and 70 percent of the region's population. By 2000 even though the six-county region as a whole had gained more than 3 million people, the city's population had dropped to 2.8 million. Its share of the regional population had fallen to 36 percent.
- Jobs have decentralized as well. In 1972 the city of Chicago had 56 percent of the region's private employment. By 1995 it had only 34 percent.
- The amount of urbanized land has increased faster than the number of households. From 1970 to 1990 the region's population increased by 4 percent, and the number of households grew by 22 percent, while the amount of urbanized land used for housing increased by 46 percent (Metropolitan Planning Council 1995).
- While regionally the trend is still toward suburbanization, the city of Chicago increased in population between 1998 and 2000. Although modest, the gain is the first upswing in fifty years. Likewise, the city has gained a few thousand jobs each year for the past five years (Illinois Department of Employment Security 1999). However, in the next twenty years, the region as a whole is expected to gain far more residents than has been the case recently, virtually ensuring continued dramatic increase in growth of the urbanized land area.

Metropolitan deconcentration is about more than just land consumption, however. The suburbanization of the Chicago region can be further identified in terms of race and class—basically, the shifting of wealth and white households from the city and older suburbs to the newer, outer suburbs.

- In 2000 an estimated 43 percent of the Cook County population was black or Latino, as compared to between 4 percent and 24 percent in each of the five collar counties (Northeastern Illinois Planning Commission 1999).
- In 1970 the median income of city residents was 86 percent of the

region's median. By 1990 median income in the city had fallen to 74 percent of the region's median. While median household income fell by 3 percent in Chicago during these years, it increased by 42 percent in suburban Lake County (after adjusting for inflation) (Summary findings . . . 2000).
- Between 1970 and 1990 the percentage of blacks living in poverty in the city of Chicago increased from 25 percent to 33 percent. At the same time, for black residents living in the ten neighborhoods that constitute the city's Black Belt, the official poverty rate rose from 33 percent to 50 percent (Wilson 1996).
- From 1980 to 1993 the real tax base per household declined in twenty-six suburbs, mostly those in south Cook County. At the same time, however, the tax base increased by more than 48 percent in seventy-seven suburbs, mostly those north and west of the city (Orfield 1996).

This development pattern and the accompanying inequalities are repeated, with variations, in metropolitan areas throughout the country. In most writing about sprawl, postwar federal highway and housing policies are identified as the main causes of suburbanization and sprawl. On the other side, those who defend this pattern of development usually argue that sprawl simply expresses the preferences of individuals and families, rational decisions by firms seeking to maximize profits, and healthy competition among local officials to offer the most attractive bundle of local amenities. This book resulted from an initiative by the Brookings Institution's Center for Urban and Metropolitan Policy to look at the role of federal and state policies across the country in bringing about this pattern. While the original idea for a tightly focused multicity analysis of this question did not totally come to fruition, colleagues in Philadelphia, Cleveland, Pittsburgh, Phoenix, and Los Angeles have been engaged in research on the same basic issue. Summary results on each city are being published in a book by the Brookings Institution. The present book consists of individual reports the Chicago case study team completed. These studies focused on a description of the nature of urban development and sprawl in Chicago; an analysis of the role of federal and state policies and programs, with an emphasis on infrastructure, transportation, housing, planning, and overall expenditures; and a set of policy recommendations.

In chapter 1 Bonnie Lindstrom reviews the history of infrastructure development in Chicago from 1830 to 1970. She shows that the city would not have developed into the metropolis it is today without the large amounts of federal, state, private, and local money invested in public works and infrastructure projects. In the nineteenth century projects were funded by the city and state. After the New Deal the federal government became more involved. As the succeeding chapters show, both the resulting infrastructure itself, and the nature of its development as a close collaboration between the public and private sectors, established a strong pattern that continues to influence development to this day.

In chapter 2 Y.Q. Wang presents the best available data about the actual changes in land use between 1972 and 1997, based on remote sensing satellite data. This confirms other data sources showing that the amount of urbanized land increased by almost 50 percent from 1972 to 1997.

After these preliminary chapters we turn to various possible explanatory factors. In chapter 3 Richard F. Dye and Therese J. McGuire analyze data on more than 100 metropolitan areas to determine whether property taxes and schools affect sprawl. Property tax differentials between the core and the collar counties had no effect on the amount of sprawl. The number of school districts had no effect on the level of sprawl. However, there is some evidence that metropolitan areas with more municipalities have more sprawl, and some evidence that there is less sprawl in states with more equalized school spending.

Chapter 4 shows that land use planning tools have lent themselves very well to metropolitan deconcentration. Jean M. Templeton shows that municipalities make wide use of boundary agreements and annexation agreements. Planning agreements between municipalities and county governments are much less common. Local governments tend to annex land as an alternative to imposing impact fees, which are restricted by the state constitution. State policies may unintentionally favor annexation over other forms of more cooperative joint planning.

Transportation, and especially federal highway policies, are usually cast as the main villain in regard to sprawl. However, Joseph DiJohn shows in chapter 5 that since the 1960s and 1970s, federal legislation has been increasingly supportive of mass transit and less willing to fund major highway projects. Federal freight railroad policy has had a neutral effect on the region's sprawl but has contributed to the region's congestion by pushing traffic to highways. Also, while highways may have contributed to decentralization by increasing accessibility, there is no empirical relationship between the regionwide rate of decentralization and the time of expressway completion. Similarly, Piyushimita Thakuriah shows in chapter 6 that the role of trucking in urban decentralization in the Chicago region has been minimal. The future needs for land for the trucking and intermodal industries are substantial, but probably will not affect population and commercial locations. Wrapping up this section on transportation, Lindstrom's chapter 7 shows that most highways proposed since the 1960s have in fact not been constructed, because of state and federal cutbacks and citizen opposition. But there is a great lack of coordination between the transportation and planning agencies in the region.

Turning to housing, in chapter 8, Charles J. Orlebeke presents a history of housing policy in the region. Long-term prosperity has been the main force propelling the housing market since the World War II. Public policy at all levels has done much to accommodate and little to restrain this demand. Now market demand is taking some new turns, away from larger houses on larger lots. However, it is unlikely that housing policy will change significantly in terms of its effect on suburbanization.

John F. McDonald and Daniel P. McMillen in chapter 9 use a unique database of major development since 1990 to show that from 1990 to 1996 industrial development was attracted to locations near O'Hare Airport, downtown Chicago, and highway interchanges, specifically outside of Cook County. Commercial development was attracted to O'Hare, highway interchanges, and suburban commercial centers. Residential development was more scattered throughout the region.

Daniel Felsenstein's chapter 10 is more speculative. He argues that the development of high technology employment alone in Chicago's outer regions has led to the consumption of 24,000 acres of land, 18,000 acres more than would have been developed if the firms had located in the city instead. At the same time, the residential behavior of high-income employees means there will be pressure on outer suburban land no matter what the location of the firms.

In probably the most ambitious chapter of the book (chapter 11), Joseph J. Persky, Haydar Kurban, and Thomas W. Lester analyze in detail the impact of federal and state expenditures on residential land absorption. Federal spending and tax expenditures have strongly stimulated peripheral land absorption, especially by consistently allowing special tax treatment of housing. The authors estimate that residential land use in the outer ring was increased by more than 20 percent as a result of such tax treatment. At the state level subsidies are directly responsible for about 3 percent of recent expansion.

The final chapter, by Wim Wiewel and Kimberly Schaffer, evaluates twenty-two potential policy remedies that come out of the preceding chapters, based on effectiveness at slowing land consumption, effect on equity, political feasibility, administrative effort, and likely secondary effects.

Our final conclusion is that federal and state policies have played a considerable role in facilitating Chicago sprawl. In most cases these policies had a wide variety of laudable purposes, and many were not even explicitly concerned with land use and population density. But the federal and state government have done little to develop a functional system of regional planning. Instead they have supported a broad range of programs in housing, transportation, land use, and local governance and taxation powers that have both encouraged and subsidized-low density development. There are many good policy ideas available whose implementation would significantly modify this pattern. So far very few of these appear likely to be pursued seriously. Combined with the expected population growth in the region, sprawl and the concomitant inequities will continue.

References

Illinois Department of Employment Security. 1999. Where Workers Work in the Chicago Metro Area. Summary Report: 1972–1997: http://lmi.ides.state.il.us/wwwork/intro.htm.
Metropolitan Planning Council. 1995. Creating a Regional Community: The Case for Metropolitan Cooperation. Chicago: Metropolitan Planning Council.
Northeastern Illinois Planning Commission. 1999. Census Bureau Releases Updated Income and Poverty Estimates for Illinois and Northeastern Illinois Counties (2/12/99). Chicago: North Eastern Planning Commission: http://www.nipc.cog.il.us/pov95.nei.htm.
Orfield, Myron. 1996. Chicago Regional Report. Minneapolis: Metropolitan Area Program.
Summary findings of the Chicago Metropolitan Case Study. 2000. Chicago: University of Illinois at Chicago.
Wilson, William J. 1996. *When Work Disappears: The World of the New Urban Poor.* New York: Alfred A. Knopf.

Suburban Sprawl

MAXINE GOODMAN LEVIN
COLLEGE OF URBAN AFFAIRS

Cleveland State University

BONNIE LINDSTROM

Public Works and Land Use: The Importance of Public Infrastructure in Chicago's Metropolitan Development, 1830–1970

Chicago is located at the southernmost part of the Great Lakes and the St. Lawrence River on the site of a short portage between the Des Plaines River (a tributary of the Mississippi River watershed) and the South Branch of the Chicago River (a tributary of the Great Lakes watershed). President Thomas Jefferson realized the strategic importance of the site as a connection for an all-water route from the Atlantic Ocean to the Mississippi River and the Gulf of Mexico. As one of his first acts after signing the Louisiana Purchase in 1803, he ordered the construction of Fort Dearborn to guard the portage link and to consolidate the federal government's hold on the Northwest Territory. The site on the southwest tip of Lake Michigan was not considered permanently habitable. The area adjacent to the mouth of the Chicago River was marshland and swamp, named *She-kag-ong*, the wild onion place, by the Potawatomi. The river itself was short, moving sluggishly across a flat prairie. On the north side of the river a shifting sandbar obstructed the discharge of its waters; on the south side the river blended indistinguishably into the marsh and swamps. The Potawatomi and early settlers considered it an unhealthy place to live.

To overcome Chicago's substantial locational disadvantages, Chicago's business and political leaders relied heavily on technological advances in infrastructure; federal, state, and local support for infrastructure improvements; and bold plans. In each of the major growth periods the innovative technological solutions utilized by city officials and civic leaders provided the basic framework for the next period's development. This chapter will examine Chicago's development in three critical periods: 1830–1870, 1871–1945, and 1950–1970. For each period the emphasis will be on the investment in public works infrastructure (water, sewage, highways and streets, railroads and public transit, and airports) by the federal, state, and local governments and the impact of these investments on the growth of Chicago and its suburbs.

Chicago, 1830–1870

The Illinois and Michigan Canal played a major role in the extraordinary growth of Chicago in the early nineteenth century. Recognizing the importance of the canal, Congress had authorized its construction in 1822—four years after Illinois became a state and eleven years before Chicago was incorporated as a town. On March 2, 1827, the federal government gave the state of Illinois approximately 286,000 acres of public land to sell to pay for the canal (Solzman 1966). In 1829 the Illinois legislature appointed a commission to plot the course of the ninety-six–mile Illinois and Michigan Canal and to finance the project. The major products carried on the canal were agricultural products from northern Illinois and products from the South—sugar, molasses, and cotton (Pierce 1940).

In 1837 the Illinois legislature supported a program of state-financed public works. The $9.5 million Internal Improvements Act empowered the state to issue bonds for eight railroads and the Illinois and Michigan Canal. The federal government supported the public works program by giving Illinois a large grant of land that the state could use as collateral or sell to raise funds directly (Cronon 1991, 64). After the Panic of 1837, the Internal Improvements program and the sixteen private railroad companies chartered by the state collapsed. The long-term consequence of the damage to the state's credit was the reluctance of the Illinois General Assembly to finance other railroad projects until the twentieth century (Young 1998).

The other major public works infrastructure necessary to develop the city was the construction of a channel through the sandbar clogging the mouth of the Chicago River. On July 1, 1833, dredges began cutting a channel through the sandbar. The federal government underwrote the project. By 1838 Congress had appropriated almost $200,000 for the original project and the repeated dredging necessary to keep the channel

PUBLIC WORKS AND LAND USE 5

deep enough to accommodate larger lake boats (Einhorn 1991). Additional appropriations totaling $55,000 were granted to the city in 1843 and 1844, and $20,000 in 1852. The city of Chicago continued to dredge the channel until 1867 when the federal government funded the extension of the north pier and constructed an outer harbor breakwater. In 1869 the federal government assumed full responsibility for preserving the entrance (Chicago 1973).

Chicago became the world's largest railroad center in the years between 1850 and 1856. The same year that the Illinois and Michigan Canal opened, the Galena and Chicago Union, Chicago's first railroad, opened with a journey of eight miles, proving that railroads would be successful in the Chicago region. The Chicago and Rock Island, the Illinois Central, and the Chicago, Burlington and Quincy were soon built. Within six years Chicago was the largest rail center in the nation, with ten different lines stretching across the continent (Young 1998). The decade of the 1850s witnessed extremely rapid railroad expansion. The amount of track expanded nationwide from 9,000 miles in 1850 to 30,000 miles by 1860. Illinois gained 2,500 miles, with almost all of the new lines focused on Chicago (Cronon 1991). Chicago became the breaking point between the eastern and western rail networks. No single railroad company operated trains east and west of Chicago (Cronon 1991). By the end of the century the railroads connected Chicago with the Atlantic and Pacific, making Chicago the center of a transcontinental network.

Economic Development

The development of the transportation network made Chicago the midcontinental commercial center. By 1870 the city had become the nation's primary corn and lumber market, the packing center of the country, and had overtaken St. Louis in the wholesale trade (Pierce 1940). The city's preeminence in shipping grain and other commodities was paralleled by the rise of industries dependent on these commodities. A signal of Chicago's new importance as a midcontinental hub for transporting grain and lumber (whether by canal or railroad), the Chicago Board of Trade was founded in 1848, as was Cyrus McCormick's reaper factory.

The city's industrial development centered on the Chicago River and the Illinois and Michigan Canal. Stockyards, slaughterhouses, grain elevators, and breweries were built along the North and South Branches of the Chicago River. The river and canal provided locational advantages to industries dependent on water for bulk transportation and waste elimination. Lumberyards, woodworking plants, and metal processing factories required access to the river because of the economies of scale derived from bulk shipping and the greater amounts of water needed in the new processing technologies. The meat packing industry, breweries, and tanneries located near the river for the easy access for waste disposal (Solzman 1966).

Technology and Public Works

The city's rapid growth in the 1850s and 1860s created major infrastructure problems. The first problem was the provision of fresh water supplies. After a cholera epidemic in 1849, the city asked the state legislature to create a Board of Water Commissioners to finance from bonds the construction of a central pumping station, lake intake tunnel, and main pipes. This quasi-private board then charged user fees to connect the water pipes to the city's buildings (Einhorn 1991).

By the 1860s, however, the Chicago River's pollution had become a serious problem. Distilleries along the North Branch emptied their wastes into the river. Meat packers along the South Branch used the river to dispose of packing wastes. Both branches meet to form the Chicago River that emptied into Lake Michigan near the water intake. The two solutions proposed were to move the water intake two miles away from shore and to deepen part of the Illinois and Michigan Canal. In order to provide safe drinking water, the board built a five-foot tunnel two miles into Lake Michigan to tap the water at the bottom of the lake. Proposed by Chicago's City Engineer E.S. Chesbrough, the project began in 1864 and was completed in 1867 at a cost in excess of $3 million. The project was financed though bonds issued for $2.5 million and by water rents (flat yearly rates based on water use) (Cain 1978).

The city is built on limestone bedrock over which is deposited layers of impermeable clay that prevent surface water drainage and create a high water table. Without a natural drainage system the unpaved streets were quagmires most of the year. There were also problems devising a sewer system that would be steep enough to work adequately. In 1855 the city council asked the state legislature to create a Board of Sewerage Commissioners similar to the water commission model. The solution for both problems by Ellis Chesbrough was to elevate the streets one grade level, raise the buildings, and install new drainage and plumbing. The waterworks and sewerage system were the most expensive public projects of the 1850s. In 1864 they were responsible for $2 million of the city's $3.5 million public debt (Einhorn 1991).

Population Growth and Annexation

The city of Chicago was incorporated in 1833. The anticipation of the construction of the Illinois and Michigan Canal led to Chicago's first boom in the 1830s (Mayer and Wade 1969; Young 1997b). The boom in land speculation, in turn, led to the plotting of towns along the canal from Bridgeport to Lockport and Joliet. In the period between 1830 and 1850, the city's population grew from 350 to 30,000. The city expanded from its original land area of 0.417 square miles when it was first organized on August 12, 1833, to 13.495 square miles by February 14, 1851, spreading from a small area adjacent to the mouth of the Chicago River in a grid pattern. The original settlement is the area now known as the Loop and included Fort Dearborn and twelve cabins. By 1837 the city of Chicago had a population of 4,200. The city included the areas north of the Chicago River to Fullerton Street, the Loop, the Near South Side, and the Near West Side (see Figure 1.1). The Germans, Irish, and Scandinavians who worked on the Illinois and Michigan Canal settled land south of the Loop. The northeastern third of what is now the Lower West Side was included within Chicago's city limits at the time of incorporation in 1837 but was not settled until the 1840s. Lincoln Park, the area from North Avenue to Fullerton and from the lake to the Chicago River developed after the Illinois and Michigan Canal Company took control of two-thirds of the land and then sold it to speculators and farmers. The city annexed the area north to Fullerton in 1857 (Miller 1995). Completed in 1848, the canal never became the intercontinental artery its promoters had promised. The canal was frozen in the winter and was too narrow and shallow to handle steamboats.

Chicago, 1871–1945

On October 8, 1871, a fire lasting three days devastated the commercial district, the Near West Side, and the Near North Side. In rebuilding the city, the Chicago City Council required that wooden structures would be banned and new construction must be made more fireproof. The down-

Figure 1.1 **Growth of Chicago by Annexations to 1899**

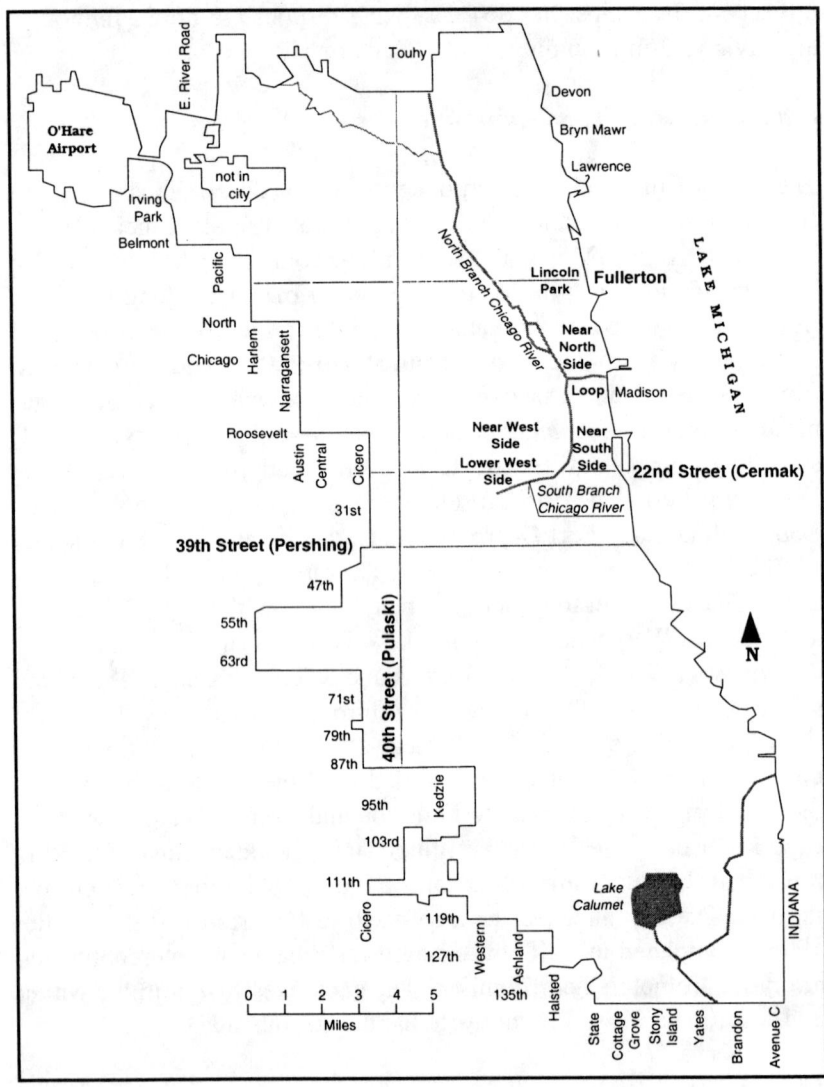

Source: Adapted from "Map of Chicago Showing Growth of the City by Annexations and Accretions," City of Chicago, Department of Public Works, Bureau of Maps and Plats (1983).

town was rebuilt with taller buildings. Apartment buildings with higher densities replaced the older frame structures, and houses within a three-mile radius were of brick construction. In rebuilding the downtown business district, new engineering advances made possible the maximum use of the constricted area available (half a square mile). The new construction technology (the invention of the steel-frame skyscraper by William LeBaron Jenney, the Otis elevator, and the caisson foundation) made higher structures possible. Designed by William LeBaron Jenney in the years 1883–1885, the Home Insurance Building was the first large commercial building constructed of metal rather than masonry walls. It was the decisive beginning of the development of the skyscraper. By combining the essential ingredients in skyscraper development (fireproof metal-frame construction with an elevator), Jenney began what became known as the Chicago School of Architecture.

The Impact of Railroads and Mass Transit

In the years after the fire, improvements in mass transit accelerated both the concentration of the nineteenth century core-oriented central business district and the expansion of the city outward. By the end of the nineteenth century the horse-drawn omnibus and horse railway permitted employees to find housing away from their workplace, extending the boundaries of the city. The increased speed and efficiency of cable cars, elevated steam railroads, and electric surface lines permitted the further rapid deconcentration of population. The development of middle-class residential suburbs along the commuter rail lines contributed to the deconcentration of households. The deconcentration of households, in turn, created distinctly differentiated land use patterns. Near the central business districts population density increased with the construction of apartment buildings and tenement buildings. At the urban edge, inner-ring suburbs developed along the commuter railroad and public transit lines.

The city was first served by an extensive system of horse-drawn streetcars. After 1890 these lines were converted to cable cars. The first elevated line was constructed to transport passengers to the Columbian Exposition of 1893. This line was so successful that plans for other elevated lines moved forward. From the 1890s through the 1920s, a system of privately funded elevated railroads were built radial from the central business district. By 1897 the "Loop" elevated line, opened circling a massive central business district that included the State Street shopping core, the LaSalle Street financial district, hotels, city government, museums, and medical buildings.

Railroads connected the satellite cities on Chicago's periphery with the rapidly expanding industrial city on the lake. The industrial satellite cities of Waukegan, Elgin, Aurora, Joliet, and Chicago Heights developed at the intersections with the Chicago Outer Belt Line (the Elgin, Joliet and Eastern Railroad). Aurora, Elgin, Joliet, and Waukegan were incorporated municipalities before the 1850s. The extension of the railroads through these municipalities accelerated their growth. Aurora, originally a stagecoach stop between Chicago and Galena on the Fox River, became a major rail center. After the Galena and Chicago Union Railroad reached Elgin, the city became a major center for the dairy industry. Joliet developed first from the barge traffic on the Illinois and Michigan Canal and then became a manufacturing hub. Waukegan, located north of Chicago on Lake Michigan, had been the site of a French fort. Although the Illinois and Wisconsin Railroad connected Waukegan to Chicago in 1855, the city did not become a manufacturing center until the Waukegan and Southern Railroad (now the Elgin, Joliet and Eastern) connected Waukegan with Elgin, Aurora, and Joliet.

Industrial facilities moved out of the city, locating where the circumferential railroads intersected the railroads radiating from the central business district. Residential, commercial, and industrial development occurred along railroad and horse-drawn omnibus lines where there was inexpensive land. The meat-packing industry, oil refineries, steel mills, brickyards, and George Pullman's railroad car works developed along the Atchison, Topeka and Santa Fe, the Chicago and Northwestern, and the Illinois Central railroads outside the city limits. These suburban communities (the towns of Lake, Hyde Park, Jefferson, and Lake View) were later annexed to the city (Teaford 1979).

By the 1870s suburban communities began to develop along streetcar and railroad lines. In 1874, for example, all of Chicago's sixty-four suburbs were located on rail lines (Keating 1988). Development companies and real estate speculators played a critical role in the growth of commuter and industrial suburbs. After platting land for new subdivisions, they persuaded the owners of the new railroads to build passenger stations. Frequently the railroads themselves undertook the new residential development (Mayer and Wade 1969; Ebner 1988; Young 1998). Along the Chicago and Northwestern line to Milwaukee, the elite residential communities of Wilmette, Winnetka, Kennilworth, Glencoe, Highland Park, and Lake Forest developed around commuter stations to Chicago's Loop. Riverside, with the Chicago, Burlington and Quincy Railroad running through the site, became the region's first planned community. Designed by Frederick Law Olmsted in 1868 as a "sylvan retreat," Riverside was laid out along the natural contours of the land, with seven hundred acres set aside for parks, open spaces, and trails.

Drinking Water, Sewage, and Storm Water Management

By the 1880s and 1890s Chesbrough's solutions for the problem of the disposal of untreated wastes (reversing the river in 1871 and pumping river water into the Illinois and Michigan canal) were not working. Wastes from homes, the stockyards, and other industries were dumped into the Chicago River and carried out to Lake Michigan. At the same time, the lake was the source of drinking water for residents in the area. The situation was particularly acute because of the animal wastes generated by the stockyards. One graphic illustration of the problem was Bubbly Creek, a tributary of the South Branch of the Chicago River. Upton Sinclair, in *The Jungle*, wrote that Bubbly Creek became an "open sewer" for the packinghouses of the Union Stockyards (Reardon 1995). The Illinois and Michigan Canal, which had opened in 1848, had partially diverted the contaminated wastes downstream but was inadequate to deal with the volume of wastes generated by the 1880s. In 1885 the rainfall from a storm washed sewage from the river past the water intake cribs. The waterborne typhoid and cholera epidemic that occurred after the storm killed between 80,000 and 90,000 Chicago area residents (Cain 1978).

After the voters gave overwhelming approval on November 5, 1889, the Illinois legislature created the Sanitary District of Chicago to construct the Chicago Sanitary and Ship Canal. The solution devised by the new agency was to construct canals and channels to reverse the flow of the Chicago and Calumet rivers. The diversion of contaminated water downstream away from Lake Michigan was possible because of the low watershed divide between the Lake Michigan basin and the Des Plaines basin. The contaminated water was diverted to the Des Plaines River, which merges with the Kankakee River to form the Illinois River, which in turn flows to the Mississippi River. On September 3, 1892, work began on the 28–mile Sanitary and Ship Canal. The canal was completed in 1900 at a cost of approximately $35 million. The project was regarded at the time as a monumental engineering achievement. Key supervisors on the project used the construction techniques developed on the project in building the Panama Canal (Dalton 1991). The North Shore Channel was completed in 1907 and the Cal-Sag Channel in 1922. In total, the district constructed 56 miles of canals. The Illinois and Michigan Canal was abandoned by 1933.

Waste diversion downstream was soon seen as an inadequate and less-than-perfect solution. By 1919 the Board of Commissions of the Chicago Sanitary District began the construction and operation of sewage treatment facilities. Sewage treatment technology had improved sufficiently to make these facilities the long-term solution for the region's waste treatment.

The first of a series of legal battles over the diversion of lake water into the Mississippi watershed began after the secretary of war authorized the diversion of water from Lake Michigan and the state of Missouri sought an injunction to prohibit the reversal of the river. When officials in the other Great Lakes states became concerned that Chicago's diversion of Lake Michigan water would lower the water level of the lake, the district installed locks at lakefront intake points to control the amount of diversion. In 1930 litigation on the diversion issue resulted in a Supreme Court decision that the district would complete the sewage treatment plants by 1939 and that the diversion would be reduced in stages over a ten-year period.

Land Use Policies, Annexation, and Regional Growth

By 1860 the city had grown to 100,000 residents (from 30,000 in 1850), with the settlement primarily in the Loop. In the next forty years the city grew to 1.7 million residents. To accommodate the growth of population and employment, Chicago experienced a period of rapid expansion and annexation in the last half of the nineteenth century. During the 1860s the city annexed north of North Avenue to Fullerton, south of Twenty-second Street to Thirty-ninth Street and west to Fortieth Street, growing from 13.5 square miles in 1850 to 35 square miles by 1870. By 1893 the city had expanded to its current municipal boundaries, approximately 185 square miles. See Figure 1.1 for the growth of Chicago by annexations.

The city's rapid expansion through annexation of adjacent communities was possible because the Charter of 1875 permitted transferring one corporate body to another by mutual consent through elections. On June

15, 1887, the Illinois legislature passed the Chicago Consolidation and Annexation Bill to clarify questions of annexation. Annexation-minded residents in Cicero, Hyde Park, Lake, Lake View, and Jefferson townships petitioned to be placed under the jurisdiction of the city of Chicago. After a series of court challenges to the legality of the petitions, a small part of Cicero Township (what is now Chicago's Austin neighborhood), the city of Lake View, and the village of Hyde Park were added to the city. Chicago added 125 square miles to its existing 43 square miles when it annexed Hyde Park and other land on the South Side in 1889 (Ebner 1987). Proponents of annexation to Chicago argued that their communities would benefit by utilizing the services (such as water) available to Chicago residents.

By 1900 the desire of suburbanites to annex with Chicago began to decline as municipalities in Cook County gained their own supply of Lake Michigan water. By 1915, 45 percent of Chicago's suburbs had piped water from Lake Michigan; by 1934, 83 percent of the suburbs within a fifty-mile radius of Chicago had Lake Michigan water. Several suburbs, such as Evanston, Wilmette, Winnetka, Kennilworth, Maywood, River Forest, La Grange, La Grange Park, Western Springs, Harvey, and Chicago Heights, constructed their own waterworks (Teaford 1979). The suburbs gained piped water from Lake Michigan through a provision in the creation of the legislation creating the Chicago Sanitary District in 1889. The legislation stated that Chicago and other municipalities bordering on the lake had to sell water to those municipalities not bordering on the lake for the same amount as they charged their residents.

In the years between 1910 and 1940, suburbs with a strong residential or industrial base able to supply quality services to their residents rejected annexation with Chicago. Voters in Evanston, Oak Park, and Cicero rejected annexation overwhelmingly. The city of Chicago continued to annex smaller communities unable to financially support the city services required by their citizens. The citizens of the working-class suburbs of Morgan Park, Clearing, Dunning, and Mount Greenwood and the middle-income suburb Beverly voted to annex to Chicago to have the city services they could not afford (Teaford 1979; Keating 1988).

Burnham's *1909 Plan of Chicago*

In 1906 Daniel Burnham was commissioned by the Merchants Club (now the Commercial Club) to develop a plan for Chicago's growth.

His *1909 Plan of Chicago* was adopted by the city of Chicago in 1910 and became the guideline for development until the Second World War. The Burnham Plan proposed a civic center, a continuous lakefront of parks and beaches, a forest preserve greenbelt encircling the developed areas in Cook County, and streets and landscaped boulevards. Based on the City Beautiful Movement in urban planning, the plan appealed to the entrepreneurial businessmen who had made the city into an industrial giant (Hall 1996; Miller 1996). Its success was based on the breadth of its vision in recognizing Chicago as preeminently a commercial city and on balancing the need for transportation and public works infrastructure with the need for a "well-ordered, convenient, and unified city" (Mayer and Wade 1969, 276). Its success can also be attributed to the efforts of the Commercial Club, who paid for the plan and promoted the municipal ordinance that established the Chicago Plan Commission to implement it. Once the Chicago Plan Commission was established, Commercial Club members dominated the executive committee of the Plan Commission, coordinating the implementation of the plan (Hall 1996).

Most of the major public projects from 1910 to 1945 were based on the Burnham Plan. In that period over a billion dollars went into new landfill and the construction of commercial and recreational facilities along Lake Michigan's shoreline. On the north side of the river, Navy Pier was completed by 1916. South of the river, Grant Park was built on landfill. The construction of the Field Museum of Natural History (1919), the Shedd Aquarium (1929), and the Adler Planetarium (1930) completed a cultural center that includes the Art Institute (1893), Orchestra Hall (1904), Fine Arts Building (1886), and the Auditorium (1889). The 1909 Plan stimulated lakefront and other open space acquisition by the Chicago Park District and the Forest Preserve of Cook County.

Chicago, 1945–1970

After the World War II, concern over Chicago's future centered on economic development. The concerns of the civic and business elites about open space and congestion at the turn of the century had resulted in the acceptance of Burnham's *1909 Plan of Chicago* with its emphasis on public buildings, highways, a park system, and river- and lakefront improvements in Chicago and a regional expressway and greenbelt system. The concerns of Chicago's civic and business elites after 1950 shifted to plans to redevelop the downtown business district and eliminate substandard housing, particularly on the South Side. In the mid-1950s the Chicago Central Area Committee, comprising members of the major downtown corporations, began outlining plans for the redevelopment of the city. This influence of this civic organization can be seen in the "Development Plan for the Central Area of Chicago" produced by the city's planning department in 1958. This plan represents a shift away from the land use and infrastructure plans for the prewar central business district. The new emphasis is on redeveloping the downtown business district by concentrating office development in a dense core. An expressway system linking the metropolitan region to the central business district (proposed in the Chicago Comprehensive Plan of 1946) and a downtown subway system were recommended. The core construct was to redevelop the downtown for management, retail, finance, and services (Squires et al. 1987).

These plans fit into the postwar involvement of the federal government in underwriting housing and transportation infrastructure development. Federal urban redevelopment policies, in particular, the Housing Acts of 1949 and 1954, and the Federal Aid Highway Act of 1956, provided the funding to implement the economic development plans developed by the Chicago Central Area Committee and the city's planning department. The two federal housing acts provided the funds to the city to clear blighted land in areas immediately adjacent to the central business district and in the area of substandard housing immediately south of the downtown. The city, in turn, sold the land to private developers or to the Chicago Housing Authority for subsidized housing. The Housing Act of 1949 provided funds primarily for slum clearance; the Housing Act of 1954 shifted the federal emphasis from slum removal to an emphasis on rehabilitation of existing structures and neighborhoods rather than demolition. More important, the Housing Act of 1954 made it possible to use federal funds for purposes other than housing (Hirsch 1983). Both housing acts were passed in order to give central cities resources to combat urban blight. One billion dollars was available in federal loans and $500 million in capital grants. Chicago, a major beneficiary of the programs, had received over $150 million by 1970 (Squires et al. 1987, 104).

The major federal housing program in the postwar period was the mortgage subsidy program provided by FHA loans that significantly benefited suburban development. The Federal Housing Administration favored low-risk loans for new single family, detached houses outside the inner city. The explicit objectives of federal policies to encourage homeownership and new construction (Checkoway 1986) were achieved in the Chicago region. By 1960, 688,222 new homes had been built in the Chicago metropolitan area; 77 percent were located in the suburbs or on undeveloped vacant land in Chicago's south, southwest, and northwest neighborhoods, and 76 percent were single-family dwellings (Hirsch 1983, 27–28).

The other major federal investment in housing was the G.I. Bill. Designed originally as unemployment insurance for returning soldiers, the most important provisions of the bill were loans for college education and low-interest housing loans. The provisions of guaranteed mortgages and low interest rates spurred a construction boom and the development of Levitt-style subdivision tract housing. Between 1945 and 1966 the federal government (FHA/Veterans Administration) under the provisions of the G.I. Bill financed one-fifth of all single-family home purchases nationwide.

Transportation Infrastructure

Planning and constructing the transportation infrastructure for the postwar city was primarily the responsibility of Chicago's political and civic elites. The city of Chicago had begun to plan for increased automobile traffic in the 1930s. Lake Shore Drive, the region's first limited access highway, opened in 1937. In 1939 the city released its first comprehensive plan for superhighways. The first steps toward a regional transportation system occurred immediately after the war with the creation of the Chicago Transit Authority and the publication of Chicago's Preliminary Comprehensive City Plan of 1946. These two events established the foundation for a regional transportation system of expressways and mass transit lines.

In 1945 the state of Illinois approved the creation of the Chicago Transit Authority (CTA) to acquire, own, and operate a transportation system in the metropolitan area of Cook County. The City Council of Chicago also passed an ordinance granting the CTA the exclusive right to own and operate a comprehensive unified local transportation system within the city. After the voters overwhelmingly approved the state and city legislation, the CTA became the second special authority (after the Chicago Sanitary District) to provide a regional service. To subsidize the purchase of the five privately owned street railway systems and the two rapid transit systems, the CTA issued revenue bonds secured by its earnings. By 1953 the CTA had purchased the privately owned streetcar and rapid transit systems at a cost of $135 million without assistance from the state or federal government (Krambles and Peterson 1993).

Chicago constructed the State Street subway in 1943 and the Dearborn Street subway in 1951 at a cost of $75 million. The federal government contributed $26 million; the city's share was provided by a fund built up from payments from passenger revenues from the privately owned transit companies for franchises to operate local services (Chicago 1973). After the Dearborn Street subway was constructed, the CTA extended the rapid transit lines by relocating an elevated line into the median strips of the Dwight D. Eisenhower, the Daniel P. Ryan, and the John Fitzgerald Kennedy expressways, and extending the system with the Skokie Swift and Englewood lines. The city pioneered in placing rapid transit lines in expressway median strips (which allowed it to fund the project with federal highway funds). The Skokie Swift extension was subsidized by a demonstration grant for mass transit from the federal government (Young 1998).

The Chicago Plan Commission's Preliminary Comprehensive City Plan of 1946 outlined the major transportation infrastructure plans for the region. The broad plan for an expressway system was to construct one that would connect residents from the metropolitan area to the central business district. This pattern, which reinforced the pattern of commuter rail lines, was designed to give automobile access to the central business district. Four expressways would radiate from the downtown business district; each would connect with another expressway or the toll highway system (see Figure 1.2).

The William G. Edens and Kennedy expressways were built north and northwest; the Eisenhower was built directly west; the Dan Ryan south; and the Adlai E. Stevenson southwest. Some of the expressway system was built before federal funds were available in 1956. The Calumet Expressway (now the Bishop Louis Henry Ford Freeway), the Edens Expressway, and the Eisenhower Expressway formed the initial structure for the region's expressway system. After the Federal Interstate Highway Act of 1956, the Kennedy, Ryan, and Stevenson were constructed.

Most of the toll highway system opened in 1958 under the control of the Illinois State Toll Highway Authority. The authority built a circumferential toll highway (Interstate 294) to bypass Chicago; Interstate 88, an east-west toll highway beginning at the western end of the Eisenhower

Figure 1.2 **Northeastern Illinois Expressways**

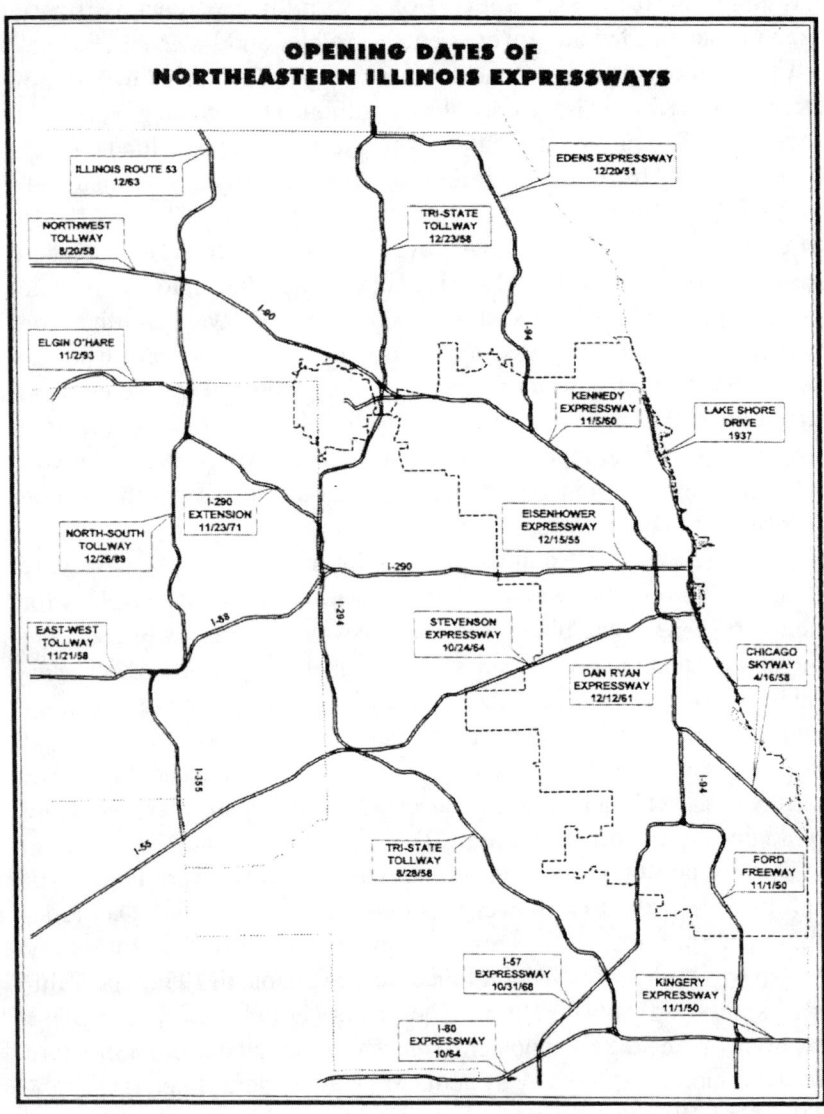

Source: Chicago Area Transportation Study 1998.

Expressway; and Interstate 90, a northwest toll highway to Rockford. The federal government paid 90 percent of the construction and land acquisition costs (see Figure 1.2 for the completed expressway/tollway system).

Midway Airport served as the region's primary airport from 1928 until O'Hare Airport opened. After the U.S. Post Office Department made the city of Chicago a center for its air mail service, the city built a first-class facility on a square mile of prairie on the southwest side in 1927 (Young 1997a). The city council first appropriated $10,000 for construction in 1927; in 1930 a bond issue of $450,000 was used for further construction and expansion (Chicago 1973). Originally the Chicago Municipal Airport, its name was changed in 1949 to honor the World War II battle of Midway Island.

By the 1950s Midway was unable to handle the new large jets. After the war Chicago acquired 1,080 acres of land northwest of the city from the Douglas Aircraft Company to construct a new regional airport and began to underwrite the construction of the facilities. The city issued revenue bonds in the amount of $120 million; the bonds were underwritten by the airlines and would be paid off by them over a period of years. The airlines also agreed to underwrite the maintenance and operating expenses of the airport (Chicago 1973). Chicago-O'Hare International Airport opened in 1955. By 1957 more than one million passengers used the airport. In 1958 longer runways were added for jets. After an eight-lane highway opened to the airport in 1960, O'Hare became the world's busiest airport. The airlines abandoned Midway, which was used primarily for private planes and charters. O'Hare soon became overcrowded. Construction of new runways at O'Hare, the development of jet aircraft with shorter runway requirements, and the reactivation of Midway met the immediate needs. Meigs Field was built on Northerly Island in Burnham Park to meet the needs of small commuter airlines and private planes.

After World War II, Navy Pier was no longer effectively able to handle the needs of oceangoing vessels, and space was problematic. The last commercial freighter was served in 1977. In 1959 the St. Lawrence Seaway began operations as an all-water link from the Great Lakes to the St. Lawrence Seaway to the Atlantic Ocean. The increased shipping meant that a deep-water port should be developed. By the 1970s the Calumet River was dredged, the Cal-Sag barge waterway connection was in place, and an inland harbor on Lake Calumet had been constructed to shelter loading and unloading. Lake Calumet, a shallow lake of 2,200 acres, became the site of the largest comprehensive terminal complex on the Great Lakes (Mayer and Wade 1969, 438). The next decade saw the heyday of cargo shipping through the port with "break-bulk" shipment. By the 1980s large containerized vessels that remained on the East Coast or went only as far in the St. Lawrence Seaway as Montreal were transporting consumer goods. The port now concentrates on bulk shipments of raw materials. Two other ports serve the metropolitan region: the Port of Milwaukee and the Port of Indiana at Burns Harbor.

Drinking Water, Sewage, and Storm Water Management

Chicago and fifty-one of the older inner-ring suburbs (built before 1950) have combined sewer systems in which rainwater mixes with normal wastewater output. During severe rainstorms when the district's treatment facilities were at capacity, the combined sewage in these antiquated systems drained directly into canals and rivers. By the 1970s the polluted water was being released into canals, rivers, and basements every three or four days (Carder 1997). In the 1960s the district began plans to construct additional pollution control projects. These projects included the construction and operation of four more water reclamation plants, the Tunnel and Reservoir Plan (TARP), and artificial aeration stations (Metropolitan Water Reclamation District of Greater Chicago 1998). Under the TARP plan, huge underground tunnels were to be constructed under the city to intercept storm water overflow and convey it to large storage reservoirs. After the storm was over the overflow could be conveyed to a treatment plant for cleaning. The United States Environmental Protection Agency provided 75 percent of the funding.

In 1955 the Illinois General Assembly authorized the Sanitary District to extend its boundaries to include all of the municipalities in Cook County and to change its name to the Metropolitan Sanitary District of Greater Chicago. In 1956 the voters in the affected area voted by a three to two majority for annexation. The annexation added 412 square miles to the district, which increased the service area to 920 square miles, and now includes 99 percent of the area and population of Cook County.

Suburban Development

Suburban population deconcentration in the immediate postwar period increased dramatically. As inner-ring Cook County suburbs became landlocked (i.e., unable to annex adjacent land), new suburbs were incorporated. There were two different types of suburban development in the postwar period. The first type was a continuation of nineteenth-century suburbanization patterns. Inner-ring suburbs and residential commuter suburbs updated their land use and zoning plans, built out from a central business district, and added new houses, retail stores, and light industry. Undeveloped land in Chicago's far northwest, southwest, and south neighborhoods also developed following this pattern. The second type was the new form of suburban development based on the automobile and access to the region's expressways. These suburbs were consciously built for low-density, automobile-dependent development. These new suburbs were planned without central business districts, access to commuter railroads or transit, and with cul-de-sac patterns of development.

Skokie's development fits the pattern of inner-ring suburban development. The village was incorporated in 1888 as Niles Center, experienced a brief real estate boom in the 1920s, and saw rapid expansion in the 1940s and 1950s. Renamed Skokie in 1940, the village developed a new zoning plan after the war. Light industry lined the railroad tracks, heavy industry was zoned for the southeast side (adjacent to Chicago), and the lots were subdivided for single-family housing. In 1956 the Old Orchard Shopping Plaza opened, one of the first suburban malls in the country. The village, one of the most rapidly growing suburbs in the Chicago area in the 1950s, had the locational advantages of proximity to Chicago and the Edens Expressway at the time that light industry and commercial development moved to the suburbs (DeVault 1996).

By the 1960s suburban development moved into a second postwar phase as the expressway/toll highway system was completed. With the opening of the Northwest Toll Highway and O'Hare International Airport, Schaumburg, Elk Grove Village, and other northwest suburbs were incorporated and grew rapidly. These suburbs were planned to take advantage of the accessibility of the airport and the expressway system. Planned without a downtown, the communities followed a distinctly suburban pattern. Schaumburg rapidly developed into an edge city, complete with office buildings and the largest indoor mall in the county. The civic leaders planned for a community with a mix of single-family and multi-unit housing and a strong tax base from light industry, corporate centers, and shopping malls.

Elk Grove Village in northwest Cook, Park Forest in south Cook, and Oak Brook in DuPage County were planned communities. Elk Grove

Village was planned by the Centrex Corporation with an industrial park adjacent to O'Hare Airport to buffer the single-family housing from the airport. Park Forest in southern Cook was the first completely planned suburb built in the United States after World War II. Originally planned as a "new town" development for returning veterans and their families, Park Forest was designed to provide affordable housing in a park setting. American Community Builders, headed by Philip M. Klutznick, planned a complete community: rental apartments, a shopping mall, and an industrial park. Oak Brook, in eastern DuPage County, was planned by Paul Butler. Recognizing its key location at the junction of the Tri-State Tollway (I-294), the East-West Tollway (I-88), and the Eisenhower Expressway, Butler began planning Oak Brook after Marshall Field and Company began building Oak Brook Shopping Center.

Conclusion

Without a substantial investment in public works infrastructure, Chicago would not have achieved its preeminence. When the city was incorporated in 1833, economic development required confronting serious water and drainage problems. Throughout the nineteenth century the federal government played a limited role in urban development. The primary federal support for economic development was through the donation of public land for major internal improvements and maritime projects through its control of national waters. The federal government donated land for the Illinois and Michigan Canal and the railroads, and subsidized the dredging of the Chicago harbor. After the Panic of 1837 the state of Illinois was unwilling to support infrastructure projects.

Without the expectation of financial support from the federal government or the state of Illinois, Chicago's leaders used their own financial resources and innovative technologies to solve the city's public works challenges. The projects to provide safe drinking water, streets, and sanitation were underwritten primarily by the residents of the city. These investments in infrastructure were critical in Chicago's growth. The city grew slowly through annexation until the 1880s. In the next twenty years Chicago added 125 square miles to its existing forty-three square miles. The voters in the outlying townships voted for annexation in order to utilize the city's services, such as drinking water.

After World War II the federal government's role increased dramatically through the G.I. Bill, FHA loans, and the Interstate Highway Act.

The federal government, states, and local governments cooperated to achieve their objectives for urban economic development. This massive federal support fueled the rapid suburbanization of the postwar period. The region's growth was also facilitated by the infrastructure developed in the nineteenth and early twentieth centuries. The public works projects necessary to support development (reversing the Chicago River, providing safe drinking water, constructing the Chicago Sanitary Canal, and storm water and sewage management) were in place. The Chicago City Council (with help from the federal government and the Cook County Board) had underwritten the basic public infrastructure projects for the past century. In the immediate postwar period Chicago, Cook County, and the federal government underwrote the first phases of the construction of the region's expressway system, established the Chicago Transit Authority, and built O'Hare International Airport. The basic infrastructure for the development of the Chicago metropolitan region had been put in place by 1970.

References

Cain, Louis. 1978. *Sanitation Strategy for a Lakefront Metropolis: The Case of Chicago*. DeKalb: Northern Illinois University Press.

Carder, Carol. 1997. Chicago's Deep Tunnel. *Compressed Air Magazine* (October–November).

Checkoway, Barry. 1986. Large Builders, Federal Housing Programs, and Postwar Suburbanization. In *Critical Perspectives on Housing*, eds. Rachel G. Bratt, Chester Hartman, and Ann Meyerson, 119–136. Philadelphia: Temple University Press.

Chicago, City of. 1973. *Chicago Public Works: A History*. Chicago: Rand-McNally.

Chicago Area Transportation Study. 1998. *1995 Travel Atlas*. Chicago.

Cronon, William. 1991. *Nature's Metropolis: Chicago and the Great West*. New York: W.W. Norton.

Dalton, Frank E. 1991. Public Involvement and Public Support in the Urban Water Management Field. In *Water and the City: The Next Century*, ed. H. Rosen and A.D. Keating. Chicago: Public Works Historical Society.

DeVault, Marjorie. 1996. Skokie. In *Local Community Fact Book: Chicago Metropolitan Area, 1990*, 311–313. Chicago: Academy Chicago.

Ebner, Michael. 1988. *Creating Chicago's North Shore*. Chicago: University of Chicago Press.

———. 1987. Re-Reading Suburban America: Urban Population Deconcentration 1810–1980. In *American Urbanism: A Historical Review*, ed. Howard Gillette Jr. and Zane L. Miller, 225–242. New York: Greenwood Press.

Einhorn, Robin L. 1991. *Property Rules: Political Economy in Chicago, 1833–1872*. Chicago: University of Chicago Press.

Hall, Peter. 1996. *Cities of Tomorrow: An Intellectual History of Urban Planning and Design in the Twentieth Century.* Malden, MA: Blackwell.

Hirsch, Arnold R. 1983. *Making the Second Ghetto: Race and Housing in Chicago, 1940–1960.* New York: Cambridge University Press.

Keating, Ann Durkin. 1988. *Building Chicago: Suburban Developers and the Creation of a Divided Metropolis.* Columbus: Ohio State University Press.

Krambles, George, and Art Peterson. 1993. *The CTA at 45: A History of the First 45 Years of the Chicago Transit Authority.* Oak Park, IL: Walsworth.

Maps of Chicago Showing Growth of the City by Annexations and Accretions. 1983. City of Chicago, Department of Public Works, Bureau of Maps and Plats.

Mayer, Harold M., and Richard C. Wade. 1969. *Chicago: Growth of a Metropolis.* Chicago: University of Chicago Press.

Miller, David. 1995. Lincoln Park. In *Local Community Fact Book: Chicago Metropolitan Area, 1990,* ed. The Chicago Fact Book Consortium, 54–56. Chicago: Academy Chicago.

Miller, Donald L. 1996. *City of the Century: The Epic of Chicago and the Making of America.* New York: Simon & Schuster.

Pierce, Bessie L. 1957. *A History of Chicago.* Vol. III. New York: Alfred A. Knopf.

———. 1940. A History of Chicago. Vol. II. New York: Alfred A. Knopf.

Reardon, Patrick. 1995. Healing Waters. *Chicago Tribune* (August 30).

Solzman, David M. 1966. *Waterway Industrial Sites: A Chicago Case Study.* Research paper no. 107. Department of Geography, University of Chicago.

Squires, Gregory, Larry Bennett, Kathleen McCourt, and Philip Nyden. 1987. *Chicago: Race, Class, and the Response to Urban Decline.* Philadelphia: Temple University Press.

Teaford, Jon C. 1979. *City and Suburb: The Political Fragmentation of Metropolitan America, 1850–1970.* Baltimore: Johns Hopkins University Press.

Young, David M. 1998. *Chicago Transit: An Illustrated History.* DeKalb: Northern Illinois University Press.

———. 1997a. Municipal Airport Starts to Spread its Wings. *Chicago Tribune* (June 3) section 2, p. 2.

———. 1997b. Canal Helps Chicago Dig in as Trade Center. *Chicago Tribune* (January 9) section 2, p. 2.

2

Y.Q. WANG

Urban Land Cover Change in Northeastern Illinois: A Landsat View from 1972 to 1997

Introduction

This chapter summarizes the general pattern of urban land cover change in northeastern Illinois between 1972 and 1997, using Landsat-acquired, remotely sensed images. The Chicago metropolitan region, like most of the other metropolitan areas in the country, experienced dramatic land cover change in the past few decades. Accompanying the redistribution of population and decentralization of metropolitan functions are the tremendous growth and development of outlying suburban areas. An important step toward a regional analysis is to understand the pattern and the quantitative results of urban land change. The objectives of this study are to obtain a quantitative description of the spatial pattern of urban land cover changes; to help in understanding the relations between urban land cover change and its driving factors; and to provide technical protocol and background data for a regional impact study. Eight northeastern Illinois counties that encompass the city of Chicago, its suburbs, and the surroundings were the study area: Cook, DuPage, Grundy, Kane, Kendall, Lake, McHenry, and Will counties.

Landsat remote sensing data provide a critical data source for this study. The Landsat Program is the longest-running enterprise for acquisition of imagery of the earth from space. The first Landsat satellite was launched in 1972; the most recent, Landsat 7, was launched on April 15, 1999. The continuous data record of the Landsat Program has proven to be an invaluable resource for earth science researchers. The multispectral capabilities of Landsat remote sensing data allow observation and measurement of biophysical characteristics, while the multitemporal and multisensor capabilities allow tracking of changes in these characteristics over time. Urban sprawl has been identified as one of the targeted research fields using Landsat 7 remotely sensed data (NASA 1999).

Remote sensing has been broadly applied in land cover mapping and land cover change detection (Green, Kempka, and Lackey 1994; Clarke and Gaydos 1998; Vogelmann et al. 2001; Wang and Moskovits 2001). Observation of urban areas over time with Landsat imagery shows where growth has been taking place and helps in evaluation of how different urban planning programs affect population growth and land use. In this study we applied three scenes of Landsat images to provide a historical Landsat view of the urban land change in the Chicago metropolitan region. Based on the processed Landsat images, we obtained the quantitative descriptions of the landscape and interpreted the patterns of urban land cover change.

Methods

To produce land cover maps of the region, we processed the Landsat Multispectral Scanner (MSS) imagery data acquired on October 2, 1972, and the Thematic Mapper (TM) data acquired on May 2, 1985, and October 10, 1997. The MSS data have 80-m spatial resolution (pixel size) with four spectral bands and the TM data have 30-m spatial resolution with seven spectral bands ranging from visible to the infrared portions of the electromagnetic spectrum. The 1972 MSS data provided the first cloud-free Landsat imagery available for the Chicago region. We geometrically rectified these digital images and georeferenced them into the Universal Transverse Mercator (UTM) map coordinate system. We applied an interpolation process to resample the MSS data into 30-m pixels so that the same spatial resolution was maintained for the MSS and TM imagery data.

We applied a classification scheme with eleven land cover categories to obtain land cover information. The categories are forest, woodland, savanna, prairie, wetland, unassociated woody vegetation, unassociated grassy vegetation, agriculture, urban grass, urban build-up, and open water. Based on the classification scheme, we identified training signatures on the 1997 TM image. These signatures tie characteristic patterns of spectral reflectance to individual types of the eleven land covers. We undertook intensive ground referencing to assist in training signature selections. We identified the training sample locations by global positioning systems (GPS). We then applied the training signatures to classify the Landsat images. We obtained historical land cover information by referencing historical aerial photographs, U.S. Geological Survey topographic maps, and county land-management records to select training signatures for the classification of the 1972 MSS and 1985 TM imageries.

To assure the greatest accuracy in analyzing land cover categories, we recoded the classified Landsat imagery data into five general categories, that is, urban land, natural area, unassociated vegetation, agriculture, and open water. Urban land includes all man-made features such as buildings, residential developments, cemeteries, roadways, landfills, quarries, and urban grasses. The natural area category includes forests, savannas, prairies, shrub lands, and wetlands. Unassociated vegetation represents a mixture of shrubs and trees and abandoned agricultural fields. Agriculture includes cropland and other types of agricultural practices.

To eliminate the influence caused by possibly misclassified individual pixels, we applied geographic information system modeling to filter the classified land cover data. We defined an area of three adjacent pixels as the minimum spatial unit. Therefore, any patches of land cover types that were less than three pixels in size (smaller than 0.5 acres) were eliminated from the change analysis. This filtering process reduced the influence of possible random noise induced by individual misclassified pixels.

The final land cover maps of the region in 1972, 1985, and 1997 are illustrated in Figure 2.1 (p. 33). One can note the increase in urban areas on the maps. The growth signifies the dramatic urban land expansion and suburban sprawl that the region has experienced during the past twenty-five years.

An accuracy assessment of land cover classification indicates that high overall accuracies were achieved. About 90 percent accuracy was obtained for the generalized 1972 land cover data and about 93 percent accuracy was obtained for the 1985 and 1997 land cover data (detailed tables available from the author upon request). For urban land, about 87 percent accuracy was achieved. This level of accuracy meets or exceeds that of the U.S. Geological Survey defined standards for their land use and land cover maps (Fisher 1991).

Regional Urban Land Cover Change

Comparison of classified land cover data of 1972, 1985, and 1997 demonstrates that urban land expansion dominated the regional pattern of land cover changes (Table 2.1). Between 1972 and 1985, urban land increased by 14.5 percent. Urban land increase and suburban sprawl accelerated to about 30 percent between 1985 and 1997. Within the twenty-five years between 1972 and 1997, area classified as urban land increased about 49 percent.

Most of the suburban land expansion occurred by consumption of agricultural land in the outer-ring and collar counties. About 22 percent and 20 percent of agricultural land were converted into other land use in the time periods between 1972 and 1985, and 1985 and 1997, respectively. A 37 percent decrease of agricultural land was observed from 1972 to 1997 (Table 2.1).

The natural areas, on the other hand, declined 7.6 percent from 1972 to 1985, and 14.5 percent from 1985 to 1997. In total, 21 percent of natural areas were converted into other types of land covers in the twenty-five years (Table 2.1).

We also noticed that the area classified as unassociated vegetation almost doubled in size during that period. This increase reflects degradation of natural lands in the absence of appropriate management and ecological restoration. It has to be pointed out, however, that the 1972 land cover data were derived from classification of Landsat MSS data. The coarser spatial resolution of MSS data made the identification of unassociated vegetation difficult. The 1985 and 1997 land cover data were obtained from classification of Landsat TM. High spatial resolution and richer spectral bandwidths of the TM data made the classification more accurate than that from 1972 MSS.

County-Level Urban Land Cover Change

From remote sensing derived land cover data we obtained the changes of land cover in the counties. We calculated both the percentages and the density of urban land changes to depict the patterns of intensity of the land transformations. As summarized in Table 2.2, the collar counties of DuPage, Kane, Lake, McHenry, and Will all experienced dramatic increase in urban land. DuPage County had over 70 percent urban land increase, with the highest change density of almost thirteen ha/km^2. Lake County ranked highest in percentage increases and second in change density. Cook County had the lowest percentage of urban land increase due to its initial high urban land concentration. Even so, about 7 ha/km^2 change density was observed. McHenry and Will counties

Table 2.1

Land Cover Change in Metropolitan Chicago Region Between 1972 and 1997

	1972 (ha.)	1985 (ha.)	1997 (ha.)	1972–1985 (ha.)	1985–1997 (ha.)	1972–1997 (ha.)
Urban land	227,487	260,498	338,612	+33,011 (14.5%)	+78,114 (30%)	+11,1125 (48.85%)
Natural area	227,047	209,796	179,061	–17,251 (7.6%)	–30,735 (14.65%)	–47,986 (21.13%)
Agriculture	599,462	468,804	375,537	–130,658 (21.8%)	–93,267 (19.89%)	–223,925 (37.35%)
Unassociated vegetation	80,644	199,355	244,716	+118,711 (147.2%)	+45,361 (22.75%)	+164,072 (203.45%)

Table 2.2

Urban Land Cover Change Between 1985 and 1997 in Northeastern Illinois Counties

Northeastern Illinois counties and the areas	Natural area to urban (in ha.)	Unassociated vegetation to urban (in ha.)	Agriculture to urban (in ha.)	Urban land cover in 1985 (in ha.)	Increase in urban land cover (%)	Change density of urban land (ha. / km^2)
Cook (2478 km^2)	6,196	6,715	4,788	101,815	17.38	7.14
DuPage (871 km^2)	2,801	4,391	3,835	15,398	71.61	12.66
Kane (1357 km^2)	1,414	2,302	3,278	3,678	70.52	5.16
Kendall (834 km^2)	109	661	1,125	3,678	51.51	2.27
Lake (1218 km^2)	265	3,435	3,444	12,370	77.07	7.83
Grundy (1115 Km^2)	363	670	733	5,031	35.69	1.61
McHenry (1581 km^2)	635	2,189	2,601	7,914	68.56	3.43
Will (2198 km^2)	2,010	3,171	6,401	16,779	69.03	5.27

experienced about 70 percent urban land increase from 1985 to 1997, with high change densities as well. Kendall and Grundy counties, which are farther away from downtown Chicago, had an observable increasing trend in urban land.

Spatial Pattern of Urban Land Cover Change

Distance from downtown Chicago is considered an important characteristic in the regional landscape. A half-ring pattern is clearly observable from both Landsat images and the derivatives of land cover maps. To quantify the spatial pattern of urban land distribution and the changes, we divided the region into five concentric zones. The zones separate the region into 0–15 km (Zone I), 15–30 km (Zone II), 30–45 km (Zone III), 45–65 km (Zone IV), and more than 65 km (Zone V) areas measured from the center of Chicago (Figure 2.2; p. 34). We compared the proportion of land converted into urban land use in different zones by calculating the percentage of increase and density of change of the urban land (Table 2.3).

The result indicates that Zone III, the area between 30 km and 45 km from downtown Chicago, had the highest change density (11.54 ha/km^2) and a high rate of urban land increase (62 percent) between 1985 and 1997. Zone IV experienced about 76 percent urban land increase and ranked second in change density (7.26 ha/km^2). This pattern agreed well with the facts that many suburban developments fell into these two zones, including the hot spots of residential and commercial developments in northwest Cook County, the southern part of Lake and McHenry counties, most of DuPage County, the eastern Kane County, and northern Will County. Development of new infrastructures, such as the I-355 toll road and the DuPage airport, were within these two-zone areas. About 22 percent of urban increase in Zone III and 37 percent in Zone IV were converted from agriculture land.

The first two zones are among the already developed areas. There was not much land left for further urban expansion. Therefore, the lower changing rate and density were expected. Zone V, the area beyond 65 km from the center of Chicago, shows an increasing trend in urban land development. In Zone IV and Zone V, most of the urban land expansion resulted from consumption of agricultural land.

Suburban sprawl has great impacts on local ecosystems and natural communities. Figure 2.3 (p. 35) illustrates the urban land cover change in a subset area of Naperville, in the southwest corner of DuPage County.

Table 2.3

Urban Land Cover Change by Distance from Downtown Chicago

Land cover change	Nature to urban (ha.)	Unassociated growth to urban (ha.)	Agriculture to urban (ha.)	Urban land in 1985 (ha.)	Urban land change (%), 1985–1997	Urban change density (ha./km²)
Zone I (0–15 km) (474 km²)	329	295	149	38,059	2.03	1.63
Zone II (15–20 km) (1188 km²)	3,559	3,232	1,335	48,037	16.92	6.84
Zone III (30–45 km) (1768 km²)	5,505	7,479	7,428	32,917	62.01	11.54
Zone IV (45–65 km) (3335 km²)	5,049	7,663	10,044	29,898	76.11	7.26
Zone V (> 65 km) (4888 km²)	1,739	4,896	6,035	23,992	52.81	4.04

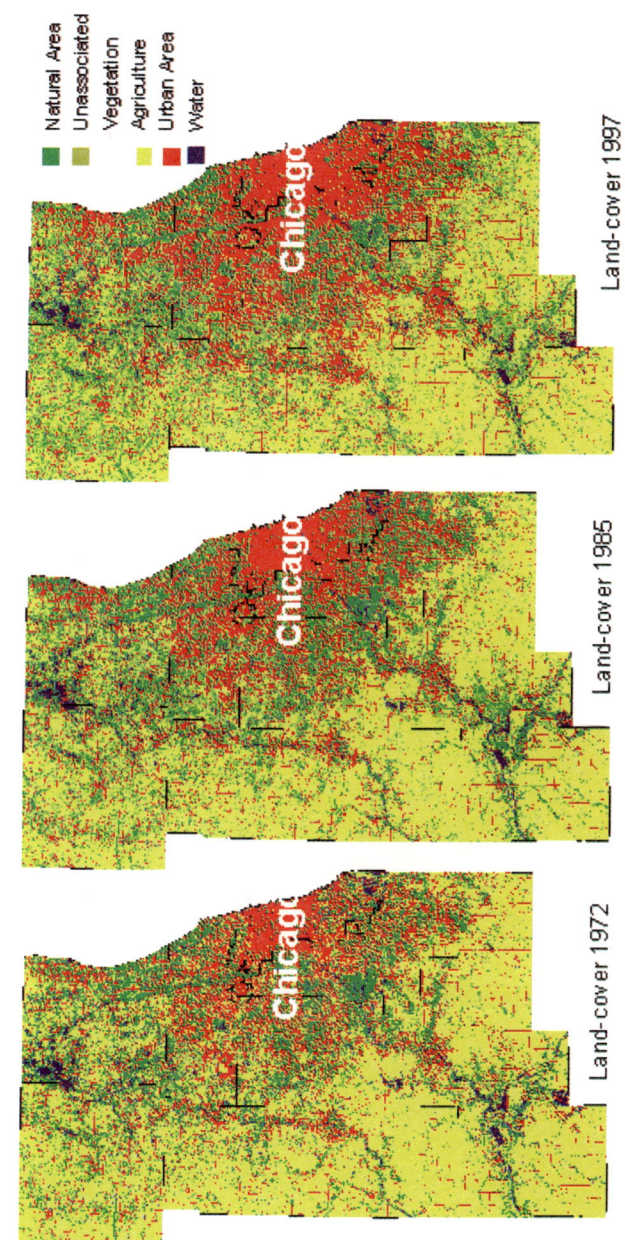

Figure 2.1 Land Cover Change of Metropolitan Chicago Region Between 1972 and 1977, Derived by Classification of Landsat Remote Sensing Data

Figure 2.2 **County Index and Distance Zones from Downtown Chicago**

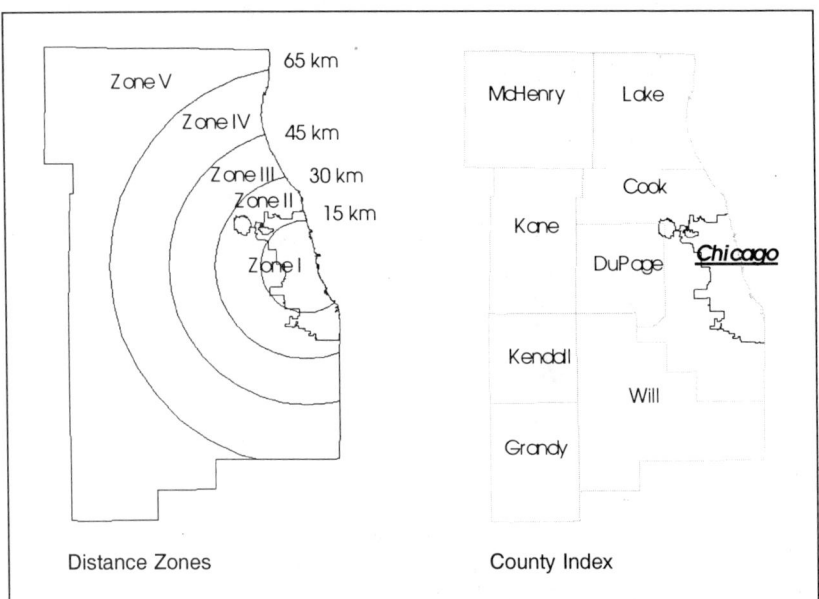

Naperville has been one of the most changed hot spots in suburban development in Illinois. Comparison of the land cover maps shows that urban land increased by 49,797 ha in this subset area. The land transformations included about 13,007 ha of natural areas, 17,766 ha of unassociated vegetation, and 19,024 ha of agriculture land into urban land use. Spring Brook Natural Preserve, a 688-ha prairie and wetland restoration site, is located in the lower left of this subset area. This preserve was purchased by the DuPage County Forest Preserve District in 1973 for prairie restoration. In the 1985 land cover map the preserve is almost entirely surrounded by agricultural land, with only the eastern portion bordered by suburban residential area. Twelve years later the preserve was almost completely surrounded by new subdivisions and commercial centers. In addition to showing the urban land expansion in the subset area, this example also demonstrates that suburban sprawl accelerates the fragmentation and isolation of natural communities and has a profound impact on natural ecosystems in the region.

Figure 2.4 (p. 36) depicts the urban land change along the I-355 corridor. Comparison of satellite-derived 1985 and 1997 land cover maps

Figure 2.3 Urban Land Cover Change in a Subset Area of Naperville, West Suburb of Chicago

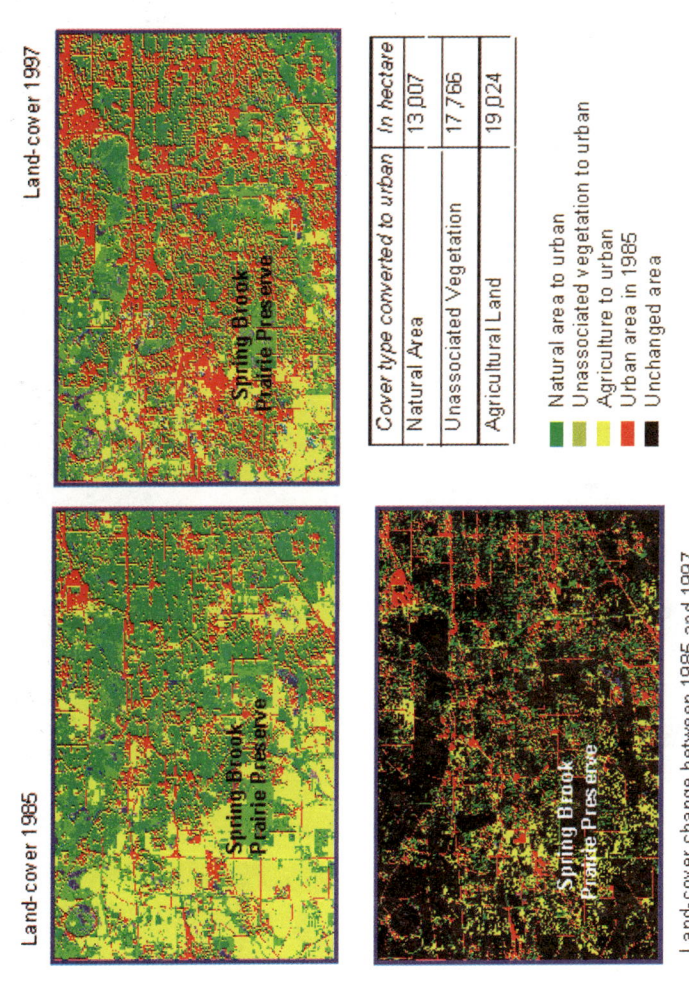

Figure 2.4 **Urban Land Cover Change of a Subset Area of I-355 Corridor in West Suburb of Chicago**

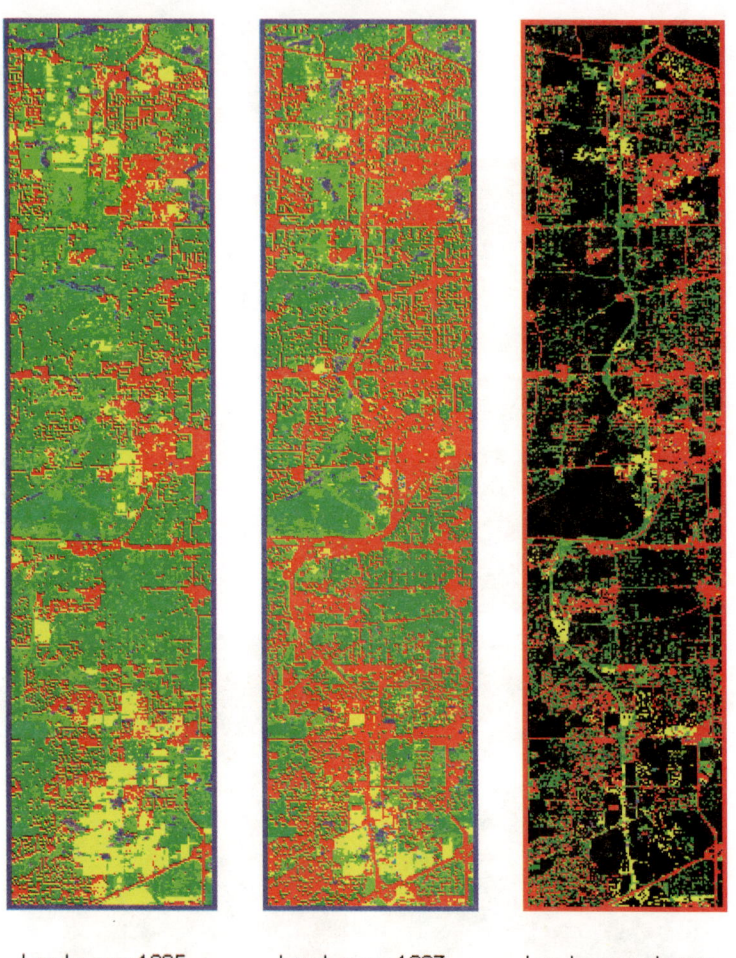

Land cover 1985   Land cover 1997   Land cover change between 1985-1997

shows that the I-355 tollway system did not exist in 1985, but it is clearly identifiable in the 1997 land cover map. Quantitative analysis of this subset area showed that an increase of 2,752 ha of urban land, including I-355 itself, occurred within the 12 years. Among land transformations, urban land expansion consumed about 1,091 ha of nature areas, 905 ha of unassociated vegetation, and 478 ha of agricultural land. Compared with the 2,705 ha of urban land in 1985, 91 percent urban land increase was experienced in this subset area, showing the impact of infrastructure development on land cover changes.

Changes in Municipality Boundaries

Many municipalities, particularly in the collar counties, have expanded their territory by annexation in the past twenty-five years. The expansion of the municipalities partially reflects the extent and potential of urbanization in the suburban areas. As a result of expansion, more planned development has been carried out within these municipalities. To depict the patterns of land expansion in the region, we extracted the changes of municipality boundaries from census data. We then obtained the relations between the urban land changes and the expansions of the municipalities using multiple year land cover data and the changes of the municipality boundaries. Population changes within the municipalities were extracted as well.

The results show that municipalities undergoing the greatest expansion lay within and around the areas of Zone III and Zone IV. The changes of the municipality boundaries were more evident between 1992 and 1997 than 1980 and 1990. Between 1980 and 1990 the municipalities of Crystal Lake, Long Grove, Naperville, Aurora, Frankfort, Antioch, Gurnee, and Wadsworth ranked near the top, increasing by over 10 km^2 in areas. Crystal Lake ranked first in area increase (about 19 km^2) but ranked only thirtieth in population increase (6,106). Naperville, on the other hand, ranked third in area expansion (16.36 km^2) but first in population increase (43,476). To reflect the intensity of urban land development, the ratio between population change and the area increase (P/A) was calculated. The P/A ratio served as an indicator for the intensity of urban development. For example, both Naperville and Wadsworth had over 10 km^2 land expansion (Table 2.4). Naperville experienced a very intensive urban development (P/A =

Table 2.4

Selected Municipalities That Changed the Most in Area Between 1980 and 1990

Municipality name	County name	Area increase (km^2)	Population change	P/A ratio
Crystal Lake	McHenry	18.99	6,106	321.54
Long Grove	Lake	18.31	2,734	149.32
Naperville	DuPage	16.36	43,476	2,657.46
Aurora	Kane	15.09	18,263	1,210.27
Frankfort	Will	13.49	2,823	209.27
Antioch	Lake	11.93	1,686	141.32
Gurnee	Lake	11.37	6,536	574.85
Wadsworth	Lake	10.95	722	65.94
Bolingbrook	Will	9.48	3,582	377.85
Bartlett	Kane	9.08	6,141	676.32
Vernon Hills	Lake	8.91	5,492	616.39
Orland Park	Cook	8.86	12,675	1,430.59
Crest Hill	Will	8.79	1,747	198.75
Lake in the Hills	McHenry	8.67	249	28.72
Buffalo Grove	Cook	8.43	14,187	1,682.92
Woodridge	DuPage	7.64	4,037	528.4
Joliet	Will	7.56	−739	−97.75
Waukegan	Lake	7.17	1,828	254.95
Lakemoor	McHenry	7.03	442	62.87

2657.46/km^2), while Wadsworth had a relatively slower pace in development (P/A = 65.94). Therefore, the municipalities with lower P/A ratio should have a greater potential or available land for urban development in the future. The lower P/A ratio also indicates that the area is in a lower density pattern of suburban development rather than an intensified pattern of new urban development.

Bolingbrook ranked ninth in area expansion between 1980 and 1990. However, this municipality ranked first in area expansion between 1990 and 1997, with 10,469 population increase (Table 2.5). The second-ranked Huntley, on the other hand, had about the same area expansion as the Bolingbrook, but its population increased by only 576 during the same time period. The big difference in P/A ratio between the top-ranked two municipalities in area expansion indicated that they were taking different development actions in the time period.

Examination of the changes for the municipalities from 1980 to 1997 shows that Naperville, Aurora, Orland Park, and Gurnee are the top four in P/A ratio (Table 2.6). Satellite-derived land cover maps agreed that

Table 2.5

Selected Municipalities That Changed the Most in Area Between 1990 and 1997

Municipality name	County name	Area increase (km^2)	Population change	P/A ratio
Bolingbrook	Will	20.86	10,469	501.87
Huntley	McHenry	20.72	576	27.80
Joliet	Will	19.04	9,532	500.63
Naperville	DuPage	16.71	21,195	1,268.40
Plainfield	Will	14.38	2,783	193.53
OrlandPark	Cook	13.40	9,937	741.57
Grayslake	Lake	12.60	6,982	554.13
TinleyPark	Cook	11.22	6,195	552.14
WestChicago	DuPage	11.20	2,084	186.07
Romeoville	Will	10.82	1,395	128.93
NewLenox	Will	10.38	3,390	326.59
LakeintheHills	McHenry	10.11	10,989	1,086.94
Algonquin	McHenry	10.01	6,326	631.97
Aurora	Kane	9.96	16,849	1,691.67
St.Charles	Kane	7.89	3,076	389.86
Channahon	Will	7.66	2,074	270.76
Montgomery	Kane	6.85	790	115.33
Harvard	McHenry	6.69	882	131.84

the most intensive urban development happened in these areas. The municipalities that ranked high in P/A ratio are mostly located within or beyond Zone IV. The combination of satellite-derived land cover maps and the changes of municipalities show that the most intense urban land consumption is occurring in the suburban areas that are the most outlying from the central city.

Discussion

This study depicts the land cover change and the change patterns of the Chicago metropolitan region during the twenty-five years between 1972 and 1997. Urban land expansion and suburban sprawl dominated the regional land cover change in this time period. Quantitative comparison and visual maps provide strong evidence of the expansion of suburban sprawl in the region.

This study agreed well with the result derived by other institutions using different methodology and technical approaches. A recent report by the Northeastern Illinois Planning Commission (NIPC), states that developed land in metropolitan Chicago increased 49 percent between

Table 2.6

Selected Municipalities That Changed the Most in Area Between 1980 and 1997

Municipality name	County name	Area changed (km²)	Population changed	P/A ratio
Naperville	DuPage	33.07	64,671	1,955.58
Bolingbrook	Will	30.34	14,051	463.12
Joliet	Will	26.61	8,793	330.44
Aurora	Kane	25.05	35,112	1,401.68
Crystal Lake	McHenry	23.53	13,590	577.56
Huntley	McHenry	22.89	1,383	60.42
Orland Park	Cook	22.26	22,612	1,015.81
Lake in the Hills	McHenry	18.78	11,238	598.40
Long Grove	Lake	18.11	4,045	223.36
Grayslake	McHenry	17.38	9,110	524.17
Plainfield	Will	17.15	3,573	208.34
New Lenox	Will	16.53	7,296	441.38
Gurnee	Lake	16.41	15,310	932.97
West Chicago	DuPage	16.32	4,342	266.05
Wadsworth	Lake	15.40	1,208	78.44
Frankfort	Will	15.38	5,250	341.35
Romeoville	Will	15.26	−23	−1.51
Algonquin	McHenry	14.08	12,185	865.41
St. Charles	Kane	13.46	8,204	609.51
Antioch	Lake	13.26	2,979	224.66

1970 and 1990, whereas its population grew by 4 percent. NIPC projected that the population of the region will increase by 25 percent over the next twenty-five years (NIPC 1998). It is certain that suburban sprawl and other urbanization processes will continue there.

Historical remotely sensed data, coupled with new Landsat 7 imagery data, are critical in development of quantitative analysis models and in simulation of the effects of urban land cover change on regional natural and cultural systems. Based on the research finding from this study coupled with the population and employment projections made by the census and planning agencies (NIPC 1998), simulation of the region's land cover change to the year 2020 is becoming possible (Wang and Zhang 2001). Modeling analysis by integration of driving factors and land cover maps derived from remote sensing will provide the data and reliable bases for anticipating suburban sprawl and its impact.

References

Clarke, K.C., and L.J. Gaydos. 1998. Loose-Coupling a Cellular Automaton Model and GIS: Long-Term Urban Growth Prediction for San Francisco and Washington/Baltimore. *International Journal of Geographical Information Sciences* 12: 699–714.

Fisher, P.F. 1991. Spatial Data Sources and Data Problems. In *Geographical Information Systems: Principles and Applications*, ed. D. Maguire, M.F. Goodchild, and D.W. Rhind. New York: Longman Scientific and Technical.

Green, K., D. Kempka, and L. Lackey. 1994. Using Remote Sensing to Detect and Monitor Land-Cover and Land-Use Change. *Photogrammetric Engineering and Remote Sensing* 60(3): 331–337.

NASA. 1999. NASA Landsat-7 Press Kit: http://pao.gsfc.nasa.gov/gsfc/newsroom/pkits/landsat7.pdf.

Northeastern Illinois Planning Commission. 1998. Population, Household and Employment Forecasts for Northeastern Illinois, 1990 to 2020 [Report]. Chicago: NIPC, 1–25.

Vogelmann, J.E., St. M. Howard, L. Yang, C.R. Larson, B.K. Wylie, and N.V. Driel. 2001. Completion of the 1990s National Land Cover Data Set for the Conterminous United States from Landsat Thematic Mapper Data and Ancillary Data Sources. *Photogrammetric Engineering and Remote Sensing* 67(6): 650–662.

Wang, Y., and D.K. Moskovits. 2001. Tracking Fragmentation of Natural Communities and Changes in Land Cover: Applications of Landsat Data for Conservation in an Urban Landscape (Chicago Wilderness). *Conservation Biology* 15(4): 835–843.

Wang, Y., and X. Zhang. 2001. Dynamic Modeling Approach to Simulating Socioeconomic Effects on Landscape Change. *Ecological Modelling* 140(1–2): 141–162.

3

RICHARD F. DYE AND THERESE J. MCGUIRE

Property Taxes, Schools, and Sprawl

That property taxes and schools have an influence on the geographical spread of population and businesses in a metropolitan area is taken as given by many observers of urban form. In fact, little systematic evidence exists to support or refute this view. There is a large empirical literature examining the question of whether property taxes are an important determinant of intrametropolitan location decisions of businesses, but these studies do not ask whether property taxes encourage geographic dispersion of business locations. In terms of the influence of schools on the dispersion of population in a metropolitan area, we have been able to find no systematic evidence.

In this chapter we provide theoretical arguments for a relationship among property taxes, schools, and sprawl, and we review the limited empirical literature relevant to these questions. We provide some new, preliminary empirical evidence on the questions of the relationship of property taxes and schools to sprawl, and we provide descriptive statistics on key variables for the Chicago metropolitan area. Concluding remarks are presented in the final section.

How Might Property Taxes and Schools Affect Urban Sprawl?

Sprawl is a dynamic process, and no single operational definition of sprawl seems satisfactory. Sprawl can refer to an increase in land area occupied by residents of a metropolitan area, a decrease of the population density of the central city, an increase in the population density of the periphery of the urban area, a leapfrogging of development from the center to the periphery, and a loss of open space in the urban area, among other definitions. Without being very precise about what we mean by sprawl, we provide various theoretical arguments about certain potential causes of sprawl.

If property taxes are a determining factor of business location decisions, and if property taxes are higher in the center of the metropolitan area relative to the urban fringe, and if population follows jobs, then differential property taxes will contribute to sprawl. As to the first assumption required for this argument, there are several studies of the effect of property taxes on intrametropolitan business location decisions including Charney (1983), who examines Detroit; Erickson and Wasylenko (1980) and Wasylenko (1980), who examine Milwaukee; Fox (1981), who examines Cleveland; McGuire (1985), who examines Minneapolis–St. Paul; and Luce (1994), who examines Philadelphia. With the exception of Erickson and Wasylenko, each of these studies finds that local taxes, typically property taxes, are statistically significant negative determinants of business location decisions (or other measures of local economic development). A more recent study of the Washington, DC, area (Mark, McGuire, and Papke 2000) finds that real property taxes were not significant determinants of population or employment growth rates across the jurisdictions in the metropolitan area. These studies are concerned with determining whether low tax jurisdictions are more attractive than high tax jurisdictions; they are not concerned with the location within the metropolitan area of the low tax jurisdictions relative to the high tax jurisdictions—an additional piece of information we need to assess whether property taxes contribute to urban sprawl. On the question of whether jobs follow people or people follow jobs, Carlino and Mills (1987) find that the relationship goes both ways—there is evidence both that job growth in an area leads population growth and that population growth in an area leads job growth.

Without providing systematic empirical evidence, several authors assert the importance of schools on urban sprawl. Downs (1994), Orfield (1998), and various participants in a 1995 conference sponsored by the Lincoln Institute of Land Policy, the Brookings Institution, and the National Trust for Historic Preservation (Young 1995) have argued that the number and quality of school districts (as well as the number of jurisdictions with zoning authority) affect the location of population within a metropolitan area. For example, Henry R. Richmond, a participant in the 1995 conference, argues that sprawl is most likely to occur "in . . . metropolitan areas . . . in which there are numerous governmental jurisdictions with zoning authority" and "in regions that show disparities in the means of financing ... education" (quoted in Young 1995, 5). The theoretical argument is as follows: If public schools are underfunded or of poor quality in the center of the metropolitan area, if there are numerous, high-quality, well-funded public schools in the outlying suburbs, and if there are not sufficient private school alternatives in the central city, then families with school-age children will choose to locate away from the center.

Related to the quality of public schools is the effect on sprawl of differences between the center and the outlying suburbs in other measures of the quality of life such as crime, grime, and congestion. Mieszkowski and Mills (1993) review the literature concerning two broad theories of suburbanization: "natural evolution theory," wherein transportation costs and income changes decrease the attraction of the core, and "flight from blight," wherein "fiscal and social problems" of the central city repel activity. They measure suburbanization or urban decentralization by decreases in population density gradients. Mieszkowski and Mills conclude that both theories are important. A key study in the "flight from blight" literature is Mills and Price (1984) in which the authors conclude that various measures of central city "social problems" such as crime, educational attainment, and taxes explain very little of the decentralization of population that occurred in metropolitan areas in the United States from 1960 to 1970. This study is the only study we have found that examines the effect on suburbanization of differences in property taxes between the central city and the suburbs, and the authors find that the variable is insignificant and its coefficient often has the wrong sign, that is, that relatively high central city property taxes, if anything, deter suburbanization of population and employment.

New Empirical Evidence

To provide new evidence as to whether property taxes and schools affect sprawl, we collected data on over one hundred of the largest metropolitan areas in the United States for the years 1970, 1980, and 1990. We examine three measures of sprawl: the share of the population outside the urban core relative to the total population of the metropolitan area, the share of urbanized land area (as defined by the U.S. Bureau of the Census 1994) relative to total land area of the metropolitan area, and the annual growth in urbanized land area.[1] We use regression analysis to relate these three measures separately to a set of explanatory variables that includes a relative core-to-suburban measure of property tax burdens, the number of school districts in the metropolitan area, the number of municipalities in the area, the state share of total public K–12 school revenues, and a measure of the degree of equalization in the state aid formula for school districts. According to the theories sketched above, we expect, other things being equal, higher core-to-suburban property tax burdens, a greater number of school districts, a greater number of municipalities, a lower state share, and a less equalizing state aid formula each to increase sprawl.

The Census definitions and designations of metropolitan areas changed over the twenty-year period, therefore we chose to standardize our set of metropolitan areas by using the 1998 designations. Because metropolitan areas comprise whole counties, we gathered data at the county level and aggregated across the relevant counties to characterize a metropolitan area. We designated one (or more) of the counties as the core (central) area and designated the remaining counties as the outlying suburban area (the "collar" area in Chicago parlance). We grouped the metropolitan areas into two data sets: one consisting of 122 primary metropolitan statistical areas (PMSAs) and metropolitan statistical areas (MSAs) and the other of 108 consolidated metropolitan statistical areas (CMSAs) and MSAs.[2] The PMSA definition better fits the traditional notion of a single set of labor, commercial, and housing markets surrounding a core city. As metropolitan areas have grown, the market boundaries of some adjacent metropolitan areas have merged, forming CMSAs. The trade-off that leads us to use both samples is that the PMSA definition might be too narrow a definition of the relevant market in some cases, while the CMSA definition includes such a large area that it may include multiple markets in some cases.

Descriptive statistics for the key variables used in the analysis are provided in Table 3.1. The first two variables shown indicate the number of counties in each metropolitan area. In the PMSA sample there is an average of 1.16 core counties and 4.79 total counties in each metropolitan area. In the PMSA sample the average metropolitan area population increased slightly from 1970 to 1990 from just below one million to just above one million. In the CMSA sample the average number of counties and population levels are slightly higher. With disproportionate growth in the collar counties, the share of population in the PMSA collar counties increased from 0.31 in 1970 to 0.35 in 1990. The share of population in the collar counties is one of the dependent variables we

Table 3.1

Variables Used in the Analysis

Variable	122 PMSA/MSAs [a]				108 CMSA/MSAs [b]			
	Mean	Std. Dev.[c]	Minimum	Maximum	Mean	Std. Dev.	Minimum	Maximum
Number of counties, core, 1998	1.16	0.58	1	5	1.40	1.30	1	13
Number of counties, total, 1998	4.79	3.58	2	25	5.69	4.92	2	33
Population, total, 1970	967,199	1,282,349	78,871	9,076,568	1,262,945	2,363,055	78,871	19,428,659
Population, total, 1980	1,045,050	1,250,324	151,196	8,274,961	1,379,647	2,395,369	151,196	18,829,146
Population, total, 1990	1,146,190	1,315,736	250,454	8,546,846	1,533,986	2,621,254	250,454	19,462,450
Share of population, collar / total, 1970	0.31	0.17	0.03	0.86	0.31	0.17	0.03	0.86
Share of population, collar / total, 1980	0.34	0.18	0.04	0.88	0.34	0.17	0.04	0.88
Share of population, collar / total, 1990	0.35	0.18	0.05	0.88	0.36	0.18	0.05	0.88
Annual growth in population, total, 1970–80 (%)	1.31	1.36	−0.92	6.51	1.40	1.37	−0.82	6.51
Annual growth in population, total, 1980–90 (%)	0.98	1.18	−0.92	5.07	1.00	1.19	−0.92	5.07
Share of total area that lies in "urbanized area," 1970	0.07	0.06	0.00	0.31	0.07	0.06	0.00	0.30
Share of total area that lies in "urbanized area," 1980	0.10	0.07	4.70E-03	0.34	0.10	0.07	4.70E-03	0.36
Share of total area that lies in "urbanized area," 1990	0.14	0.12	0.01	0.78	0.12	0.07	0.01	0.37
Annual growth in urbanized land area, 1970–80 (%)	4.40	3.31	0.28	15.76	4.38	3.29	0.34	15.76
Annual growth in urbanized land area, 1980–90 (%)	1.64	1.41	−0.62	9.69	1.63	1.37	−0.62	9.69
Ratio of property tax per capita, core / collar, 1972	1.39	0.58	0.45	5.54	1.41	0.60	0.45	5.54

Ratio of property tax per capita, core / collar, 1982	1.31					0.44	3.33
Ratio of property tax per capita, core / collar, 1992				1.32	0.50	0.44	2.90
Number of school districts, total, 1972	1.30	0.49			0.48	0.56	
Number of school districts, total, 1982	39.80	0.48		1.32		2	700
Number of school districts, total, 1992	39.71	51.86	2	50.19	90.28	2	715
Number of municipalities, total, 1972	38.72	51.86	2	50.18	91.47	2	712
Number of municipalities, total, 1982	57.61	50.14	2	48.97	89.70	5	714
Number of municipalities, total, 1992	59.23	70.46	5	69.90	101.63	5	714
	60.09	70.87	5	71.93	102.20	5	722
		71.03		73.08	102.99		
State share of school district revenue, 1970*	0.43	0.11	0.20	0.44	0.11	0.20	0.61
State share of school district revenue, 1980*	0.48	0.10	0.20	0.48	0.10	0.20	0.69
State share of school district revenue, 1990*	0.47	0.11	0.25	0.48	0.11	0.27	0.73
State coefficient of variation of equal state aid per pupil minus state coefficient of variation of actual state aid, 1972*	2.11	5.14	−20.67	2.12	5.20	−20.67	9.81
State coefficient of variation of equal state aid per pupil minus state coefficient of variation of actual state aid, 1982*	2.19	3.87	−8.06	1.77	3.44	−8.06	8.08
State coefficient of variation of equal state aid per pupil minus state coefficient of variation of actual state aid, 1992*	4.77	4.62	−5.41	4.25	4.23	−5.41	14.11

Notes:
* Weighted if mulitstate.
See Data Appendix for sources of variables.
[a] Primary metropolitan statistical areas/metropolitan statistical areas.
[b] Conslidated metropolital statistical areas/metropolitan statistical areas.
[c] Standard deviation.

employ as a measure of sprawl. Our other two measures of sprawl are the share of urbanized land relative to total land area of the metropolitan area and the growth rate of urbanized land area.[3] For the PMSA sample the urbanized share of land area increased from 0.07 in 1970 to 0.14 in 1990. The mean annual growth rate in urbanized land area for the PMSA sample was 4.40 percent from 1970 to 1980 and 1.64 percent from 1980 to 1990.

The remaining variables summarized in Table 3.1 measure differences in fiscal or governmental structures. In the PMSA sample the ratio of property taxes per capita in the core county to property taxes per capita in the collar counties declined from 1.39 : 1.00 to 1.30 : 1.00 from 1972 to 1992. For both the number of school districts in the metropolitan area and the number of municipal governments in the metropolitan area, there is little variation over time, but, as can be seen by the large standard deviations or the large range between the minimum and maximum numbers, enormous variation across metropolitan areas. The last two measures (last six variables) match state-level data on school aid to each metropolitan area.[4] The state-supplied share of local school district revenues increased between 1970 and 1990 for both samples. A measure of the degree of cross-district equalization in the distribution of state aid increased dramatically between 1982 and 1992 (from 2.19 to 4.77 for PMSAs and from 1.77 to 4.25 for CMSAs) and has exhibited a large range across metropolitan areas.[5]

We estimate equations that relate our three measures of sprawl to the set of explanatory variables described above. Higher values of our three measures of sprawl—the share of total population residing in the collar counties, the share of total land area categorized as urbanized, and the growth in urbanized land area—indicate greater sprawl. Thus, a positive (negative) coefficient on an explanatory variable in our empirical models indicates that higher values of the variable are associated with greater (lower) levels of sprawl. We report six regressions in Table 3.2, defined by the two samples and the three dependent variables. In regressions (5) and (6) the change in urbanized land area from 1970 to 1980 (1980 to 1990) is regressed on values of the independent variables for 1970 (1980). The first five explanatory variables test various hypotheses concerning the effect of property taxes, local government structure, and school funding on sprawl. We also include control variables for total population (or growth in total population) and for the three census years covered in the analysis (1970 is the omitted year).

According to the theories sketched above, the predicted effects for the key variables are: a positive effect on sprawl of the ratio of core property taxes per capita to collar property taxes per capita, a positive effect on sprawl of the number of school districts, a positive effect on sprawl of the number of municipalities, a negative effect on sprawl of the state share of total school district revenues, and a negative effect on sprawl of the degree of equalization in the state aid formula. The results in Table 3.2 are consistent with some but not all of these predictions. Our results indicate that there is no effect on sprawl of the ratio of core-to-collar property taxes per capita (the variable is insignificant in all six regressions). Thus, higher relative property taxes in the core county (or counties) do not appear to increase sprawl. Our measure of relative property taxes is admittedly crude, and our inability to construct a better measure may be the explanation for our finding of no effect, but nonetheless the consistent results across the six regressions indicate that, in general, higher property taxes in the core relative to the collar do not increase sprawl.

A greater number of school districts is predicted to increase sprawl because parents of school-age children have more choice over school districts and a greater ability to flee school districts in the core and the central city. We find no evidence to support this hypothesis.

The variable is not significant in any of the six regressions, and in regression (2), in which the variable is marginally significant, the coefficient has the "wrong" sign. A greater number of municipalities is expected to result in a higher level of sprawl because municipalities can use their zoning authority to tailor their municipalities to fit the diverse tastes of the population. We find some evidence that metropolitan areas with a greater number of municipalities have a greater level of sprawl. The variable is highly significant in three of the six regressions (columns 1, 2, and 4), and the sign of the coefficient in these three regressions is positive. Casting some doubt on this finding are the result in column (3) in which the variable is marginally significant and has a negative effect, and the insignificant coefficients in columns (5) and (6).

The results for the two variables characterizing state aid are also mixed. A greater share for the state in funding schools and a greater degree of equalization in the state aid formula are expected to decrease sprawl. Higher values for either variable should reduce disparities across school districts and therefore diminish the desire of parents with school-age

Table 3.2

Regression Results for Three Measures of "Sprawl" (absolute values of t-statistics in parentheses)

Dependent variable	Share of total population in collar counties		Share of metropolitan area that lies in "urbanized areas"		Annual growth in urbanized land area	
Sample (specification)	PMSA [a] (1)	CMSA [b] (2)	PMSA (3)	CMSA (4)	PMSA (5)	CMSA (6)
Independent variables						
Ratio of property tax per capita, core / collar	0.0081 (0.45)	0.0005 (0.03)	-0.0029 (0.37)	-0.0019 (0.30)	-0.0034 (1.22)	-0.0041 (1.41)
Number of school districts, total	2.21E-04 (0.69)	-5.22E-04 (1.69)	-9.12E-06 (0.06)	-2.00E-05 (0.20)	-5.55E-05 (1.02)	-4.13E-05 (1.27)
Number of municipalities, total	4.65E-04 (2.39)	5.64E-04 (3.07)	-1.51E-04 (1.73)	1.91E-04 (3.14)	2.68E-05 (0.84)	2.20E-05 (0.75)
State share of school district revenue	-0.1084 (1.13)	-0.1830 (1.80)	-0.0233 (0.55)	-0.0892 (2.65)	0.0589 (3.63)	0.0584 (3.64)
Degree of equalization in distribution of state aid	-0.0043 (2.02)	-0.0072 (3.07)	0.0031 (3.26)	0.0012 (1.51)	-0.0013 (3.51)	-0.0014 (3.85)
Population, total	1.30E-08 (1.25)	1.20E-08 (1.30)	5.04E-08 (8.70)	8.47E-09 (2.77)		
Annual growth in population, total					(5.14) 0.6831	(4.44) 0.5994
1980	0.0347 (1.57)	0.0330 (1.43)	0.0315 (3.19)	0.0375 (4.91)	-0.0292 (9.69)	-0.0300 (9.74)
1990	0.0589 (2.55)	0.0620 (2.61)	0.0502 (4.95)	0.0480 (6.11)		
Constant	0.3033 (5.86)	0.3794 (7.11)	0.0433 (1.85)	0.0855 (4.84)	0.0179 (2.11)	0.0204 (2.57)
Number of observations:	366	324	344	324	212	210
Adjusted R-squared:	0.0952	0.0725	0.3991	0.4041	0.4628	0.4558

Notes: 1970 is the omitted year. [a] Primary metropolitan statistical area. [b] Consolidated metropolitan statistical area.

children to relocate to the fringes of the area in order to escape underfunded core-county and central-city school districts. The coefficient for the state share variable is negative as predicted in the first four regressions, but the variable is statistically significant in only two of these regressions (strongly so in column 4, marginally so in column 2). In contrast, the coefficient on state share is positive and significant in the two regressions with growth in urbanized land area as the dependent variable (columns 5 and 6). The sign of the coefficient for the degree of equalization variable flips among the three measures of sprawl. The variable has a negative effect as predicted on the share of total population residing in the collar counties and on the growth in urbanized land area, but a positive effect on the share of total land area categorized as urbanized. It may be possible to explain these opposing results by examining our three measures of sprawl. It seems at least plausible that the share of the population residing in the collar counties might decline as state aid became more equalizing and more parents of school-age children chose to stay in the core, while the spread of population *density* across the metropolitan land area (our second and third measures of sprawl) might increase as more people chose to live in the area as state aid became more equalizing.[6]

To comment briefly on our control variables, there is some evidence that metropolitan areas with larger populations experienced higher levels of sprawl (columns 3 and 4); evidence that sprawl was greater in 1980 relative to 1970 (especially with respect to the amount of land that is urbanized); and strong evidence that sprawl was greater in 1990 relative to 1970.

Our dependent variable for the share of total population in the collar counties is crude because it is measured at the county level. Several metropolitan areas have unusual county configurations. For example, the Phoenix MSA consists of only two counties, one designated core and the other collar, and only a very small fraction of the total population resides in the collar county (see Table 3.3). To investigate the robustness of our results in columns (1) and (2) to the influence of these "outlier" metropolitan areas, we re-estimated the equations with several different samples in which we excluded observations for metropolitan areas at both ends of the distribution for the dependent variable. For the PMSA samples, the results in column (1) were not sensitive to elimination of outliers. For the CMSA samples, the results were not sensitive to elimination of outliers at the lower end of the distribution (i.e., the omis-

Table 3.3
Variable Values for Selected Metropolitan Areas

Variable	Chicago PMSA[a]	Cleveland PMSA	Philadelphia PMSA	Phoenix MSA[b]	Pittsburgh MSA	Chicago CMSA[c]	Cleveland CMSA	Los Angeles CMSA	Philadelphia CMSA
Number of counties, core, 1998	1	1	1	1	1	2	2	1	3
Number of counties, total, 1998	9	6	9	2	6	13	8	5	14
Population, total, 1970	7,099,321	2,418,809	4,884,456	1,039,807	2,683,970	7,947,855	3,098,048	9,980,861	5,679,574
Population, total, 1980	7,246,048	2,277,949	4,781,235	1,600,093	2,571,223	8,114,844	2,938,277	11,497,549	5,649,031
Population, total, 1990	7,410,858	2,202,069	4,922,175	2,238,480	2,394,811	8,239,820	2,859,644	14,531,529	5,892,937
Share of population, collar / total, 1970	0.23	0.29	0.60	0.07	0.40	0.24	0.27	0.29	0.56
Share of population, collar / total, 1980	0.27	0.34	0.65	0.06	0.44	0.29	0.31	0.35	0.60
Share of population, collar / total, 1990	0.31	0.36	0.68	0.05	0.44	0.32	0.33	0.39	0.62
Annual growth in population, total, 1970-80 (%)	0.20	-0.60	-0.21	4.31	-0.43	0.21	-0.53	1.41	-0.05
Annual growth in population, total, 1980-90 (%)	0.22	-0.34	0.29	3.36	-0.71	0.15	-0.27	2.34	0.42
Share of total area that lies in "urbanized area," 1970	n.a.	0.28	0.20	0.03	0.13	0.21	0.26	0.06	0.17
Share of total area that lies in "urbanized area," 1980	n.a.	0.29	0.26	0.04	0.16	0.25	0.27	0.07	0.23
Share of total area that lies in "urbanized area," 1990	0.27	0.29	0.31	0.05	0.18	0.29	0.29	0.09	0.27
Annual growth in urbanized land area, 1970-80 (%)	n.a.	0.28	3.00	5.02	2.35	2.09	0.34	2.08	3.18
Annual growth in urbanized land area, 1980-90 (%)	n.a.	0.13	1.60	1.45	0.89	1.17	0.50	1.92	1.35
Ratio of property tax per capita, core / collar, 1972	1.52	1.29	0.53	0.83	1.76	1.51	1.26	1.15	0.57
Ratio of property tax per capita, core / collar, 1982	0.81	1.29	0.54	0.72	1.79	0.85	1.24	0.89	0.63
Ratio of property tax per capita, core / collar, 1992	0.96	1.19	0.49	0.77	1.85	0.99	1.17	0.93	0.60

Number of school districts, total, 1972	360	80	209	78	111	414	108	221	283
Number of school districts, total, 1982	342	84	199	80	106	396	114	220	281
Number of school districts, total, 1992	334	84	198	80	105	386	114	215	269
Number of municipalities, total, 1972	288	113	354	24	407	344	144	141	426
Number of municipalities, total, 1982	292	114	354	28	410	350	144	152	428
Number of municipalities, total, 1992	293	115	354	32	412	351	146	172	428
State share of school district revenue, 1970*	0.31	0.27	0.42	0.49	0.46	0.32	0.27	0.32	0.43
State share of school district revenue, 1980*	0.38	0.46	0.40	0.39	0.41	0.39	0.46	0.66	0.41
State share of school district revenue, 1990*	0.33	0.43	0.43	0.44	0.44	0.35	0.43	0.67	0.44
State coefficient of variation of equal state aid per pupil minus state coefficient of variation of actual state aid, 1972*	4.24	4.82	3.95	-0.42	4.63	4.16	4.82	0.06	2.67
State coefficient of variation of equal state aid per pupil minus state coefficient of variation of actual state aid, 1982*	5.94	-0.56	6.40	0.66	5.15	5.21	-0.56	0.81	6.20
State coefficient of variation of equal state aid per pupil minus state coefficient of variation of actual state aid, 1992*	1.96	2.85	8.28	0.53	6.56	1.86	2.85	4.43	8.16

Notes:
* Weighted if multistate.
See Data Appendix for sources of variables.
[a] Primary metropolitan statistical area.
[b] Metropolitan statistical area.
[c] Consolidated metropolitan statistical area.

sion of metropolitan areas such as Phoenix with little population in the collar area), but the coefficients on a few variables are somewhat sensitive to elimination of outliers at the high end of the distribution. For example, if we eliminate from the sample the top twenty-one metropolitan areas with share of total population in the collar counties greater than 65 percent, we find that the coefficient on the state share of school district revenue becomes insignificantly different from zero.

Property Taxes, Schools, and Sprawl in Chicago: 1970, 1980, and 1990

Table 3.3 presents variable values (the same measures as Table 3.1) for selected metropolitan areas—the six metropolitan areas given case study status in the Brookings project. We focus our remarks on the Chicago metropolitan area, a nine-county group in the PMSA sample and a thirteen-county group (the Chicago-Gary-Kenosha, Illinois-Indiana-Wisconsin CMSA) in the CMSA sample. In terms of population and number of counties, the Chicago metropolitan area shown in Table 3.3 is much larger than the average metropolitan area from Table 3.1. Chicago shows the same increase in total population and decrease in the core-county share of population as the average metropolitan area. The two school aid variables for Chicago show different patterns than the "average" metropolitan area—between 1980 and 1990 Chicago (actually, the state of Illinois) exhibited a sizable decrease in both the state share of school district revenues and the degree of equalization in the distribution of those revenues.

The remaining columns in Table 3.3 show variable values for the Cleveland-Lorain-Elyria, Ohio PMSA, the Philadelphia, Pennsylvania-New Jersey PMSA, the Phoenix-Mesa, Arizona MSA (which is in both samples), the Pittsburgh, Pennsylvania MSA (which is in both samples), the Cleveland-Akron, Ohio CMSA , the Los Angeles-Riverside-Orange County, California CMSA,[7] and the Philadelphia-Wilmington-Atlantic City, Pennsylvania-New Jersey-Delaware-Maryland CMSA. By most measures, including population and number of jurisdictions, these six metropolitan areas are relatively large.

For Chicago, more specifically for the six surrounding counties defined as metropolitan in 1970, we have much more detailed information on property taxes than we do for the other metropolitan areas. In Figure 3.1 we display the aggregate effective property tax rates for municipalities in the Chicago metropolitan area in 1996.[8] Note that the highest aggregate effective tax rates (9.76% or higher) are almost entirely in Cook County. Similarly, most of the municipalities with aggregate effective tax rates in the third quartile (7.797% to 9.75%) are in Cook County. The city of Chicago has a 9.47 percent tax rate, which places it in the third quartile. There is a concentration of municipalities in the lowest quartile of tax rates (6.83% or lower) in DuPage County. Figure 3.1 indicates that property tax rates are highest in Cook County, the core county of the metropolitan area. Preliminary results from an ongoing research project on the Chicago metropolitan area suggest that higher property tax rates may discourage economic activity (Dye, McGuire, and Merriman 2001). Thus, property taxes may be a factor in encouraging sprawl in the Chicago metropolitan area.

Conclusion

In a survey of the literature we found very few studies that directly addressed the question at hand: Is urban sprawl affected by property taxes and schools? Several authors and commentators suggest a connection, but little systematic evidence exists. In an attempt to provide some evidence on the question, we gathered data on over 100 of the largest metropolitan areas in the United States and measured the level of sprawl over a twenty-year time period. We used regression analysis to relate our measures of sprawl to variables characterizing local government structure, local finances, and schools in metropolitan areas. We found that property tax differentials between the core and the collar and the number of school districts had no or little effect on the level of sprawl. We found some evidence in support of the notion that a greater number of municipalities in a metropolitan area is associated with greater sprawl, and some evidence for the hypothesis that sprawl is lower in states with a larger and more equalizing role for the state in financing local school districts.

The Chicago metropolitan area differs from the average metropolitan area on the three variables for which we find evidence of a relationship with sprawl. The Chicago PMSA and CMSA are clearly outliers in terms of the number of municipalities with, for example, the Chicago PMSA at 293 municipalities in 1992 compared with an average of 60. The state share of school district revenues was lower in the Chicago metropolitan area over this time period, while, in contrast to other states, the degree

56 RICHARD F. DYE AND THERESE J. MCGUIRE

Figure 3.1 **Aggregate Effective Property Tax Rates with Respect to Equalized Assessed Value. Municipalities in the Chicago Metropolitan Area, 1996**

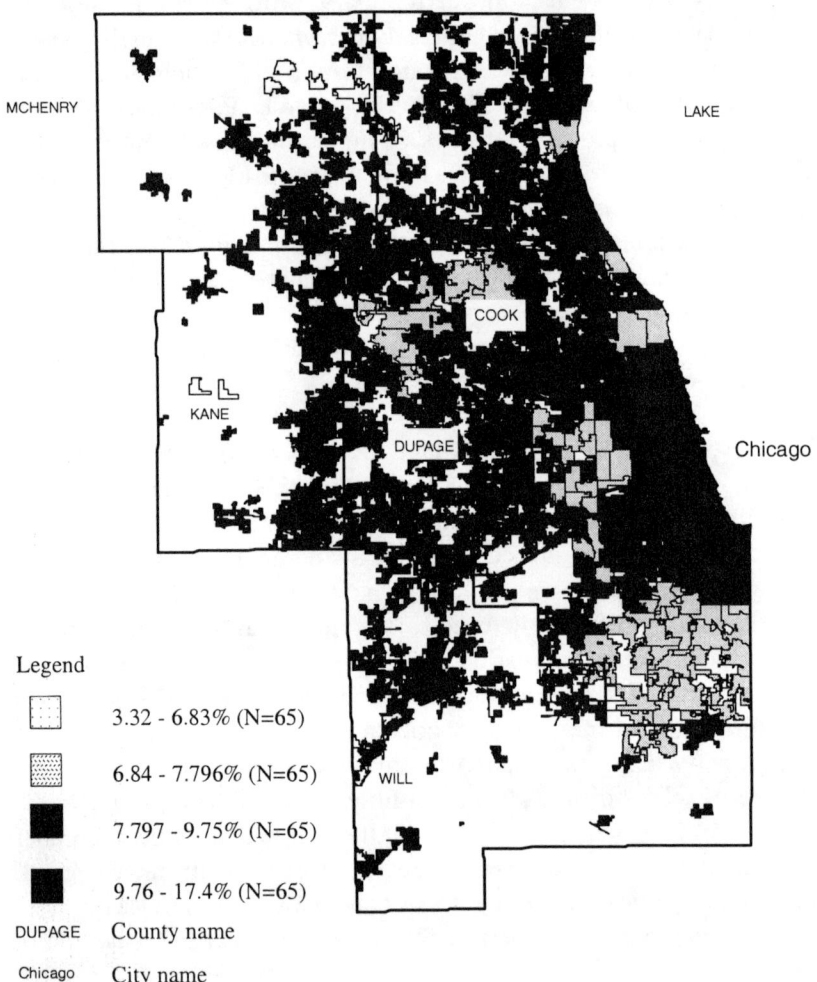

Legend

☐ 3.32 - 6.83% (N=65)

▨ 6.84 - 7.796% (N=65)

■ 7.797 - 9.75% (N=65)

■ 9.76 - 17.4% (N=65)

DUPAGE County name

Chicago City name

Source: Data from the Illinois Department of Revenue. Map by the Institute of Government and Public Affairs, 1999.

of equalization of the state aid in Illinois fell dramatically from 1982 to 1992. Given our empirical findings, these nonaverage values for Chicago may have contributed to sprawl in the Chicago metropolitan area. In other words, the large number of municipalities in the Chicago area and the small role for the state in financing education may have been contributing factors explaining the level of sprawl in the area in recent decades.

Data Appendix

Metropolitan Area Definitions

We use the June 30, 1998, definition of metropolitan areas given by the Census Bureau (www.census.gov/population/estimates/metro-city/98mfips.txt). New England County Metropolitan Area (NECMA) definitions are also from the Census Bureau (www.census.gov/population/estimates/metro-city/98nfips.txt). Metropolitan areas may be either MSAs (metropolitan statistical areas), CMSAs (consolidated metropolitan statistical areas), PMSAs (primary metropolitan statistical areas), or NECMAs (New England county metropolitan areas). A CMSA is formed by the joining of two or more PMSAs and is indicative of a metropolitan area created by the fusing of multiple smaller metropolitan areas. PMSAs exist only as divisions of a CMSA. New England metropolitan areas typically are composed of towns and partial counties; the NECMA definition, which uses entire counties, is more useful to us as most of our data were gathered at the county level. A NECMA may be equivalent to a PMSA or to an MSA.

Metropolitan areas (PMSAs, CMSAs, MSAs, and NECMAs) were chosen for our samples based on the following criteria: The metropolitan area must have a 1990 population of at least 250,000, and it must contain more than one county. For PMSAs and MSAs, 124 metropolitan areas met the criteria. Two of these cases were later dropped due to difficulties in selecting a core county. For CMSAs and MSAs, 108 metropolitan areas met the criteria. The two PMSAs dropped from the PMSA sample are included within their respective CMSAs in the CMSA sample.

Number of Counties

The number of counties in each metropolitan area is determined by the metropolitan area's Census Bureau definition. The designation of core counties was done manually, based on relative 1970 population and population density, and does not correspond to the Census Bureau's core county indicator. The county or counties containing the primary city of the metropolitan area were always designated as the core; other counties were also included if the metro area had more than one central city. In every case, we made an effort to minimize the number of core counties. The core counties we selected for the PMSAs automatically became core counties in the CMSAs.

Population

Population data at the county level is from the decennial Census: www.census.gov/population/estimates/county/e7079co.zip and e8089co.zip (1970 and 1980), and www.census.gov/population/censusdata/90den_stco.txt (1990).

Land Area

Land area in square miles by county, 1990, is from the 1990 Census: www.census.gov/population/censusdata/90den_stco.txt.

Land Area, Urbanized Areas

Data for land area of urbanized areas come from the 1972 County and City Data Book (1972); the 1980 Census of Population Supplementary Report, Population and Land Area of Urbanized Areas for the United States and Puerto Rico (Mills 1984); and the 1990 Census of Population and Housing Supplementary Report, Urbanized Areas of the United States and Puerto Rico (U.S. Bureau of the Census 1993). We include urbanized areas whose named city is located inside the metropolitan area.

Property Tax Revenue, Counties

Property tax revenue data by county comes from the 1972, 1982, and 1992 Census of Governments, volume 4, number 5. Figures represent the sum of all property tax revenues collected by local governments within each county border.

Number of School Districts

Number of school districts in each county is from the 1972, 1982, and 1992 Census of Governments, volume 1, number 1. Figures include both independent and dependent K-12 public school districts.

Number of Municipalities

Number of municipal governments in each county is also from the 1972, 1982, and 1992 Census of Governments, volume 1, number 1. In the states of Connecticut, Massachusetts, Minnesota, New Hampshire, New Jersey, New York, Pennsylvania, Rhode Island, and Wisconsin, township governments are added. In Virginia, we added counties to the municipal count since county governments in that state provide general purpose government functions and exist only in areas with no municipal or township governments.

State Share

State share of school district revenue, by state, 1970, 1980, and 1990, comes from the National Center for Education Statistics, "State Comparisons of Education Statistics: 1969–70 to 1996–97." NCES 98–018.

Degree of Equalization

See note 5 for the definition and source of this measure.

Notes

1. We explored a fourth measure of sprawl—the population density of the suburban area relative to the population density of the total metropolitan area—but the results obtained with this variable were weak and not robust to changes in specification. Hence we do not report results for this measure.

2. In order to have both "core" and "collar" counties in each metropolitan area, one-county metropolitan areas are not included in the sample. In the six New England states the unit is the New England county metropolitan area (NECMA). A consolidated metropolitan statistical area (CMSA) contains more than one primary metropolitan statistical area (PMSA). For definitions of the metropolitan area concepts see U.S. Bureau of the Census (1994).

3. Census "urbanized areas" can cross county lines and in some cases include

land outside the counties in the metropolitan areas. For urbanized areas that cross PMSAs we were able to allocate by county for 1990 only; thus we lose some observations and our sample size for this variable is 122 in 1990, 110 in 1980, and 112 in 1970.

4. For metropolitan areas that cross state lines, the population-weighted average of the state variables is calculated. An alternative of using just the largest state has no substantial impact on the estimates presented below.

5. Our measure of the degree of equalization in the state aid formula is the difference between the coefficient of variation across school districts of hypothetical state aid distributed on a per pupil basis and the coefficient of variation across school districts of actual state aid. Thus a higher value of this measure means more equalization. We would like to thank Sheila Murray for providing us with this variable. For a description of the data set from which this was taken, see Murray, Evans, and Schwab (1998).

6. Tables 3.1 and 3.3 both show that the variable meant to represent "the degree of equalization in state school aid" is quite volatile. This measure is not ideal since there can be sources of variation in state aid across districts other than formula-based equalization.

7. Los Angeles is excluded from the PMSA sample since it is a one-county PMSA.

8. The effective tax rate is calculated from Illinois Department of Revenue data as the ratio of "current total extensions" to "equalized assessed value" (equalized assessed value in Illinois is one-third of market value). There are over 1,200 local governments with property-taxing authority in the six-county Chicago metropolitan area—counties, municipalities, school districts, library districts, and other special districts. The pattern of overlap in these governments creates thousands of different combinations or "tax codes." We assign each municipal government a single tax code—a unique set of overlying governments. Thus for each municipality we can calculate the aggregate effective tax rate as the sum of the effective tax rates for the list of overlying governments.

References

Carlino, Gerald A., and Edwin S. Mills. 1987. The Determinants of County Growth. *Journal of Regional Science* 27(1) (February): 39–54.

Charney, Alberta. 1983. Intraurban Manufacturing Location Decisions and Local Tax Differentials. *Journal of Urban Economics* 14: 184–205.

Downs, Anthony. 1994. *New Visions for Metropolitan America*. Washington, DC: The Brookings Institution.

Dye, Richard F., Therese J. McGuire, and David F. Merriman. 2001. The Impact of Property Taxes and Property Tax Classification on Business Activity in the Chicago Metropolitan Area. Mimeo. Institute for Government and Public Affairs, University of Illinois at Chicago, Chicago.

Erickson, Rodney, and Michael Wasylenko. 1980. Firm Location and Site Selection in Suburban Municipalities. *Journal of Urban Economics* 8: 69–85.

Fox, William. 1981. Fiscal Differentials and Industrial Location: Some Empirical Evidence. *Urban Studies* 18: 105–111.

Luce, Thomas F., Jr. 1994. Local Taxes, Public Services, and the Intrametropolitan Location of Firms and Households. *Public Finance Quarterly* 22(2) (April): 139–167.

Mark, Stephen T., Therese J. McGuire, and Leslie E. Papke. 2000. The Influence of Taxes on Employment and Population Growth: Evidence from the Washington, DC, Metropolitan Area. *National Tax Journal*. 53: 105–123.

McGuire, Therese J. 1985. Are Local Taxes Important in the Intrametropolitan Location of Firms? An Empirical Analysis of the Minneapolis–St. Paul Metropolitan Area. *Journal of Urban Economics* 18: 226–234.

Mieszkowski, Peter, and Edwin S. Mills. 1993. The Causes of Metropolitian Suburbanization. *Journal of Economic Perspectives* 7(3) (Summer): 135–147.

Mills, Edwin S., and Richard Price. 1984. Metropolitan Suburbanization and Central City Problems. *Journal of Urban Economics* 15(1) (January): 1–17.

Mills, Karen M. 1984. 1980 Census of Population, Supplementary Report: Population and Land Area of Urbanized Areas for the United States and Puerto Rico, 1980 and 1970. Washington, DC: U.S. Bureau of the Census, Department of Commerce.

Murray, Sheila E., William N. Evans, and Robert M. Schwab. 1998. Education Finance Reform and the Distribution of Education Resources. *American Economic Review* 88(3) (September): 789–812.

Orfield, Myron. 1998. *Metropolitics: A Regional Agenda for Community and Stability*, rev. ed. Washington, DC: The Brookings Institution.

U.S. Bureau of the Census, Department of Commerce, Economics and Statistics Administration. 1994. *Geographic Areas Reference Manual*. November: www.census.gov/geo/www/garm.html.

———. 1993. *1990 Census of Population and Housing, Supplementary Reports: Urbanized Areas of the United States and Puerto Rico*. Washington, DC: U.S. Bureau of the Census.

———. 1972. *1972 Census of Population and Housing, Supplementary Reports: Urbanized Areas of the United States and Puerto Rico*. Washington, DC: U.S. Bureau of the Census.

Wasylenko, Michael. 1980. Evidence of Fiscal Differentials and Intrametropolitan Firm Relocation. *Land Economics* 56: 339–349.

Young, Dwight. 1995. *Alternatives to Sprawl*. Report based on a conference in Washington, DC, in March 1995 cosponsored by the Lincoln Institute of Land Policy, the Brookings Institution, and the National Trust for Historic Preservation. Cambridge, MA: Lincoln Institute of Land Policy.

4

JEAN M. TEMPLETON

Land Use Planning Tools in Illinois: Preventing or Promoting Sprawl?

Introduction

Discussions about urban sprawl that blame municipal governments for sprawl-related problems often fail to consider the structure of relationships that govern land use decisions. It is often assumed that local governments are united in their pursuit of uncontrolled growth strategies or that the metropolitan area is composed solely of fragmented decision-making processes that are characterized by competition rather than cooperation. This view also does not tell the whole story about local land use decision making in metropolitan regions.

In most places land use regulations are issues of local concern. Illinois is no exception to this general rule. However, there are a number of areas where state level policies and other substate policies play an important role in structuring the arena in which land use regulation decisions are made.

This chapter will explore the overall framework for land use regulation in the Chicago metropolitan region and will address three specific land use tools in use by Illinois municipalities: municipal boundary agreements, annexation, and impact fees. Particular emphasis will be placed on examining the interrelationships among state, county, and municipal authority and the limitations imposed on each. The discussion about the framework of land use regulation in Illinois will be organized in the following way. First, a very brief explanation and evaluation of the impact of the 1970 constitution on local government powers will be presented. Second, an analysis of the ways in which land use regulatory powers are distributed between differing layers of government—such as municipal, county, and state, will be presented. The chapter will then turn to a more specific discussion about the land use tools described above. Some examples of recent efforts and practices on the developing fringe of the Chicago metropolitan area will be discussed.

As we will see, there is in fact a fair amount of cooperation among municipalities through voluntary municipal boundary agreements. However, the ease of annexation has placed few obstacles in the way of continuing suburban sprawl. The difficulty of imposing impact fees has also put few financial obstacles in the way of developers. Thus, land use planning legislation in Illinois has generally been favorable to continued outward expansion of the metropolitan area.

The 1970 Constitution

Illinois adopted its most recent constitution in 1970. It replaced the constitution adopted one century earlier and sought to address some of the shortcomings in that document that had become apparent over the years. One of the central themes for discussion in the crafting of the new constitution was the scope of powers to be given to local governments. The constitution of 1870 did not contain any general grant of powers to local governments.[1] The general interpretation of this relationship was that municipalities had only those powers expressly conferred on them by the legislature or those that could be fairly implied therefrom. This rule applied to the smallest cities in the state as well as to cities like Chicago.

One of the motivating forces behind the constitutional convention in 1970 was to address this perceived dependency by local government on the state legislature. The importance of local governmental issues in the convention is demonstrated by the fact that there was a separate convention committee dealing only with local government. The committee examined home-rule provisions in a number of states and noted that they varied widely from state to state. The committee's majority report expressed the view that home-rule provisions should be included in the new constitution in order to provide local governments with creative and extensive powers to contribute effectively to solving problems created by increasing urbanization.[2]

Despite the strong support for the proposed home-rule provisions, there was opposition to the broad grant of home-rule powers proposed for the 1970 constitution. Comments considered by the committee included some observations that now seem eerily prophetic:

Many problems have grown beyond city limits, but the city's power to cope with a situation ends abruptly at its boundary lines. In addition to local inability to provide many services, individual communities may damage their neighbors' interests by their own policies—by excluding moderate-cost housing or polluting rivers, for example. . . . Where everybody is concerned but no one unit has the power to act, what purpose is served by local popular control? The Commission shares the view expressed by Luther Gulick that municipal home rule in the mid-twentieth century is not the right to be left alone behind legally defined bulwarks, but rather the right to participate as an equal partner in arriving at decisions which affect community life. (U.S. House 1966, 123–124)[3]

While recognizing the potential problems that could exist in urbanized areas, the majority of the local government committee members believed that the solution to the potential fragmentation problem did not lie in denying much needed powers to local governments, but rather in encouraging maximum cooperation between local governments to solve their problems.

The framers of the state constitution achieved the goal of the adoption of broad home-rule powers through two means: first, by using language that granted extensive powers and second, by conferring home-rule powers on municipalities automatically, without the need for any action by the municipality. This constitutional grant of power provides that a home-rule unit in Illinois may "exercise any power and perform any function pertaining to its government and affairs."[4] Home-rule powers are conferred by the constitution on any municipality with a population of more than 25,000. Unlike some other states that adopted home rule, no action by the local government was required in order to become a home-rule unit—the provisions of the constitution were self-executing. Home-rule provisions supersede other governmental regulations, including county or state regulations.

Land use decisions made within the corporate boundaries of a municipality fall under home rule, but in extraterritorial matters, the operation of home-rule provisions may be severely restricted. A municipality that desires to expand its territory by annexation, for example, must do so in strict conformance with state statutes.[5] Municipalities have been granted certain extraterritorial powers by state statute, and their ability to operate outside of their boundaries usually conforms closely to those provisions.

Despite the broad grant of local decision-making power under the home-rule provisions of the Illinois constitution, there are provisions for preemption of home-rule power. The state has explicitly preempted municipal home-rule authority in a variety of situations where the state's interests are deemed to be superior. In addition, the Illinois courts have also occasionally found preemptions by implication. This situation arises only where the state has legislated extensively in an area and where the subject matter of the legislation is clearly a matter of statewide concern, as opposed to purely local concern, such that uniform state regulations are perceived as important; for example, local environmental regulations that are more stringent, or more liberal, than the state's are not a proper exercise of home-rule powers.[6]

State Level Policies

Illinois has little in the way of explicit land use planning policies at the state level. There are various state agencies with some planning authority, such as the state's Department of Transportation with general authority for planning of highways throughout the state, and the Department of Commerce and Community Affairs, which has general authority for economic development planning. No cohesive or coherent system of land use regulation exists at the statewide level, aside from regulations that either enable planning by local governments or which prohibit local governments from preventing certain kinds of activities in order to avoid NIMBY situations.[7] There is state-level legislation that authorizes regional planning of a sort through the Northeastern Illinois Planning Commission (NIPC), but the planning activities authorized under that legislation are generally advisory and not binding.

In recent years, Governor George Ryan has expressed a commitment to a "smart growth" agenda for the state. This agenda includes farmland protection measures, directing growth to established communities and distressed areas, respect and reliance on local and regional decision making, and a process that will not involve state-directed mandates. In general this appears to be consistent with the state's current policy, which devolves most land use regulation to local, rather than state, government. Specific initiatives that fit into this agenda include funding for redevelopment of dilapidated industrial land, an investment in infrastructure in existing communities, and the preservation of open space. The state also created the new Illinois Open Land Trust Act, which, among other things, authorizes the Department of Natural Resources to acquire real property for conservation and recreation purposes and to provide grants and loans to units of local government and nonprofit corporations to also acquire real property for the same purposes.

It also established the Smart Growth Task Force, which has as a partial list of its objectives to conduct public hearings on a plan for twenty-first-century farmland preservation, land use, and transportation needs for different state regions; strengthen laws that promote farmland preservation and promote compact development; examine how state fiscal policy affects land use and farmland preservation; and to recommend action steps to create a statewide smart growth land use plan based on statewide public hearings. Thus, it is clear that there is a good deal of legislative interest in the general topic of growth management in the state.

Government Powers and Intergovernmental Relationships

Leaving aside the issue of the scope of home-rule powers in Illinois, there remains a complex web of interrelationships governing land use in Illinois. Generally speaking, land use decisions are developed and implemented at the local level. However, in many areas, state statutes provide for specific powers to be allocated to differing levels of government in an array of overlapping responsibilities. Intended to foster cooperation, such regulations may, indeed, have the opposite effect. In Illinois different levels of government carry out different public missions. County level government has overall responsibility for operation of the state court system. Some counties, such as Cook County, also operate substantial healthcare operations and may even operate hospitals and clinics. Many of the counties in northeastern Illinois also act as distributors of Federal Community Development Block Grant funds to their municipalities. Finally, counties also have significant responsibilities for certain "housekeeping functions," such as tax collection, tax assessment, real property tax classification, and highway improvements and maintenance.

Illinois also has township governments in some counties in the state. Townships are units that are geographically smaller than counties, but usually larger in area than municipalities. Township government has limited responsibility in Illinois, and most townships in the metropolitan region are responsible for some highway maintenance, some tax assessment and collection responsibilities, and some regional social service activities.

Local general-purpose governments in Illinois have fairly extensive responsibilities for managing local concerns. Functions include general municipal services such as garbage collection, street maintenance, fire and police protection, sewer and water services, enforcement of health and safety regulations such as building codes and restaurant licensing, general business licensing and regulation, zoning authority, planning and development authority, and various financial responsibilities related to local tax collection and enforcement.

Under state law, municipalities have the primary responsibility for developing local land use plans.[8] Included with the responsibility for developing comprehensive plans is the explicit authority to develop subdivision regulations, which may be considered part of the comprehensive plan. This planning power includes the authority to develop a comprehensive plan for areas outside of the corporate limits of the municipality, within 1.5 miles of its boundaries. Municipalities are also authorized to approve plats of subdivision or resubdivision for areas lying within their comprehensive plan, and they may through that process require that lands be dedicated for public purposes such as park sites and school sites. Municipalities are also granted separate authority to develop zoning ordinances and to similarly exercise their zoning powers within the 1.5-mile boundary area outside of their territorial limits. However, municipal zoning powers over the extraterritorial property within the 1.5-mile limit may not be exercised by the municipality if the county in which the municipality is located has adopted a zoning ordinance.

Counties and townships also have the power to develop land use plans and zoning/subdivision regulations.[9] Those regulations are not effective within the confines of any incorporated municipality—local zoning regulations take precedence. County regulations take precedence only in unincorporated areas, and township regulations are restricted even more, as they do not apply at all in counties that have adopted zoning requirements.

However, unless the local government in question has land-banked a substantial amount of vacant land, it is likely that development will occur somewhere outside of the incorporated boundaries of the municipality. Such development is governed jointly by the municipality and the county. While the municipalities are given the power to adopt official comprehensive plans in territory located outside their boundaries, those plans are deemed advisory only. If the county in which the municipality is located has adopted a county zoning ordinance, then the county zoning provisions will apply within this 1.5-mile area. As a result, although the municipality is the one charged with the responsibility for designating land use and development patterns in this extraterritorial area, it is the county that will actually be responsible for developing zoning ordinances that may or may not coincide with the municipality's land use plans.

Land Use Tools

Despite the overall devolution of land use power to local municipalities, there are constraints on the ability of local governments to exercise control over how land is developed. These constraints are most often apparent in the context of regulations that either involve extraterritorial actions or that involve exactions that might be viewed as unduly burdensome on property owners. Among the long list of land use regulation tools available to municipalities, this chapter will examine three: municipal boundary agreements (including joint planning agreements), annexation, and impact fees. The first two, municipal boundary agreements and annexation, involve attempts by a municipality to control development outside of its political boundaries. The third land use tool, impact fees, may be operative within the municipality and sometimes outside of the municipality, since subdivision controls adopted to implement a comprehensive plan may govern development in this extraterritorial area. Impact fees are also constrained by constitutional limitations on their application. Each of the three is a potentially powerful tool for any municipality, although these tools are generally most useful to those municipalities that find themselves growing, rather than declining.

Boundary Agreements and Joint Planning

As municipalities grow, and in more densely settled sections of the metropolitan region, obvious conflicts develop with respect to land use planning decisions. There are situations where these 1.5-mile planning boundaries surrounding municipalities overlap. This may lead to conflicting land use patterns, since one municipality may designate its boundary area for residential use, while the next municipality may designate the property on just the other side of the line for heavy industry. There is little that can be done to alleviate such conflicting patterns, since municipalities are free to adopt comprehensive plans that provide for their own vision of how development should occur.

More important, one of the municipalities may decide to annex some of the unincorporated territory within the 1.5-mile boundary, thus shifting this line. The decision by one municipality to do this can eliminate a buffer area between two municipalities. An example is the controversy that erupted in suburban Kane County, where the city of Elgin and the separate village of South Elgin found themselves in litigation over a proposed annexation by the city of Elgin in the late 1980s.[10] A developer sought to join some 150 acres of property to the city of Elgin; this not only took up all of the space in the boundary planning area, eight acres of it wound up on the side of the line in the planning area belonging to the village of South Elgin. South Elgin attempted to stop the annexation by arguing that the 1.5-mile planning boundary prevented Elgin from annexing territory lying on South Elgin's side of the boundary. The court did not accept the reasoning by the village of South Elgin, finding that there was nothing in the statutory scheme creating the extraterritorial planning areas that prevented either municipality from annexing land and permitted the annexation to go forward. As a result of this annexation, the boundary planning area of the city of Elgin shifted substantially.

Municipal Boundary Agreements

Illinois municipalities have attempted, over a period of many years, to bring some level of certainty to this situation by entering into voluntary agreements, authorized by state statute, which would allocate the planning responsibilities between them. Many of these agreements also included promises by the contracting municipalities with respect to annexation of particular parcels. Generally, such agreements would include a statement by the parties that each agreed not to annex certain parcels or that if parcels were annexed, the property would be zoned in a certain way. In a series of court decisions in the 1980s, agreements containing such annexation prohibitions were found to be invalid and unenforceable.[11]

The cases, which went to the Appellate Court, all involved municipalities located in fast-growing sections of the metropolitan area such as southern Lake County and DuPage County.[12] In each case, the boundary agreement not only attempted to establish a buffer zone and/or planning boundary, but also sought to establish commitments on the issue of future annexations. By articulating a clear position about what property each municipality might or might not annex, the municipalities sought to fix future growth in a more substantial way than merely by articulating "planning" considerations.

One of the cases involved two villages in southern Lake County, Long Grove and Kildeer, both of which were characterized by large-lot residential uses. The agreement was entered into in the early 1960s and stated that neither village would annex land beyond its respective boundary line. In the late 1970s, however, Kildeer repudiated the agreement. Several years later the village of Kildeer annexed a thirty-two-acre parcel that overlapped the established boundary line between the two municipalities, and Long Grove sued to prevent the annexation on the basis of the boundary agreement. The court held that while the municipalities could certainly engage in binding agreements to establish planning boundaries, they did not have the legal power to promise not to annex property. As a result, the annexation by Kildeer was viewed as perfectly legal, regardless of the boundary agreement.

The authorizing statute was subsequently amended specifically to include agreements to annex as one of the matters about which municipalities could agree in a jurisdictional boundary agreement.[13] Boundary agreements that regulate annexation activities have been upheld under this statute, even against arguments by a landowner that the annexation limitations contained in such an agreement harmed his prospects for future development.

Municipal boundary agreements continue to present both opportunities and challenges in the metropolitan area. They can be used not only to provide a natural buffer between municipalities but also to control unwanted commercial development. The villages of North Barrington and Hawthorn Woods, upper-income residential villages right on the border of southwestern Lake County and northwestern Cook County, were engaged in a highly charged controversy over a proposed development lying in an unincorporated area between their two villages.[14] A developer proposed a 1.1 million-square-foot shopping mall in the area between the two municipalities. While some development in that area is not necessarily opposed by either municipality, the size of the proposed commercial development (and the potential for a windfall in taxes) has led to controversy between the two. The developer approached North Barrington first, but then shifted his sights to Hawthorn Woods after village officials reportedly offered a substantial rebate of sales taxes associated with the mall. During the controversy, North Barrington officials held what one reporter described as an "early morning meeting" and summarily approved a request for annexation to North Barrington that had been proposed by the developer some time previously but never withdrawn by him. They also rezoned the property. Both actions were deemed invalid by the county state's attorney's office as violating the Open Meetings Act.[15] North Barrington then chose to approve a municipal boundary agreement that had been previously approved by Hawthorn Woods, which gave the property in question to North Barrington and dedicated 30 percent of the sales tax revenue to Hawthorn Woods. After approving the agreement, North Barrington filed suit in the spring of 1999 to enforce it.

In an attempt to resolve litigation, the village of North Barrington proposed in April a municipal boundary agreement containing the following provisions: (1) limiting the commercial development on the 110-acre site to 35–50 acres, (2) requiring that the rest of the property be devoted to single-family and multifamily (primarily townhouses) residential use, (3) granting Hawthorn Woods control over the entire site, (4) requiring that North Barrington receive 40 percent of the sales tax generated for the next ninety-nine years, along with 35 percent of the commercial building fees. The proposal to limit the commercial development to 35 to 50 acres would effectively kill the proposed shopping mall. Municipal officials in North Barrington and Hawthorn Woods did, ultimately, reach agreement on the terms for resolving this dispute. Under the agreement, the property would be on the Hawthorn Woods side of the boundary line, and revenue from development would be divided between Hawthorn Woods and North Barrington. Hawthorn Woods rejected the notion of the shopping mall, and the agreement contains terms that therefore make the development of the shopping mall as proposed extremely unlikely. North Barrington has agreed to drop its claim for annexation of the parcel, so the property currently remains outside of the limits of both municipalities and is undeveloped. Although the immediate crisis is over, concerns remain on the part of some officials that the developer may try to locate some other municipality that might be in a position to annex the property.

Joint Planning for Land Resource Management

About the same time much of the early litigation between municipalities over boundary agreements was going on, the legislature also adopted a new act, effective in 1985, that sought to encourage a better planning process with respect to land management practices. The Local Land Resource Management Planning Act[16] has as its stated purpose to "encourage municipalities and counties to protect the land, air, water, natural resources and environment of the State and to encourage the use of such resources in a manner which is socially and economically desirable through the adoption of joint or compatible Local Land Resource Management Plans." Under the act, a Local Land Resource Management Plan is defined to include a map of existing and proposed land use as well as written policy statements adopted by the county or municipal government. In addition to generalized land use issues, such plans may also include sewer and water systems, energy distribution systems, recreational facilities, public safety facilities and their relationship to natural resources, air, water, and land quality management programs.

Plans under the act may also adopt goals and procedures for resolving conflicts in relation to a rather extensive list of objectives, including such diverse topics as agricultural preservation, economic activity, energy conservation, governmental cooperation, housing, and open spaces.[17] Local governments wishing to benefit from the new act were required to (a) Adopt implementing ordinances, zoning, and subdivision ordinances as authorized by law, (b) adopt a three-year capital improvement and maintenance program for the jurisdiction that would consider reasonably anticipated growth and that was designed to accommodate contiguous development, (c) adopt a statement of goals compatible with the "local situation," and (d) develop a system and timetable to review and update the plans at least once every ten years.

In return for engaging in this planning process, local governments were authorized under the act to enter into enforceable joint agreements with other municipalities and with their counties for planning, land resource management, and zoning enforcement, notwithstanding the general statutory limitations concerning county and municipal zoning. The act also provided for a system of planning grants, administered by the state Department of Commerce and Community Affairs for the development, administration, and implementation of such plans.

Following the adoption of the new act, five of the six counties in the Chicago metropolitan region adopted local land resource management plans.[18] While several of the counties had previously engaged in countywide planning efforts, the new plans focused with greater specificity on some of the growth management issues articulated in the act.

Indeed, the three fastest-growing counties in the Chicago metropolitan region (DuPage, Lake, and Kane) each have land use resource management plans that specifically articulate a planning goal of attracting new growth into areas that currently exist within municipal boundaries, and identify one important tool toward accomplishing that growth, namely the implementation of municipal boundary agreements. Officials in these counties acknowledged less success in getting joint planning agreements between the municipalities and the counties themselves. One of the barriers to more rapid progress has been that there just are not many incentives to induce municipalities to engage in joint planning with the county. Although the statute provides that the Department of Commerce and Community Affairs may offer planning grants to municipalities who engage in this process, the General Assembly has never appropriated funds to support the grants.

Annexation

In Illinois, annexation procedures are governed by state statute. A home-rule unit in Illinois has the same power that non-home–rule units do to annex property, and they must complete their annexation process in strict compliance with the state-level policies concerning the addition of territory. Annexation in Illinois has its own colorful history. During the nineteenth century a number of municipalities sought to connect themselves with the city of Chicago, perhaps in the hope of acquiring, among other things, better water and sewer services. This annexation frenzy led to referenda in 1889 that, in one fell swoop, added 120 square miles of territory to the city of Chicago, effectively doubling its size.[19] Annexation continues to be a popular method by which municipalities seek to control growth around their borders, basically by bringing new territory within their corporate boundaries.

A detailed discussion about the various methods for annexation of property into a municipality is beyond the scope of this chapter. Illinois provides a menu of annexation choices for varying circumstances, some of which involve referenda or court approval, and others that require only the approval of the corporate authorities.[20] In most situations annexation is a voluntary act that can be initiated by interested landowners. Depending on the circumstances, referendum approval by the voters residing in the territory to be annexed may also be required. The circumstances under which annexations occur and the methods followed vary based upon the size of the territory, its proximity to other municipalities, and whether it is vacant or occupied. There are, however, two key issues pertaining to annexation in Illinois. The first is that under the annexation statutes, an interested developer and a willing municipal council can annex appropriate land quickly and within in a fairly short time. The second key point is that annexation done in conformance with the requirements of the state statutes is almost exclusively within the discretion of the local municipal authorities—there is little or nothing that County government or other landowners can do to prevent the annexation.

Municipalities gain substantial benefits by annexing land. First, if they are home-rule units, they gain substantial power over the management of the land use, including the power granted by state statute to zone. Second, they gain tax revenue that the land produces, since tax burdens and benefits in Illinois are distributed based upon incorporated municipal boundaries. They also may extend their planning boundaries, since they will be entitled to engage in extraterritorial land use planning within their new 1.5-mile boundary, provided that this area is not included in the incorporated limits of any other municipality.

More important, however, municipalities wishing to annex a parcel of property may engage in negotiations with a developer to produce an annexation agreement that will control both the timing of the annexation and the contributions made by the developer to the municipality. Annexation agreements may specifically include agreements relating to subdivision controls and zoning by the municipality, as well as "contributions of either land or monies, or both, to any municipality and to other units of local government having jurisdiction over all or part of land that is the subject matter of any annexation agreement."[21] There are no restrictions or requirements that the developer's contributions be limited to remedying the impacts of his proposed development, and since annexation is a voluntary act, the municipality is free to negotiate with the developer for whatever it can get.

While municipalities may enter into annexation agreements for a period not to exceed twenty years for property that is noncontiguous, they can only actually annex property that is contiguous to their boundaries. In consensual annexations, the property owner and the municipal authorities may conclude the annexation process simply by the passage of an ordinance and the agreement of all of the landowners if the property is vacant. No court proceedings are required, nor is the approval of any higher level of government. There is little that any other municipality or governmental unit can do to prevent the annexation.

County level land resource plans within the metropolitan region generally articulate a goal of preventing or discouraging "defensive" annexations by municipalities that seek to pre-empt development or grab land. Instead, the county plans generally favor annexation processes that define a municipal planning boundary and then proceed with annexation consistent with those boundary definitions. However, these statements in the county land resource plans are merely expressions of planning goals, and the fact remains that county policies may have little impact on annexation decisions.

Annexation is more of an issue on the developing fringe where there is still land available for growth than it is for those areas of the metropolitan region where substantial development has already occurred. DuPage County, for example, has been one of the fastest growing counties in the metropolitan region for some period of time. Located immediately to the west of Cook County, where the city of Chicago and Chicago's O'Hare airport are located, DuPage has felt the pressure of this fast growth. By 1992, farmland in DuPage County represented only 8.2 percent of the land area of the county. This represented only slightly more farmland that was available in the county of Cook, the region's most urbanized county (6.9 percent). The next fastest growing county in Illinois, Lake County, had only 25 percent of its farmland remaining in 1992, as compared with roughly 60 percent remaining in McHenry, Kane, and Will counties.

Despite the rather rapid conversion of farmland in Lake County, the Lake framework plan does not seek to prevent municipal annexation or growth. Instead, it merely seeks to try and channel that growth into areas where development is already taking place. Goals are also articulated for attempting to preserve what are termed "countryside" districts to maintain the essentially "rural" character of the county.

The place where annexation is a more important issue is on the western, developing fringe of the metropolitan area, particularly in Kane County. Kane has experienced rapid growth within the last decade and its position immediately to the west of the expanding Fox Valley industrial corridor make it a likely target for continued growth into the next century. Two communities, Aurora and Huntley, both located at least partly in Kane County, have used the annexation process as a means of acquiring desirable land to aid in their expansion. In one sense their actions may be construed both as attempts to control sprawl and as examples of sprawl itself. Both communities exist on the urban fringe of the metropolitan area but are extremely different in their history and expectations for future growth.

Kane County is essentially rectangular in shape, with its north-south border longer than its east-west border. Agriculture has been a mainstay of its economy for much of its history, although the county is also home to two of the four "satellite cities" located in Chicago's metropolitan areas. The county is bordered on its eastern edge by DuPage County, with the Fox River running in a generally north-south direction in the eastern third of the county. The existence of the Fox River as both an early means of transportation and an early water source for drinking water and for water for industrial use resulted in a substantial agglomeration of small cities in the eastern edge of the county, with a substantially less-developed western border.

Aurora, Illinois

Aurora, Illinois, is located on the extreme southwestern fringe of the Chicago metropolitan region. It was originally established in the 1830s, with settlements on both the east and west banks of the Fox River.[22] By the middle of the nineteenth century it had attracted sufficient industry to establish itself as a significant city in its own right. By the 1970s and 1980s, however, Aurora joined other cities in the rust belt and suffered severe losses in its industrial base.[23] Aurora has experienced burgeoning growth more recently, and the city now is located not only in Kane County but also in DuPage, Will, and Kendall counties as well.

Aurora is one of the group of cities on the metropolitan fringe referred to as "satellite cities." There are four such cities located in the metropolitan region: Aurora, Elgin, Joliet and Waukegan. All four were formally incorporated in the mid-nineteenth century within a few years of one another. By 1870 all of them had achieved significant populations, although Aurora was the largest by far. By 1900 Aurora, Elgin, and Joliet had all reached populations in excess of 20,000. There was steady population growth throughout the early part of the twentieth century, and by 1950 Aurora and Joliet each had 50,000 people, and Elgin and Waukegan hovered around 40,000. These population figures have nearly doubled for each of the satellite cities, and by 2000 Aurora had some 142,990 (as per 2000 U.S. Census) people.

As population within these satellite cities grew, so did the land area they encompassed. According to 1960 census figures, the incorporated portions of the satellite cities ranged from nine square miles to thirteen square miles. By the 1990 census, Elgin, Joliet, and Waukegan had all doubled their land areas, while Aurora had more than tripled its incorporated land area and had grown to nearly thirty-nine square miles by 1998.[24]

Aurora's growth since the 1970s is the result of a series of annexations that brought large tracts of developable land within the limits of the city. In 1973 the city welcomed a proposal for a mixed-use development on the eastern border of Aurora in DuPage County. This development, called Fox Valley East, contained plans for residential development and the construction of a new shopping mall. This development alone brought over 3,000 acres of land into the corporate limits of Aurora in one proposal.

In the mid- to late 1970s another large development brought more land within Aurora on its northeast side. This development, called Butterfield, also included a mixture of residential, commercial, and other business development. The next really large-scale addition to Aurora occurred in 1989–1990, through a planned development on the city's west side. This development again included a plan for mixed uses, with a golf course, single-family homes, higher density residential and some residential parcels with zero lot lines (i.e., without setbacks allowing construction of the property boundary), commercial development, some business/industrial development, and other parcels that could be developed as either office or commercial.

The year 1995 saw the expansion of Aurora for the first time into Will and Kendall counties, which border the city to the south. This development, by the Aurora Group, again brought in a large parcel of land to the city through annexation. The plan for development included both residential and commercial activity at the site, and at least some of the proposed residential development was higher density development. With this last annexation Aurora now spans four counties (Kane, DuPage, Will, and Kendall).

The comprehensive plan for the city does articulate a planning area into which the city might expand. The borders of that planning area have not yet been reached. Aurora has entered into boundary agreements with some its neighbors that will limit its expansion in certain directions. Agreements are in force with Naperville to the east, Batavia to the north, and Montgomery to the south. There are no boundary agreements with Sugar Grove to the west of Aurora, or with Oswego and Plainfield to the south and southwest. As a result, Aurora has no limitations on its growth in those directions.

More important, a boundary agreement with the separate city of North Aurora expired in 1991. That agreement had defined the boundary between the two cities as the I-88 tollway. In the last twenty years, the I-88 tollway has become a "high-tech" corridor, with a concentration of businesses located on both sides virtually from its eastern end near the edge of the city of Chicago to its western edge just past Aurora. It is a highly traveled and highly visible traffic corridor. In the years since the expiration of this boundary agreement, landowners in the area north of I-88, formerly within the planning sphere of North Aurora, have approached the city of Aurora about the possibility of annexation. This development would bring into the city some prime business property, with high visibility on the I-88 corridor. While no annexation has yet taken place, planning officials have developed a plan for the parcel should it ultimately become a part of the city.

Huntley, Illinois

In some ways, the town of Huntley, Illinois, represents the polar opposite of Aurora. Situated at the northern end of Kane County and the southern edge of McHenry County, Huntley was incorporated as a village in 1851. It has long been classed as a rural farming center. For most of its history, information about Huntley was not even included in census reports because its population fell below the smallest census place designation of 2,500. Huntley finally made it into census published reports in 1990, when its population reached the 2,500 mark.

Huntley is situated on the northwestern fringe of the metropolitan area. It was, for much of its history, located exclusively in McHenry County, which is primarily a rural county. The area has begun to feel development pressures from northwestern Cook County and western Lake County, however. Prior to 1990 Huntley's only major highway connection was State Route 47. It had no immediate connection to a toll highway, although the Northwest Tollway ran past Huntley several miles to the south.

The 1990 census indicated that Huntley's incorporated territory consisted of 2 square miles. Commencing in about 1991, the village began to annex surrounding vacant land to add to its territory. One of the early annexations, with a developer called the Prime Group, brought over 2,000 acres of land within the corporate limits of the village. It also extended the village's boundary down to the Northwest Tollway exchange in neighboring Kane County. The village has also annexed land on its northern boundary, including a 750-acre parcel. As a result of these annexations, the village currently comprises a territory of eleven square miles, more than five times its size ten years ago.

Nearly all of these annexations were completed relatively quickly. Most of the parcels were owned by one owner, often a professional development company. The parcels were almost always unoccupied, which meant that Illinois annexation rules did not require a referendum or court approval on the annexation. All that was required to add this property to the village was an agreement with the developer, and a vote by the village board of trustees. Virtually all of the annexation agreements between the village and the developers included substantial contributions. These included such things a new sewage treatment plant, building of sewer extensions to connect the new development to existing sewage treatment plants, new water systems or extension of existing water systems to serve proposed residential development, and new zoning standards, which were spelled out in the agreement. The agreements often also provide for a per unit cash payment to the village to compensate it for other development impacts. Other contributions may include either land for new parks or contributions of improvements to existing parks, donations for the school and library districts, and donations to compensate the village for increased fire protection needs. In addition, one developer widened State Route 47 in front of his development from a two-lane country road to a four-lane divided highway with left-turn lanes.

One of the major developments in the area is the new Del Webb "Sun City." This is a development targeted for active seniors, and includes the development of town houses and recreational facilities. A new designer outlet mall, strategically located at the tollway interchange, has now been in operation for several years. There are also discussions under way in the village about attracting additional commercial development along its Route 47 corridor, which runs north to south through the center of the village.

In addition to this substantial development on the village's southern edge, the village has also annexed 750 acres on its northern boundary. Annexed in 1993, that parcel is also being developed by one owner and has a variety of uses scheduled for the site.

Huntley's annexation activity has been spurred, in part, by growth in the surrounding metropolitan fringe. One of the adjoining villages to the east of Huntley is Lake in the Hills, which has been ranked as the fastest growing municipality in Illinois. In the 1990 census Lake in the Hills had a population of nearly 6,000. By 1996 its population had nearly tripled to just over 16,000. Present estimates put its population at more than 20,000. Although Huntley has made use of municipal boundary agreements to control its borders on the developing eastern fringe of its boundary, it has still felt the substantial impacts of this growth. Village officials point to the development in Lake in the Hills of a 900-unit subdivision on the northern borders of Huntley. While the land is in the area controlled by Lake in the Hills, the residents of this development are in the Huntley school district, which will have to bear the burden of expanding its facilities to accommodate the children who will attend its schools.

Much of the development in adjoining villages has been in residential development. Officials in Huntley have pursued a slightly different strategy, and many of the annexation agreements that brought property into the village included a mix of residential and commercial/business development. It appears to be the intention of Huntley officials to balance both their own residential growth, and the residential growth in other areas, with a suitable amount of commercial/business development.

While Huntley's growth along its eastern border is constrained by a number of municipal boundary agreements, there is little in the way of development or competing villages to constrain development along its western border. As a result, further expansion is possible, although village officials seem content at present to work through the many projects that are currently on the drawing boards.

Annexation Lessons to Be Learned

The ability to annex vacant land in a simple and straightforward process has been an advantage to municipalities on the developing fringe of the metropolitan area, and has made it both easy and attractive to keep expanding. Municipalities located in more well-developed areas of the metropolitan region do not have the ability to engage in this rapid growth. Many of these older municipalities, such as the city of Chicago itself, are effectively landlocked and unable to bring new property within their boundaries without extensive legal efforts, usually requiring referenda.

The addition of new property to a municipality is not without problems, however, as the local government now becomes responsible for providing a host of services to the new development, including fire, police, and school facilities. Some municipalities are clearly able to secure contributions from those interested in joining the locality to cover the cost of the initial capital improvements. Continuing operations, however, must also be funded and may add significantly to local area budgets.

Ironically, despite the vast difference in size and history between these two municipalities, both Aurora and Huntley have pursued similar strategies in the plans for their annexed development. The large parcels annexed to both municipalities include a mixture of residential and business/commercial uses. Some of the residential development involved in these annexations is proceeding based on higher densities than the typical, large-lot suburban subdivision.

Impact Fees

Generally speaking, impact fees are charges levied on a developer by a municipality or other governmental unit to compensate the municipality for costs relating to infrastructure improvements required as a result of the new development. Typically, these may include contributions for road improvements, sewer systems, water lines, fire equipment, or dedications of land for park or school purposes.

For many years Illinois has had a more restrictive attitude than some other jurisdictions about impact fees. In Illinois the general rule is that a developer may be required to assume only those costs that are "specifically and uniquely attributable to his activity."[25] State statutes give to local municipal authorities the power to approve the plat of a subdivision before it is filed with the county to subdivide the land, and this provides an opportunity for the local government to shift the burden of paying for the infrastructure related to the new development to the developer in certain circumstances. The most common exactions involve dedications of land for school or park purposes, although there are other forms of impact fees such as water service or fire protection. There is considerable variance between municipalities both in the method by which such fees are imposed and the purposes for which fees or exactions are sought.

State-level policies in Illinois on developer exactions can be best summarized by observing that in order to be permissible, such exactions must be designed to compensate for the impacts actually resulting from the development, and that they are primarily focused on compensating the municipality for infrastructure investments. Beyond these general parameters, there has been little in the way of explicit state-level policy that either promotes or inhibits the imposition of impact fees by individual municipalities.

This situation changed somewhat, however, as a result of legislation passed in the late 1980s. In 1989 the General Assembly created a statutory scheme pertaining to road impact fees.[26] The new act applied to all counties with a population in excess of 400,000 and all home-rule municipalities. Of the counties in the metropolitan Chicago region, only three had populations in excess of 400,000: Cook (the region's largest county), DuPage, and Lake. The act sought to create a method whereby local governments could recoup the cost of road construction resulting from new development.[27]

Although the act suggests that one of its purposes is to ensure the ability of local municipalities to impose impact fees for road improvements, the provisions contained within the act make it rather clear that it is also intended to provide developers with an opportunity to critique the assumptions made in connection with the development of impact fee ordinances. In order to impose roadway improvement impact fees, a municipality or county must follow a complex and expensive set of mandated procedures to comply with the state statute. Notable among these requirements is the mandate that the governmental unit establish an "advisory committee" which must have 40 percent of its members from the real estate, development, and building industries. The advisory committee has a direct role in the process of developing the road impact fees, including the opportunity to make specific recommendations on the land use assumptions that underlie the impact fees. The advisory committee is also given general powers to monitor the implementation of the road improvement plan and impact fees, and to report to the municipality on its land use assumptions.

The process required is detailed, time-consuming, and potentially expensive. In addition to this complex process, the statute also includes two specific substantive requirements that any road impact fee ordinance must meet. Those two requirements are that: (1) the improvement for which an impact fee is imposed must be specifically and uniquely attributable to the traffic demands generated by the new development paying the fee, and (2) the impact fee must not exceed a proportionate share of the costs incurred or the costs that will be incurred by the unit of local government in the provision of road improvements to serve the new development. The municipality or county is further mandated to consider in determining the "proportionate share," of the costs incurred whether there are credits that the developer should receive. These credits can include offsets for donations of land made by the developer, credit for the increased payments the municipality might receive as a result of the new development, and other available sources of funding for road improvements.

In addition to this comprehensive process and specific direction to consider two separate issues, the statute also mandates that in making a determination about "proportionate share" the municipality must consider eight factors. Those factors include things such as other means of financing roads, the extent to which the new development has already contributed to costs of improving the roads through prior payments or tax assessment, and the extent to which the developer should receive a credit for providing road improvements without charge to other properties within the service area.

DuPage County enacted ordinances imposing road impact fees following the passage of the state statute. The DuPage County ordinances divided the county into eleven districts and created a formula for the calculation of fees to be paid for road improvements for county roads. The ordinance also took into consideration, as required by the statute, credits due to developers for contributions made by them. As a result of these calculations, there were actually three zones in DuPage County where no impact fees were charged because those areas contained fewer miles of county roads and the credits due to developers under the ordinance would have exceeded the impact fees.

Despite fairly close adherence to the statutory requirements, the DuPage County impact fee ordinances were almost immediately challenged by the development industry. But the county road impact fee scheme survived the challenges brought by the development industry. The opinion from the Illinois Supreme Court was issued in 1995, however, some six years after the state statute authorizing the imposition of road impact fees was enacted.

Lake County has not been able to enjoy the benefits contained in the provisions of the act. Although Lake County has adopted a road impact fee ordinance, funding has not been available to implement the ordinance fully. As a result, the county does not currently impose road improvement impact fees at the county level.

Kane County, where a great deal of development is currently going on, does not meet the population requirements of the 1989 statute and thus has been unable to impose county-level road impact fees. Planning officials in Kane County suggested that, for the most part, impact fees within the county tended to be consistent with what most other municipalities were doing; that is, they sought dedications for park and school land. Thus, DuPage County remains the only county to have imposed such fees.

Conclusion

The way in which local governments have used land use tools available to them indicates, to some degree, the impact these state-level policy choices can have. Local governments make wide use of municipal boundary agreements, which include not only demarcations of boundaries between municipalities, but also agreements about which municipality will annex what land. These agreements are the result of voluntary negotiations between local governments, and the level of participation is reflective of the fact that there are real and tangible benefits to be derived from these agreements. Implementing and enforcing such agreements is not unduly complicated.

Planning agreements between municipalities and county-level government, on the other hand, are far less common. The lack of real incentives, the absence of funding for planning activities, and the inability of county government to coerce compliance results in far less cooperation. County governments are left to rely on gentle persuasion and endless discussion as a means of trying to effectuate something that resembles a regional policy on land use. While planning officials in the region may undertake sincere efforts to accomplish laudable goals, these efforts have born little fruit to date despite some intensive efforts.

In addition, planning officials also have serious obstacles to overcome when municipalities straddle more than one county. The city of Aurora presently sits in four separate counties; even the small village of Huntley has managed to expand itself into two separate counties. Since county level development policies can also vary within the region, counties may find themselves in a defensive posture with respect to trying to control someone else's development.

While impact fees are available to local governments as a tool to compensate them for the effects of development, their scope in Illinois is restricted by state constitutional constraints. Local governments can certainly make the case that various likely impacts should be compensable, but the requirement that they establish that the impacts are "uniquely attributable" to a specific development places a significant burden on local officials. The statutory process for imposing impact fees for road improvements has resulted in a rather complex process, ripe with the potential for mistakes that may subject local governments to potentially costly litigation, and that is not inexpensive to implement. The only county to undertake this program, DuPage, endured several years of litigation in order to establish its right to impose such road impact fees. Many smaller municipalities may lack the resources to develop the kind of extensive plans required by the statute and may also lack the resources required to defend any lawsuit challenging their process.

Finally, it is clear that local governments have identified voluntary annexation processes as a viable alternative to merely imposing impact fees. Where land is available, local governments do not hesitate to engage in annexation activities, thus bringing within their boundaries potentially valuable developments. There are few incentives to avoid annexation—municipalities lose little from engaging in this activity, and have substantial benefits to gain. Indeed, the fact that annexation agreements are specifically permitted even for property that is not yet eligible for actual annexation suggests that local governments are encouraged to look well beyond their borders to assess their growth potential. There is little to constrain their annexation activity, since such annexation decisions are almost exclusively the province of the local government.

While there is nothing improper about municipalities choosing to annex available land, it seems apparent that state level policies have produced a climate that favors annexation over other forms of more cooperative joint planning. The ease with which annexation can take place and the benefits that accrue to local governments from engaging in this activity make it a logical course of action for municipalities to pursue if they have suitable land surrounding their borders. To the extent that state-level policies are now directed toward identifying potential solutions for growth problems, consideration should be given to the strong sprawl-promoting tendency of Illinois's annexation policies, and the serious limitations of current impact fee legislation.

Notes

1. Proceedings of the Constitutional Convention of 1970, Report of the Local Government Committee, p. 1603.
2. Ibid., p. 1605.

3. Comments supplied by the U.S. House Advisory Commission on Intergovernmental Relations, "Metropolitan America: Challenge to Federalism," Intergovernmental Relations Subcommittee of the House Committee on Government Operations, 89th Congress, 2d Sess. 123–124 (1966).

4. Illinois constitution, Article VII, Sec. 6.

5. *City of East St. Louis v. Touchette*, 14 Ill. 2d 243 (1958); *People ex rel. Hanrahan v. Village of Wheeling*, 42 Ill. App. 3d 825 (1976).

6. *City of Des Plaines v. Chicago and Northwestern Railway*, 65 Ill. 2d 1, 357 N. E. 2d 433, 2 Ill. Dec. 266 (1976).

7. The state will act to limit local government authority where there is the perception that local government will seek to shift the burden elsewhere. So, for example, although municipalities generally have broad authority over land uses within their borders, local government's siting authority with respect to landfills and incinerators is strictly limited by the Environmental Protection Act to prevent the exclusion of these facilities from cities and villages. 415 ILCS* 5/39.2.

8. Under 65 ILCS 5/11–12–4, municipalities are authorized to create plan commissions and planning departments; 65 ILCS 5/11–12–5 authorizes the development of a comprehensive plan that can be made applicable to territory located within 1.5 miles of the boundary of the municipality, provided that such territory is not located within some other municipality.

9. Townships exist in Illinois as an intermediate level of government between the local municipality and the county government, although their powers are generally quite restricted. Under 60 ILCS 1/110–5, township governments may exercise zoning authority when authorized to do so by the voters; township zoning authority cannot be exercised in any county in which the county has adopted a zoning ordinance, and township zoning regulations do not apply to any area that is governed by a municipal zoning ordinance. County zoning power is found at 55 ILCS 5/5–12001. The county is authorized only to exercise its zoning power in areas of the county that are outside the limits of an incorporated municipality.

10. *Village of South Elgin v. City of Elgin*, 203 Ill. App. 3d 364, 561 N.E. 2d 295, 149 Ill. Dec. 17, 1990.

11. The cases involved Northbrook and Glenview, both in northern Cook County, Kildeer and Long Grove, both in Lake County, and Lisle and Woodridge, both located in DuPage County.

12. The cases were: *Village of Long Grove v. Village of Kildeer*, 146 Ill. App. 3d 979, 497 N.E. 2d 319, 100 Ill. Dec. 341 (1986), both located in Lake County; *Village of Lisle v. Village of Woodridge*, 192 Ill. App,. 3d 568, 548 N.E. 2d 1337, (1989) both located in DuPage County.

13. Statutory authority for municipal boundary agreements is found at 65 ILCS 5/11–12–9. The amended statute provided that "on and after September 24, 1987, such agreement may provide that one or more of the municipalities shall not annex territory which lies within the jurisdiction of any other municipality, as established by such [municipal boundary] line."

14. "North Barrington offers plan to kill mall: Village officials put hot potato in lap of rival Hawthorn Woods," *Daily Herald*, March 26, 1999.

---

*ILCS = Illinois Compiled Statutes, a database of recent state laws.

15. The state's Open Meetings Act requires that public bodies provide a certain interval of notice prior to convening any meeting to discuss public business. Failure to comply with the provisions of the act can invalidate official action taken at any such meeting.

16. 50 ILCS 805/1.

17. The complete list of objectives that such plans may remedy is as follows: (1) agricultural preservation, (2) air and land resource quality, (3) archaeological, cultural and historic places, (4) areas subject to natural disasters and hazards, (5) economy of the area, (6) energy conservation, (7) forest lands, (8) governmental cooperation, (9) housing, (10) natural resources, (11) open spaces, (12) public facilities and services, (13) recreational needs, (14) transportation, (15) urban design, (16) water, (17) citizen involvement, and (18) data collection.

18. For many years, the county of Cook, which is the largest and most urbanized county, had not updated its countywide land use plan. Much of the land area in Cook is located within the borders of incorporated municipalities, although there are some unincorporated areas of the county.

19. Louis Cain provides an interesting analysis of those who did choose to annex versus those who did not in "To Annex or Not? A Tale of Two Towns: Evanston and Hyde Park," *Explorations in Economic History* 20 (1983): 58–72.

20. The annexation statutes themselves are contained in 65 ILCS 5/7-1-1, *et seq.* There is an excellent description of the various annexation options under Illinois law in a handbook for Illinois legal practitioners entitled "Illinois Municipal Law" published by the Illinois Institute for Continuing Legal Education. Chapter 11 is devoted exclusively to annexation.

21. 65 ILCS 5/11-15.1-2, (d).

22. Chicago Fact Book Consortium. 1995. *Local Community Factbook, Chicago Metropolitan Area 1990.* Chicago: Chicago Fact Book Consortium, Department of Sociology, University of Illinois at Chicago.

23. Aurora Consolidated Plan for 1995 Executive Summary: www.hud.gov/cpes/il/aurorail.html.

24. The 1990 land area, according to data released on the World Wide Web in 1996, was as follows: Aurora: 33.5 sq. miles, Elgin, 21.9 sq. miles, Joliet 27.8 sq. miles and Waukegan, 22.2 sq. miles.

25. *Rosen v. Village of Downers Grove*, 19 Ill. 2d 446 (1960). The Supreme Court of Illinois also established requirements for road impact fees in *Pioneer Trust and Savings Bank v. Mount Prospect*, 22 Ill. 2d 375, 176 N.E. 2d 799 (1961).

26. The original statute did not contain the requirement that the local government establish that the road impact fees be "uniquely attributable" to the development upon which the fees were to be imposed. The statute was subsequently amended to require that impact fees for road improvements be "uniquely attributable" to the development. A discussion of the original statute is contained in the recent opinion by the Supreme Court upholding a later version of the statute, *Northern Illinois Home Builders v. County of DuPage*, 165 Ill. 2d 25, (1995) at page 31.

27. 605 ILCS 5/5-901, the Road Improvement Impact Fee Law, which took effect in 1989.

5

JOSEPH DIJOHN

Transportation in the Chicago Metropolitan Region Since 1970

Introduction

This chapter is a historical and political analysis of surface transportation in the Chicago metropolitan region and its relationship to growth, development, travel behavior, and decentralization. The area consists of the six-county region of northeastern Illinois including the city of Chicago, suburban Cook County, and the five collar counties: Lake, McHenry, Kane, DuPage, and Will. The time frame ranges from 1970 to the present time. The modes of transportation studied are mass transit, highways, and railroad freight transportation. Federal legislation since 1970 and the impact on each mode will be reviewed. The history of state, regional, and local decisions affecting transportation will be examined as well as how the region's travelers are using the transportation systems.

Transit

Federal Transit Legislation

A key question about federal transportation funding is whether it has a bias toward private transportation and against public transit. In this first section we deal with federal transit funding; later we address questions related to highway construction.

The federal government first began funding transportation projects in 1961 when demonstration grants for transit projects were made available under the Housing and Urban Development (HUD) Act. In 1964 the Urban Mass Transit Administration (UMTA), the predecessor to today's Federal Transit Administration (FTA), was created under HUD. Two years later UMTA was put under the newly created U.S. Department of Transportation (DOT). The UMTA Act provided capital grant subsidies for public transportation projects. Since private operators provided much of the transit during this period, public bodies were created to channel newly funded capital equipment to private operators. Funding was also expanded under the DOT (Smerk 1991).

Although the focus of our study is from 1970 to the present time, it is important to note that it was only several years earlier that the federal government acknowledged the mass transit need and provided the much needed financial assistance, and by 1970 the program was well established. The rest of the decade saw an increased federal commitment to funding mass transit programs. In 1973 the federal share of capital projects was increased from 66.67 percent to 80 percent. Also in that year the principle of flexibility between highway and transit was established when Federal Aid Urban Systems (FAUS) and Interstate Transfer Funds (ITF) were made available for transit purposes. This was a landmark for transit that has been carried forward and expanded in subsequent legislation. In 1974 transit funding was again increased and expanded to include both capital and operating funds. In 1978 grant funds were expanded to include categories for fixed guideways and for areas outside of urban areas.

The decade of the 1980s continued the federal government's commitment to the nation's transit needs. In 1982 a one-cent-per-gallon tax from the Highway Fund Account was dedicated to the mass transit account. This would be increased later to 1.5 cents in 1990, 2 cents in 1993, and 2.86 cents in 1997 (APTA [American Public Transit Association] 1999).

The Intermodal Surface Transportation Efficiency Act (ISTEA) of 1991 was landmark legislation in several ways. It:

- provided multiyear funding through 1997,
- vastly increased the amounts of funding for mass transit,
- provided flexible funding from highway for mass transit projects,
- required comprehensive regional planning by metropolitan planning organizations (MPO), and
- reorganized and renamed UMTA to the Federal Transit Administration (FTA) (APTA 1999).

In 1998 new legislation called the Transportation Equity Act for the 21st Century (TEA 21) was passed and continued the principles of ISTEA through 2003. In addition, it provided for additional optional levels of funding if Congress so approves. Other features included funding for job access and reverse commute grants, funding for the development of Intelligent Transportation Systems (ITS) and an increase in the amount of tax-free benefit for employees receiving transit subsidies to $65 per month. Operating funding was discontinued for metropolitan areas over 100,000 population, although provisions were made to allow the use of capital funds for certain limited operating uses (U.S. Department of Transportation 1998).

Certain nontransportation legislation impacted the transit industry. In 1990 the Clean Air Act contained provisions requiring employers to reduce the use of single-occupant automobiles to worksites. This would have provided incentives for increased transit use. However, in 1995 the Environmental Protection Agency (EPA) made compliance voluntary. Also in 1990 the Americans with Disabilities Act (ADA) imposed accessibility requirements on the nation's transit systems, significantly increasing transit capital and operating costs. Finally, in 1995, drug and alcohol testing requirements were imposed on transit agencies, which increased costs and reporting requirements (APTA 1999).

Overall, one can conclude that federal policy and programs since 1970 have been supportive of mass transit. Not only have funding levels increased, but features such as flexibility to use highway funds for transit and regional planning requirements likewise supported and encouraged the increased use of transit.

History of the Region's Transit System

The history of the region's public transit is one of frequent funding crises that finally resulted in a relatively stable system of a regionally financed, but decentralized operating system.

The decade of the 1970s began with a transportation financial crisis, one of many in the region's long history. Prior to 1970 the legislative history of passenger transportation was one of regulation. The city and ultimately the state, through the Illinois Commerce Commission, regulated fares and services of private carriers by virtue of the operator's monopoly power. Other significant legislation occurred in 1945 with the formation of the Chicago Transit Authority (CTA), which consolidated the Chicago Surface Lines, Chicago Rapid Transit Co., and later, the Chicago Motor Coach Co. under public ownership. The legislation did not provide funding or taxing power to the CTA but did provide authority to refinance the debt by the issuance of revenue bonds. The legislation also assisted CTA by exempting it from certain taxes (Krambles and Peterson 1993).

In 1970 the state of Illinois held a constitutional convention that provided a constitutional foundation that allowed for the provision of assistance to public transportation, a necessary requirement for future legislation. This stipulated that:

> Public Transportation is an essential public purpose for which public funds may be expended. The General Assembly by law may provide for, aid, and assist public transportation, including the granting of public funds or credit to any corporation or public authority authorized to provide public transportation within the state. (Tecson 1975)

> The federal government had already recognized the importance of transit financial assistance by authorizing the Urban Mass Transportation Act of 1964. This act provided an impetus for states to develop programs and provide the local match to attract federal grants. The capital funds could not be used to directly subsidize private carriers, which gave rise to the creation of single purpose, a municipal entity whose objective was to obtain federal capital grants and lease needed equipment to private operators. In 1970, with the exception of the CTA, most transit in the Chicago region was provided by privately owned for-profit businesses. (Young 1998)

The financial circumstances in the beginning of the 1970s were bleak. The fare-box revenue failed to cover operating expenses, not to mention capital expenses. Fare increases provided some immediate relief but discouraged usage and resulted in lower ridership. At the time, there was no source of public subsidy to make up the operating deficits. Suburban bus lines were on the verge of bankruptcy except for the few satellite cities where the municipality took over the operations of the private carriers to maintain local bus service. Several of the commuter rail services were marginally profitable, while the majority of lines were incurring losses and were threatening major fare increases and service discontinuance. The region had already experienced the demise of the interurban electric rail lines north and west of the city.

The movement of employers from the central business district (CBD) to the suburbs resulted in nontraditional city-to-suburb and suburb-to-suburb commutes. These demographic forces along with the accompanying financial difficulties put transit operators in the very difficult circumstance of fighting a superior competitor, the automobile, in a declining market without a public funding source.

By 1973 circumstances worsened. The CTA threatened fare increases and major service cutbacks, the commuter railroads filed petitions for substantial rate increases, and the private suburban bus lines teetered on bankruptcy. The General Assembly formed a Transportation Study Commission and held public hearings that resulted in legislation to provide bridge operating loans and capital assistance, and signed into law the creation of a six-county Regional Transportation Authority (RTA) subject to voter referendum for approval. This was a very controversial issue resulting in acrimonious political debate.

Representation on the new agency was split evenly between the city and suburbs; each member had four votes. The chairman was to be elected by a two-thirds majority of the directors. After an extensive search and lengthy negotiation, the controversial stalemate was broken when the chairman of the CTA was named first chairman.

The RTA was organized to provide financial support and oversight of the transportation agencies, although the RTA had the authority to operate service directly. The RTA Act provided the new organization with a funding source by diverting existing funding, not by the imposition of new taxes. There were three funding sources: $3/_{32}$ of the sales tax collected in the region, $14 of each motor vehicle registration fee collected by the state from the city of Chicago, and a $5 million contribution from Chicago before any aid could be given to the CTA. In addition, the RTA was given bonding authority and became the recipient of federal capital and operating funds that were provided by UMTA on a matching basis (Tecson 1975).

The RTA entered into the operating arena during the 1970s by purchasing the private suburban bus companies. The RTA board at that time did not envision directly operating transit service. This policy changed later when the Rock Island Railroad declared bankruptcy and the line was being liquidated. The RTA contracted with the Chicago and North Western Railroad on an emergency basis to continue operations on the Rock Island. After many difficulties the RTA formed the Northeast Illinois Rail Corporation (NIRC) and began direct operations of the Rock

Island, and later, the Milwaukee Road, which also declared bankruptcy (Young 1998).

Mass transit service during the 1970s and into the 1980s faced the continued cost pressures of an inflationary economy and the inability of the RTA's funding sources to provide adequate ongoing operating assistance. Then again in 1981, the RTA faced a financial crisis similar to the crisis of 1973, only worse.

In 1981 the shortfall in funding resulted in RTA terminating the payments to carriers required under the purchase of service and financial assistance agreements. Faced with the prospect of shortfalls in funding, the carriers threatened massive fare increases and service cuts. The looming crisis became a hot topic in Springfield with the legislative leaders, the governor, and the mayor of the city of Chicago taking sides in what was essentially a continuation of the city versus suburb controversy that began with the referendum in 1974. Suburban interests felt it was another bailout of the CTA. The RTA board and the first two chairmen of the RTA were viewed as being closely identified with the interests of the city of Chicago.

The financial crisis of 1981 left the region's mass transit in a shambles that it could not fully recover from even decades later. Faced with funding shortfalls, the CTA increased its base fare by 50 percent. The commuter railroads, having had their purchase of service contracts breached, implemented fare increases of 80 percent to 100 percent and proposed service cutbacks, even abandonments. Suburban bus lines followed the CTA fare increase of 50 percent but, having little, if any, financial resources, faced a complete shutdown of service. During the ensuing two years CTA ridership fell by 11.6 percent, commuter rail ridership decreased 25.6 percent, and suburban bus lines lost 29.2 percent of their riders. During this period the system lost 113 million rides (CTA 1999, Metra 1999, and Pace 1999).

Finally, in the fall of 1983, two years after the crisis, the General Assembly passed and the governor signed legislation reforming and reorganizing the RTA, hopefully putting it on a sound financial basis. The compromise legislation was a settlement of city and suburban interests that provided increased funding to the CTA and gave the suburbanites control of suburban transportation by creating the Commuter Rail and Suburban Bus Boards, which were divisions of the RTA. The CTA remained an independent agency. Some key features of the reorganization were:

- RTA was limited to financial oversight, planning, and coordination of transit;
- the service boards were given authority to operate, set fares, and establish the nature and levels of service;
- imposition of a one-cent sales tax in Cook County and a quarter of a cent tax in the five collar counties that were distributed by a formula assuring that a portion of the funds raised in that county would be distributed to the service board serving that jurisdiction;
- provision for a new state subsidy equal to 25 percent of the sales tax raised;
- elimination of cost-of-living-agreements (COLA) in labor contracts, a major cause of escalating costs during the inflationary economy in the late 1970s and early 1980s;
- provision for a suburban majority of the board based on the census of 1980 and the principle of "one man, one vote." However, a supermajority is required to pass a budget, thereby assuring compromise of political interests; and
- finally, the act mandated the RTA must maintain a fare box recovery ratio of at least 50 percent, the highest such requirement in the United States (RTA Act, 70 ILCS as amended by Public Acts 83–885 and 83–886).

In the period since the reorganization of the RTA as a financial oversight and planning agency and the creation of Metra (commuter rail transit) and Pace (suburban bus line), there has been relative stability of the region's transit finances. Fares have remained stable compared to inflation, although there have been a number of small increases to the region's fare structures. Financially, the RTA system has met and exceeded the mandated 50 percent fare-box recovery ratio every year since 1985. In the most recent five years, CTA has averaged just over 52 percent, Metra around 56 percent, and Pace just above 36 percent (RTA 1996).

Since 1970 the state has provided transit-funding packages in the form of issuing bonds in 1979, 1983, 1989, and 1999. There is currently a backlog of more than $3 billion in unfunded capital projects.

Expansion of Service

During the last three decades there have been several major new services proposed and implemented. The CTA extended the Blue line to

O'Hare International Airport in 1984 and constructed the new Orange line to Midway Airport in 1993. They also completed a major rehabilitation of the Green line in 1996. However, two rail proposals within the city of Chicago were dropped due to lack of funding and/or political support. The first was the downtown distributor that would have replaced the "Loop" elevated structure with a subway. This project ended with the abolishment in 1976 of the Chicago Urban Transportation District, which had been established to provide a local tax and to construct the facility. Likewise, in 1996 the downtown circulator project was abandoned. This light-rail project was designed to expand transit options in the Loop including McCormick Place and North Michigan Avenue (Young 1998).

Metra undertook a study of possible rail extensions in the late 1980s called the "FAST" plan. In 1987 they extended their Milwaukee West line approximately three miles to Big Timber and in 1997, completed the first new commuter rail line in seventy years with the North Central service to Antioch. The FTA recently approved a grant to build a second track to enable Metra to expand service on the line. Metra is also studying a series of rail extensions and new lines, most notably in the Inner Circumferential Line between O'Hare and Midway Airports and the Outer Circumferential Line along the Elgin, Joliet, and Eastern Line between Joliet and Waukegan (Metra 1998a). No funding has been identified for these projects.

Pace has implemented a series of new service proposals aimed at carrying reverse and suburb-to-suburb commuters. Their VIP vanpool program that began in 1991 has over 300 vans in operation, making it the second largest vanpool service in the nation. In 1992 when Sears moved from Sears Tower in downtown Chicago to Hoffman Estates, Pace provided not only vanpools, but also designed subscription buses and express buses for these nontraditional commuter trips. In 1996 they began operation of shuttle buses from Metra's Lake-Cook Road station to the many large suburban employers along that corridor.

The RTA proposed a Personal Rapid Transit (PRT) system in 1994 that would utilize small vehicles along an overhead track to carry commuters in the Rosemont area. The project was abandoned in 1999. In 1998 the RTA initiated an alternatives study along the Northwest Corridor between the city limits and the Woodfield-Schaumburg-Hoffman Estates area along the Northwest Tollway. Among the alternatives for consideration are an extension of the CTA Blue line, commuter rail, and express bus and high occupancy vehicle (HOV) lanes (RTA 1998).

Table 5.1

Regional Transportation Authority Annual Ridership (in millions)

Year	CTA	Metra	Pace	RTA total
1973	595.5	66.6	17	679.1
1974	625.4	69	19.7	714
1975	612.5	68.7	21.9	703.2
1976	633.2	67.2	21.7	722.1
1977	643	68.6	24.5	736.1
1978	659.6	72.2	28.9	760.6
1979	716.1	79.1	35.6	830.9
1980	696.6	81.9	38.2	816.8
1981	643.3	70.4	27.4	741
1982	616.1	60.5	27.7	704.3
1983	614.6	59.2	31.2	705
1984	638.2	62.1	36.2	736.5
1985	644.4	64.5	38.4	747.2
1986	611.7	64.5	36.1	712.3
1987	608.9	66.5	35.6	711
1988	577.3	69.8	36.7	683.9
1989	569.4	71.2	37.9	678.4
1990	569.9	69.3	40.3	679.6
1991	528	69	40.5	637.5
1992	494	70.2	39.4	603.5
1993	445.6	69.9	38.3	553.8
1994	448.2	72	38.6	558.8
1995	426.6	70.4	37.2	534.2
1996	427.3	70.6	37.5	535.4
1997	419.2	72.3	37.9	529.4
1998	424.1	74.5	39.3	537.9

Source: CTA (1999), Metra (1999), and Pace (1999).

Table 5.1 shows that ridership on the transit system as a whole has fallen from 679 million rides in 1973, the year the RTA was created, to 538 million rides in 1998, a decrease of 21 percent. CTA lost over 171 million rides, a decrease of 29 percent. This reflects the shift of population and employment from the city and near-in suburbs to the outer suburban area. From 1970 to 1990 the city of Chicago experienced a decrease in population of 17 percent and a decrease in employment of 21 percent as shown on Table 5.2.

Suburban commuter rail and bus ridership gained 30 million rides from 1973 to 1998, an increase of 36 percent (Table 5.1). The population and employment in suburban Cook and the five collar counties grew by 24 percent and 80 percent, respectively, between 1970 and 1990 (Table 5.2).

Government transit subsidies, both operating and capital, basically support the existing transit system that is designed to serve the central city and the most urbanized areas of the region. The impact of these subsidies has been to make the central city more accessible by providing efficient and effective mobility alternatives to users. This tends to counteract the region's sprawl by offsetting some of the demographic trends of the movement of population and jobs to the outlying suburban area.

Transit usage, however has declined both absolutely and relatively in spite of the federal and state programs. There was a significant loss of riders resulting from the financial crises that occurred since 1970. Losses resulted from service cutbacks, interruptions, fare increases and a general loss of confidence in the system. The crises resulted from the inability of political leaders to compromise on the interests of the city and suburbs. The political bickering and resulting impacts on the region's transit services likely hastened the shifting of population and employment to the suburbs.

Highways

Federal Highway Legislation

In 1956 Congress passed the Federal-Aid Highway Act, which authorized $25 billion to construct 42,500 miles of Interstate highways. In the Chicago region the construction of the Interstate Highway System was essentially completed in 1972. There was, however, significant highway legislation beginning in 1970 with the Clean Air Act amendments, which required state implementation plans to deal with pollution from mobile sources: automobiles and trucks. In 1973 flexibility was allowed for the substitution of transit projects for nonessential highway funds. This flexibility was later expanded in 1976, further allowing for substitution of transit projects for Interstate Highway funds while also increasing planning requirements (Smerk 1991).

In 1990 flexible funding became a principle of ISTEA and its successor legislation in 1998, TEA 21. This legislation required regional planning, land use considerations, an analysis of transit alternatives, and public input on highway projects. TEA 21 also provided increased fed-

Table 5.2

Six-County Employment and Population Decentralization Between 1970 and 1990

	1970 Employment	1990 Employment	1970–1990 Change	Change %	1970 Population	1990 Population	2000 Population	1970–1990 Change	Change %
Cook	2,700,000	2,775,300	75,300	2.8	5,493,766	5,105,067	5,376,741	–388,699	–7.08
Sub Cook				55.7					9.3
DuPage	146,400	530,700	384,300	262.5	487,966	781,666	904,161	293,700	60.19
Kane	103,300	145,300	42,000	40.7	251,005	317,471	404,119	66,466	26.48
Lake	116,400	228,500	112,100	96.3	382,638	516,418	644,356	133,780	34.96
McHenry	36,300	65,500	29,200	80.4	111,555	183,241	260,077	71,686	64.26
Will	82,500	99,400	16,900	20.5	247,825	357,313	502,266	109,488	44.18
Total	3,184,900	3,844,700	659,800	20.72	6,974,755	7,261,176	8,091,720	2,864,214.11	

Source: CATS, Transportation Facts (1996) and U.S. Bureau of the Census.

eral funding of both transit and highways and continued the policy of flexible uses of funds as determined by local decision makers (U.S. DOT 1998).

History of the Region's Highway System

The system of expressways and tollways in the Chicago region began with the construction of Lake Shore Drive in 1937 (Table 5.3) and was essentially completed in its present form with the completion of I-355, the North-South Tollway, in 1989 and U.S. Route 20, the Elgin-O'Hare Expressway, in 1993 (Christopher and Custodio 1997). Most expressway construction took place between 1958 and 1965.

The majority of federal and state funding for highways is for maintenance and improvement of the existing system. The shortage of funding for new highways has resulted in major projects being scrapped or delayed, such as the Fox Valley Freeway and Wacker Drive. New roadway construction projects and major improvements, such as extensions and widenings, are increasingly being opposed by local residents and environmental groups. Two such projects, the I-355 extension in Will County and the Route 53 extension in Lake County, are delayed as a result of local opposition and environmental concerns.

Since 1970 the state of Illinois has authorized four highway-funding packages: in 1979, 1983, 1989, and 1999. The 1979 funding authorization provided for $400 million in bonds funded by 5.5 percent of the state sales tax to the road fund. In 1983, $1 billion in bonds was financed through a tax increase of 5.5 cents per gallon on gasoline, 8 cents for diesel, and an increase of the motor vehicle registration fee to $48. The funding package in 1989 provided for $1 billion in bonds with a 6-cent-per-gallon increase in the motor fuel tax. According to the Illinois Department of Transportation, the unfunded highway need over the next five years to upgrade the highway system to a good condition is $16 billion. The minimal need is in the neighborhood of $4 billion. In 1999 the legislature passed and the governor signed the Illinois FIRST (Funding for Infrastructure, Roads, Schools, and Transit) legislation, which provides $4.1 billion for highway projects (Schlickman 1999).

Since 1970 there have been a number of new highway construction projects that have been scrapped or delayed for various reasons. In 1979 the Crosstown Expressway, a corridor along Cicero Avenue to divert traffic from the heavily used Kennedy and Dan Ryan Expressways, was

Table 5.3

Completion Dates of Major Chicago-Area Expressways

Expressway	Date first leg completed	Date completed
North Lake Shore Drive	1937	1954
Edens Expressway	1951	1959
Northwest Tollway	1958	1958
East-West Tollway	1958	1974
Tri-State Tollway	1958	1958
Kennedy Expressway	1958	1960
Eisenhower Expressway	1956	1960
Bishop Ford Expressway	1956	1962
Chicago Skyway	1958	1962
Dan Ryan Expressway	1961	1962
Stevenson Expressway	1956	1964
I-57 Expressway	1963	1970
I-270 Extension	1961	1971
North-South Tollway (I-355)	1989	1989
Elgin-O'Hare Expressway	1993	1993

Source: Christopher and Custodio (1997).

scrapped due to local grassroots opposition from city residents. The federally allocated funds for this project were diverted under the Interstate Transfer Fund provisions to other transit and highway projects in the city and suburbs (Young 1998). In 1990 the state proposed building an expressway along the Fox River Freeway. This project was dropped due to lack of funding as well as local opposition. Around the same time, the state transferred to the Illinois State Toll Highway Authority (ISTHA) two extension projects due to lack of funding; the I-355 extension south into Will County and the Route 53 extension north into Lake County (Dewberry and Davis 1997). These projects engendered much local opposition and resulted in a lawsuit by advocacy groups claiming that inadequate environmental impact studies were made by the tollway. Early in 1999 the state appellate court upheld the lower court decision requiring further environmental analysis and causing several years of delay to the projects.

Highways and Sprawl

The relationship between highways and sprawl in the Chicago region is complex. There has been a variety of contributing factors other than highways that have contributed to sprawl since the beginning of the century. By the 1920s, when the city had its greatest decennial population increase, the area within four miles of the Chicago central business district lost population. There were no expressways, but decentralization was firmly in place. Population was decentralizing then for many of the same reasons common today such as property values, traffic congestion, inability to secure ample space, lack of choice locations, legal restrictions and city-suburban controversies (Colby 1933). During this period prosperity was the principal contributing factor to urban residential decentralization, as it is today (Sen et al. 1998).

In the first three decades of this century there were rapid population increases in communities on the edge of the city and then in the suburbs. This decentralization could be attributed to several factors associated with increasing prosperity, namely declining household size and increasing household formation, home ownership, and increasing lot sizes. Each of these directly contributed to the per capita consumption of residential land (Sen et al. 1998). These three factors have fueled urban decentralization for many decades both prior to the era of highway construction and since 1970, when little new highway construction has taken place. While highways facilitate mobility in the region, they are not the primary cause of sprawl.

History of Sprawl and the Role of Prosperity

The relationship between population decentralization and the development of the expressway system in the Chicago is not obvious. While most assume that the region has decentralized because of the new expressways, there are several factors that contributed to population decentralization before the first major expressway was completed. First, the outer belt railway connecting Waukegan, Elgin, Aurora, Joliet, and Gary, Indiana, was built in response to the movement of major employers seeking low-cost sites beyond the immediate Chicago area. This was one of the earliest signs of employment decentralization. Second, the population of Chicago has been decentralizing since the late 1800s, that is, the core areas were declining in population and the outer fringe was growing. Third, the decentralization process has been strongest during periods of economic growth such as the 1920s and 1950s. Clearly there is a worldwide association between population decentralization (densities in urban areas) and standard of living. The highest-density urban

Table 5.4

Population Densities and per Capita GDPs of Selected Urban Clusters

Urban cluster[1]	Density[2]	Per capita GDP[3]
Lagos, Nigeria	142.8	230
Dhaka, Bangladesh	138.1	200
Jakarta, Indonesia	130.0	630
Mumbai (Bombay), India	127.5	380
Cairo, Egypt	120.2	720
Shanghai, China	88.9	360
Manila, Philippines	54.0	720
Seoul, Korea	49.1	6,300
Sao Paulo, Brazil	41.5	2,540
Mexico City	40.0	3,200
Tokyo, Japan	25.0	19,100
Paris, France	20.2	18,300
New York	11.5	22,470
Los Angeles	9.1	22,470
Chicago	8.6	22,470

Source: Sen et al. (1998), using U.S. Census data.
Notes:
[1] Portion of the urban area with at least 5,000 residents per square mile.
[2] Persons per square mile within the urban cluster, in thousands (1991).
[3] Per capita gross domestic product in urban cluster's country, in U.S. dollars.

areas are in third world nations, while the lowest-density urban areas are found in first world nations, particularly in the United States (Table 5.4). In Europe and Japan urban areas are much more densely populated than those in the United States but are relatively low in density compared to third world urban clusters. The role of prosperity in sprawl is very evident, as measured by population density.

Moreover, many think of decentralization as a post–World War II phenomenon associated with postwar reconstruction. In the Chicago area this association stems partly from the time when the city reached its maximum population, just after the end of the war. Had the city limits been larger, the size of Jacksonville, Florida, the population would have continued to grow until 1970 (Table 5.5). Conversely, had the city limits been the size of San Francisco, the population would have peaked in 1920.

After approximately 100 years of population decentralization, the phenomenon is beginning to exhibit a tipping point. In the last decade the outward growth is continuing, but what is new is the growth in the core and inner ring of suburbs. Between ·1990 and 2000 seven of the ten

Table 5.5

Year of Maximum Population with Different Hypothetical City Limits

Area (square miles)	City of that size	Decennial year of maximum population if Chicago were of this size
35	Miami	1910/1920
45	San Francisco	1920
100	Milwaukee	1930
225	Chicago	1950
500	Los Angeles	1960
750	Jacksonville, FL	1970

Source: Sen et al. (1998).

core community areas experienced population growth. The Loop population grew by 37 percent and the Near South Side grew by 40 percent. The Near North Side added 10,000 residents or 16 percent to its 1990 total.

Even more impressive has been the growth in the inner ring of suburbs, especially north of Chicago. Between 1970 and 1980 and again from 1980 to 1990, all of the ten suburbs on Chicago's northern border or on Lake Michigan in Cook County lost population. After twenty years of population decline all of these suburbs gained population from 1990 to 2000. The same applies to the first two suburbs into Lake County, Highland Park and Deerfield. This is a remarkable turnaround.

Moreover, all but two suburbs in northern Cook County gained inhabitants in the 1990s; Golf and Barrington Hills lost a total of less than 300 residents. By contrast, Skokie grew by almost 4,000, Glenview by 4,500, and Des Plaines by more than 5,000. To the west, Cicero grew by 18,000 and Berwyn by more than 8,000. While growing affluence continues to fuel growth in the fringe, there is also now growth in core areas.

Sprawl and Highway Use

It is inevitable that with sprawl travel will grow. As new fringe neighborhoods are developed, services are commonly some distance from homes. Indeed many seek housing at some distance from neighbors or other forms of urban activity. This contributes to long average trip lengths, and Table 5.6 shows the growth in vehicle miles traveled (VMT). Since 1970 there has been a significant increase in automobile and highway usage. Table 5.6 shows that from 1970 to 1995 the number of registered vehicles in the six-county area grew by 65 percent. Likewise, the VMT

Table 5.6

Percentage Change in Vehicle Registrations and Vehicle Miles Traveled

	Vehicle registrations (%) 1970–1995	Vehicle miles traveled (%) 1973–1993
Chicago	+4.1	+42.7*
Suburban Cook	+66.8	
DuPage	+182.8	+116.2
Kane	+114.3	+61.3
Lake	+138.0	+84.1
McHenry	+203.0	+131.5
Will	+151.8	+60.5
Total region	+65.0	+57.6

Source: CATS, Transportation Facts (1996).
Note: *All of Cook County.

on area roadways increased by 58 percent from 1973 to 1993. This growth occurred at greater rates in the collar counties than in Cook County. VMT grew by 132 percent in McHenry County and 116 percent in DuPage County, while the region as a whole grew at half this rate. This has resulted in increased congestion, much of it occurring in the suburban area. In the suburban counties the growth in VMT was smaller than the growth in registered vehicles but much greater in Chicago. This is likely related to a reverse commuting and travel to suburban shopping centers and other attractions throughout the region.

Sprawl and Congestion

Two important factors have contributed to the association between sprawl and congestion. First, the prosperity that fuels sprawl also contributes to the number of cars on the road. The car population would grow with prosperity even if cities did not sprawl; this is occurring throughout the world. Second and perhaps more important is that the growth in personal vehicles is not matched with a commensurate increase in highway capacity.

The highway system has not expanded its capacity to handle the growth of highway usage. Table 5.7 shows that during the period of 1985 to 1995 vehicle miles traveled increased by almost 32 percent while lane

Table 5.7

Percentage Change in Vehicle Miles Traveled and Highway Lane Miles, 1985–1995

County	Vehicle miles traveled	Highway lane miles
Cook	+21.5%	+1.7%
DuPage	+56.5%	+16.4%
Kane	+48.1%	+5.2%
Lake	+37.2%	+10.7%
McHenry	+60.7%	+2.9%
Will	+66.6%	+5.0%
Total	+31.8%	+5.1%

Source: CATS (1996).

miles of highways increased by only 5 percent. Traffic has increased at a rate faster than the capacity of the system to handle the increase resulting in worsening congestion.

The slow growth in lane miles can also be seen relative to population increase. Figure 5.1 illustrates how population in McHenry County is growing much more rapidly than lane miles. From 1983 to 1995 the number of lane miles per 1,000 inhabitants has dropped from over twenty-four to under seventeen or by approximately 30 percent. With the increase in population and vehicles, roads and streets that had very low traffic volumes in the past now have congested conditions during the peak periods. While the levels of congestion are often much lower than those experienced in the core areas of Chicago, they are much higher than in the recent past and consequently there is substantial public concern over the rate of change in traffic volumes.

The fact that there are fewer lane miles in the core areas per urban activity can be seen in Table 5.8. Cook County, the central county, has fewer lane miles per four different measures of traffic generation than the collar counties, with the exception of retail activity in DuPage County. As Figure 5.1 indicates, the suburban lane miles per population are declining, but at present they are still substantially higher than in Cook County. Dividing the 1995 lane miles by the 1990 and 2000 populations show that the gap is closing. Although the number of lane miles is fixed in this comparison, we know that the growth in lane miles is minor and there is growing pressure on existing roadways. With the even greater

Figure 5.1 **Lane Miles per 1,000 Population in McHenry County, 1983–1995**

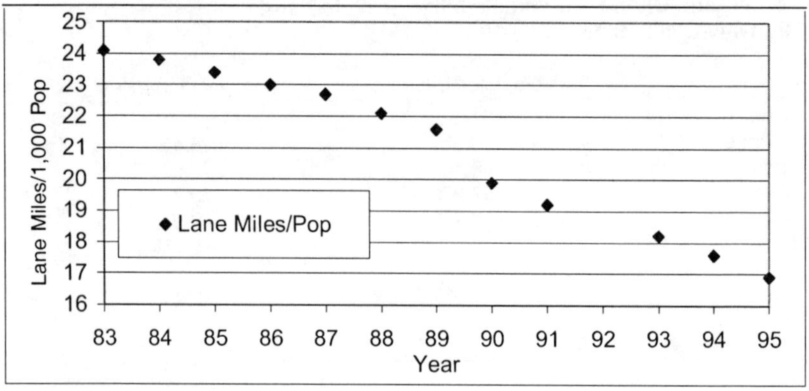

```
25
24 ◆
23     ◆
22        ◆
21           ◆
20              ◆
19                 ◆ Lane Miles/Pop
18                                    ◆
17                                       ◆
16                                          ◆
   83 84 85 86 87 88 89 90 91 92 93 94 95
                     Year
```

Source: Sen et al. (1998).

increase in vehicles, it is not surprising that congestion is a growing concern to suburban residents.

Travel Behavior

Changes in Trip Length and Duration

With the decentralization, population and urban activity is scattered over a large territory, and as Table 5.6 indicates, the VMT is rising. This would also apply to individual trips lengths. Table 5.9 shows that work trips less than ten miles (air line distance) are declining and longer trips are becoming more common.

To most commuters the number of minutes of travel is as important as or more important than the number of miles traveled. This would certainly be true of public transit users.

To the extent that travel time is critical in commuting choice, Table 5.10 shows the change in trip duration from 1970 to 1990. While there was a higher proportion of trips in 1970 under ten minutes, a higher proportion were over forty minutes. With the bold figures showing the larger percentage in each duration category there does not appear to be an appreciable change in overall travel times. To some extent faster speeds in the outlying areas are compensating for longer commutes (Table 5.10) and on balance the travel times show little change.

TRANSPORTATION IN CHICAGO METRO REGION SINCE 1970 107

Table 5.8

Number of Lane Miles per Four Measures of Traffic Generation

County	Population 1990[1]	Population 2000[1]	Employment[2]	Vehicles[3]	Retail[4]
Cook	5.2	4.9	11.2	9.7	4.1
DuPage	8.4	7.3	14.0	11.7	4.1
Kane	12.5	8.3	29.4	20.3	10.7
Lake	10.3	9.8	22.5	16.5	7.0
McHenry	16.9	11.9	55.3	26.7	20.3
Will	14.9	10.6	56.2	25.5	19.8

Source: Sen et al. (1998).
Notes:
[1] Number of 1995 lane miles per 1,000 inhabitants in 1990 and in 2000.
[2] Number of 1995 lane miles per 1,000 employees in 1990.
[3] Number of 1995 lanes miles per 1,000 registered vehicles.
[4] Number of 1995 lane miles per million dollars of retail wages in 1992.

Table 5.9

Chicago-Area Automobile Work-Trip Lengths, 1970 and 1990

Trip length (miles)	Percent of trips	
	1970	1990
0–5	54.1	50.8
5–10	23.6	23.0
10–15	11.2	12.5
15–20	5.4	6.7
20–25	3.1	3.6
25–30	1.3	1.7
30–35	0.7	0.7
> 35	0.6	1.0
Total	100.0	100.0

Source: Sen et al. (1998), using CATS data.

Trip Chains

A series of trips starting at home and ending at home is known as a trip chain. Over time these chains have become more complex. Table 5.11 illustrates the growing complexity of travel in DuPage County from 1970 to 1990 for all chains and separately for shopping chains (a shopping chain is a journey in which at least one stop is for the purpose of shopping). Note that while the population of the county grew by 60

Table 5.10

Chicago-Area Automobile Work-Trip Durations, 1970 and 1990

Trip duration	Percent of trips	
(minutes)	1970	1990
0–10	24.8	24.3
10–20	26.5	26.8
20–30	22.4	21.4
30–40	7.1	10.2
40–50	9.3	8.7
50–60	6.2	5.1
> 60	3.8	3.5
Total	100.0	100.0

Source: Sen et al. (1998), using CATS data.
Note: Totals may not add up exactly due to rounding.

percent, the total number of trip chains increased by only 28 percent. Of course since the complexity of chains increased, the increase in the number of destinations reached is much greater than 28 percent. This suggests that suburban residents are adjusting to congestion and the greater scatter of their destinations by combining trips. While this contributes to more efficient travel, one negative aspect is that many of these trips are made during the peak periods, on the way to and from work. This then may add more to congestion than to the total number of miles traveled.

Freight

Railroads

Since 1970 the railroad industry has seen major changes in the regulatory environment that have impacted the very structure of the industry. Prior to 1970 the federal government heavily regulated the railroad industry. The Interstate Commerce Commission (ICC) regulated all economic aspects of the industry: freight rates, passenger fares, service and line abandonments, and mergers and acquisitions. Railroads did have antitrust immunity to set rates and tariffs and did so through rate associations or bureaus. Since Chicago is the major rail hub of the nation, many of these changes had an impact on the region.

The creation of Amtrak in 1971 allowed railroads that joined the system to discontinue their money-losing passenger trains without ICC

Table 5.11

Complexity of Trips in DuPage County, 1970 and 1990

No. of trips in chain	No. of trip chains (000s)		No. of shopping trip chains (000s)	
	1970	1990	1970	1990
2	481	499	103	71
3	85	138	47	54
4	33	84	13	28
5	10	37	4	15
>5	9	37	3	17
Total	620	792	171	185

Source: Kim et al. (1995) using CATS data.
Note: Totals may not add up exactly due to rounding.

approval (Smerk 1991). The number of intercity passenger trains was reduced significantly. The impact of the creation of Amtrak had the following effects on the Chicago region:

- It decreased the number of intercity trains serving the region.
- It reduced the number of intercity terminals to one, Union Station.
- The private railroads closed their passenger offices in Chicago.

The overall impact was to reduce the passenger activity and the importance of Chicago as a passenger rail hub of the nation.

In the area of freight, regulatory reform began with the Regional Rail Reorganization Act of 1973, which was passed primarily to restructure the railroads in the northeast. In 1976 the act was strengthened with the Railroad Revitalization and Regulatory Reform Act that relaxed regulation of railroad rates, mergers, and abandonments. The goal of the 1976 act was to rescue the industry by giving it more flexibility to respond to market forces. This legislation never met its objective, so in 1980 the Staggers Rail Act was passed to significantly reduce regulation of all railroad procedures and operations. This sped up the timetable for mergers, acquisitions, and abandonments of lightly used and duplicative lines. Finally, in 1995 the Interstate Commerce Commission was abolished and replaced with a much smaller Surface Transportation Board (U.S. DOA 1998). The impact of this relaxation of regulation was a series of mergers and consolidations that reduced the number of class-one (large) railroads from 71 in 1970 to 33 in 1982 to 8 in 1998 (U.S. DOT 1996).

The increased merger activity resulting from the deregulation resulted in a significant loss of the number of railroads and railroad and shipper associations in the Chicago region. In 1970 seven class-one railroads were headquartered in Chicago. In 1999 the last major railroad that maintained its headquarters in Chicago, the Illinois Central, was acquired by the Canadian Pacific Railroad. Likewise, the number of railroad, shipper, and railroad associations dwindled. In 1970 there were approximately two dozen such agencies headquartered in Chicago while in 1998 only about half a dozen remain (National Railway Publication Co. 1972). Nationally, railroad employment fell from 566,000 employees in 1970 to only 190,000 in 1994, a decrease of 66 percent (U.S. DOT 1996). Chicago, being the rail center of the nation, experienced a significant loss of employment as well. The deregulation and resulting consolidation of the industry reduced Chicago's importance as a rail hub and resulted in a reduction of railroad employment in the region and a decline in activity in the downtown central business district.

Freed from economic regulation, railroads became more efficient competitors for freight. While the number of companies and employment decreased, the amount of traffic the railroads were carrying increased. Between 1970 and 1994 railroad traffic expressed in ton-miles increased by 57 percent (U.S. DOT 1996). In some instances, particularly on the Union Pacific, increased rail traffic caused congestion and delays costing shippers millions of dollars. Congested railroad yards also resulted in highway traffic congestion and delay in the Chicago region. This was due to grade crossing blockages due to an increased number of trains and delay while trains waited to enter the congested yards. The increase in intermodal traffic, that is, truck trailers or containers, resulted in increased intermodal transfers between railroad yards by truck. In 1996 there were 14,200 daily truck movements of containers transferring between intermodal facilities. This number is forecasted to double by 2020 (Rawling 1997).

The region's commuter rail service was also negatively impacted by freight congestion. Metra reported that increased freight interference resulted in their on-time performance to slip from 97.3 percent to 95.8 percent in October of 1998 (Metra 1998b).

The Chicago region experienced a decline in importance as a rail hub and a loss of employment resulting from deregulation of the rail industry. It also witnessed a significant increase in rail traffic that resulted in both increased congestion of the railroad facilities and the highway system.

Conclusions

Because there have been many factors contributing to sprawl and because sprawl has occurred for such a long period, the role of the transit and highways systems is difficult to assess. Increasing wealth has been a major contributor to urban sprawl in the Chicago area but household formation and increasing rates of home ownership are also factors. These factors have characterized the Chicago area throughout the entire twentieth century, not just since World War II. Because the city limits of Chicago are rather substantial, the city did not lose population until the end of the 1940s, but the core areas of the city started losing population around the beginning of the 1900s. Therefore it is commonly believed that sprawl started in the 1950s. While it is clear that sprawl has occurred for approximately one hundred years, the role of transportation systems is less clear. Many urban residents who seek low-cost housing find it on the fringe of the region and tolerate high commuting costs. McHenry County is a good example. It has been the fastest growing county in the state of Illinois for several decades and yet it has no freeway interchanges. Still, transportation plays a role, and an understanding of federal and state policy on transportation is essential in understanding the role of transportation in sprawl.

Transit

Federal legislation has been increasingly supportive of mass transit. In the last three decades programs have been expanded, funding increased, transit planning required, and flexible funding with highway programs encouraged. The state has recognized the importance of transit, provided legislation to create the Regional Transportation Authority and a state-operating subsidy, and through four bonding programs provided capital funds to replace aging infrastructure. But in the past financial crises resulting from operative fund shortfalls have caused major disruptions to the system resulting in losses in ridership. Infrastructure was allowed to decay without timely replacement programs. The passage of Illinois FIRST in 1999 was the first state funding package in a decade. Locally, the lack of city and suburban cooperation has led to financial crises and a lack of coordinated, comprehensive, regional transportation planning, although the individual entities have made innovations in service in their respective areas. Despite these many efforts on all levels of government, transit ridership fell in both absolute and relative terms. Ridership in the city of Chicago fell drastically while suburban bus and rail ridership increased at a modest rate. The net effect of government transit programs on the region's sprawl has been positive but not to the extent that it could have been.

Highways

Since the Interstate Highway program essentially came to an end in the early 1970s, there has been little federally funded new highway construction in the region. The federal government has increasingly treated highway and transit more evenly by combining them into one single multimodal legislation. Regional planning, public input, transit alternatives analysis requirements, along with increasingly flexible funding, have all been supportive of transit alternatives to highway projects. At the state and local level there has been little new highway construction in the last thirty years. Illinois FIRST will also provide funding to maintain and improve the highway system, the first bonding package in a decade. There is a backlog of projects just to get the system into satisfactory condition. Four major new construction projects have been scrapped or delayed for various reasons, including lack of funding, lack of political support, local opposition, legal and environmental issues. But measures of automobile usage, such as vehicle registrations and vehicle miles traveled, have increased significantly while the highway capacity has not grown to the same extent in the region, contributing to worsening congestion.

Travel Demand and Travel Behavior

While the relationship between highways and sprawl is complex, state and federal highway policy since 1970 has not been a major cause of the region's sprawl. The large increase in the size of the labor force and the increase in productivity have contributed to a prosperous region in which home and car ownership has increased. Even with the greater miles traveled and the growing congestion, travel time is not increasing. Not only are many residents driving in fringe areas with moderate congestion, those who are not are modifying their travel behavior to compensate for the greater scatter of destinations by combining many destinations in one journey, called trip chaining. Trip chaining represents a fundamental change in travel behavior in the last several decades. It is largely attributable to the growth of multiworker households but also to increasing traffic congestion. When many destinations are combined into one journey, daily travel is more efficient and the total daily time spent traveling is not increased.

Railroads

Economic deregulation of the railroad freight industry resulted in the elimination of numerous railroad companies located in the region and the loss of tens of thousands of jobs, thereby lessening Chicago's role as the nation's transportation hub. Increased rail traffic volumes have resulted in added congestion of both rail and highway facilities, much of it from truck transfer of intermodal containers. Rail freight congestion has resulted in increased highway congestion by making the region's transit system less effective. Federal policy in the area of freight railroads has had a neutral effect on the region's sprawl but has contributed to the region's congestion.

References

American Public Transit Association (APTA). 1999. *Transit Fact Book.* 50th ed. Washington, DC: APTA.
Chicago Area Transportation Study (CATS). 1996. *Transportation Facts* 13(4) (October).
Chicago Transit Authority (CTA). 1999. *CTA Ridership.* Chicago: CTA.
Christopher, E.J., and Maryanne Custodio. 1997. *A History of Northeast Illinois Expressway System.* Working Paper 97-04. Chicago Area Transportation Study.
Colby, Charles. 1933. Centrifugal and Centripetal Forces in Urban Geography. *Annals of the American Association of Geographers* 22 (March).
Dewberry and Davis. 1997. *Technical Audit,* ed. Sidney O. Dewberry. Chicago: Illinois State Toll Highway Authority.
Kim, Hyungjin, Ashish Sen, Siim Sööt, and Ed Christopher. 1994. Shopping Trip Chains: Current Patterns and Changes since 1970. *Transportation Research Record* 1443, National Research Council, 38-44.
Krambles, George, and Arthur H. Peterson. 1993. *CTA at 45: A History of the First 45 Years of the Chicago Transit Authority.* Oak Park, IL: Walsworth.
Metra, Commuter Rail Division of the RTA. 1999. *Metra Ridership.* Chicago: Metra.
———. 1998a. *1999 Program and Budget Document.* Chicago: Metra.
———. 1998b. *Metra Faces Challenges of Rail Industry's Second Wind? On The (Bi) Level.* Chicago: Metra.

National Railway Publication Co. 1972. *Official Guide of the Railways* 104(12).
Pace, Suburban Bus Division of the RTA. 1999. *Pace Ridership*. Arlington Heights, IL: Pace.
Rawling, Gerald. 1997. *Statistical Summary and Value of the Intermodal Freight Industry of Northeast Illinois*. Chicago Area Transportation Study.
Regional Transportation Authority (RTA). 1996. *Annual Report*. Chicago: RTA.
———. 1998. *Market Analysis: Northwest Corridor Transit Feasibility Study*. Chicago: RTA.
Regional Transportation Authority Act. (70 ILCS 3615/1.02).
———. (70 ILCS as amended by Public Acts 83–885 and 83–886).
Schlickman, Steve. 1999. Summary of SB 1028– Transportation Revenues and RTA Bonding. Memo to Business Leaders for Transportation, June 3.
Sen, Ashish et al. 1998. *Highways and Urban Decentralization*. Chicago: Urban Transportation Center, University of Illinois at Chicago.
Smerk, George. 1991. *The Federal Role in Urban Transportation*. Bloomington: Indiana University Press.
Tecson, Joseph. 1975. The Regional Transportation Authority in Northeastern Illinois. *Chicago Bar Record* (May–August).
U.S. Department of Agriculture (DOA). 1998. *Transportation Challenges for the Twenty-First Century*. Washington, DC: DOA.
U.S. Department of Transportation (DOT). 1998. *Transportation Equity Act for the 21st Century*. Washington, DC: DOT.
———, Bureau of Transportation Statistics. 1996. *National Transportation Statistics*. Washington, DC: DOT.
Young, David. 1998. *Chicago Transit: An Illustrated History*. DeKalb: Northern Illinois University Press.

6

PIYUSHIMITA THAKURIAH

Commercial Motor Carrier Operations in the Northeast Illinois Region: Impacts on Land Use Trends Since 1970

Introduction

The northeastern (NE) Illinois region has historically been a hub of freight transportation. Today the Chicago area leads the nation in the volume of freight moved by trucks. The number of daily truck trips is very large and is expected to keep rising. It has been estimated that between 1973 and 1993, about 41 percent of the growth in total vehicle miles traveled (VMT) in the northeastern Illinois region can be attributed to truck and other nonpersonal transportation (Sen et al. 1998).

This chapter considers if (a) governmental policies relating to the motor carrier industry and (b) trucking activities initiated by motor carrier industry have implications on decentralization of land use in the NE Illinois region. To this end, the paper considers some of the key policy issues and trends in the motor carrier activities that could potentially have impacted land use in the region.

The region consists of six counties: Cook (including the city of Chicago and suburban Cook), DuPage, Lake, McHenry, Will, and Kane. The period of examination is post-1970. County-level data on various indices were used for the analysis.

The motor carrier industry has a number of stakeholders. Outcome measures (such as increase in truck traffic contributing to congestion, location of trucking and warehousing facilities, and so on), which could be construed as the mechanisms relating the motor carrier industry to land use changes, are mediated through the actions of these stakeholders. These stakeholders operate within a framework laid out by governmental policies and general economic and industry trends.

Trucking activities may have impacted land use patterns in NE Illinois in two major ways.

A. The first trend of impact may have been operationalized by the following mechanisms:

1. By reducing a key price of production (namely, cost of transporting input factors of production and the cost of distributing finished products), the trucking industry may have facilitated decentralization of industry in general.
2. By increasing congestion in urbanized areas of the road network, the trucking industry may have contributed to a reason for households to move outward to avoid congestion.
3. By having to offer shippers and receivers competitive prices, there is a need to keep costs of operations down, providing incentive to move to locations where trucking operations can be consolidated and are more cost-effective relative to other locations.
4. By using trucks with larger bodies that have difficulty maneuvering in older city streets, there is an incentive for trucking firms to locate in newer developments where land is more easily available.
5. By having to operate in ways that require considerable land for loading/unloading and drayage operations, thereby locating in areas where land is inexpensive.

B. The second trend whereby trucking activities may have impacted land use trucking emerges from the fact that trucking is a derived demand. Hence, it may be speculated that trucking activities that are related to land use are simply a response to factors such as:

1. Movement along with other decentralizing industries and services to outlying regions of the northeastern Illinois metropolitan area.
2. Outward movement as population in general decentralized.

The relationship of trucking to land use patterns in the NE Illinois region are combinations of both types of trends. Trucking activities have certainly followed the patterns established by other sectors; on the other hand, there is reason to believe that trucking has also strengthened the pattern of decentralization in the region. It is beyond the scope of this chapter to speculate whether these decentralization trends would have continued to occur without the pattern of trucking activities that the region witnessed in the post-1970 period. Furthermore, data at a much finer geography and time scales are required to fully explore the topic of this chapter. County-level data may be too aggregate for the purposes of such a study.

General Trends and the Motor Carrier Industry in Northeast Illinois

The possibility has been raised that by reducing a key price of production (namely, cost of transporting input factors of production and the cost of distributing finished products), the trucking industry may have facilitated decentralization of industry. However, little evidence of this speculation holds for the continuing decentralization trends in the Chicago area, especially in the post-1970 period.

Industry decentralization has been ongoing in the Chicago region for several decades. Chapter 5 (Table 5.2) shows the share of employment in the six counties for 1970 and 1990 and the percent change between these employment figures. DuPage County had the largest percent gain in employment followed by Lake, McHenry, and Kane counties. Cook County has the smallest increase in employment, while the city of Chicago experienced a decrease in employment (of –2 percent, from 1,864,000 in 1970 to 1,473,200 in 1990). Table 5.2 also shows the patterns of population decentralization. Cook County experienced a 7 percent decline in population during this time, while the outer counties, especially DuPage and McHenry, experienced substantial amount of population growth.

The trends in the spatial distribution of employment growth in the trucking industry (given in Table 6.1) are similar to those of all industries (Table 5.2). DuPage and Lake counties particularly saw phenomenal growth rates (of over 1000 percent) in trucking-related employment.

It may be speculated that some of this outward movement of industry was facilitated by the availability of affordable and reliable trucking

Table 6.1

Six-County Employment Decentralization Trends and Trends in Trucking and Courier Firms Between 1970 and 1990

	1970 Employment	1990 Employment	1970–1990 Change	Change %
Cook	49,142	44,673	–4,469	–9.09
DuPage	732	13,454	12,772	1,733.98
Kane	N/A	1,858		
Lake	668	1,562	894	133.83
McHenry	428	1,010	582	135.98
Will	446	1,836	1,390	311.66
Total	51,416	64,393	12,977	25.24

Source: Economic Census, Geographic Data Series, U.S. Department of Commerce.

services. The hypothesis here would be that industries moved out first—with the availability of trucks to distribute goods and services to consumers, there was no longer a need to be physically close to consumers or to suppliers of other components in the production process. At best, the evidence to support this hypothesis is mixed because a number of other reasons exist because of which firms located in the outer suburbs.

In an examination of company location preference, based on a stated preference survey of firms currently located in DuPage County, Thakuriah (1998) found that the primary factors determining company location varies significantly by type of industrial category that the firm belongs to. I have considered the example of one of the important factors cited by firms surveyed—availability of land. The availability of large plots of land was of greatest importance to manufacturing and service firms. These firms tend to be physically larger than other types of firms. About 42 percent of the firms surveyed with facilities larger than 100,000 square feet belong to the manufacturing industry. Another 42 percent of facilities with such large physical dimensions belong to the service industry. For these firms, lack of constraints on physical growth and land availability were important factors in locating outside the urban core in NE Illinois.

Firms also vary tremendously on their level of dependence on trucks. Thakuriah (1998) found that in DuPage County the type of firm and the number of times per week that trucks access the facility are significantly related. More trucks accessed firms in the manufacturing and transportation, communications, and utilities sector than facilities in any other industrial sectors.

Hence, although trucking may have facilitated the outward movement of industry to some extent, (a) the level of this impact of this factor on the decentralization of industry has had tremendous variations by type of industry, (b) the impact might not have occurred unless other facilitating factors had existed for companies to move out, and most important (c) the overall trends in the location patterns of trucking establishments were not different from other establishments. Moreover, the impact may have been stronger in the earlier decades of this century; however, in the post-1970 period, the effects were probably minimal.

It has also been speculated that the impact of trucking activity on land use was simply a by-product of the response to general decentralization trends in the NE region. The demand for trucking is primarily a derived demand—derived from the level of economic activity in the nation. The demand for freight transportation is most closely related to the goods production component of the gross domestic product (GDP). But the caveat exists that while GDP measures production in dollars, the demand for freight transportation is more strongly related to the production of bulk commodities (low value per ton) such as household goods and agricultural products. On the whole, time series data tell us that expansion in the national or regional economy result in increases in overall freight demand, while contractions in the economy result in reductions in this demand.

Figure 6.1 shows wages earned per unit of population for the six counties in NE Illinois for each year from 1983 to 1995. The wages have been adjusted for inflation using the consumer price index (CPI). The first figure shows that the spending potential is the greatest in DuPage County for each year examined, followed by Lake County. The overall trends in all counties show an increase in spending potential over time. This trend translates into an increasing demand for shipment of goods and commodities, with the greatest demand stemming from DuPage and Lake. As the buying power has decentralized over the six-county area, so have trucking establishments and the pattern of trucking activity. Although county-level data are too aggregate to show these relationships, it may be speculated that locating in suburban areas allowed most trucking establishments an easily accessible "catchment area" that included shopping centers and other sites where retail purchases were made.

Figure 6.1 **Wage per Unit of Population in the Six Counties in Northeast Illinois from 1983 to 1995**

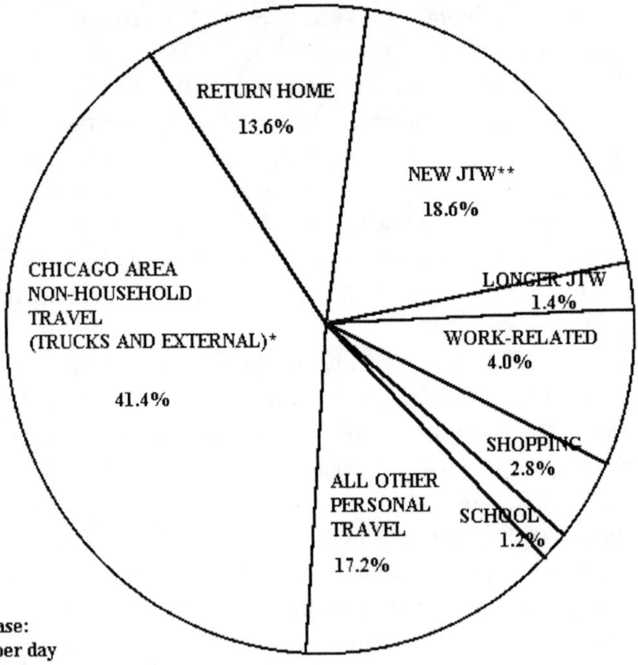

- RETURN HOME 13.6%
- NEW JTW** 18.6%
- LONGER JTW 1.4%
- WORK-RELATED 4.0%
- SHOPPING 2.8%
- SCHOOL 1.2%
- ALL OTHER PERSONAL TRAVEL 17.2%
- CHICAGO AREA NON-HOUSEHOLD TRAVEL (TRUCKS AND EXTERNAL)* 41.4%

Twenty-year increase:
49.5 million VMT per day

* Includes all additional traffic not included in 1970 and 1980 CATS Household Travel Surveys

** JTW: Journey-to-work

Impacts of Trucking Activities on Congestion Levels

By increasing congestion in urbanized areas of the road network, the trucking industry may have contributed to a reason for households to move outward to avoid congestion. Between 1973 and 1993 there were only modest increases in average trip lengths for personal (as opposed to commercial trips). Yet, "congestion" in terms of delays in travel has increased substantially during this time. Between 1973 and 1993 the area vehicle miles traveled (VMT) grew from 85.9 million miles per day to 135.4, or an increase of 49.5 million miles per day, almost a 60 percent jump.

Figure 6.2 gives an idea of the spatial distribution of the demand for road capacity in NE Illinois. This is intended to provide a very rough picture of this demand, because clearly the demand is related to the

Figure 6.2 **Road Capacity Relative to Population, Number of Employed Persons, Number of Vehicles Registered, and Wages Earned in Six Counties in Northeast Illinois: Trends from 1983 to 1995**

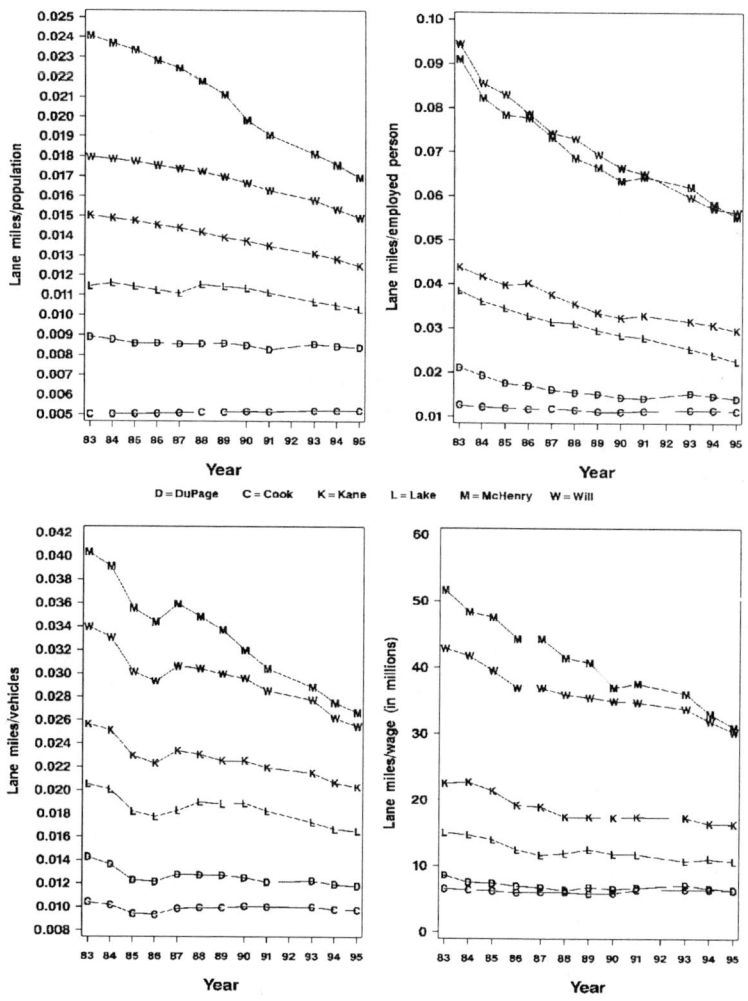

routes chosen by travelers, many of whom may originate outside the particular counties shown in the figure. The figure has four parts: Part I shows lane miles per population, according to which the road capacity relative to population has been steadily decreasing at the fastest rate in McHenry, Will, Kane, and Lake counties. This index has been relatively stable for DuPage and Cook counties over the period examined. Parts II, III, and IV show lane miles per employed person, per vehicle registered, and by wages earned. For all these indexes, DuPage and Cook counties are relatively stable whereas McHenry, Will, Kane, and Lake counties have steadily declined over time.

In a study of factors contributing to the large increases in VMT in the six-county Chicago metropolitan area, (Sen et al. 1998) identified several major factors and their share of VMT. These are given in Figure 6.3. This figure shows that approximately three-quarters of the increase in VMT between 1973 and 1993 can be attributed to an increase in the size of the labor force, increased external traffic and growth in trucking. Moreover, because trucks are the equivalents of two or three automobiles, their contribution to activity on the road is even greater than their VMT indicates.

The authors concluded that the growth in truck traffic reflects several factors. First, the increase in the labor force indicates that with the resources earned we are consuming more, and trucks transport these goods and services. Second, despite the information and electronic age, truck-based delivery services are becoming more numerous. Also, shopping at home requires home delivery. Third, while the manufacturing era was more dependent on the railroad, contemporary industries as a whole have become more truck-dependent. These reasons are similar to the ones raised in the discussion of trucking as a derived demand.

Of interest to us is whether the increase in congestion generated by truck traffic has provided incentive for households and employment in the NE Illinois region to move to outlying areas with the expectation that they will "flee" congestion. The literature on the sociodemographic and socioeconomic reasons for sprawl is extensive, and there is no single reason or sets of reasons that explain population and economic movement to outlying areas. Further, the greatest rates of decentralization in the Chicago area were in the 1950s and the 1960s, although the greatest rates of growth in truck VMT is much more recent (Sen et al. 1998). Hence, the evidence to support the speculation that increases in congestion (a large share of which has been contributed to by trucks) may have contributed to a reason for household and employment to move outward in NE is mixed.

Impacts of Public Sector Policies and Land Use

In this section I will examine key public sector policies pertaining to the motor carrier industry that have had the potential of decentralizing popu-

COMMERCIAL MOTOR CARRIER OPERATIONS IN NE ILLINOIS 123

Figure 6.3 **Major Contributors to Percentage Increase in VMT in the Chicago Area from 1973 to 1993**

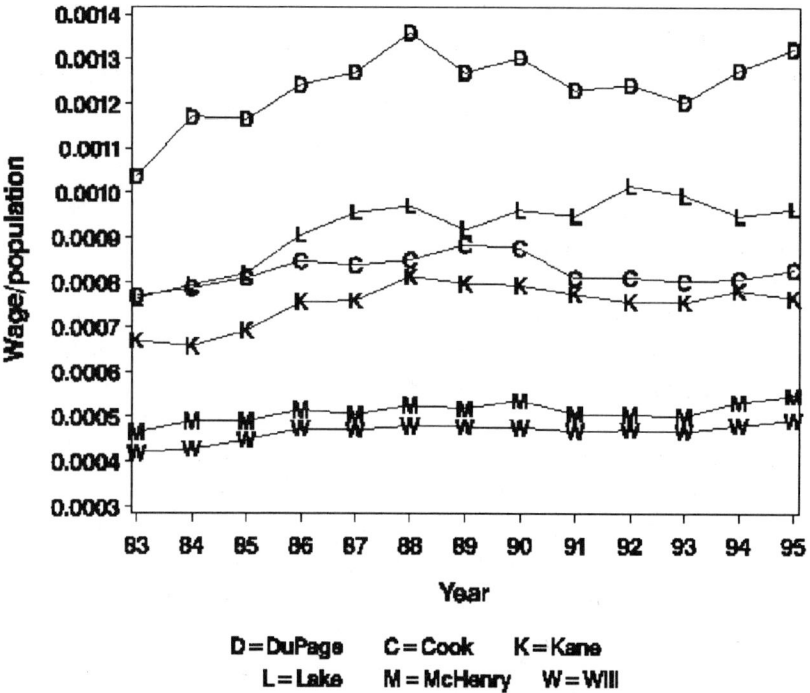

D = DuPage   C = Cook   K = Kane
L = Lake   M = McHenry W = Will

lation and employment. It would appear that as the demand for motor carrier transportation has increased, trucking companies took decisions for efficient operations that may perhaps have had (inadvertent) impacts on land use. But in what ways has the demand for motor carrier services increased (relative to an alternative mode of transporting goods, say, railroads) and what has been facilitating regulations that provided the incentive to carriers to move outward? We will examine such issues in this chapter.

The freight industry has typically not been a part of the public sector regional planning process. The Chicago Area Transportation Study (CATS), which is the metropolitan planning organization (MPO) for the NE Illinois region, established an Intermodal Advisory Task Force for the 2020 regional transportation planning process. This task force provided a forum for representatives of the rail, truck, air freight, and water carrier industry, as well as shippers, businesses, and other users, to provide input into the metropolitan transportation planning processes relating to intermodal and freight industry needs and issues. One objective of such public sector initiatives has been to "mainstream" the freight industry by integrating it into the regional planning, programming, and investment cycle as well as by identifying the freight component of proposed projects and identifying the benefits of such projects, in an effort to qualify it for a public sector program (CATS 1998).

Deregulation and the Trucking Industry: The Motor Carrier Act of 1980

The possibility has been raised that by having to offer shippers and receivers competitive prices, there is a need to keep costs of operations down, providing incentive to move to locations where trucking operations can be consolidated and are more cost-effective relative to other locations. The competitive nature of the trucking industry rose with the Motor Carrier Act (MCA) of 1980, which led to substantial easing of restrictions on the entry of motor carriers into new markets. The open competition that resulted from the changes brought about by this act has enabled well-managed motor carriers to enter many markets and forced many inefficient carriers out of the market. In this section we will examine to what extent, if any, the MCA has affected the pattern of decentralization in the NE Illinois region.

As a result of deregulation, the motor carrier industry in NE Illinois, as elsewhere, became structured along several predominant organizational lines on the basis of organization of the carrier and operations of the carrier. On the basis of ownership, the trucking industry is organized into "for-hire" and "private" carriers. Private carriers are owned and operated by businesses as private fleets for their purposes (for example, many of the nation's largest grocery and retail stores, manufacturers, oil companies, wholesalers, and distributors own and operate their own trucks).

For-hire firms, as the name suggests, provide trucking service to other industries and firms for a price. Traditionally, for-hire companies have specialized in either common or contract trucking. Common carriers transport goods for the public and charge published rates (tariffs) while contract carriers haul goods for specific companies under contract. One small but important component of the for-hire industry are independent contractors or owner operators. Estimates suggest that there may be as many as 100,000 owner-operators across the nation (Transportation Research Board 1987).

In the Chicago metropolitan area, approximately one-half of the carriers located in each county are for-hire carriers and the remaining half are private carriers. For example, in Cook County, 49.90 percent of the carriers are for-hire and about 44 percent are private (information was obtained from the Office of Motor Carrier, Federal Highway Administration's 1999 Motor Carrier Management System). In DuPage County, about 54 percent are for-hire and about 45 percent of the carriers are private. There appears to be no trends with respect to location of for-hire and private carriers in the NE Illinois region, at least at the county level.

On the basis of operations, for-hire and private carriers specialize in one of two kinds of shipments: truckload (TL) freight and less-than-truckload (LTL). TL operations are of a single shipment from one shipper to one receiver, and that single shipment constitutes the entire load of the truck. Because of the nature of TL operations, many carriers lack substantial investment in communications, management, and sales staff. LTL carriers carry several small shipments in one load of the truck from multiple shippers to multiple receivers. LTL operations in the United States today are extremely efficient and sophisticated, but because of the cost of hiring and training high-quality personnel and the need to establish and maintain sophisticated equipment, it is difficult to get into the LTL business. Indeed there are fewer than 500 LTL carriers today (including Yellow Freight, Consolidated Freightways, Roadway, UPS, and so on). This organizational picture is very different from the structure of the TL industry; according to the Office of Technology Assessment (1988), there are more than 25,000 for-hire carriers and some 50,000 private carriers in the United States providing TL service. Data were not available by type of carrier operations for firms located in NE Illinois.

The major outcome of the MCA of 1980 was "decentralization" in decision making. Each motor carrier firm became free from a large number of regulatory constraints in their operations. At the same time, when the market opened up to newer firms, competitive practices in these firms soared. This resulted in various carrier-level decisions that were intended to provide shippers and receivers with efficient, low cost services. One decision that emerged was the choice of location of trucking facilities and warehousing. Easy access to the highway system and the ability to conduct loading and transfer operations became increasingly important.

Another factor that is often cited to be an important outcome from the deregulation act is the "consolidation" of services. Consolidation can occur at two levels—that of ownership (merging of companies) and

Table 6.2

Number of Trucking and Courier Establishments in the Six Counties from 1970 to 1996 and the Percentage Change in the Number of Large Establishments*

County	No. of trucking establishments			% Change between 1970 and 1990	% Large establishments of all establishments			
	1970	1980	1990		1970	1980	1990	1996
Cook	1,531	1,333	1,494	-2.42	14.04	12.98	8.50	2.36
DuPage	86	187	316	247.44	2.32	5.88	5.70	6.05
Kane	88	83	124	40.91	7.90	3.61	4.03	3.85
Lake	68	73	130	91.18	2.94	3.85	3.07	3.85
McHenry	31	37	87	180.65	6.45	10.81	2.30	3.82
Will	52	83	117	125.00	0	1.20	1.70	3.63

Source: Economic Census, Geographic Data Series, U.S. Department of Commerce.
*Defined as establishments with fifty or more employees.

consolidation of activities within a company. From a land use perspective, consolidation of terminal and warehousing facilities is likely to lead to less fragmented development but perhaps to an increase in vehicle miles traveled (VMT), as trucks will have to be dispatched over greater distances to reach their destinations.

Growth in the number of trucking and courier establishments (an establishment is the same as a facility; two establishments may have the same owners, but they are located in separate sites) have occurred at different rates in the six counties of the northeastern Illinois region. Table 6.2 shows that while there has been an increase in the number of trucking establishments in all six counties, the rate of growth has been greatest in the collar counties. However, contrary to the concept of consolidation of services, the number of establishments with more than fifty employees (which can be considered to be large establishments) in fact went down from 228 in 1970 to 196 in 1996. It can be seen from Table 6.3 that the large trucking establishments in Cook County have decreased from 14.04 percent to 2.36 percent of all Cook County trucking establishments from 1970 to 1996.

In McHenry and Kane counties also, large trucking establishments as a percent of all trucking establishments decreased from 1970 to 1990. Large establishment share increased in DuPage County during this period. In fact, while the number of trucking establishments increased by

Table 6.3

Average Number of Trucks and Number of Drivers Employed with Commercial Driver's License (CDL) in Companies Located in the Counties in Northeast Illinois

	Trucks		CDL	
	Mean	Std. Dev.	Mean	Std. Dev.
Cook	8.47	60.20	5.15	63.60
DuPage	69.08	1521.35	17.94	249.97
Kane	13.38	153.16	8.50	112.78
Lake	10.50	74.25	13.91	174.43
McHenry	5.79	24.94	3.13	21.57
Will	N/A	N/A	N/A	N/A

Source: Office of Motor Carrier, Federal Highway Administration, U.S. Department of Transportation. 1998. Census Files.

about 244 percent during this period, the percent increase in the share of large establishments is about 800 percent.

A better measure of the size of a motor carrier firm and its impact on the road network are the number of trucks it owns and the number of drivers it employs. By these measures, the larger trucking companies are located in the suburban counties. Table 6.3 shows the average number of trucks and number of drivers employed with commercial driver's licenses (CDL) in companies located in the counties in NE Illinois.

The mean number of trucks owned by firms located in DuPage County is about sixty-nine; however, the standard deviation is almost twenty-two times the mean. Also, motor carrier firms in DuPage have the highest mean number of employers with CDL. Cook and McHenry county firms own comparatively fewer numbers of trucks. It should be noted that this table shows fleet size and driver pool by location of headquarters only and not by location of individual trucking terminals, warehouses, or other subsidiary type of trucking establishments.

The data in this section show that while deregulation opened up the market for increased competition in the motor carrier industry, the choice of location of trucking establishments, including firms, are due to a large number of reasons. Although large trucking establishments as a percent of all trucking establishments is greater in the collar counties (in 1996), the trends toward consolidation that one would have expected after deregulation has not been strong. Further, the small share of large establishments as a percent of all trucking establishments in Cook County probably indicate the emergence of "niche" trucking services that carry goods and commodities transferred from large trucks that have difficulty moving in older city streets into inner city areas.

Truck Size and Weight Policies

One of the speculations raised is that using trucks with larger bodies that have difficulty maneuvering in older city streets creates an incentive for trucking firms to locate in newer developments and within easy access of high-capacity highways. Larger trucks are the result of various federal policies on truck size and weight limitations.

As a result of deregulation and changing nature of markets, timely and reliable delivery of goods has become critical for carriers to remain competitive. But cost of operation is a key issue with trucking industries. Competition is keen and carriers need to be cost-effective in their operations. Morris, Kornhauser, and Kay (1998) noted the following factors as the most frequently cited barriers to freight transportation in metropolitan areas on the basis of a survey of industry professionals who had extensive operational experience in managing their firm's transportation needs: congestion and consequent delays faced by truckers, inadequate docking space, inadequate curb space for commercial vehicles, narrow streets that make it particularly arduous for trucks to bring large shipments to the central business district (CBD) area, and limited or nonexistent parking, which creates extreme difficulties in unloading freight and security. It may be noted here that a large number of these "complaints" pertain to physical accessibility.

In assessing these accessibility concerns, one needs to take the size of trucks into account. The size of trucks allowed on highways have become larger over the years. Federal policies on truck weights and sizes may have contributed to the desire of trucking firms to relocate to the outer suburbs. The Federal-Aid Highway legislation of 1956 set the maximum gross weight on interstate highways at 73,280 lbs. In the Federal-Aid Highway Amendments Act of 1974, Congress increased the gross weight limit to 80,000 lbs, an increase that was viewed as an energy conservation measure as a quid pro quo for reducing the speed limit to 55 miles per hour in the same legislation.

The number of registered trucks in the northeastern Illinois region in 1995 that are over 8,000 lbs of gross vehicle weight is 212,775 (CATS 1998a). The daily movements or trips in the region made by trucks over

Table 6.4

Differences in Distances Traveled by Trucks Between 1970 and 1986

	Truck types	Trip length (miles)
1970	Light	4.4
	Medium	6.5
	Heavy	11.1
1986	Light	9.6
	Medium	10.5
	Heavy	24.9

Source: CATS (1998).

8,000 lbs is 417,865. As indicated earlier, truck movements have led to an increase between 1973 and 1993 of about 41 percent of the total growth in VMT (Sen et al. 1998). The northeastern Illinois region has not only seen an increase in the number of trips made by trucks, but also an increase in heavier and larger trucks. Table 6.4 provides a comparison of truck trip lengths between 1970 and 1986 in the Chicago region. The table shows that trip lengths by all categories of trucks have increased, but trip lengths by heavy trucks have increased the greatest amount (1986 is the latest year for which these data are available).

Many national carriers today subcontract the last leg of the trip to niche carriers with smaller trucks whose drivers can cope with the problem of moving goods into the CBD area (Morris, Kornhauser, and Kay 1998). Larger trucks face more accessibility problems. Accessibility problems translate to costs for the carriers in terms of delays, safety issues, and other such factors. It is natural that given the competitive nature of current trucking operations, a desire for cost-effectiveness would encourage location of carriers in areas with fewer physical constraints and accessibility barriers, which is often to be found outside the inner core of urban areas. Thus increases in truck sizes has probably contributed to a desire by trucking firms to locate in collar counties.

Policies Emphasizing Intermodal Traffic and Newer Trucking Operations

The need for a high volume of intermodal (rail to truck or air to truck) operations has put a new demand on the trucking industry. For surface transportation, the interface between the trucking industry and the railroad industry, which is a core component of intermodal operations, is a major challenge. The intermodal infrastructure includes intermodal yards that accommodate rail tracks, containers and trailers, truck parking, access and egress points, and road network connectors between intermodal facilities and other destinations. As reported by CATS (1997), the Chicago area has extensive intermodal infrastructure and operations. Chicago acts as a hub of intermodal freight operations in the upper Midwest region. Much of the intermodal business in the Chicago area is also tied to the Pacific Rim trade, which is a major generator of container traffic.

The Intermodal Surface Transportation Efficiency Act (ISTEA) of 1991 called for plans and programs that would lead to the development and operation of an integrated intermodal system, including the efficient movement of freight. Following this, CATS formed an Intermodal Advisory Task Force consisting of private and public sector representatives. An objective of the task force was to include an intermodal component into the 2020 Regional Transportation Plan for the Chicago area.

The 2020 Plan notes that the intermodal freight industry accounted for approximately $8.7 billion or 6 percent of the gross regional product in NE Illinois in 1996. The scale of intermodal freight operations involves moving an estimated 4.2 million tons of freight daily in the region. Intermodal agreements have played a major role in the development of rail intermodal services over the past several years. Between 1980 and 1994 nationwide intermodal movements grew from 3.5 million trailers and containers to 8.2 million—a 134 percent increase. Most new domestic intermodal traffic previously was being shipped entirely by truck, but some portion was also moving by train. Intermodal agreements with shipping companies also have resulted in the diversion of some truck traffic to doublestack trains and container trains and some to go by ship through the Panama Canal.

A major component of the 2020 Plan was a set of six intermodal policies to identify and address the operational needs of the intermodal freight industry and to enhance the efficiency of freight transportation. These policies are intended to lead to the development of a comprehensive regional network of intermodal facilities connected by necessary intermodal connectors and to improve the operational characteristics of these connectors.

The intermodal industry makes extensive use of the region's expressways and major arterials. An example provided in the CATS documentation indicates that thirty key intermodal connectors to the National

Highway System (NHS) have been identified to provide 46.7 miles of access to twenty-eight major intermodal facilities. Most of the region's current intermodal facilities are located within Cook County, with a few in DuPage County. However, there will be a need for the development of large intermodal facilities in the near future.

Approximate calculations by CATS staff (1998a) shows that, based on conservative growth trends, the land needed for intermodal operations for the year 2020 at current levels of service would be about 7,020 acres. The land use needs of individual intermodal companies can be as high as 700 acres—such high contiguous acreage is likely to be hard to find within already developed areas. This need may translate to greater land consumption. However, even if sites for new facilities are eventually located far away from the current urbanized areas and are located along currently existing transportation routes, in the absence of supporting economic and social infrastructure, human and industrial settlements may not necessarily follow.

Railroad Policies

Railroads are best suited for long-haul transportation and for carrying bulk commodities. The low-rolling friction of the rail and the high power of the diesel engine allow railroads to carry a large volume of traffic at low ton-mile costs. These characteristics make railroads the best mode for carrying dry bulk commodities. However, for short-haul movement of goods, the relative advantages of trucking over rail need not be elaborated. However, loss of rail service shifts freight movements to trucks, which increases wear and tear of highways in addition to adding to highway congestion.

Since railroads are the major modal competitor to trucking, it is pertinent to review if federal railroad policies could have facilitated lesser dependence on trucks by instituting polices that would have increased the rail mode share of goods and commodities. The Interstate Highway System made trucking services ubiquitous with respect to space. Barriers to exit kept railroads from abandoning unprofitable tracks with the result that operations could not be streamlined to meet demand and compete effectively with trucks. The passage of the Staggers Rail Act of 1980 led to significant reduction in regulation of railroad procedures and operations. The impact of the Staggers Act was a series of mergers and consolidations of inefficient railroad companies. The Chicago area saw a significant reduction in the number of railroad companies and associations since 1980.

The nature of trucking and railroad services inherently makes trucking the more favorable mode in all but the longest trips. This is true for the shipment of all types of commodities, including bulk agricultural products. This is because arrival time reliability of commodities has become increasingly important to shippers and receivers over time. Further rail capacity cannot shift quickly to meet quick fluctuations in demand.

Trucking has been the dominant mode of choice for shipments for the last several decades. This issue has less to do with governmental policies than with the inherent limitations of railroads as a mode in meeting the new and emerging needs of the commodities market.

But railroads share of commodities shipped has increased in recent years. The estimated daily volume of freight moved in trucks in NE Illinois in 1986 was 1,359,920 tons, the estimate for 1996 was 1,591,106 tons, and the forecast for year 2020 is 2,267,326 tons (CATS 1997). The daily volume of freight moved by rail in 1996 was 2,459,982 tons and the forecast for 2020 is 4,375,231. However, even if the share load shipped by railroads continue to increase, the needs for greater amounts of land by the freight industry will continue in future in the Chicago area. Further, delays to road traffic by rail operations have increased in recent years. But the scope exists that some of the other reasons by which trucks facilitate decentralization may reduce if investments on railroads increase.

Conclusions and Recommendations

The major conclusions from this chapter are:

1. The role of trucking in urban decentralization in the NE Illinois region has been minimal. Impacts, if any, probably would not have occurred in the absence of a variety of other facilitating factors. These factors include general household and economic trends. Overall, the trends in the location of trucking establishments are similar to all other business and industrial establishments. On the household side, trucking activities have followed buying power as population continues to decentralize.

2. Overall, government policies appear to have a minimal role on any

impact that trucking may have had on urban decentralization. While the government had a substantial role in restructuring the industry with the deregulation act of 1980, this role does not appear to have any direct negative impact on urban land use. A majority of trucking operation policies and industry structure as they relate to land use are the result of decisions made by private industry. However, policies pertaining to truck weight and size may have contributed to decentralization by encouraging trucking establishments to locate in lower density areas. In addition, it may be possible that government-funded construction of the Interstate Highway System may have subsidized trucking relative to railroads.

3. The extent of trucking activity may not reduce unless significant costs are incurred by a number of industries and individual households. This is because trucking is mostly derived demand and occurs due to the needs of industry and the purchasing power of individuals. Further, lack of adequate trucking services are more likely to negatively impact certain industries compared to others. There may also be differential impacts by geographic areas within the NE Illinois region in terms of the goods and services that can be accessed by population groups in those areas.

4. The future needs for land for the trucking and intermodal industry are substantial. However, even if sites for new facilities are eventually located far away from the current urbanized areas and are located along currently existing transportation routes, in the absence of supporting economic and social infrastructure, human and industrial settlements may not necessarily follow.

5. Data at much finer geography and time scales are required to fully explore the topic of this chapter. County-level data may be too aggregate for the purposes of such a study. Hence the findings in this chapter should be taken as overall trends. To find detailed cause-and-effect relationships would require much better data than available here.

References

Chicago Area Transportation Study (CATS). 1998a. Discussion Paper/Presentations on the Subject of Intermodal Planning, Working Paper 97–17, January.

———.1998. The 2020 Regional Transportation Plan: Destination 2020, August.

———. 1997. Statistical Summary and Value of the Intermodal Freight Industry to Northeast Illinois, Working Paper 97–03, July.

Morris, A.G., A. Kornhauser, and M.J. Kay. 1998. Urban Freight Mobility: Collection of Data on Time, Costs, and Barriers related to Moving Products into the Central Business District. Paper presented at the Transportation Research Board Annual Conference, Washington, DC, January.

Office of Motor Carrier, Federal Highway Administration, U.S. Department of Transportation. 1998. Census Files. Washington, DC.

Office of Technology Assessment. 1988. *Gearing Up for Safety*. Congress of the United States. Washington, DC.

Sen et al. 1998. Highways and Urban Decentralization, Final Report, Appendix 6, Urban Transportation Center, University of Illinois at Chicago.

Thakuriah, P. 1998. Land Use and Company Location. Paper presented at the Regional Science Association International Annual Meetings, Santa Fe, November.

TransCore in association with HNTB, Barton-Aschman Associates, Inc. 1999. Northeast Illinois Strategic Early Deployment Plan, May.

Transportation Research Board. 1989. Providing Access for Large Trucks, Special Report 223.

7

BONNIE LINDSTROM

The Role of Regional Planning Agencies in Suburban Deconcentration

Planning Agencies in Northeastern Illinois

The six-county northeastern Illinois region does not have a single, general purpose metropolitan planning agency. Planning in the Chicago metropolitan region is the joint responsibility of the Northeastern Illinois Planning Commission (NIPC) and the Chicago Area Transportation Study (CATS). NIPC, functioning as the regional council of governments with its board comprising of elected officials, is responsible for developing comprehensive land and water use plans and the long-range population and employment forecasts for the region's transportation plans. CATS, whose board comprises transportation professionals, is the designated metropolitan planning organization (MPO) with the primary responsibility of programming the federal funds for transportation infrastructure in the region. The agencies jointly prepare transportation plans for a twenty-year time period. The most recent plan, *The 2020 Regional Transportation Plan: Destination 2000* (Chicago Area Transportation Study, 1998a), was completed in 1997 for the year 2020.

In order to analyze the effect this bifurcation in responsibilities has had on regional growth, this chapter will first briefly review the historical background, organizational structure, and responsibilities of each agency. Second, the chapter will examine two earlier regional transportation plans (the 1980 plan and the 1995 transportation system plan), the most recent transportation plan, and plans for land and water use developed by NIPC. Third, the chapter will analyze the strengths and weaknesses of the two agencies and the role they have played in the region's growth. Finally, the chapter will examine proposals from civic and advocacy organizations to change the mandates of the two agencies to better meet the challenges confronting the region.

The Chicago Area Transportation Study

The Chicago Area Transportation Study (CATS) is the metropolitan planning organization in the northeastern Illinois region designated to develop one-year and five-year transportation plans for the region, do long-range planning for transportation investment based on available and projected estimates of funds, and program the federal funds for regional transportation projects. These projects include major new infrastructure facilities, major facilities expansions to existing expressways or mass transit lines, and existing system improvements. It has no authority to implement its proposals. However, if a transportation project is not included as part of CATS's evaluation of regional transportation projects, the project will receive no federal funding. CATS also serves as a liaison with local and state agencies. As the designated MPO for the six-county area, CATS collects information on transportation needs and is responsible for determining whether the region's transportation planning is consistent with federal air quality requirements.

The Chicago Area Transportation Study was created in 1955 by an intergovernmental agreement among the state of Illinois, the city of Chicago, and Cook County. The first study was funded by the city of Chicago, Cook County, the state of Illinois, and the U.S. Bureau of Public Roads. CATS began solely as an advisory body. Its mandate was to make recommendations to the sponsoring agencies that had the responsibility to implement the proposals. CATS operated from the Division of Highways of the State of Illinois and all personnel were hired by the state (McDonald 1988). After the U.S. Department of Transportation required that each urbanized region of the county establish a metropolitan planning organization in 1973, the governor of Illinois designated CATS as the metropolitan planning organization for the northeastern Illinois region. The original study area included Cook and a portion of DuPage County; the northeastern Illinois region now includes the six counties in northeastern Illinois: Cook, DuPage, Kane, Lake, McHenry, and Will. Under an interagency agreement, the state department of transportation has fiduciary and administrative responsibility for the agency.

The twenty-member Policy Committee of CATS is permanently chaired by the secretary of the Illinois Department of Transportation (IDOT). The chair of the Council of Mayors is the only elected official. All the other members of the Policy Committee are appointed and represent specific transportation agencies or are policy-level representatives of local governments.[1] The Council of Mayors comprises the elected officials of the 270 municipalities in the six-county region. The councils prioritize the federal aid funds from the Surface Transportation Program (STP) allocated for locally initiated projects.

The budget is funded by federal, state, and local government agencies with the portions paid by the different levels of government allocated by agreement. The Illinois Department of Transportation contributes the local share of operating costs. The agency also derives income from contract work for local agencies and private concerns (Fiske 1989). In turn, CATS suballocates federal planning funds to other regional transportation agencies. In 1998 CATS suballocated planning funds to NIPC, the Chicago Department of Transportation, the Chicago Transit Authority, the Regional Transportation Authority, Pace (suburban bus), Metra (suburban rail), and the subregional councils of mayors. CATS, for example, funds 80% of the salaries of the transportation planners in each subregional council of mayors.

The Northeastern Illinois Planning Commission

The Northeastern Illinois Planning Commission (NIPC) is the state-chartered comprehensive regional planning agency for the six counties in northeastern Illinois. Governor William Stratton signed into law the Northeastern Illinois Metropolitan Area Planning Act on July 6, 1957. The agency was mandated to develop and adopt a comprehensive plan to guide the development of the six-county region, specifically in the areas of public health (water supply, storm water management, and sewage and garbage disposal), transportation, and land use; to offer technical assistance and advice to local governments; and to conduct research and collect data for regional planning. The name was changed in 1967 to the Northeastern Illinois Planning Commission.

Representation on NIPC's board is fixed by statute, with appointments for a fixed four-year term. The board comprises elected officials, representatives appointed by the governor, and representatives of transportation, park districts, and wastewater agencies.[2] Advising the board are technical committees, task forces, advisory committees, and NIPC staff. The technical and advisory committees and task forces comprise representatives from agencies and organizations involved in specific planning issues.

NIPC has neither taxing authority nor a fixed source of income. It receives funding from state and federal grants, contributions from local governments and foundations, and contracts for specific projects. Each year NIPC asks for membership dues from the units of local government in the region. The formula for the financial contribution is based on general revenues as reported to the state comptroller.

NIPC has no authority to implement or enforce its plans. The 1957 enabling legislation explicitly states that NIPC is to act solely as an advisory body. Its decisions are not binding on units of local government or state and federal agencies.

Regional Forecasts and Plans: 1962–1998

In 1962, when the first CATS plan was completed with projections and plans for 1980, the major expressways outlined in the Chicago Plan Commission's preliminary comprehensive city plan of 1946 were built or under construction. These expressways were primarily radial from the central business district. The region's tollway system opened in 1958 under the authority of the Illinois State Toll Highway Authority. The toll highway system included the Tri-State (I-294) planned as a circumferential tollway bypassing Chicago; the Northwest Tollway (I-90) to Rockford, Illinois; and the East-West Tollway (I-80) from the Eisenhower Expressway to Aurora. This committed system was in place by 1966.

Plans for transportation infrastructure to expand the existing and committed system of highways and transit lines were first proposed by the Chicago Area Transportation Study in 1962. Subsequent plans were developed in conjunction with the Northwestern Indiana Regional Planning Commission and the Northeastern Illinois Planning Commission. The majority of the highway projects proposed by the planning agencies since 1962 have not been implemented; the extensions of the mass transit lines have been achieved. The lack of implementation of the projects proposed is a function of the plans themselves and a changed fiscal, regulatory, and political environment.

The 1980 Transportation Study

The 1980 transportation study was a three-volume study sponsored by the state of Illinois, Cook County, and the city of Chicago in cooperation with the U.S. Department of Commerce. The work began in 1956, was completed in 1962, and was planned with a twenty-year time horizon. The 1980 plan was based on the forecast that the region's population would increase to 7.8 million by 1980, average family income would increase, and consumers would prefer more single family housing in low-density settings. Therefore, there would be a shift from public transit to private passenger cars and toward greater suburban growth.

The CATS 1980 Plan proposed to supplement the committed radial system developed under Chicago's 1946 comprehensive plan with a system emphasizing north-south and east-west segments and an expanded mass transit system. The plan consisted of six new crosstown connections for the existing system. The mass transit proposals were to extend the system along the median strip in the Kennedy and Dan Ryan expressways, build an elevated line from Evanston to Skokie, and extend an elevated line from 63rd Street to Midway Airport. The plans CATS developed in 1962 to complete the committed system, however, were not implemented. By 1980 no additional expressways had been constructed other than those in the Chicago Commission's 1946 Plan, while two of the transit projects had been accomplished.

There were several reasons for the failure to implement the expressway projects presented in the 1980 plan. First, there were failures in the planning process itself. The CATS forecast for the region's population seriously overestimated the actual growth by 1980[3] and underestimated the extent of suburban deconcentration. Second, the CATS planners did not sufficiently incorporate the objections of the city of Chicago and so had limited support from the city of Chicago and Mayor Richard J. Daley for the proposed expressways. More critically, the policy and fiscal environments for continued expressway construction had changed by the 1970s. Nationwide, the "freeway revolt" of urban neighborhoods and funding cutbacks from the state and federal government seriously constrained new expressway construction. In the Chicago region the Crosstown Expressway, which was the one new segment of the plan that Mayor Daley supported and which had funding, encountered serious opposition from grassroots groups and was eventually canceled. By the late 1960s the federal government considered the interstate system complete and began supporting other transportation projects such as mass transit systems. These two factors were critical reasons for the failure to implement the expressway projects of the 1980 plan.

At the same time, the political and fiscal environment had become more positive for transit projects. In 1964 Congress passed the Urban Mass Transit Act, which authorized funding for transit projects for the first time. In 1968 the Urban Mass Transportation Administration was created, which paid for the extension of the Red line in the Dan Ryan median strip and the Blue line in the Kennedy median strip.

The 1995 Transportation System Plan

In 1974 the Chicago Area Transportation Study and the Northwestern Indiana Regional Planning Commission, with the assistance of the Northeastern Illinois Planning Commission and the Department of Development and Planning of the city of Chicago, proposed the 1995 transportation system plan. The plan was to provide an improved transportation system for the residents of the eight-county region that encompasses six counties in northeastern Illinois and two counties in northwest Indiana. The plan seriously overestimated the prospective population for the six-county region by forecasting that the region would have 10,200,000 residents by 1995 (CATS and NIRPC 1974, 28). The population forecasts seriously underestimated the effects of decreasing household size and women's entry to the workforce.[4] NIPC's household and employment forecasts were on target.

The 1995 transportation system plan was fairly restrained in its proposals for new projects. The 1995 plan proposed no new additions and three extensions to the existing commuter rail system and four rapid transit additions with five extensions to the existing system. The plan proposed seven additions to the expressway system. The same nationwide conditions that prevailed for the 1980 plan continued through 1990. The federal government continued to reduce its involvement in highway construction, while citizen opposition to new highways did not abate. In the Chicago region, grassroots opposition to new highways was instrumental in canceling the Fox River Valley Expressway in 1993. Only a 6.6-mile segment of the Elgin-O'Hare Expressway was completed in 1993; the eastern part of the expressway that would bypass O'Hare Airport has not been constructed due to regional conflict on expanding O'Hare (see below). The other expressway projects were not constructed.

By the 1980s the region's major infrastructure funding came from the dedesignation of the Crosstown Expressway. An Interstate Transfer Fund was created to distribute the $2 billion the federal government had earmarked for the project. The city of Chicago used its share of these funds to build a rapid transit line to Midway Airport, extend a rapid transit line from Jefferson Park to O'Hare International Airport, and construct or rehabilitate sixteen other rapid transit stations. The suburbs used their share of the funds to enhance capacity by widening and improving their existing roads (rather than building new ones) and to upgrade Metra stations (Crimmons 1994).

In order to circumvent grassroots opposition to new expressways and to find a stable source of funding for highway construction, the Illinois General Assembly turned to the Illinois State Toll Highway Authority to complete the highway projects proposed in the earlier plans. In 1983 the General Assembly authorized the Illinois State Toll Highway Authority to undertake construction of the first leg of an outer circumferential tollway first proposed as an expressway in the 1980 plan. The North-South Tollway (Interstate 355) from Army Trail Road in DuPage County south to Interstate 55 in Will County was completed in 1989 as the first addition to the existing system.

The 2020 Regional Transportation Plan

The *2020 Regional Transportation Plan* (*2020 RTP*) was developed under the new planning requirements of the Intermodal Surface Transportation Efficiency Act of 1991 (ISTEA). Under these new requirements, metropolitan planning organizations must meet three new federal regulations: The process must have more public involvement; transportation projects must reflect reliable revenue projections; and the process to identify which transportation projects to fund must operate through a consensus building relationship with local governments, transit agencies, and the state department of transportation. These new provisions substantially altered both the planning process for the *2020 RTP* and the plan itself.

The *2020 RTP* planning process was begun in 1994 in response to changing growth and development patterns in northeastern Illinois and to incorporate the new requirements of ISTEA. CATS developed the plan, working closely with NIPC. NIPC was responsible for the population and employment forecasts used to develop and evaluate the plan. In addition, CATS and NIPC worked cooperatively to analyze the relationship between land use and transportation. The *2020 RTP* was adopted in 1997, with new population and employment forecasts and new proposals for expanding the region's transportation system. The plan integrated land resource management strategies and air quality goals. The *2020 RTP* population forecasts were that the region will grow by 25 percent (from 7.2 million in 1990 to 9 million people by 2020) and that job opportunities will increase by 37 percent. This growth is predicated on Hispanic in-migration (1.2 million new residents) and an increase in the African American population (0.6 million new residents). NIPC's forecast for the region's population is increasingly "black, brown, and grey."

The transportation projects proposed in the *2020 RTP* differ significantly from the earlier plans. First, the emphasis is on maintenance of the existing system. The *2020 RTP* proposes that 80 percent of the projected resources should be allocated to maintain the current highway and transit system. Second, the capital improvements proposed include major extensions of the rail transit system and significant capacity enhancements of the highway system. There are two highway extensions proposed. The *2020 RTP* proposes twenty major capital improvements to expand the existing expressway and transit capacity. The transit improvements include an enhancement to one Metra line; three new transit lines; and one extension. The highway improvements include nine projects to add lanes to existing expressways, an extension of the tollway, an extension of an expressway, one new interchange, and one High Occupancy Vehicle (HOV) lane addition (see Figure 7.1).

This new direction reflects the maintenance needs of an aging infrastructure, the reality of the success of rail transit improvements in the region, and new federal requirements. The rail transit plans, in particular, include both improvements to the city of Chicago's mass transit system and major extensions of the system (the Mid-City Transitway) and major new commuter rail extensions for Metra (the Outer Circumferential and the South Suburban Commuter Rail Corridors). The highway projects are designed primarily to complete projects proposed in earlier plans (the Elgin-O'Hare Expressway), to add additional lanes to the committed system, and to extend I-355 north into Lake County and south into Will County. The new direction reflects the changed federal guidelines for funding transportation projects.

The provisions of the Intermodal Surface Transportation Efficiency Act also had an effect on the specific projects in the *2020 RTP*. First,

REGIONAL PLANNING AGENCIES IN SUBURBAN DECONCENTRATION 143

Figure 7.1 *2020 RTP* Highway and Transit Projects

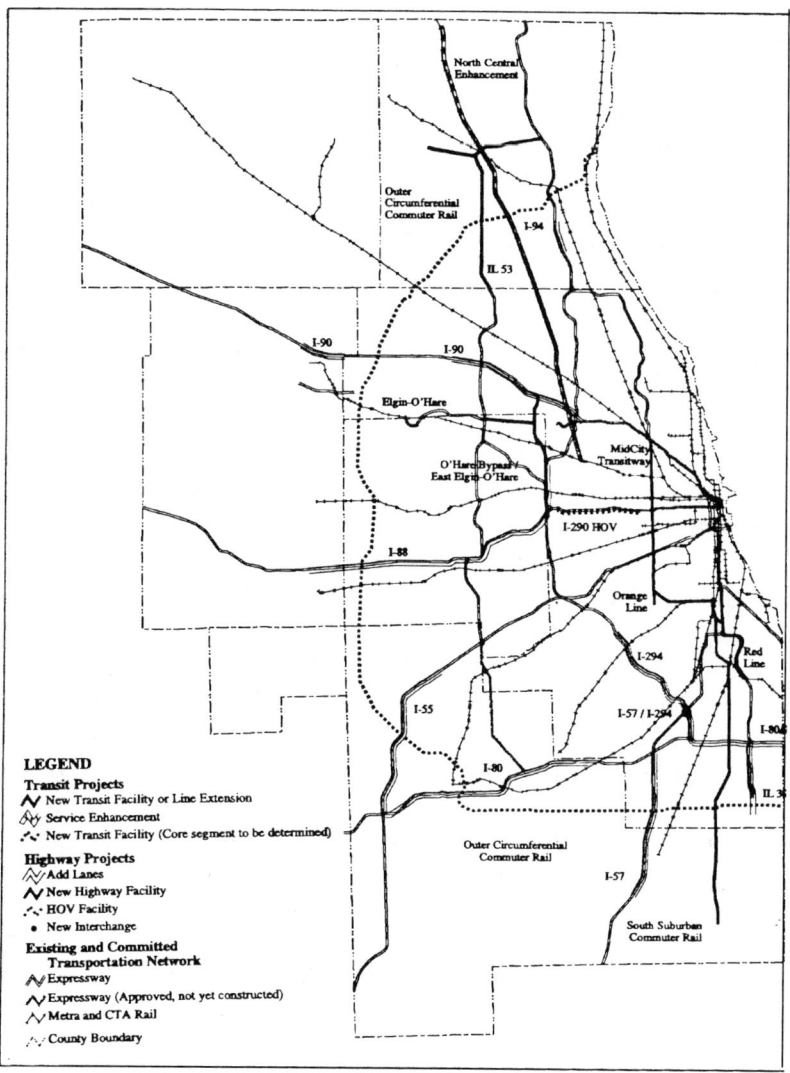

Source: Chicago Area Transportation Study (1998).

CATS and NIPC jointly developed the plan, with input from regional agencies, governments, and citizen's groups. Second, agreeing that one primary goal was to not jeopardize federal funding, the two agencies only included those transportation projects for which there was a regional agreement. This decision meant that the plan does not address the fundamental question of whether to construct a third regional airport or to accommodate future air travel needs at O'Hare and Midway airports. These two regional airports are owned and operated by the city of Chicago. The question whether to add additional capacity to O'Hare or to build another major regional airport has been controversial for over twenty years. Faced with the lack of consensus on the issue, the *2020 RTP* does not address the feasibility and desirability of either scenario. Rather than recommending one option, the *2020 RTP* presented network-level evaluation results for two scenarios: one scenario for improvements at the existing airports (i.e., O'Hare and Midway) and one for the South Suburban Airport. NIPC also did two separate demographic and employment forecasts, one with the South Suburban Airport and one with improvements to the existing airports.

The proposals to extend the region's expressway/tollway system detailed in the *2020 RTP* are encountering the same obstacles that previous expressway projects have encountered in the past thirty years. The possibility of constructing any of the proposed expressway additions near O'Hare (the eastern part of the Elgin-O'Hare Expressway and a western O'Hare bypass) is problematic given the conflict between the city of Chicago and the state Republican leadership. For the first time in the past forty years, one major participant in the regional planning process (the DuPage County Board) refused to endorse the regional plan unless it would be modified to include the stipulation that O'Hare area road improvements would "not be constructed until there is a ban on future runways at O'Hare and a decision is made to construct a third regional airport" (DuPage County Board Resolution 1997). This refusal to endorse the plan is consistent with the DuPage County Board's position that the board would support a western bypass and access to O'Hare only if the access project would use land at the southwest corner of the airport and so preclude new runway construction.

Similarly, the extension of I-355 south to I-80 in Will County and the Route 53 extension in Lake County by the Illinois State Toll Highway Authority has encountered strong opposition. The extension of I-355 has been temporarily delayed by a lawsuit filed by environmental advocacy organizations and grassroots groups. After then-Governor Jim Edgar signed the legislation for the extension, the Environmental Law and Policy Center of the Midwest, the Business and Professional People for the Public Interest (BPI), the Sierra Club-Illinois Chapter, and South Corridor Against the Tollway (SCAT) sued the authority over the adequacy of its environmental impact statement. In 1997 the federal judge agreed with the plaintiff's argument, halting the southern extension of the tollway. In January 1999 after fighting Judge Conlon's ruling on appeal, the toll authority and IDOT announced it would abandon the appeal and conduct the studies ordered by Judge Conlon.

NIPC's Land Use and Water Resource Plans

NIPC adopted its first plan for the orderly development of the six-county area in 1968. The Comprehensive General Plan, amended in 1976 and 1977, established the broad policies for land use and the framework for functional plans relating to transportation, wastewater service, and open space. In the 1970s, NIPC developed a series of regional plans in accordance with its statutory mandate to meet the planning requirements for federal capital grants. Although the A-95 review process was eliminated by the Reagan administration in 1983, NIPC continued its responsibilities to review regional plans. The 1984 Regional Land Use Policy Plan was an advisory plan designed as a bridge between the broad concepts of the Comprehensive General Plan and the specific, highly detailed plans of the municipalities and counties for land use, wastewater service, and open space (NIPC 1984). The 1984 plan was used as a template in preparing reviews of public and private development proposals, developing plans for major public investment in infrastructure, evaluating the impact of capital investment programs, and guiding population and employment forecasts. Using the plan as a template, NIPC reviewed grant applications from state and local governments for federal funds, conducted reviews of development proposals upon request, and evaluated annually the degree to which the Transportation Improvement Program for the region is supportive of regional policies. The 1992 Plan calls for networks of trails and parks, protecting farmland, encouraging affordable housing in the suburbs, discouraging suburban sprawl, and encouraging redevelopment of inner city neighborhoods.

NIPC's mandate is to develop policies for regional water resources and review regional wastewater and point source proposals. In 1997 the commission's Water Resources Committee assessed the water resource management plans developed since 1976. The conclusion was that the commission's plans for storm water management and wastewater treatment plant improvements had been successful, but that due to changing circumstances about the availability of Lake Michigan water and lack of knowledge of nonpoint source pollution, NIPC's plans in these areas had not been implemented (NIPC 1997b). In 1997 NIPC began a process to identify the water resource issues confronting the region. The Illinois Environmental Protection Agency has designated NIPC the responsible agency to review the Facility Planning Area requests of local governments to provide water and sewer services to unincorporated areas, a preliminary step to annexation.

The Strengths and Weaknesses of the Two Agencies and Suburban Deconcentration

The two planning agencies in northeastern Illinois operate within constraints established and maintained since the 1950s. First, mandated to develop regional plans for transportation, neither agency was given the statutory authority to implement its proposals. Implementation is the responsibility of state and local governments and the region's public authorities (the Regional Transportation Authority, the Chicago Transit Authority, Metra, Pace, and the Illinois State Toll Highway Authority). Second, rather than one agency with the responsibility for transportation and land use, there are four agencies with responsibility for transportation planning in the six-county region: CATS; NIPC; the Illinois Department of Transportation (IDOT); and the Regional Transportation Authority (RTA), comprising the Chicago Transit Authority, Metra (commuter rail), and Pace (suburban bus). Each of the twelve councils of mayors has responsibility for planning for surface transportation projects. NIPC is the only agency with responsibility for land use planning. Third, both agencies were established without a predetermined local contribution, which has made them financially vulnerable.

Implementation Authority

The Northeastern Illinois Planning Commission and the Chicago Area Transportation Study have no authority to implement the plans they develop. Implementation is the responsibility of the state department of transportation and the two regional public authorities (the Regional Transportation Authority and the Illinois State Toll Highway Authority). Without the authority to implement the plans they developed and therefore the need to prioritize the projects, the two planning agencies developed regional transportation plans from 1962 to 1992 that were unconstrained wish lists of expressway and transit projects dependent upon the state and local governments to implement. The ultimate effect on regional growth was that the expressway projects proposed in those thirty years were not constructed while the transit projects were. The political and fiscal environment of those thirty years precluded new expressways in the collar counties, while those same factors encouraged new transit lines.

The expressway system constructed after the war was funded by the bonds issued by Cook County and by Interstate Highway funds. However, the federal government began disinvesting from its earlier support for new expressways in the late 1960s. By the 1970s extensions of the system in the collar counties required funding from the state. The combination of grassroots groups' opposition to new expressways and middle-class suburban taxpayer revolts effectively precluded extending the region's expressway system. The fiscally and politically constrained state government turned to the Illinois State Toll Highway Authority to construct the North-South Tollway (I-355) and to complete an outer circumferential tollway. The Illinois State Toll Highway Authority, however, is not legally required to defer to the plans developed by CATS.

The extension of the mass transit system has not been handicapped by the same the fiscal and political constraints hindering expressway development. First, expansion of transit systems does not provoke grassroots opposition. Business, neighborhood, and environmental groups strongly support extensions of mass transit. The major opponents of mass transit are highway advocates competing for scarce transportation funding. Second, regional political fragmentation does not have the same effect on transit projects. The mass transit system in the region is controlled and operated by the Regional Transportation Authority and its three service branches, the Chicago Transit Authority, Metra (commuter rail), and Pace (suburban bus). The city of Chicago and the Chicago Transit Authority have utilized available funding to extend the rapid transit lines to O'Hare and Midway airports. Similarly, when New Start and Congestion Mitigation and Air Quality (CMAQ) funds were available from the federal government in the 1990s, Metra used the funds to construct the North Central line, the first new commuter rail line in the region in forty years.

One of NIPC's critical weaknesses in land use planning is that the agency's plans for managed regional development (e.g., the 1992 Plan) would require regulatory changes that the leadership in the Illinois General Assembly currently is unwilling to consider. NIPC took the lead in proposing the Intergovernmental Planning Act that would have renamed and amended the existing Local Land Resource Management Planning Act to provide permissive authority for voluntary cooperation among local governments. The legislation would have given local governments the authority to prepare intergovernmental plans for land use and boundary agreements, and the authority to enforce these plans, and would have provided new incentives for cooperation in areas such as agricultural preservation, housing, natural resources, water, transportation, subdivision improvements, and open spaces (NIPC 1996).

NIPC and local municipalities spent six years preparing the Intergovernmental Planning Act. The act had bipartisan support in the Illinois General Assembly; it had easily passed the Illinois House and would have passed in the Senate if it had been brought to a vote. The bill was killed in the Senate Rules Committee in December 1998 by Illinois Senate Majority Leader James "Pate" Philip, who criticized the bill as an insufficient compromise with the wishes of the Homebuilders Association (NIPC 1998c).

Divided Responsibility for Transportation and Land Use Planning

The success of mass transit in the region is also attributable to the manner in which CATS has suballocated transportation planning funds. Because CATS as the MPO for the region is not the sole planning agency, CATS suballocates federal planning funds to NIPC, the RTA, the CTA, Metra, Pace, the Chicago Department of Transportation, and the councils of mayors. This suballocation, in turn, has meant that these agencies and councils have been able to develop transit planning capacity during the 1970s and 1980s when the primary regional planning concern was highway construction. When funds were available, either through the designation of the Crosstown Expressway or through New Start and Congestion Mitigation and Air Quality funds in the 1990s, the transit authorities were ready with new projects.

The development of the North Central line, which operates on the Wisconsin Central freight tracks from Antioch near the Wisconsin border to Chicago, exemplifies the importance of building planning capacity within the transit agencies and the councils of mayors. First included in the *2010 Plan*, the project was proposed by Metra in 1986. In 1988, the North Suburban Mass Transit District (NORTRAN) began to work with municipalities along the line. When NORTRAN transferred the operation of its bus system to Pace in 1991, the Northwest Municipal Conference formed the Wisconsin Central Mayoral Task Force to continue the subregional planning necessary for the line and to secure local commitment (Fowler 1994).

The division of responsibility for transportation and land use between the two agencies, however, has the potential to be one of the more critical weaknesses for the future. CATS, with a Policy Committee composed of transportation professionals, works with local governments specifically on transportation projects. NIPC's board comprises elected officials from throughout the region. The policies for land use, wastewater and storm water management that NIPC develops are not necessarily incorporated in the transportation plans developed by CATS. Under the new regulations of ISTEA and TEA 21, this bifurcation in planning responsibilities could adversely impact the region's ability to meet the federal requirements for future transportation projects.

Financial Vulnerability

One of the critical weaknesses of the region's planning agencies is their financial vulnerability because they have no assured legislative revenue streams. When funding sources are uncertain, agencies can be threatened by politicians more concerned about maintaining their political advantage than serving the needs of the residents in the region (New Serious Look 1972). NIPC's dependence on voluntary contributions from local governments has made the agency vulnerable to pressure from local governments angered by the agency's planning decisions.[5] The lack of a guaranteed revenue source also makes NIPC dependent on contracts from state agencies.

Agencies in which the state department of transportation has administrative and fiduciary responsibility, on the other hand, can be criticized on the basis that the governor and state department of transportation dominate regional transportation planning. Critics of CATS, for example, argue that the agency is a department of the Illinois Department of Transportation (IDOT), with the secretary of the IDOT as the permanent chair of the policy committee and its staff employees of the IDOT.[6] Other critics point to the lack of representation of elected officials on CATS Policy Committee. In addition, this representation is not proportional demographically. The city of Chicago, with almost 3 million residents, has one vote, as does McHenry County with 250,000 residents (Pierce 1998). The overrepresentation of transportation rather than elected officials and its lack of demographic proportionality has led to criticism that its emphasis is on highways rather than mass transit (Black 1990) and on suburban rather than city projects.

Proposals to Change the Mandates of the Two Agencies

Regional competitiveness, concerns about the economic viability of the region, and the forecasts of regional growth from the 2020 RTP are driving the civic and public advocacy communities of the region to develop a consensus on regional objectives and plans to proactively manage the predicted growth. This consensus includes decisions on the future of the two agencies. The Civic Committee of the Commercial Club has taken the lead in proposing new regional governance structures for the planning agencies.[7] Another civic organization, the Metropolitan Planning Council (MPC) has as its priorities to: (1) update the current intergovernmental agreement between CATS, NIPC, RTA, and IDOT in order to better respond to the transportation, land use, and policy changes in the region; (2) expand public involvement in CATS's decision-making processes; and (3) apply project criteria that connect transportation and development decisions. The MPC is now in a coalition with NIPC and the Regional Transportation Authority in the Campaign for Sensible Growth. The Metropolitan Mayors Caucus, a caucus of the region's 270 mayors, has prepared a response to the Chicago Metropolis 2020 Project that does not support the creation of a regional superagency. The Metropolitan Mayors Caucus has recently recommended a "mutual adjustment" model of regional governance (Savitch and Vogel 1996) that consists of interlocal agreements and private-public partnerships rather than the creation of a superagency (Metropolitan Mayors Caucus 1998, 3). The Center for Neighborhood Technology and the Chicagoland Transportation and Air Quality Commission, a coalition of 140 groups working for alternative planning strategies to meet the needs of inner-city residents, have been working to restructure CATS to make the agency more proportionally representative or to fold the agency into NIPC.

The new requirements under the ISTEA and the Transportation Equity Act for the 21st Century (TEA 21) are also driving inquiries into how the agencies can best fulfill their regional mandates. The Center for Neighborhood Technology has twice introduced bills into the Illinois General Assembly relating to CATS. In 1997 the Center introduced a bill to restructure CATS to make it more proportionally representative so that it would reflect its constituent population and a bill to have CATS folded into NIPC. CATS seriously underrepresents the residents of Cook County and Chicago—with 70 percent of the population, they have only two to three members on the CATS Policy Task Force (or approximately 10 percent of the votes). The center's drive to reinvent CATS is part of a nationwide movement to decentralize transportation policy from state transportation departments to regional MPOs (Gage and McDowell 1995).

NIPC's new president is also working to better integrate the agency's land use projections with CATS and the region's other two transportation authorities. The eighteen-year-old intergovernmental agreement that designates the responsibilities of IDOT, NIPC, CATS, and the Regional Transportation Authority in coordinating regional planning is under review.

In 1995 NIPC adopted a new strategic plan that envisioned new strategic directions for the agency. NIPC has held an annual forum on regionalism for the area's officials for the past three years. NIPC and the Regional Transportation Authority have sponsored a series of forums on transit-oriented development (TOD) to encourage increased densities near transit and Metra stations. NIPC is a coalition partner on the Campaign for Sensible Growth, a collaborative effort to balance regional economic growth with environmental quality, and is directing its efforts toward smart growth legislation in the Illinois General Assembly.

Conclusion

The major questions raised by this research are: (1) What role have the two agencies played in the region's development for the past thirty years; and (2) what will their future role be? An analysis of how successfully the transportation and land use plans they developed from 1962 to 1992 were implemented reveals the importance of outside factors over which the agencies have little control. However, the strengths and weaknesses of the two agencies and the planning process itself have contributed to the region's development in unanticipated ways. Specifically, the successful extension of the region's mass transit system since the 1970s is a function of the political fragmentation of the region, the constraints imposed on the agencies since the 1960s, and CATS's planning processes.

In the immediate post-World War II period, transportation planners in Chicago and Cook County laid out an extended system of highways based on a radial system with east/west and north/south expressways to complete the grid. The plan that they laid out became the infrastructure "footprint" for the region. The radial highways converging on Chicago's central business district and a circumferential interstate toll highway (I-294) provided the basic template for regional development. Major business development occurred around O'Hare International Airport and at interstices of the expressway and railroad grid (McMillen and McDonald 1998). Residential growth followed the expressways and then began an "infill" process.

Since the adoption of the 1980 metropolitan transportation plan in 1962, the majority of the new highways proposed by the Chicago Area Transportation Study and the Northeastern Illinois Planning Commission have not been constructed. In the same period many of the proposed transit projects have become part of an expanding transit system in both Chicago and the suburbs. The expressway projects proposed were not completed primarily because state and federal funding cutbacks for new highways occurred at the same time that grassroots groups successfully opposed further expressway construction. Available state and federal highway revenues were used to enhance capacity on the existing system rather than construct new expressways. The one major addition to the system was the North-South Toll Highway (I-355). From 1992 to 1997, new revenues for highways were available through ISTEA. In that five-year period, although one 6.6-mile expressway and 70 miles of arterials were added to the system, 65 percent of the funds were spent for roadway improvements on approximately 1,060 miles (Johnson 1999).

One significant aspect of the planning process in the region is the autonomy that the other transportation agencies have to develop their own infrastructure plans. The effect of this autonomy can be seen in the way the city of Chicago and the suburban municipalities utilized the Interstate Transfer funds. In the 1980s, when revenue was available through the cancellation of plans for the Crosstown Expressway, the city of Chicago utilized its funds to improve and extend its mass transit system and enhance its arterials; the suburbs used their funding for road improvements and Metra stations.

The national regulatory environment for transportation planning has changed significantly in the 1990s. ISTEA's new regulations promote multimodal, financially constrained planning developed with greater public input. The projects proposed in the *2020 RTP* represent this new regulatory reality. The national and state fiscal environment changed significantly in the 1990s. With the passage of the $204 billion transportation bill by Congress in 1998 and the Illinois FIRST bill passed by the Illinois General Assembly in 1999, federal and state funding is available for the region's transportation projects.

In the new fiscal and regulatory environment of ISTEA and TEA 21 and in a metropolitan region as politically fragmented as the six-county northeastern Illinois region is, cooperation and consensus is the sine qua non for successful implementation of transportation projects. Politically fragmented governance structures severely constrain the possibility of financing and implementing contested transportation projects. This constraint can be seen in the conflict over O'Hare, which has precluded cooperation on airport-related projects (including the Elgin-O'Hare Expressway) for twenty years. If the regulatory environment of ISTEA and TEA 21 and a politically fragmented governance structure constrain the possibilities for developing financial packages for new projects, the same environment and governance structures facilitate the success of grassroots opposition to new expressways.

The challenges confronting the region are formidable. These include poor air quality, severe traffic congestion, regionwide service inequities, and increased threat to wetlands and greenfields. The region ranks as a severe nonattainment area under the Clean Air Act Amendments of 1990 and by 1999 was rated third worst in the nation in terms of traffic congestion (Texas Transportation Institute 1998). The lack of affordable housing in areas with high employment growth, continued high indicators of urban distress in some Chicago neighborhoods, and inner-ring suburbs, and inequitable regionwide service delivery systems seriously impacts the region's economic vitality (Orfield 1996). In addition, if recent trends of higher land consumption per capita unrelated to either population growth or economic development continue, developed land in the region could increase by 55 percent by 2008 (Openlands Project 1999).

The forecasts for regional growth in the *2020 RTP* predict a population increase of 25 percent and an employment increase of 37 percent. Without a regional consensus, coordinated planning by the two agencies, and implementation of the plans, the predicted growth will have major negative impacts on the region. The success of the *2020 RTP* will depend on a regional political consensus to pressure lawmakers for state and federal funds to construct the projects. The major question for the region is the ability of the civic, business, and political leadership to cooperate in order to realistically plan to meet the challenges confronting the region. Given the forecasts of the *2020 RTP*, the ability of the two planning agencies, transportation authorities, local governments, and the business leadership to work together to achieve a regional consensus on transportation and land use policies for the region is critical.

Notes

1. Policy Committee members include the chair of the Council of Mayors Executive Committee, the executive director of the Illinois State Toll Highway Authority, the commissioner of the Chicago Department of Transportation, representatives of the six county governments, representatives from the four regional transportation agencies (the Regional Transportation Authority; the Chicago Transit Authority; Metra; and Pace), representatives from two federal transportation agencies (the Federal Highway Administration and the Federal Transit Administration), NIPC, and regional transportation providers.

2. There are five commissioners appointed by the governor of Illinois; five appointed by the mayor of Chicago (three of whom are required to be Chicago aldermen); eight mayors elected by the Assembly of Suburban Mayors; eight county board members appointed by county board chairmen (three are from Cook County and one from each of the collar counties); representatives of the Regional Transportation Authority, the Chicago Transit Authority, Metra, and Pace; one member from the Metropolitan Water Reclamation District of Greater Chicago; one from the board of the Illinois Association of Park Districts; one from the board of the Chicago Park District; and one from the board of Illinois Association of Wastewater Agencies.

3. The 1962 population forecast was 9.5 million, 2.2 million too high (McDonald 1988).

4. In 1990, the population of the city of Chicago was 2,783,700; the population for suburban Cook and the other five counties was 4,477,726.

5. In 1971 the Metropolitan Sanitary District of Chicago (now the Metropolitan Water Reclamation District of Greater Chicago) sharply reduced its contribution to NIPC when the commission refused to recommend the district for an A-95 federal matching grant. NIPC and the Metropolitan Sanitary District had earlier disagreed over the location of a sewer. In November 1998 the DuPage County board voted to withhold the county's contribution to NIPC because the commission was taking a neutral position on the advisability of a third regional airport, but reversed its decision in April 1999 (see below).

6. This objection was first voiced by the city of Chicago in 1977 before the governor of Illinois designated CATS as the metropolitan planning organization for the six county region and continues to be articulated by critics of the agency.

7. The Civic Committee of the Commercial Club financed the Chicago Metropolis 2020 Project. The report calls for restructuring the regional planning agencies by first creating a new metropolitan planning agency comprising the Northeastern Illinois Planning Commission, the Chicago Area Transportation Study, and the planning department of the Regional Transportation Authority. This new agency would be adequately funded to eliminate the need to seek voluntary contributions; be mandated to create a new land use and transportation program consistent with the goals of the Chicago Metropolis 2020 plan; initiate capital improvement projects of strategic importance; set priorities for federal revenues and allocate new revenues collected through user fees and vehicle-pricing; approve or reject toll highway expansions within the region; and develop new regional transportation plans. The second step would be to create a more powerful regional coordinating mechanism that would have the authority to issue bonds to finance capital improvement projects; develop long-range strategic plans for transportation, land use, housing, wastewater, storm water and water-supply services; approve or deny access to sewer systems and wastewater treatment facilities; provide grants to foster transit-oriented land use planning; and receive and distribute revenues to moderate fiscal and service inequities in the region (Johnson 1998).

References

Black, Alan. 1990. The Chicago Area Transportation Study: A Case Study of Rational Planning. *JPER* 10(1) 27–37.
Chicago Area Transportation Study. 1998. The 2020 Regional Transportation Plan: Destination 2020, August.
———. 1962. Transportation Plan: Volume III, April.
Chicago Area Transportation Study and Northwestern Indiana Regional Planning Commission. 1974. Summary Description: 1995 Transportation System Plan.
Crimmons. Jerry. 1994. The Crosstown Legacy: Expressway's Demise Paves the Way for a Load of Infrastructure Projects. *Chicago Tribune* (March 7) section 2, p. 2.
DuPage County Board. 1997. Opposition to the CATS Destination 2020 Regional Transportation Plan (DT-0061–97).
Fiske, Barbara Page. 1989. *Key to Government in Chicago and Suburban Cook County.* Chicago: University of Chicago Press.
Fowler, Mark. 1994. The Wisconsin Central: A Model of Intergovernmental Cooperation. Prepared for the Regional Transportation Authority, January.
Gage, Robert W., and Bruce D. McDowell. 1995. ISTEA and the Role of MPOs in the New Transportation Environment: A Midterm Evaluation. *Publius* 25(3) (Summer): 133–154.
Hemmens, George C. 1998. Planning and Development Decision Making in the Chicago Region. In *Metropolitan Governance Revisited: American/Canadian Intergovernmental Perspectives,* eds. D. N. Rothblatt and A. Saction, 121–159. Berkeley, CA: Institute of Governmental Studies Press.

Johnson, Charles. 1999. Investment of Highway Funds in Northeastern Illinois, 1992–1997. CATS Working Paper 99–02, May.
Johnson, Elmer. 1998. Chicago Metropolis 2020: Preparing Metropolitan Chicago for the 21st Century. Executive summary, a project of the Commercial Club of Chicago in association with the American Academy of Arts and Sciences, November.
McDonald, John F. 1988. The First Chicago Area Transportation Study Projections and Plans for Metropolitan Chicago in Retrospect. *Planning Perspectives* 3: 245–268.
McMillen, Daniel P., and John F. McDonald. 1998. Suburban Subcenters and Employment Density in Metropolitan Chicago. *Journal of Urban Economics* 43: 157–180.
Metropolitan Mayors Caucus. 1998. Review of Metropolis 2020 Project Recommendations, November.
A New Serious Look at NIPC: Are Too Many Cooks Spoiling the Broth? 1972. *Planning* (April): 59–61.
Northeastern Illinois Planning Commission. 1997b. Assessment of the Status of Water Resource Management Plans of the Northeastern Illinois Planning Commission, July.
———. 1996. NIPC Will Push for Improved Intergovernmental Planning Legislation. NIPC Reports, February.
———. 1984. Regional Land Use Policy Plan, March.
Openlands Project. 1999. Under Pressure: Land Consumption in the Chicago Region: 1998–2028.
Orfield, Myron. 1996. Chicago Regional Report. Report prepared for the John D. and Catherine T. MacArthur Foundation, October.
Pierce, Kevin. 1998. *Viewpoint.* Newsletter of the Chicago Design Consortium (January/February/March).
Savitch, H.V., and R.K. Vogel, eds. 1996. *Regional Politics: America in a Post-City Age.* Thousand Oaks, CA: Sage.
Texas Transportation Institute. 1998. Urban Mobility Study. Texas A&M University, College Station, Texas.

8

CHARLES J. ORLEBEKE

Housing Policy and Urban Sprawl in the Chicago Metropolitan Region

Introduction

One of the most frequently cited statistics relating housing to urban sprawl is that between 1970 and 1990 "the [Chicago] region has increased only 4 percent in population, but the amount of land developed for residential uses has increased by 46 percent" (MPC 1995). The purpose of this chapter is to explore the role of housing policy in shaping the development of the Chicago region. It begins with a brief outline of federal, state, and local roles in housing and then moves on to discuss the federal policy role in greater detail, including federal initiatives in the 1970s to influence the regional distribution of housing in response to the twin crises of urban decline and suburban sprawl. This is followed by an account of the Chicago region's response to these federal policies. Finally, the chapter examines the reemergence of the sprawl debate in the 1990s as the region anticipates a new period of rapid growth, posing questions as to where housing policy fits in the "smart growth" agenda.

Federal, State, and Local Roles in Housing

The federal government has helped shape housing development patterns in important ways through a wide variety of incentives, subsidies, and regulations. In addition, federal nonhousing policies such as the Interstate Highway System, water and sewer programs, various grants to cities and suburbs, environmental regulations, immigration policies, the tax structure, location of federal facilities and military bases, airport sitting decisions, and procurement practices have also influenced indirectly the demand for and location of housing. The feds have not, however, sought to promote, much less impose, any particular type of residential settlement patterns on the nation's metropolitan areas. The most assertive period of federal housing policy, as we shall see, was from the late 1960s to the late 1970s, when a confluence of initiatives, including a 1968 statutory requirement that regional planning bodies prepare specific housing plans for all income groups, was in place. But the steam behind these initiatives had dissipated by the late 1970s, and the federal government would never again venture into the politically volatile territory of regional housing planning.

Potentially, state governments have a large role to play in housing because of their broad constitutional powers to regulate land use, building codes, and other environmental matters. States may also directly administer various housing subsidy programs, often drawing on federal grants and tax incentives as the main source of funds. But states, with the possible exception of New Jersey, have not asserted their inherent constitutional prerogatives to achieve particular housing objectives, either statewide or at regional and local levels. So too in Illinois, which has never articulated a state "housing policy" or "plan," nor has it sought to intervene in or regulate local land use decisions that affect housing.

Local governments act within the context of the national economy and federal policies. They must also function within the constitutional and regulatory framework established by state government. But local control of land use, including housing, is a prerogative that is tenaciously defended; as a practical matter, local governments make the key planning and zoning decisions regarding what sort of housing is to be built, where it will be located, and, indirectly, the kind of people who will live in it. These decisions are of course constrained by local circumstances prevailing at the time they are made; these circumstances include the availability of undeveloped land, market demand, local citizen sentiment and political leadership, and the blandishments of housing developers. Since housing, once built, is semipermanent, successive generations of local officials must live with the consequences, good and bad, of accumulated previous decisions.

Housing: The Direct Federal Role

In this section, I discuss federal policies that have explicit housing aims and their possible effects on urban sprawl.

Homeownership

The first major federal intervention in housing happened in the 1930s in response to the Great Depression. Unemployment and chaos in the banking system combined to cause massive mortgage defaults among the nation's homeowners. Federal action transformed the mortgage finance system for homeownership, first by setting up the Home Owners Loan Corporation to rescue families in default on their mortgages, and then creating the Federal Housing Administration, which pioneered the low down payment, long-term mortgage instrument, the industry standard ever since.

As signaled by the federal rescue of homeowners in the Depression, homeownership has traditionally occupied a favored position in national policy. In promoting homeownership, the federal government has provided mortgage insurance, generous tax advantages through the deductibility of mortgage interest and property taxes, and sometimes direct subsidies, which reduce the market price of housing. The federal government has also sponsored publicly held corporations, known as Fannie Mae (Federal National Mortgage Association) and Freddie Mac (Federal Home Loan Mortgage Corporation). "Fannie" and "Freddie" provide a secondary market for mortgages originated by local banks and thereby insure a constant flow of available mortgage capital.

These policies have been successful. Before World War II the homeownership rate stood at only 43 percent of all households, but by 1980 the rate had hit 65.6 percent. The rate dipped slightly in the late 1980s to about 64 percent and then resumed its climb in 1995, hitting an all-time record of 67.5 percent by 2001.

The federal government's enthusiastic sponsorship of homeownership coincides with and buttresses an almost universal American preference for this form of tenure—invariably referred to as the American dream. Homeownership is believed to confer family stability, civic virtue, better educational performance for children, and a good measure of economic security. A potent homebuilder and real estate lobby in Washington also plays on these themes and helps ensure a friendly political environment for the industry. Part of the background music to these themes is that the American dream is always out of reach for millions of Americans and therefore more must be done to encourage homeownership, and nothing should be done to tamper with incentives already in place.

Because single-family homes typically take up a lot more space per household than apartments do, it seems reasonable to conclude that national policies favoring homeownership also contribute in some ways to urban sprawl. However, a direct link remains difficult to determine.

A recent report by the U.S. General Accounting Office (1999) on federal influences related to sprawl includes a brief literature review on the homeowner tax preference issue. The GAO notes that "very little research" has focused directly on the tax preference-urban sprawl connection, and that the studies that do are inconclusive. For example, GAO points to a 1983 study by Dixie Blackley and James R. Follain, which concluded that "in general, the impact of the preferences on locational choice was ambiguous" and that some models suggest "that the preferences may, in fact, be a countervailing force to suburbanization." Also cited by GAO, a more recent (1997) study by Joseph Gyourko and Richard Voith concludes that tax advantages by themselves do not cause population decentralization effects, but that they may interact with other aspects of the housing market, such as restrictions on land-use and how local amenities are funded.

Until quite recently the capital gains treatment of home sales probably was a contributor to sprawl because of the homeseller's incentive to buy a more expensive house in order to postpone payment of capital gains tax on the sale. However, as noted later in this chapter, the incentive was removed in 1997 in favor of eliminating the capital gains tax altogether in most cases, which may now be encouraging older owners of large houses to "trade down" to smaller units, thereby reducing the sprawl effect.

Rental Assistance Programs

The federal government's role in rental assistance also traces back to the Depression of the 1930s. In 1937 the public housing program was enacted, a program that paid the full construction cost of rental housing to be administered by local housing authorities. Initially, public housing was intended as transition housing for the temporarily unemployed. Always controversial, public housing did not achieve significant scale until the 1950s and 1960s, the heydays of urban high-rise public housing. As the financial and social problems of the "projects" multiplied, the federal government shifted its rental assistance strategy in the late 1960s and 1970s to concentrate primarily on privately financed new construction. Under the two major production programs, Section 236 (enacted in

1968) and Section 8, which replaced Section 236 in 1974, some 1.3 million units were built throughout the nation. The high cost of these programs, together with fears of the social consequences of concentrating poor families in subsidized projects, drove yet another policy shift in the early 1980s, this time toward a housing voucher strategy that subsidizes the individual housing consumer to find suitable housing in the private market. The housing voucher strategy has dominated federal policy throughout the 1980s and 1990s.

The connections between rental assistance programs and urban sprawl are not easy to sort out. In general, the impacts were larger when the federal government was directly encouraging the new construction of big developments with deep subsidies. The most conspicuous example is urban high-rise public housing, which became concentrations of poverty and social pathology, seriously blighting large areas of central cities and probably contributing to the flight to the suburbs by both whites and middle-class African Americans. Privately financed assisted housing has generally had a better track record with regard to neighborhood impacts. Most developments were built in urban locations, but they were smaller, better built, and more dispersed than public housing. And although most suburbs resisted such developments, a surprising number were in fact built in suburban locations, partly as a result of deliberate federal policy to give preference to suburban sites (discussed below). The net impact on sprawl of most privately financed assisted housing is probably small.

Although the federal government have almost entirely withdrawn as a direct financial partner in new housing construction, they have in the 1990s supplemented the dominant voucher strategy with some key initiatives. These initiatives are providing new housing resources to cities, urban counties, and states; they are also quite flexible in their application and probably have a net positive effect on constraining urban sprawl by making cities more attractive places to live. The 1990 HOME Investment Partnership Act provides block grants to big cities (over 50,000 population), to urban counties, and to states; HOME grants can be used for a wide variety of housing purposes that benefit low and moderate income families, both renters and homeowners. The Low Income Housing Tax Credit, first enacted in 1986 and made permanent in 1993, gives generous tax write-offs to investors who help finance rental housing for families meeting federal income criteria. Tax credit deals are frequently combined with HOME money and several other layers of public and private funds to create a financially feasible affordable housing development, either by new construction or major rehabilitation. Another important federal initiative is the HOPE VI program, which explicitly acknowledges the failure of urban high-rise public housing and commits the federal government to a strategy combining demolition; some replacement with new, mixed-income housing; and extensive use of vouchers to disperse current public housing tenants into the private housing market.

The policy initiatives of the 1990s continue the steady process of federal disengagement from a direct role in deciding what sort of publicly assisted housing should be built and where. Such decisions, where they involve new construction or rehabilitation, have been effectively ceded to local and state governments. The increasing use of vouchers, on the other hand, puts the housing choice in the hands of the eligible housing consumer, who may or may not be guided in that choice by counseling as to location options. These policy shifts, as the city of Chicago's five-year Affordable Housing Plan notes, are "devolving onto states and cities a wholly new amalgam of responsibilities, burdens and demands. Major players, resources, markets, policy tools, and approaches to community development are all in flux" (City of Chicago 1998).

Federal Policy Meets Urban Sprawl: The 1960s and 1970s

In view of the current burst of interest in urban sprawl, it is sobering to note how little the policy rhetoric has changed from that of thirty years ago. In the 1960s the critique of metropolitan development gone awry came against the backdrop of economically declining central cities and, by middecade, the outbreak of racially charged civil disorders. The flip side of the "urban crisis" was uncontrolled suburban growth that sucked jobs and talent out of the city even as it also consumed meadow and farmland on the fringe at an alarming rate.

As HUD Secretary George Romney (1969) testified in October 1969 to a House Subcommittee on Urban Growth:

> Never before have our people been so widely separated in space on the basis of their income and their race. And with this separation came a lessening of equality of access to good schools, to good jobs, to medical services, and to recreational opportunities. It is no wonder that we see in our country an increase in the spirit of divisiveness.

HOUSING POLICY AND URBAN SPRAWL IN CHICAGO METRO REGION 163

The problems of slums and blight, unequal economic and social opportunity, air and water pollution, clogged traffic arteries, disappearing open spaces, destruction of natural resources—all these have been aggravated, if not directly caused, by the way our national growth took place.

Echoing the HUD secretary, Congress declared presciently in the "Findings and Purpose" section of the 1970 Urban Growth and New Community Development Act "that continuation of established patterns of urban development, together with anticipated increase in population, will result in (1) inefficient and wasteful use of land resources . . . (5) unduly limited options for many for many of our people as to where they may live, and the types of housing and environment in which they may live . . . (8) further separation of people within metropolitan areas by income and by race; (9) further increases in the distances between the places where people live and where they work and find recreation; and (10) increased cost and decreased effectiveness of public and private facilities for urban transportation" (U.S. Department of Housing and Urban Development 1970).

Housing policy at the federal level was importantly shaped by this context of urban crisis and suburban sprawl. Responding to housing analysts' predictions of a shortage of new housing in the 1970s, Congress in 1968 established a ten-year numerical housing goal of 26 million units, six million of which would be federally subsidized for low- and moderate-income families. Two new subsidy programs, one rental and one for new homeowners, were enacted to further the subsidized housing goal.

The 1968 housing act also mandated that regional planning bodies must prepare a "housing element" as part of their comprehensive planning mission, a provision that HUD Secretary Romney called "extremely important and far-sighted legislation" (Romney 1970, 13). At the time, the federal government was already funding regional planning bodies for general planning and had charged these bodies with responsibility for reviewing and "clearing" all major federal grants for consistency with regional plans—the so-called "A-95 review." Yet another 1968 milestone was passage of the first national fair housing law, which put the federal government on the side of minorities wanting to break out of the urban crisis ghetto.

Thus, by 1970 the stage was set for a period of unprecedented activism in regional planning, including housing as a specific component.

Generous congressional appropriations quickly pumped up subsidized housing production to an annual level of more than 400,000 units, almost all produced by private developers using FHA mortgage insurance and interest subsidies that reduced the cost of borrowing to only one percent. An issue for HUD—one of many—was how to direct or at least influence the location of this subsidized housing production surge so as to avoid further poverty concentrations in cities on the one hand, and on the other to open up housing opportunities in the suburbs for lower income and minority families.

HUD pursued a two-pronged strategy aimed at its dispersal objective. First, HUD hoped that the "housing element" planning requirement would prompt regional planning bodies to develop regional fair share plans for the distribution of subsidized housing: the theory was that wary suburban politicians would accept a limited number of units if they could be assured they would not be inundated. The Dayton, Ohio, area had made promising moves in this direction, and HUD urged others to follow. Few did. Instead, regional planning officials pleaded that they did not know what a housing element was or how to prepare one. (They had a point, since there was no definition nor known methodology for a housing element.) HUD responded by contracting with the American Institute of Planners to write a technical guide, but the guide was not issued until 1972, four years after the statutory requirement was passed. The guide had little effect. Showing some impatience, Congress in 1974 set a three-year deadline (1977) for regional bodies to complete a housing element or face a cutoff of all planning funds. This turned out to be an empty threat: by the late 1970s political support for any federal role in funding metropolitan planning was rapidly eroding and would soon disappear.

Even if the housing element initiative had been more successful in creating regional housing plans, it was not at all clear how they would be implemented on the ground. Neither the policy nor the bureaucratic connections were in place to link housing plans with housing production. Congress enacted the 1968 subsidy programs without any reference whatever to the housing element requirement. Within HUD the Federal Housing Administration (FHA) bureaucracy concerned itself with meeting unit production goals through its traditional dealings with homebuilders and developers. FHA processing of builder applications typically focused on market and financing feasibility of individual projects, not on fuzzy notions of metropolitan planning and "open communities" that were being promoted by HUD's leadership. Similarly, at the local level, regional planning bodies lacked the institutional and political levers that had a chance of transforming a regional housing plan into anything like reality.

As the weaknesses of the regional housing planning strategy became increasingly apparent, HUD moved to strengthen the second prong of its dispersal initiative, which was to use its leverage with private developers. Beginning already in 1969, HUD Secretary Romney had informally instructed FHA field offices to keep up-to-date maps showing the distribution pattern of approved developments. Builders were given the message that if they wanted to benefit from HUD subsidies, they had a better chance of winning approval if they brought in sites that were away from areas of minority concentration already containing a lot of subsidized housing, and if the sites were convenient to transportation and job opportunities. In 1972 HUD formalized by regulation its developer-driven strategy by issuing Project Selection Criteria used to evaluate and rank competing applications for subsidy funds. Preliminary analysis by HUD's evaluation staff indicated that the new regulations were in fact stimulating builders to propose more suburban sites for subsidized housing; however, the issue soon became moot when President Richard Nixon in January 1973 abruptly suspended the high volume subsidy programs passed in 1968. Production resumed during the Gerald Ford and Jimmy Carter administrations under the new rental subsidy program called Section 8, but the number of units constructed would never again come close to the 1.6 million units started during the first Nixon term. And, with the shift to a housing voucher policy in the 1980s, the federal government lost whatever leverage it had to induce new subsidized developments in suburbs.

Housing and Urban Sprawl: The State Role in Illinois

Unlike the federal government, the state government of Illinois has not asserted a direct state interest in sprawl issues as they relate to housing. Although housing advocates have frequently called on the state to set statewide standards for building codes, site development, impact fees, and other regulatory matters—all actions that might contribute to higher density housing in suburban areas—the state legislature has chosen to stay out of such issues and leave decisions in the hands of local officials.

The state's main housing activity is the Illinois Housing Development Authority (IHDA), created in 1967 as a financing vehicle for low and moderate-income multifamily developments and for first-time homebuyers who could qualify for a below-market rate mortgage. Renter subsidies were funded by federal production programs in the seventies and later by federal low income housing tax credits and by the federal HOME block grant for housing. A small additional subsidy is provided by IHDA's ability to issue bonds that are not subject to either federal or state income taxes. For first-time homebuyers, IHDA also issues mortgage revenue bonds, the proceeds of which are allocated to lenders who in turn passed along the slightly lower (1–2 percent) mortgage interest rates to the buyer. As a self-supporting state authority, IHDA operates according to a business model that stresses the quality and financial soundness of the projects it sponsors. By all accounts IHDA does its job well, but its mandate does not include a broader planning focus that could conceivably influence established residential patterns.

**Federal Housing Planning Mandates:
The Chicago Response**

Federal planning mandates for housing included the "housing element" requirement enacted in 1968 and HUD's pressure on regional planning bodies to develop "fair share" plans for the distribution of subsidized housing throughout a metropolitan area. In Chicago these mandates fell on the Northeastern Illinois Planning Commission (NIPC). The NIPC response, particularly at the professional staff level, was moderately activist.

In 1973 NIPC released "An Interim Plan for the Balanced Distribution of Housing Opportunities for Northeastern Illinois"; the plan identified a need for 229,400 housing units over a ten-year period for low- and moderate-income households, although it did not specify the location of these units. Then, in 1976, NIPC planners identified fifty-three communities with high job growth potential but with a minority population of under 2 percent and little or no housing for low- or moderate-income workers. NIPC hoped to use the A-95 federal grant review process, which is merely advisory to the federal agency involved, to induce these communities to begin planning for housing for a broad range of income groups and on a nondiscriminatory basis. The rapidly developing western suburb of Oak Brook became the test case.

Oak Brook applied in 1976 for a $750,000 federal grant for a street-widening project, but refused to acknowledge any responsibility to plan for the housing needs of the thousands of retail and office workers being attracted to Oak Brook's jobs. NIPC was urged by civil rights and prohousing groups to give the application a negative review, but in the end, the NIPC commissioners split down the middle on whether to recommend that the project be funded by the U.S. Department of Transportation. The tie vote meant the project was forwarded to the state highway agency without NIPC endorsement. The state agency, which administered federal transportation grants, declined to get involved in the issue, and the project was funded (Orlebeke 1999).

In the aftermath of the Oak Brook controversy, NIPC paid a price for venturing into local housing issues. Some local governments canceled their contributions to NIPC's budget. As one village president recalled: "We all said, 'What the hell do you [NIPC] have to do with housing?'" (Reid 1982).

Despite the Oak Brook setback, NIPC continued to compile data on housing conditions, trends, and needs. In 1978 NIPC issued its "Regional Residential Policy Plan," which proposed a plan for distributing an estimated 6,000 to 7,000 units of federally subsidized units being allocated annually by HUD. NIPC's approach was to divide the region into eleven subregions—one for the city of Chicago, five in suburban Cook, and five for the collar counties—and then to estimate subsidized housing needs in each subregion and present a housing distribution scheme that would not overwhelm individual communities with "assisted" housing.

NIPC also hoped that its Regional Residential Policy Plan would provide a framework for carrying out the federal court's order in the *Gautreaux* litigation. The plaintiffs in this case, brought against the Chicago Housing Authority (CHA) in 1966 by the American Civil Liberties Union, charged that the CHA had systematically concentrated public housing in black neighborhoods, thereby depriving low-income black tenants and those on the public housing waiting list from housing opportunities in unsegregated areas. One part of the court's decision in this complex and protracted litigation was that "*Gautreaux* class plaintiffs" should have access to subsidized housing, to the extent available, dispersed throughout the Chicago region. NIPC aspired to be the broker between CHA, local governments, the *Gautreaux* plaintiffs, housing developers, and HUD (which had become a codefendant in the case with the CHA), and thus "encourage a comprehensive solution for the plaintiffs and final disposition of the case" (NIPC 1978).

Despite NIPC's efforts to promote regional housing planning, it lacked the political leverage to make much difference. NIPC could study and recommend and encourage, but it could not tell a single local government, housing developer, or federal agency what to do and make it stick. Related to NIPC's political impotence was the administrative complexity that somehow had to be cut through if NIPC's plan was to be implemented. Dozens of local governments, as well as numerous bureaucratic fiefdoms in HUD and other federal agencies, would need to give up their usual ways of doing business and cooperate with each other. Such cooperation is rare, even when agencies presumably share objectives: HUD and NIPC, for example, were unable to agree on how NIPC would participate in the processing and approval of specific development proposals in the HUD pipeline.

NIPC's foray into regional housing planning was effectively ended by two major changes in federal policy taking effect in the early 1980s: the elimination of all federal support for comprehensive planning at the regional level, and the shift in housing policy from subsidized production programs to housing vouchers.

The Region's Housing Patterns: How Did We Get Here?

Many economic, demographic, social, and political forces have conspired to produce NIPC's remarkable statistic that in the 1970–1990 period, housing consumed 46 percent more land while the population increased by only 4 percent. This section of the chapter outlines some of these forces.

Raw population trends clearly have some bearing on trends in the housing stock, but other factors are probably more important. At the top of the list is the strength of the economy: housing prospers when the economy prospers and slumps when the economy lags. For example, in 1981 when the economy was in recession, builders sought permits for only 9,567 units in the entire Chicago region, but as the economy picked up in the mid-1980s, the number of permits more than tripled to around 30,000 in 1985 and 1986, mostly for single-family homes in the suburbs.

Economic conditions also have a critical bearing on the rate of household formation—the rate at which people decide to set up new households by getting married or divorced, or living alone instead of with family or roommates. Hard times and high interest rates restrain both housing construction and household formation because the cost of money to both builder and consumer puts the cost of housing beyond the reach of a greater proportion of the housing market: people will tend to double up or stay together when they might prefer not to. But when times are good, people have the money to act on their preferences, and the building industry strives to provide products to meet market demand. Although the economy and household formation rates have had ups and downs, the long-term trend, nationwide and in the region, is clear: Increasing numbers of persons have had the means to make choices resulting in steadily decreasing household size—in the Chicago region, from 3.14 persons per household in 1970 to 2.72 in 1990. Thus, the rate of household growth generally exceeds population growth, and it is not unusual that a moderate population decline will be accompanied by an increase in households. This happened in Cook County in the 1980s when population loss in Chicago and many inner suburbs caused a countywide decline of about 148,000 persons even as the number of households increased slightly.

Household formation as the driver of housing demand is also closely linked with demographic trends, which in turn influence the type of housing that builders seek to market. The most powerful demographic force of the last half century is the post-World War II baby boom. In the 1970s and 1980s boomers were raising families and creating an enormous market for single-family homes in the suburbs. But now that the boomers are entering their fifties and their children have (they hope) moved on, the homebuilding industry is responding with a variety of products: "active adult communities" such as Del Webb's 2,000-acre Sun City spread in the tiny McHenry County community of Huntley, town houses and condominiums in established suburban downtowns such as in Arlington Heights and Highland Park, and upscale lofts that once housed factories and offices in and around Chicago's downtown.

A social force that has also influenced housing demand is so-called white flight—the tendency of white families to move away, usually to nearly all-white suburbs, after African American families begin to move in. For a thirty-year period following World War II, large areas of Chicago on the South and West Sides flipped from nearly all white to nearly all black in ten years or less. The same process occurred in some close-in suburbs such as Maywood. In the 1980s and 1990s, increasing numbers of middle-class African American families have also left the city for the suburbs, usually clustering in communities south of the city. Again, although the process is less dramatic, resegregation appears to be occurring as whites move out, usually to more distant suburbs (Gordon 1997). All of these moves from city to close-in suburb to distant suburb, whether motivated by racial prejudice or other factors, are facilitated, and probably accelerated, by the sustained economic growth that the region has been enjoying, including high rates of job creation, low interest rates, and rising incomes.

The consumption of land by housing development involves a nexus between homebuilder, local government, and the consumer. The homebuilder, or developer, plays a critical role. Unless housing is built on publicly owned land, nothing can be built anywhere until a developer acquires a site, often several years before actually breaking ground. The developer has a lot at stake and a lot can go wrong. As one developer put it: "A developer needs a high capacity for risk, a gambler's mentality and optimism" (Young 1999). At the suburban fringe where "sprawl" is a threat, the builder's site, perhaps a former farm, is likely to be large and located on unincorporated land near a small town. As an entrepreneur, the builder seeks a profit on his or her investment, and that means marketing a product that must satisfy two masters: the local authorities who control land use of the site, and the potential consumers of the product.

Both masters can be capricious. If local government blocks the builder's proposal or even takes too long to decide (time is money), the builder loses his gamble and may go broke. The same thing happens if the project is built but does not sell, possibly because of a sudden updraft in mortgage rates, or because the market has become saturated by overbuilding of that kind of product—a fact not apparent until shoppers fail to appear. In that event, the developer's options are to sell out at a loss to a competitor or call in an auctioneer to salvage what he can. Even in the current hot market for home sales, builders can miscalculate and fail. The Sundance firm, for example, an established developer of more than 6,000 homes in twenty-eight communities, lost money in 1997 and 1998, defaulted on $67 million in loans, and sold to Centex Homes eleven developments in progress plus 1,600 lots (*Crain's Chicago Business* 1999; Benderoff 1999).

Before the housing consumer gets to weigh in, the developer's options for offering a product are constrained by local government's control of land use and the conditions under which it is willing to allow a developer to proceed. In the Chicago region, this means that housing development decisions are highly decentralized among some 270 municipalities, plus many others that lie outside the traditional six-county regional boundaries but are in the path of development. Each municipality has some sense of its own past—the accumulated decisions over time that brought it to its present state—and some general sense of what it hopes to look like in the future. In those communities where developers are eager to build housing, local authorities have already indicated through zoning what type of housing is to be permitted, from apartment buildings or town houses all the way up to five-acre luxury estates. But a zoning classification is not immutable and can merely be the starting point of negotiations between a builder and local officials. Zoning is only one area of negotiations; others could involve impact fees charged to the developer for the privilege of building in a community, or donations of land for open space, parks, or schools.

On the urban fringe where developer-owned land is often in unincorporated areas, negotiations may be conducted in the context of a proposed annexation to a nearby municipality. Builders seek annexation because of the marketing advantage of offering municipal services, and they are willing to sign agreements that compensate, within reason, the annexing municipality, or that impose other conditions such as minimum lot size. In Lake County's South Barrington, for example, the village requires five-acre minimum lot sizes in annexation agreements with developers, but in practice, developers are expected to come back to the village seeking somewhat higher densities (*Chicago Tribune* 1998).

Depending on the persons involved and particular local circumstances, negotiations of agreements can go smoothly because of mutual trust or successful political lobbying, or they can be lengthy and contentious. Here are a few examples of recent negotiations. In Grayslake in booming Lake County, the village board haggled with a developer over the density of the proposed Hidden Pond subdivision: The developer wanted fifty-four lots, the village board would prefer about forty. Another issue is whether the development would include a private park not available to other Grayslake residents. In Crystal Lake, also in Lake County, the city council debated with a developer about thirty proposed "town houses" on a seven-acre site. The town houses, however, would not be attached to each other, so are they really town houses or are they single-family homes? This is more than a semantic quibble because of Crystal Lake's impact fee policy: Town houses are charged $324 per unit and single-family homes $5,100. A "hybrid formula" will need to be negotiated. In Harvard, located in fast-growing McHenry County, the city council has imposed a freeze on multifamily housing; however, a developer proposing nine 16-unit apartment buildings has been allowed to petition the city's zoning board of appeals for an exception (*Chicago Tribune* 1999).

In Villa Park, an older western suburb, an abandoned Ovaltine factory is being converted to a 344-unit apartment complex in the center of town. A village trustee hoped the project could be reduced to about 320 units because of "density concern." Traffic impact, parking, and green space were also discussed (DeDolph 1999).

As one can glean from these examples and numerous others that might be cited, a frequent point of contention between builders and local officials is the density of a proposed development. In general, builders can make more money if they can put as many units on a site as can be successfully marketed; local officials, on the other hand, tend to have a well-entrenched bias in favor of single-family homes on large lots, which, according to standard fiscal impact analysis, have lower public service demands (especially schools) in relation to property tax generated. (The local position on the density issue must, of course, also be grounded to some degree in market realities—a municipality cannot arbitrarily limit new home construction to million-dollar homes on three acres unless there is a reasonable prospect that millionaires, who can live wherever they want, will be attracted to their community.) Builders contend that market forces such as "empty nesters" who want smaller, low maintenance houses or in-town condominiums should influence density standards. As one developer put it, "Buyers today want smaller lots; they're tired of cutting all that grass. Customers would be happy with smaller lots, especially those that back on open space." However, he went on, "there's a lot of resistance to new thinking. . . . We have been frustrated by governmental bodies that will not veer from large-lot zoning" (Handley 1998).

Not incidentally, developers are not the only persons at risk in these negotiations; local elected officials and professional staff are also vulnerable to losing their jobs if caught on the wrong side of development issues. South Barrington again provides an example: In the April 1999 elections three "antidevelopment" candidates for the village board beat two incumbents and the village clerk for control of the board. In May the mayor fired the acting village manager, acknowledging "that the two had not seen eye to eye on development issues" (Scott 1999).

In short, the widely cited increase in the consumption of land by housing is not a single story with a clear plot line but rather a multitude of episodes played out in hundreds of municipalities between builders and local officials over the half century since World War II. The prerogatives of local government to control land use outcomes, whether for a single lot or thousands of acres, are deeply embedded in the Illinois constitution, in state law, and in tradition. The result, like it or not, is what we have today, and the story goes on. According to real estate consultant Tracy Cross, "Nearly 850 active projects are underway" currently in the Chicago suburbs (DeBat 1999). Each one has its own dynamic.

A common theme one hears among gatherings of builders is the frustration they feel in dealing with the differing requirements among the scores of municipalities, with the whims of local planners and elected officials, and with the irrationalities of vocal citizens' groups. If only the development review process could be shortened and "streamlined," they say, then we could deliver a better product at a more affordable cost to the housing consumer. Although these frustrations are no doubt genuine, it is also true that organized homebuilder interests have no active legislative agenda calling for changes in state law needed to address their complaints. The reason is that the prevailing system, though complex and often unpredictable, has so far in a rough way served their interests. Local officials, for their part, have also been disinclined to give up their traditional powers. The question is: What are the prospects for change?

Housing Policy and the Smart Growth Agenda

According to U.S. Census estimates, population growth in the Chicago region since 1990 has already outstripped the increase in the previous two decades (1970–1990)—in raw numbers, 306,000 compared to 282,000. Looking ahead, in contrast to the often-cited 4 percent population increase between 1970 and 1990, NIPC (1997) projects a growth spurt of 25 percent or about 1.8 million people between 1990 and 2020 for a total population of just over nine million people. If NIPC's projection is in the ballpark, does it also portend an even more frightening rate of land consumption than was recorded in the 1970–1990 period when population growth was slow? NIPC, for one, does not think so. Current research at the university at Illinois at Chicago (UIC) Urban Transportation Center (Sööt 1999) also suggests that the high rates of household formation characterizing the postwar period may be tapering off, and further, that the recent rapid increases in the homeownership rate in the Chicago region—from 54.7 percent in 1986 to 65.8 percent in 1996— are not likely to continue. Both of these points indicate less pressure on land consumption.

NIPC sees the 1970 to 1990 growth pattern as essentially a *shift* of population from the city of Chicago and the inner suburbs farther out to northwest and southwest Cook County, DuPage County, south central Lake County, and northern Will County. But looking ahead to 2020, NIPC offers forecasts that "most definitely do not suggest a continuation of past development patterns." NIPC describes its growth scenario as follows: "If three concentric circles are imagined around a regional center defined as Chicago and inner suburban communities, signs of renewed growth will be seen in the center. Population in the first ring will be relatively stable. The second ring, including most of the area that experienced rapid growth over the last twenty years, will show only modest growth. Substantial growth will occur in the outer ring."

NIPC's optimistic outlook is "based on the Commission's expectation that public policy and investment will give increased emphasis to the maintenance of existing communities, revitalization of declining areas, and cost-effective and environmentally-sensitive new development. These assumptions developed from a series of meetings with regional leaders in 1996 . . . and also reflect the expectations of the 207 municipalities (of 270) which participated in the development of these [forecasts]." However, NIPC cautions, "the forecasted growth patterns will not happen without the active and continuing efforts of governments in northeastern Illinois and the State of Illinois."

The policy umbrella for this regional agenda is the Campaign for Sensible Growth, a coalition of government, civic, and business groups led by the Metropolitan Planning Council (MPC) and NIPC. The campaign embraces the principles of "smart growth," which include the discouragement of "leapfrog" development in favor of infill development in cities and suburbs where infrastructure is already in place. When economic and population pressures require development of raw land on the fringe, smart growth advocates call for the coordination of infrastructure and development investments, and for development featuring compact, walkable neighborhoods with a variety of housing choices and ready access to local stores, professional services, recreational opportunities, and public transportation. New housing should be near jobs in order to cut down on car use, commuting time, and related traffic and air pollution problems; it should also be affordable to the "average worker," not just high-paid executives. Another key part of the smart growth agenda is the preservation of farmland and environmentally sensitive open space, using public funds to acquire such land and keep it out of the hands of developers.

Closely associated with the Campaign for Sensible Growth is Chicago Metropolis 2020, a project of the Commercial Club of Chicago. The author of the recently issued *Chicago Metropolis 2020* report is Elmer W. Johnson (1998), a former General Motors executive. Chicago Metropolis 2020 is headed by George A. Ranney Jr., former Inland Steel CEO and member of MPC's Executive Advisors Group. Although Chicago Metropolis 2020 also aligns itself with smart growth principles, its agenda is far broader and more ambitious, including education reform, a many-pronged challenge to the "auto culture," property tax reform, and consolidation and strengthening of regional planning entities. As articulated by Johnson, the mission of Chicago Metropolis 2020 is driven as much by a commitment to social justice and equality of opportunity as it is to economic prosperity:

> Economic and social goals . . . are intertwined. Without a strong regional economy, we will not have the resources to address the social issues. And as we succeed in putting real teeth and meaning into the ideal of equality of opportunity, we will bring about levels of human productivity and social cohesion that reinforce our economic objectives. (Johnson 1998, 2.)

Ranney's Chicago Metropolis 2020 organization, which raised $4 million in corporate and foundation support, will be responsible over the next twenty years for building up the research base of the agenda, for organizing task forces on specific issues, and for mobilizing coalitions to bring about legislative and administrative implementation of its recommendations. The Campaign for Sensible Growth and Metropolis 2020, with their overlapping leadership and funding sources, can be expected to work together closely, parceling out various pieces of the agenda according to their strength with somewhat different constituencies—Metropolis 2020 with its corporate sponsors, and MPC/NIPC with their ties to local officials, professional planners, developers, and universities, as well as to the business community.

In order to implement the specific housing components of the smart growth agenda, the Campaign for Sensible Growth and Metropolis 2020 are counting on a combination of education, persuasion, and legal institutional change. Education and persuasion involves convincing skeptical constituencies, particularly homebuilders and the officials of Chicago's famously fragmented metropolitan region, that smart growth principles really are in their long-range best interests, and furthermore, that their decisions relating to the location, price range, density, and design standards of new housing development should flow logically from smart growth principles. The educational campaign also includes showcasing good examples of how smart growth can work in specific cases, as MPC (1998) has done with its publication *Growing Sensibly: A Guidebook of Best Development Practices in the Chicago Region*.

So far the campaign and Metropolis 2020 have been effective in getting people to focus on smart growth as a promising concept through conferences, attractive publications, and positive media coverage. Even at the state government level, not known for much interest in planning innovation, the House of Representatives formed a Smart Growth Task Force in 1998 Governor George Ryan also espoused smart growth principles in general terms. But state politicians have been close to inaudible on housing-related smart growth measures: The House Task Force's Final Report issued in January 1999 focused mainly on the loss of "prime farmland to suburban sprawl at an alarming rate" (Illinois House Smart Growth Task Force 1999, 1) and its list of ten "recommendations for immediate action" include nine that address farmland preservation. Before adjourning in 1999, however, the state legislature did authorize continuation of a Smart Growth Task Force with members from both the House and the Senate.

Governor Ryan's agenda has emphasized his highly popular $12 billion Illinois FIRST infrastructure development program, which promises to deal with the state's shoddy road system, Chicago's battered transit system, and a host of other capital projects. Ryan has also successfully advanced another key part of the smart growth agenda by gaining legislative approval to create the four-year, $160 million Illinois Open Land Trust for public acquisition of open space. The governor has not, however, presented any proposals to the legislature that would disturb the traditional local control over land use and housing decisions. Politically, action on housing is further, much further, down the list on the smart growth agenda.

Meanwhile, both MPC and Metropolis 2020 are hoping to enlist major employers in the cause of affordable housing in the rapidly developing areas of the region. The premise is that in a scarce labor market, employers have an interest in seeing that their employees and potential employees can live within reasonable commuting distance of their jobs; in addition, as good corporate citizens, they should also care about such issues as traffic, pollution, and regional economic health. MPC has already moved to set up pilot employer-assisted housing programs with several major suburban employers; under these programs, employee housing would be a focused concern of company human resources offices, which would provide employees and applicants with housing market information, counseling, and possibly modest financial support such as down payment assistance. MPC hopes also that employers, once engaged in housing issues, will use their corporate clout in their communities to advocate for affordable housing. An idea being pursued by Metropolis 2020 is that major employers sign a "social compact" obligating them to give strong weight, when planning new operations or expansions of existing ones, to localities that "(1) have provided for the creation of housing that is affordable to employees and their families in that area; (2) are making efforts to create a statutory framework supportive of affordable housing; and (3) are working to curtail low-density sprawl in favor of compact, transit oriented development" (Johnson 1998, 18).

In addition to leveraging employer influence in housing opportunity, Metropolis 2020 calls on "[Local], state, and federal agencies [to] create policies and programs to reduce the isolation of poor minority residents and expand the availability of affordable housing across the region" (Johnson 1998, 20). Suggested policies include adoption of a statewide building code that would preempt local codes, expansion of the Low Income Housing Tax Credit for the construction of low and moderate income housing, and increased availability of Section 8 vouchers along with counseling programs to encourage voucher recipients to seek housing throughout the region. All of these proposals, if adopted, would only "lessen the impacts of sprawl and provide some counterbalance to racial and economic segregation in the region" (Johnson, 20).

For "major progress," according to Metropolis 2020, the region must confront the necessity for "fundamental changes" in its system of governance and taxation. The main change proposed is the creation of a "regional coordinating mechanism" that would have the authority to "develop long-range strategic plans and goals for transportation, land use, housing, wastewater, storm water, and water supply services" (Johnson, 22). It would also have the authority to issue bonds for capital projects, as well as to raise and redistribute revenues reducing fiscal disparities among the region's local governments. One of the benefits of the new entity would be a "more rational distribution of housing types throughout the region" (Johnson, 22).

Metropolis 2020 acknowledges that many details relating the structure, funding, and powers of the new body remain to be worked out, and "it could take many years to establish" (Johnson, 23). In the meantime, the state and region should move ahead with several "interim steps," including the consolidation of the planning functions of NIPC, the Chicago Area Transportation Study, and the RTA. This transitional body would "create a new regional-transportation and land-use vision," but would evidently focus mainly on transportation issues—allocation of new vehicle pricing revenues, control of toll road expansions, and a new post-2020 Regional Transportation Plan are mentioned as tasks, but housing is not on the list.

Even if one is pessimistic about the political feasibility of the Metropolis 2020 interim and long-term agenda for institutional change, there are important market and demographic forces that could moderate the housing contribution to urban sprawl in the next few decades. As baby boomers age, they are forming a huge market segment that requires smaller units on less land than when the children were growing up, whether that unit is in Sun City, a town house in the suburbs, or a condo in downtown Chicago. The impulse to trade down is being fueled in part by the latest goody in the array of federal homeownership benefits—the virtual elimination in 1997 of capital gains taxation on the sale of one's house, an action that reverses the previous incentive to trade up to a more expensive house in order to postpone paying capital gains tax until age fifty-five. Under the new law, an owner of any age can sell his or her house, buy a less expensive one, and pocket the difference. Although surely not enacted as an antisprawl measure, it seems to be working out as one, particularly as long as a strong economy and low interest rates prevail.

In addition to the boomer factor, there are broader demographic trends toward later marriages, smaller families, and increasing numbers of nontraditional households—all of which points toward greater demand for smaller units than the traditional house in the suburbs surrounded by a big lawn. This market pressure, not just developers' desire to make more money, is at the heart of the long-running debate between developers and local officials about density. If one believes that market forces have a way of eventually prevailing, then we should be seeing more apartments and more six- to eight-units-per-acre town house developments in fast-growing suburbs.

Conclusion

Long-term prosperity has been the main force propelling the housing market since World War II. Until the 1990s, this force has translated into consumer demand for bigger houses on more land; public policy at all levels has done much to accommodate and little to restrain this demand—hence the dramatic increase in farmland and other open land consumed by housing development. Now, market demand is taking some new turns, and a formidable array of opinion leaders has enlisted under the smart growth banner.

Even the National Association of Home Builders (NAHB) has signed on; recently running full-page ads headlined "Smart Growth—Making the American Dream Better than Ever!" and "Smart Growth—The Call of the Wild!" as an American bald eagle soars overhead. "We believe the answer is SMART GROWTH, a common-sense approach to the development of communities across our country," the ad states. But the six-page NAHB (1999) smart growth policy statement adopted March 15, 1999, is more carefully nuanced. The statement points to polls that show a strong preference for the suburban single-family home, takes a poke at those "who want to turn Smart Growth into a tool to stop or slow growth" (NAHB, 3), admonishes communities "setting aside meaningful open space" to "rezone other land to assure there is an ample supply of land available for residential development" (NAHB, 4), and calls for smart growth discussions to begin at the local level "because the politics of growth are uniquely local and because the authority to determine land use is vested in local government" (NAHB, 3). NAHB's ambivalence is summed up nicely in this paragraph near the end of the statement:

> NAHB supports higher density development and innovative land-use policies to encourage mixed-use and pedestrian-friendly developments with access to open space and mass transit. Generating greater public support for this type of development, however, will require a change in thinking by people opposed to higher density development in their own backyards, by local governments that have erected barriers to higher density development and are easily influenced by citizen groups opposed to any new growth, and by typical housing consumers who continue to favor a single-family home on an individual lot. (NAHB, 5)

"A change in thinking" is the linchpin phrase in this statement. Political realism suggests that where housing is concerned, institutional change imposed from above by metropolitan or state authority is at best a distant prospect. Perhaps, as the easier pieces of the smart growth agenda—better roads, transit, and open space preservation—fall into place, housing also will follow. Meanwhile, at the local level where housing decisions will be made for the foreseeable future, the power of persuasion and good examples will need to serve as the main levers for change.

At the federal level, housing policy, as we have seen, has historically been marked with both pro-sprawl and anti-sprawl features. The federal embrace of the social value of homeownership, including generous tax benefits, has probably on balance contributed to higher rates of housing and land consumption. In addition, the federal funding of new subsidized projects, particularly public housing, in the 1960s and 1970s was concentrated in central cities and led both to urban blight and an accelerated rush to the suburbs. More recent policy initiatives, however, are probably working against sprawl by strengthening central cities. These initiatives include the shift from a production to a voucher strategy for housing subsidies in the eighties and the addition in 1990 of a housing block grant to cities and states.

Unlike the federal efforts in the 1970s to link housing policy to the control of sprawl, recent federal initiatives, such as the Bill Clinton administration's proposed "Livability Agenda," have had no explicit housing policy component. As former Vice President Al Gore has said, "The federal government is not a national zoning board. Washington should not be making local planning decisions" (Harris 1999, 3). Rather, the focus of the Livability Agenda was on infrastructure improvements and such "green" initiatives as "Better America Bonds" and a $1 billion "Lands Legacy Initiative" for parks, farmland, wetlands, and forests. Gore called this "giving you the tools and resources you need to create the communities you want" (Harris, 3). It is clear that if there are to be changes in housing patterns, communities must "want" them.

References

Benderoff, Eric. 1999. Buyer Expresses Fear As Building Company Sold. *Chicago Sun-Times*, Home Life (March 5), p. 3.

City of Chicago, Department of Housing. 1998. Housing Opportunities Into the New Century: Affordable Housing Plan 1999–2003.

DeBat, Don. 1999. Suburbs Still Appeal to Most Homebuyers. *Today's New Homes/ Pioneer Press* (March 10), pp. 5, 8.
DeDolph, Meg. 1999. Stirring Up Discussion. *Chicago Tribune* (April 24), p. 7.
Gordon, Danielle. 1997. "White Flight" Taking Off in Chicago Suburbs. *Chicago Reporter* 26(8): 1, 4–10.
Handley, John. 1998. A Growing Dilemma. *Chicago Tribune* (November 22), section 16, p. 4.
Illinois House of Representatives Smart Growth Task Force. 1999. Final Report.
Harris, Elaine. 1999. Smart Growth Should Happen at the Local Level, Gore Says. *Nation's Cities Weekly* (May 10), p. 3.
Is Sundance Facing Its Last Waltz?1999. *Crain's Chicago Business* (February 22), p. 1.
Johnson, Elmer W. 1998. *Chicago Metropolis 2020. Executive Summary*. Commercial Club of Chicago.
Metropolitan Planning Council. 1995. Housing for a Competitive Region.
———. 1998. Growing Sensibly: A Guidebook of Best Development Practices in the Chicago Region.
National Association of Home Builders. 1999. NAHB's Statement of Policy On Smart Growth. Washington, DC, March 15.
Northeastern Illinois Planning Commission. 1978. Regional Residential Policy Plan (Public Hearing Draft).
———. 1973. An Interim Plan for the Balanced Distribution of Housing Opportunities for Northern Illinois.
———. 1997. Population, Household and Employment Forecasts for Northeastern Illinois 1990 to 2020.
Orlebeke, Charles J. 1999. Interview with Lawrence B. Christmas and Deborah Washington, former and current directors of the NIPC, April 20.
Reid, Gil. 1982. Doubts Over Future, Cutbacks Cloud NIPC's 25th Anniversary. *Suburban Sun-Times* (June 25), p. 17.
Romney, George. 1969. Testimony to the Subcommittee on Urban Growth, U.S. House of Representatives, October.
———. 1970. Statement before Senate Select Committee on Equal Educational Opportunity, August 26.
Scott, Anika. 1999. Changing of Guard Shakes Up Village Hall. *Chicago Tribune* (May 19), p. 1.
Sööt, Siim. 1999. Personal interview, July 26. (See also *Highways and Urban Decentralization*. 1998. Urban Transportation Center, University of Illinois at Chicago. Appendix 5: Effects of Decentralization on the Cost of Housing.)
Suburban Report: South Barrington. 1998. *Chicago Tribune* (November 22).
Suburban Report: Grayslake, Crystal Lake, Harvard. 1999. *Chicago Tribune* (May 29).
U.S. Department of Housing and Urban Development. 1970. Excerpts from Urban Growth and New Community Development Act of 1970.
U.S. General Accounting Office. 1999. *Community Development: Extent of Federal Influence on "Urban Sprawl" Is Unclear*, 37–40.
Young, David. 1999. Unnecessary Sacrifice. *Chicago Tribune* (May 15), section 4, p. 10.

9

JOHN F. MCDONALD AND DANIEL P. MCMILLEN

Employment Subcenters and Subsequent Real Estate Development in Suburban Chicago

Introduction

The ongoing decentralization of American cities is often characterized by the pejorative term "sprawl." This imprecisely used term generally is applied to new, low-density, scattered development located at ever-increasing distances from the traditional urban core. At the same time, many suburban areas now have large subcenters with significant effects on nearby population density, land values, housing prices, and employment density.[1] A city that grows by adding to relatively densely populated subcenters is more centralized than one that grows by pushing firms and households to a rapidly expanding urban periphery. Little is known about the spatial patterns of suburban development because existing data are usually highly aggregated spatially.

This chapter examines the spatial patterns of real estate development in the suburban areas of metropolitan Chicago in the 1990s. Although still a highly centralized city, Chicago is an interesting case study because it has large suburban subcenters and its recent growth has been biased toward the periphery.[2] Data on individual real estate developments that were completed during the period 1990–1996 are used to test hypotheses regarding the influence of various features of the suburban economic geography. Of particular interest is the possible influence of suburban employment subcenters that were identified in our previous research (McMillen and McDonald 1998a). Industrial, commercial, and residential developments are studied separately.

Our results indicate that industrial and commercial development, although widely scattered, is nonetheless attracted to traditional measures of access to the urban transportation network. Industrial development is attracted to locations near O'Hare Airport, downtown Chicago, and highway interchanges. It is also attracted to locations outside of Cook County (probably by the high property tax rate on industrial property in Cook). However, industrial development is not attracted to suburban employment subcenters. Commercial development is attracted to locations near O'Hare Airport and, in contrast to industrial development, is more likely to have occurred in locations proximate to highway interchanges or suburban employment subcenters. The industrial and commercial results are similar to McMillen and McDonald's (1998b) results for population density in metropolitan Chicago in 1980. McMillen and McDonald find that population density is strongly positively related to proximity to commuter rail stations and the nearest suburban employment (but not highway interchanges).

The results presented in this paper indicate that recent residential development is following a different spatial pattern, one that is scattered relative to existing concentrations of population as well as to new developments in industry and commerce. The probability that a location has residential development is negatively related to distance to O'Hare Airport and downtown Chicago as expected, but housing is not being attracted to sites with favorable access to commuter rail stations, highway interchanges, or suburban employment centers. Indeed, proximity to highway interchanges and suburban employment centers have negative effects on the probability that housing development takes place. In addition, the size of the residential development (measured in housing units) declines with distance to O'Hare Airport, but increases with distance to downtown Chicago and commuter rail stations.

The low density and scattered pattern of Chicago's recent development is consistent with the term "sprawl" over this period. The employment subcenters attracted commercial development, but residential and industrial development was more dispersed. However, it is important to note that Chicago is characterized by a traditional transportation system with spokes coming out of the central city. Earlier development took place by moving out along the spokes, leaving gaps between the highways and rail lines. New development is filling in the gaps, but at lower density.

Chicago's Suburban Employment Centers

Distance to the nearest employment subcenter is a critical variable in our empirical analysis. Chicago's subcenters were identified in McMillen and McDonald (1998a). Here we briefly review the methods and results obtained in that paper. A map showing the location of the subcenters is available in our earlier paper.

Although various methods for the identification of employment subcenters exist, most have followed McDonald (1987) by designating as subcenters locations with relatively large values for *gross* employment density (i.e., employment divided by total land area). The data used in McMillen and McDonald (1998a) and in this study pertain to small areas that are 0.25 square miles in area (quarter sections). We follow Giuliano and Small (1991) and define as potential subcenters a set of "nearby" quarter sections that have gross employment density of at least ten employees per acre in either 1980 or 1990 and together have an average over these two years of at least 10,000 employees.[3] We raise the cutoff point to twenty employees per acre in the area near O'Hare Airport and in the northern suburbs because otherwise its high density leads to a single "subcenter" of more than 400,000 employees.

This procedure identifies twenty employment subcenters in the Chicago suburbs. McMillen and McDonald (1998a) informally group them into the following categories based on age, location, and industrial composition:

- Old satellite cities—Aurora, Elgin, Waukegan
- Old industrial suburbs—Chicago Heights, Harvey, McCook
- Post-World War II industrial suburbs—Addison, Des Plaines, Franklin Park, Niles, Norridge, O'Hare
- New industrial/retail suburbs—Northbrook, Palatine
- Edge cities—Naperville, Oak Brook, Schaumburg
- Service and retail centers—Burbank, Evanston, Maywood

The five subcenters with the most rapid employment growth over the 1980–1990 period are the two newer industrial/retail suburbs and the three edge cities. Each of the other four categories include some subcenters with positive growth and others with negative growth rates. Of the fifteen subcenters in these four groups, nine had positive employment growth and six declined over the decade. The two subcenters in these groups with the fastest growth rates are Addison and O'Hare, two centers immediately adjacent to O'Hare Airport.

The empirical results for employment and population density patterns from McMillen and McDonald (1998a, 1998b, 1998c) can be summarized briefly. Employment density in both 1980 and 1990 is strongly positively related to proximity to commuter rail stations, highway interchanges, and the nearest employment center (especially those with more than 15,000 employees). Population density follows roughly a similar pattern, except that proximity to a highway interchange does not affect population density.

Real Estate Development Data

We obtained data on real estate developments in metropolitan Chicago from the Northeastern Illinois Planning Commission (NIPC) for the years 1990 to 1996. The data cover the six-county northeastern Illinois area, which includes Cook, DuPage, Kane, Lake, McHenry, and Will counties. Developments and their components must involve at least one acre of land, 10,000 square feet of building, or $1 million in expenditure to be included in the NIPC data. Hence, our study is one of real estate developments that are at or above one of these thresholds. Components of larger developments are listed separately in the data because such components are usually constructed in sequence rather than simultaneously. NIPC obtained information from a number of published sources and unpublished sources, including Dodge Construction News, *Chicago Sun-Times, Chicago Tribune,* individual developers, local newspapers, local governments, and NIPC's Project Review Department. NIPC believes that the data covers the great bulk of development activity, but no claim is made of complete coverage of all activity meeting the stated criteria.

The information recorded for each development (and each of its components, if relevant) includes the following:

- status: for example, planned, approved, under construction, completed, suspended, etc.
- land use category: commercial, industrial, residential, other
- location coded by quarter section
- number of housing units
- square footage for commercial, industrial, and other types of developments
- acreage of the development
- cost of the development

Table 9.1

Suburban Developments

Land use category	No. of developments	No. of quarter sections with development	% of quarter sections with development
Industrial	296	143	1.00
Commercial	617	393	2.75
Residential	620	442	3.09

Developments are included in this study if they were coded as completed, which means that they were recorded as completed during the 1990–1996 period. We examine industrial, commercial, and residential developments separately. Acreage and cost were reported for only a fraction of the developments, so these variables are not used in this research.

Industrial developments include manufacturing; industrial, not elsewhere classified; warehousing; and distribution. Commercial is a broad category that includes retail, shopping centers, auto, business parks, hotels, office, public storage, research, parcel distribution, and commercial, not elsewhere classified. Residential developments include single-family detached, single-family attached, multifamily, general residential, and congregate housing.

Our study is restricted to quarter sections located in Chicago area suburbs. Quarter sections in the city proper are excluded. There are 14,299 quarter sections in the six-county area outside the city of Chicago. Of these, we omitted ten observations with missing data. Some quarter sections contain more than one development in a land use category. The total number of developments and the number of quarter sections with any development are given in Table 9.1. We see that development during the seven-year period is an event of low probability for a quarter section chosen at random.

Explanatory Variables

The empirical analysis consists of two parts. We first use a probit model to estimate the probability that a quarter section has any development of a given type (industrial, commercial or residential), and then use ordinary lease squares (OLS) to estimate a model of the amount of development given that development took place. The chapter appendix presents a theoretical justification for this approach to modeling recent development choices in the metropolitan area.

It is hypothesized that the probability of development in a quarter section depends on several factors. Distance to O'Hare Airport is included because O'Hare is the center of the air transport system and is adjacent to a very large freight rail yard and to several highways.[4]

We expect this variable to have a negative sign for all three uses because O'Hare is a large employment center that attracts both employers and households that want to live near their workplaces. Similarly, distance to downtown Chicago is expected to have a negative sign for all three uses because greater distance to downtown means less access to workers, suppliers, and so forth for firms and a longer commute for workers.

The next three variables are entered as the *inverse* of distance to a particular feature. This specification permits the marginal effect of distance to fall off rapidly, which is our expectation for this group of three variables.[5] Distance to the nearest commuter train station, highway interchange, and nearest employment center are entered into the model as inverses. We expect the inverse of distance (i.e., proximity) to a highway interchange to have a positive effect for industrial and commercial development to indicate that the probability of development is negatively related to distance to a limited-access highway. The effect is unclear for residential development because industrial and commercial firms tend to bid more for quick highway access than do residential uses, which could lead residential development to sites away from the interchanges. Proximity to commuter train stations is most prized by households and least valued by industrial firms, so the expected sign of this variable is positive for residential development and negative for industrial development. Alternatively, proximity to commuter train stations may appear to deter development for all three uses if these sites are already developed.

The models also include the proportion of the quarter section that is devoted to railroad use, water, parks and open space, and agriculture.[6] We expect that railroad facilities will attract industrial development, but they should have little effect on commercial development and may repel residential development. The other three variables are used to account for the availability of land for development since new building is much less likely in previously developed suburban areas. Other land uses listed by NIPC reduce the probability of new development because they reduce the space available for new building.[7] Quarter sections with more undeveloped land are more likely to have new development, but the current use of the undeveloped land may matter. We expect that water deters development because these sites are either lakes or wetlands that are costly to develop. Parks and open space also are expected to deter development because parks cannot be built upon, and open space is unused land. Land does not go unused in the Chicago area unless it is difficult to develop. The remaining land use, agriculture, is prime land for development. Unlike unused land, it can be developed relatively easily because it is flat, cleared of trees and underbrush, and serviced by roads and other infrastructure.

Employment subcenters have agglomeration economies that attract industrial and commercial firms and may also attract residential development because of the employment located there. However, the effect of proximity to an employment subcenter is ambiguous because subcenters tend to have high land values, which may deter new development (especially residential development). A fourth distance variable entered as an inverse is distance to the nearest employment subcenter *if* that subcenter is dominated by manufacturing.[8] Manufacturing employment is the one major sector of employment that has been stagnant in metropolitan Chicago, so we hypothesize that development will not be attracted to industrial employment subcenters in any of the sectors.

The probit model also includes several additional variables. One reflects the fact that the nearest employment subcenter is one of the twelve that are dominated by manufacturing. The expected sign on this variable is negative for all uses because development should not be attracted to an area with declining employment. The other variables represent locations outside Cook County. They are included to capture differences in property tax rates along with other unmeasured differences among the counties. Cook County uses a classification system that assesses industrial and commercial property at higher rates than other types of property, whereas the other counties have a uniform assessment rate. Estimates of the average effective property tax rates by county for 1988 (due in 1989) are presented in Table 9.2. Cook County has relatively high industrial and commercial property tax rates and is already highly developed, so we expect development in all three sectors to be attracted to the other counties. Will County has a low industrial tax rate, but its attractiveness to industrial development is unclear because of its distance from Chicago.

Table 9.2

Average Effective Property Tax Rates in 1988

County	Industrial (%)	Commercial (%)
Cook	5.19	4.63
DuPage	1.91	1.83
Kane	1.99	1.98
Lake	2.05	1.95
McHenry	2.07	2.11
Will	0.92	2.31

Our output measure varies by sector. For the industrial and commercial sectors, we have information on the square footage of the developments. We have information on the number of units in new residential developments, but not on their square footage. The estimates of development size turn out to be imprecise for all three sectors. To improve the precision, we include only a subset of the explanatory variables discussed above for these models—distance to O'Hare Airport; distance to downtown Chicago; the variables measuring proximity to commuter rail stations, highway interchanges, and the nearest employment center; and the dummy variable representing a Cook County location.

Spatial Patterns of Industrial Development

There were 314 industrial developments (or components) located in 143 suburban quarter sections completed during 1990–1996. Complete data on square footage are available for 118 of these quarter sections. For those quarter sections with any industrial development, the amount of development ranges from 12,000 square feet to 1,100,000 square feet, with a mean of 203,000 square feet. Figure 9.1 shows the quarter sections with any industrial development (including those inside the city of Chicago). We note that there is some clustering of industrial development in north-central DuPage County, northwest Will County, and near O'Hare Airport. Otherwise, development is scattered mostly around the fringe of the urban area. The estimated probit model for industrial development in a quarter section is shown in the first result's column of Table 9.3. In this equation most of the coefficients have the expected sign and attain statistical significance. The probability of industrial development is strongly negatively related to distance to downtown Chicago and negatively related to distance to O'Hare Airport. The probability of development is higher if the quarter section is closer to a highway interchange or farther from an employment subcenter if that subcenter is *not* dominated by manufacturing. Proximity to an employment subcenter that is dominated by manufacturing has essentially no effect ($-0.675 + 0.942$) on the probability of development. The proportion of land used by railroads has a weak positive effect, whereas water and parks and open space have negative effects on the probability of development.

The proportion of land in agriculture has a positive effect that is highly statistically significant ($t = 6.34$). This is strong confirmation of the hypothesis that agricultural land represents land that is potentially available for development. It is true, of course, that most agricultural land is located at great distances from downtown Chicago, and distance to downtown has a strongly negative effect on development. It is therefore important to recognize that the effect of the proportion of land in agriculture on development is strongly positive at a given distance to downtown. Lastly, location outside of Cook County has a statistically significant and positive effect on the probability of industrial development. DuPage, McHenry, and Will counties all have statistically significantly higher probabilities of attracting development than does Cook County.

Regression models of the amount of development in a quarter section (given that development took place) are shown in last two columns of Table 9.3. Of the 143 quarter sections with industrial development, 118 had complete tallies of square feet of developed space. It is assumed that these 118 quarter sections are a fair representation of the larger group from which they are drawn. Various ordinary least squares models were tried, but very few statistically significant results were obtained. A typical result for all locations is shown in the second column of regression results. In this equation, Cook County has a strongly negative effect on square footage. The coefficient of the inverse of distance to an employment subcenter has a negative coefficient of marginal statistical significance, which implies that the size of the industrial development increases as distance to the employment subcenter increases. The results in the last column show that the effect of distance to an employment subcenter loses its marginal statistical significance when an adjustment is made for selection bias.

To summarize, the probability that any industrial development took place in a quarter section was strongly influenced by its location, largely in ways that can be expected. The probability of industrial development in a quarter section is larger if the quarter section:

EMPLOYMENT SUBCENTERS AND REAL ESTATE DEVELOPMENT 191

Figure 9.1 **Post-1990 Industrial Development**

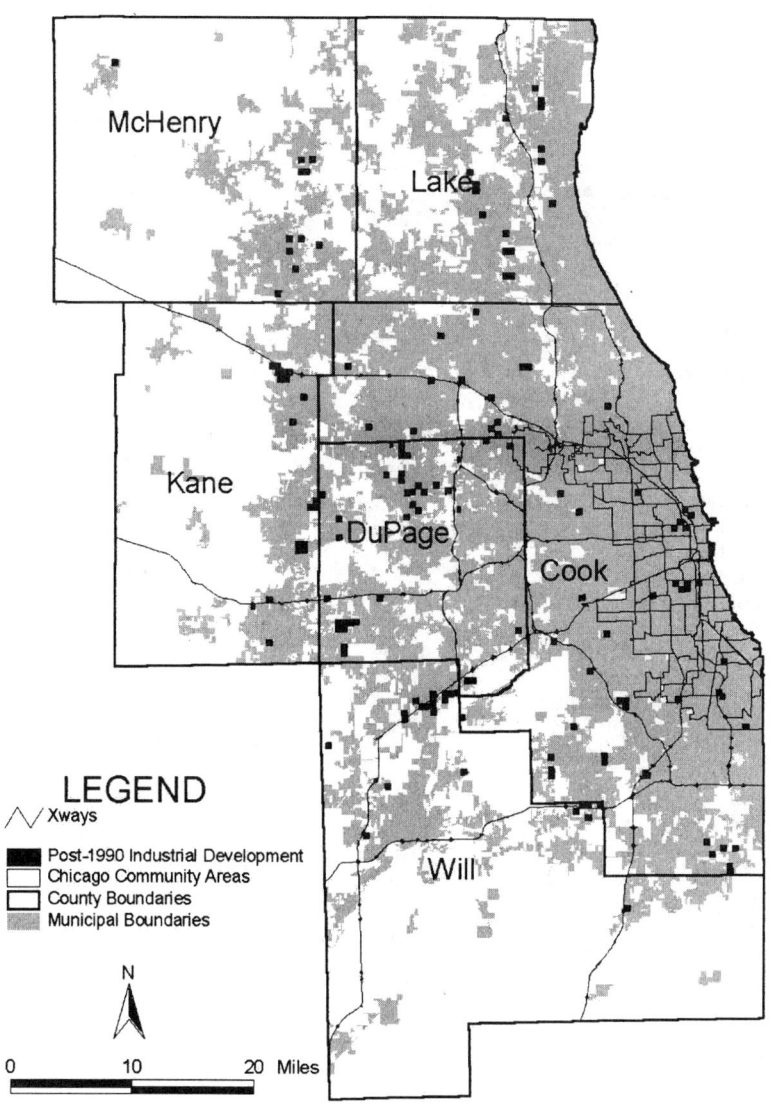

Note: Xways = expressways.

Table 9.3
Industrial Development

Dependent variable	Presence of development in quarter section	Log of square footage in developments	Log of square footage in developments
Estimation method	Probit	OLS	OLS, adjusted for selection bias
Constant	−1.385	5.592	6.463
	(6.394)	(10.664)	(8.963)
Distance to O'Hare Airport	−0.022	0.001	0.017
	(3.320)	(0.089)	(1.095)
Distance to downtown Chicago	−0.316	−0.201	−0.065
	(3.530)	(1.046)	(0.331)
Inverse of distance to commuter rail station	−0.091	0.070	0.172
	(1.160)	(0.246)	(0.612)
Inverse of distance to highway interchange	0.121	0.132	0.089
	(2.439)	(0.876)	(0.616)
Inverse of distance to nearest employment subcenter (D)	−0.675	−0.667	−0.369
	(2.194)	(1.779)	(0.884)
D x nearest employment subcenter is manufacturing	0.942		
	(2.975)		
Proportion of quarter section: railroad rights of way	1.196		
	(1.739)		
Proportion of quarter section: water	−3.961		
	(2.119)		
Proportion of quarter section: parks and open space	−0.573		
	(1.474)		
Proportion of quarter section: agriculture	0.985		
	(6.342)		
Nearest employment subcenter is manufacturing	−0.204		
	(1.769)		
Cook County location		−1.060	−0.810
		(4.337)	(3.182)
DuPage County location	0.232		
	(2.083)		
Kane County location	0.365		
	(2.065)		
Lake County location	0.129		
	(0.837)		
McHenry County location	0.598		
	(2.638)		
Will County location	0.077		
	(0.554)		
Inverse Mills ratio			−0.733
			(1.953)
Standard error			1.197
ρ			−0.613
R^2		0.169	0.194
Number of observations	14,289	118	118

Note: Unsigned asymptotic *t*-values are in parentheses.

EMPLOYMENT SUBCENTERS AND REAL ESTATE DEVELOPMENT   193

- is located closer to O'Hare Airport, downtown Chicago, or a highway interchange;
- is located farther from a commuter train station or a suburban employment subcenter (unless that subcenter is dominated by manufacturing employment);
- contains less land devoted to parks and open space or covered by water, or contains more land devoted to agriculture;
- is not located in Cook County (probably because of property tax rates).

The size of the industrial development is smaller if it is located in Cook County, and possibly is larger the greater is the distance to the nearest employment subcenter.

Spatial Patterns of Commercial Development

Commercial development is a heterogeneous collection of 673 developments (or components) located in 393 quarter sections. We have estimated the same probit models for the probability of development and the same OLS models for the square footage of development as for the industrial category. The quarter sections with commercial development are shown in Figure 9.2. Quarter sections inside the city of Chicago with commercial development are shown in Figure 9.2, but as noted above, the city is not included in the econometric analysis. Figure 9.2 shows that commercial development appears to have some tendency to follow the major highways to the southwest, west-southwest, northwest, and north. This impression is generally confirmed by the econometric results.

The probit models are displayed in the first column of results in Table 9.4. Most of our hypotheses are strongly confirmed by these results. The probability of commercial development is negatively related to distance to O'Hare Airport, a highway interchange, and the nearest employment subcenter (the last with only marginal statistical significance). Also, commercial development is less likely to have occurred in quarter sections with more water or parks and open space. The proportion of land in agriculture has a statistically significant positive effect, confirming its use as a measure of land potentially available for development. The other variables, including location outside of Cook County, do not have statistically significant effects.

The square footage of the commercial development in a quarter sec-

Table 9.4
Commercial Development

Dependent variable	Presence of development in quarter section	Log of square footage in developments	Log of square footage in developments
Estimation method	Probit	OLS	OLS, adjusted for selection bias
Constant	−1.239	4.898	7.985
	(9.848)	(13.626)	(7.973)
Distance to O'Hare Airport	−0.024	−0.017	0.024
	(5.689)	(1.602)	(1.493)
Distance to downtown Chicago	−0.076	−0.096	−0.012
	(1.405)	(0.813)	(0.095)
Inverse of distance to commuter rail station	−0.026	−0.213	−0.104
	(0.620)	(2.557)	(1.185)
Inverse of distance to highway interchange	0.139	0.228	0.015
	(4.354)	(2.997)	(0.150)
Inverse of distance to nearest employment subcenter (D)	0.165	0.114	−0.146
	(1.941)	(1.054)	(1.065)
D x nearest employment subcenter is manufacturing	0.066		
	(0.576)		
Proportion of quarter section: railroad rights of way	−1.336		
	(1.496)		
Proportion of quarter section: water	−0.986		
	(1.665)		
Proportion of quarter section: parks and open space	−0.377		
	(2.481)		
Proportion of quarter section: agriculture	0.282		
	(3.028)		
Nearest employment subcenter is manufacturing	−0.039		
	(0.555)		
Cook County location		−0.151	−0.144
		(0.891)	(0.853)
DuPage County location	−0.009		
	(0.120)		
Kane County location	−0.026		
	(0.229)		
Lake County location	0.032		
	(0.348)		
McHenry County location	−0.075		
	(0.492)		
Will County location	−0.187		
	(1.831)		
Inverse Mills ratio			−1.859
			(3.258)
Standard error			2.085
ρ			−0.892
R^2		0.074	0.099
Number of observations	14,289	310	310

Note: Unsigned asymptotic *t*-values are in parentheses.

Figure 9.2 **Post-1990 Commerial Development**

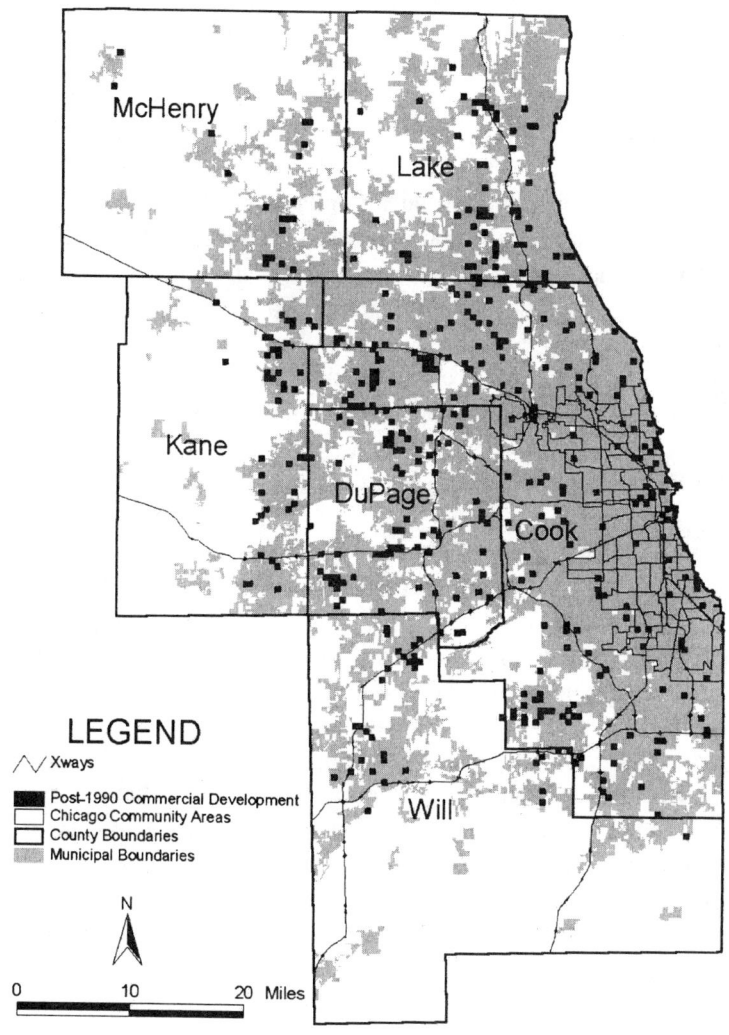

tion is examined in the last two columns of Table 9.4. Complete data on square footage are available for 310 out of the 393 quarter sections with commercial development. Square footage ranges from 5,000 to 2,323,000, with a mean of 165,000. The OLS regression results show that the size of the development is negatively affected by proximity to a commuter rail station and positively related to proximity to a highway interchange. Proximity to a commuter rail station most often means that the quarter section is already highly developed with little room for additional commercial space. The more important result is that highway interchanges attract larger commercial developments. However, the results in the last column of Table 9.4 show that both effects lose statistical significance when the adjustment is made for selection bias.

The results for commercial development can be summarized briefly. Commercial development is negatively related to distance to downtown Chicago and O'Hare Airport, and is attracted to quarter sections with proximity to a highway interchange and a suburban employment subcenter. The commercial development may contain more square feet of space if the quarter section is located nearer to a highway interchange. Clearly the importance of highway interchanges has been highlighted in these results, but the positive effect of proximity to an employment subcenter also is found.

Spatial Patterns of Suburban Residential Development

The spatial patterns of suburban residential development are especially important because new residents demand public services and infrastructure, especially schools. There were 668 residential developments recorded for 442 quarter sections over the 1990–1996 period. Complete housing unit data are available for 436 of the quarter sections, so coverage by this variable is good. The mean number of housing units in a quarter section with residential development is 171; units in a quarter section vary from 4 to 1,747. It is important to recall that the data set does not contain smaller residential developments below the thresholds mentioned previously (see Real Estate Development Data). The quarter sections with residential development are shown in Figure 9.3, which suggests large clusters of development to the north and to the west of O'Hare Airport. Otherwise, residential development appears to be quite scattered around the fringe of the urban area.

As with the industrial and commercial sectors, our tasks are to determine the factors that are related to (1) the probability that a suburban quarter section experienced residential development, and (2) the size of the development (i.e., housing units) given that new development has taken place. One hypothesis is that housing development in the suburbs is attracted to locations that are closer to O'Hare Airport, downtown Chicago, commuter rail stations, highway interchanges, and suburban employment subcenters. Alternatively, it can be hypothesized that such

Figure 9.3 **Post-1990 Residential Development**

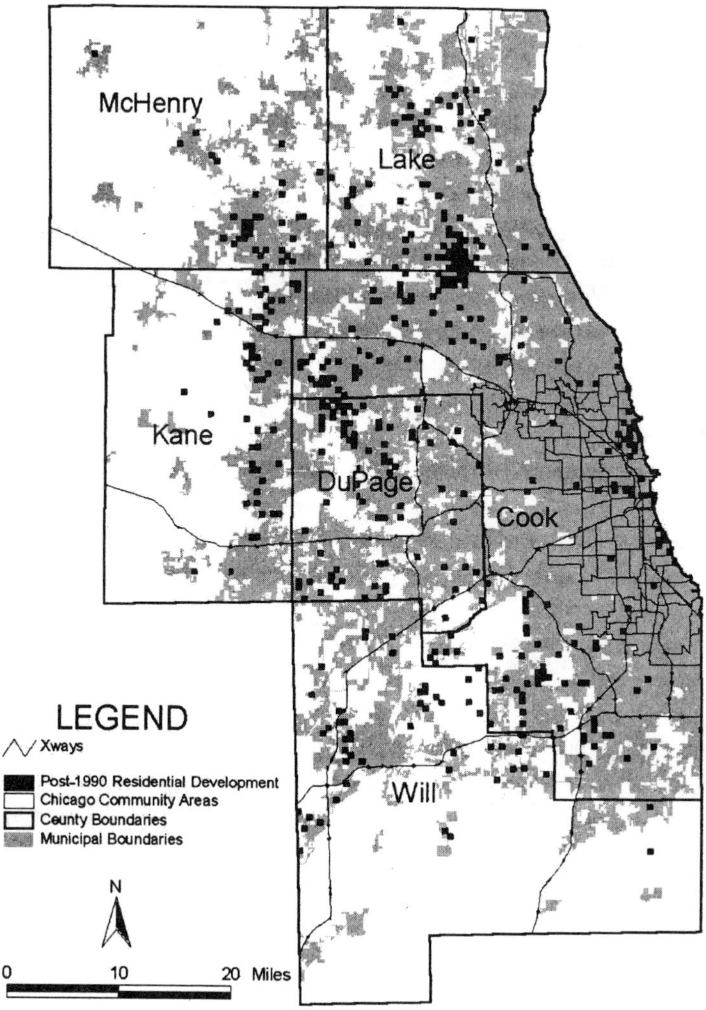

sites are already rather fully developed and unable to accommodate additional housing. Recall that both employment and population density were positively related to proximity to these types of locations in 1980. For sites with such favorable accessibility features that remain for development, residential development may not be able to outbid other uses. The issue turns on the empirical evidence.

Table 9.5
Residential Development

Dependent variable	Presence of development in quarter section	Log of number of units in developments	Log of number of units in developments
Estimation method	Probit	OLS	OLS, adjusted for selection bias
Constant	−0.884	4.857	5.322
	(6.879)	(17.460)	(10.541)
Distance to O'Hare Airport	−0.030	−0.054	−0.043
	(6.736)	(6.394)	(3.237)
Distance to downtown Chicago	−0.110	0.370	0.391
	(2.093)	(4.486)	(4.623)
Inverse of distance to commuter rail station	−0.002	−0.317	−0.288
	(0.043)	(4.689)	(3.912)
Inverse of distance to highway interchange	−0.185	0.016	0.101
	(3.781)	(0.149)	(0.741)
Inverse of distance to nearest employment subcenter (D)	0.040	0.049	0.060
	(0.395)	(0.242)	(0.290)
D x nearest employment subcenter is manufacturing	−0.377		
	(2.050)		
Proportion of quarter section: railroad rights of way	−2.460		
	(2.037)		
Proportion of quarter section: water	−0.277		
	(0.673)		
Proportion of quarter section: parks and open space	−0.093		
	(0.679)		
Proportion of quarter section: agriculture	0.451		
	(4.947)		
Nearest employment subcenter is manufacturing	0.040		
	(0.547)		
Cook County location		−0.093	−0.072
		(0.779)	(0.607)
DuPage County location	0.017		
	(0.240)		
Kane County location	−0.001		
	(0.008)		
Lake County location	0.138		
	(1.594)		
McHenry County location	0.007		
	(0.053)		
Will County location	−0.071		
	(0.737)		
Inverse Mills ratio			−0.395
			(1.083)
Standard error			1.061
ρ			−0.372
R^2		0.141	0.144
Number of observations	14,289	436	436

Note: Unsigned asymptotic *t*-values are in parentheses.

Probit models of the probability of residential development in a quarter section are shown in the first column of results in Table 9.5. Distance to O'Hare Airport has a negative and highly statistically significant effect on the probability that there was residential development. Comparing the results in Tables 9.3 to 9.5, we see that distance to O'Hare has a similar negative effect in all three sectors. Distance to downtown Chicago also has a negative effect that is statistically significant. So far the results are as anticipated, but the coefficients of the other distance variables tell a very different story.

Note that proximity to a commuter rail station, a highway interchange, and the nearest employment subcenter do *not* attract residential development to a quarter section. Indeed, the probability of residential development is higher at greater distances from a highway interchange (with a highly statistically significant coefficient). Proximity to a commuter rail station and proximity to the nearest employment subcenter have no effects at all (if that subcenter is *not* dominated by manufacturing employment). If the subcenter is one of the twelve manufacturing subcenters, proximity reduces the probability of residential development in the quarter section. These results say that residential development is not being attracted to suburban quarter sections with these favorable accessibility features; in fact, housing is being pushed away from highway interchanges and employment subcenters dominated by manufacturing.

The remaining probit results show that, as we expect, housing development is less likely in quarter sections with more railroad land use. The effects of more land in water or parks and open space are zero, but the effect of land in agriculture is once again strongly positive. Also, a location outside of Cook County has no effect on the probability of housing development. This finding is expected because the property tax treatment of housing does not differ a great deal across counties (as it does in the industrial and commercial sectors).

The last empirical results in this study pertain to the size of the residential development (measured in housing units) in a quarter section, given that development took place. The OLS results for the entire suburban data set are shown in the last two columns of Table 9.5. The 436 quarter sections there have the requisite data on housing units. The results show that the size of the housing development is negatively related to distance to O'Hare Airport and to proximity to a commuter rail station. However, the effect on the number of housing units of distance to downtown Chicago is strongly positive. Introduction of the adjustment for selection bias (results shown in the last column) makes no change in these results.

The results for residential development tell a reasonably clear story. Although the probability of residential development falls with distance to O'Hare Airport and distance to downtown Chicago as expected, housing is not being attracted to suburban quarter sections with favorable access to commuter rail stations, highway interchanges, or suburban employment subcenters. Indeed, the evidence is strong that residential development is avoiding highway interchanges and those employment subcenters dominated by manufacturing. Furthermore, although the size of the residential development (i.e., number of units) is negatively related to distance to O'Hare Airport, size increases with distance to downtown Chicago and commuter rail stations. In short, the empirical evidence presented here largely shows that residential development has been, in some important respects, assuming a spatial pattern that is rather scattered. The costs and benefits of this pattern of housing development are not assessed here, but the nature of the pattern is documented rigorously for the first time.

Summary and Conclusions

This article presents empirical results for the spatial patterns of real estate developments completed in metropolitan Chicago during the years 1990 to 1996. The industrial, commercial, and residential sectors are studied separately. The data on these real estate developments were provided by the Northeastern Illinois Planning Commission.

The results for industrial developments show that they are few in number and that they are more likely to occur at locations nearer to downtown Chicago or O'Hare Airport. Developments are attracted to highway interchanges but not to suburban employment centers. Commercial developments are far more numerous and are more likely to locate near O'Hare Airport, a highway interchange, or a suburban employment center, but distance to downtown Chicago has no effect. Holding other factors constant, both types of development are attracted to locations with more land devoted to agriculture.

Residential developments are more likely to occur at locations nearer to downtown Chicago and O'Hare Airport, but locations with proximity to commuter rail stations, highway interchanges, and suburban employment centers did not attract housing over this period. As with industrial and commercial development, a greater amount of land in agricultural use is associated with a higher probability of residential development. Furthermore, the size of the residential development (measured as number of housing units) increases with distance to downtown and commuter rail stations and decreases with distance to O'Hare Airport. This seemingly rather scattered pattern of residential development calls for further investigation.

Appendix:
Modeling the Allocation of New Developments to Sites

The basic modeling question of this analysis concerns the discrete choice of location for new real estate developments, given the characteristics of sites. Urban economic models of discrete choice of intraurban residential location were developed by Quigley (1976), Anas (1982), and Ellickson (1981). Lee (1982) adapted Ellickson's model to the study of location choice by firms in Bogota. A more recent use of the Lee (1982) model by Shukla and Waddell (1991) examines firm location choice in Dallas-Fort Worth. Carlton (1983) developed a similar model to study intermetropolitan area location decisions by establishments. Rosenthal and Helsley (1994) and Munneke (1996) follow a similar approach to ours to analyze the redevelopment decision, but their emphasis is different because redevelopment is primarily an inner-city phenomenon.

In our case, firms develop and sell real estate of a particular type—industrial, commercial, or residential. The firms must decide both the location and the size of the developments. These decisions result in certain locations being chosen for development and, given that a location is chosen, in the amount of development at that location. In essence, we study the propensity of a location to attract development (above a threshold size as defined in the data). Locations are identified as quarter sections. A relatively small time period, 1990–1996, is represented in our data set. Market conditions did not change dramatically across the Chicago region during this period. With each site experiencing nearly the same change in economic conditions, the probability of development depends on relative bid rents and a site's idiosyncratic characteristics rather than on changes in the economic environment.

The analysis is complicated by two features of our data set. First, only a small minority of the quarter sections have any new development. Second, some quarter sections have more than one development, sometimes of different types. Standard discrete choice models such as Lee's do not apply directly when having a commercial development on a site does not preclude having a residential or industrial development. More complex models that account for multiple developments are problematic when only a small percentage of sites have any development.

We choose instead to model each development type separately, using probit models. The current land value at site s is a function of standard explanatory variables such as distance to highway interchanges:

$$V_{0s} = \beta_0' X_s + u_{0s} \qquad [1]$$

where V_{0s} is the existing land value at the site, X is the vector of explanatory variables, and u_0 is an error term. The land value for alternative use i follows a similar form:

$$V_{is} = \beta_i' X_s + u_{is} \qquad [2]$$

where i denotes industrial, commercial, or residential use. Development is more likely to occur as V_{is} rises relative to V_{0s}. If the error terms are normally distributed, the probability of observing development in use i is simply

$$\Phi\left(\frac{(\beta_i - \beta_0)' X_s}{\sigma_i}\right) \qquad [3]$$

where Φ denotes the normal cumulative density function and $\sigma_i^2 = var\ (u_{is} - u_{0s})$. This last expression defines a standard probit model, where the dependent variable is the probability that a location (i.e., a quarter section) attracted development of a particular type i.

The probit model follows from our assumption of only two (current and an alternative) of an enormous number of potential land uses. Our data set permits us to distinguish between four types of new developments (industrial, commercial, residential, and "other"), and nineteen varieties of existing land uses. In principle, we could allow β_0 to vary by the existing land use, and the choice of new development category could be handled by multinomial logit or probit. We rejected these approaches because of data limitations. We did not allow β_0 to vary with the existing land use because our experiments produced an unacceptably large number of insignificant coefficients. Only 7.2 percent of the observations in our data set have any new developments. When the categories are split further by development type and existing land use, the number of observations within any category is very small. Multinomial logit is inappropriate because the errors are almost certainly correlated across development category. Probit models can be estimated for multiple regimes, but the estimates will be imprecise when the number of observations is small within any category. Despite a small geographic unit, our data are necessarily aggregated in that some observations have more than one development and sometimes more than one type of development. An explicit model of the number of units developed and the type of development would be very inefficient in a data set dominated by zeros for the dependent variable. Our approach is a compromise between potential bias caused by using simple estimation procedures and the imprecision associated with applying complicated procedures to less than ideal data.

In addition to location choice, the real estate development data include a measure of output for those developments that were actually completed. The output measure for the industrial and commercial sectors is square feet of floor space, and the number of housing units is recorded for residential developments. The production function for real estate of type i is

$$Q_i = f_i(L, K; X_s) \qquad [4]$$

where Q is output, L is land, K is capital, and X_s is the vector of site characteristics. Given output price, $P_i(X_s)$, the rental rate on capital, P_k, and land rent, $R(X_s)$, the optimal input choices for K and L generate the following supply function for a firm of type i that chooses location s:

$$Q_{is} = g_i(P_i(X_s), P_k, R(X_s), X_s) + \varepsilon_{is} \qquad [5]$$

where ε_{is} is another error term.

Given that P_k is constant while output prices and land rents are determined by X_s, this last equation reduces to an equation that says that output is a function of site characteristics and a random error:

$$Q_{is} = h_i(X_s) + \varepsilon_{is} \qquad [6]$$

The error terms in equations [2] and [6] are likely to be correlated because they control for unobserved site characteristics. The possibility of correlation between the errors means that OLS estimates of equation [6] must be corrected for selection bias. We use a modified version of the Heckman (1976) two-stage estimation procedure. The first step is to estimate the probit model for the probability that any development took place, and the implied inverse Mills ratio is used as an additional explanatory variable in the second-stage OLS estimates for output.[9] We use a modified version of the Heckman method in the sense that the output measure does not exist for a few sites with development. All sites are used in the estimation of the probit model, but only sites with output reported are used in the estimation of equation [6]. We do not attempt to control for spatial autocorrelation because only a small number of observations are available for estimating equation [6] and existing spatial models rely heavily on asymptotic results. In small samples or in probit models with few unit values for the dependent variable, attempts to correct for autocorrelation can increase the mean squared error of the estimates.

Notes

1. For example, see Giuliano and Small (1991), Gordon et al. (1986), Heikkila et al. (1989), McDonald and Prather (1994), McMillen and McDonald (1998a; 1998b; 1998c), and Sivitanidou (1996; 1997).

2. According to data from the Northeastern Illinois Planning Commission, the city of Chicago's population grew by 0.65 percent between 1990 and 1998 (reversing forty years of decline), and the rest of Cook County grew by 2.77 percent. Nearby DuPage and Lake Counties grew by 11.22 percent and 14.66 percent, respectively, whereas the more distant counties of Kane, McHenry, and Will had growth rates of 18.86 percent, 23.95 percent, and 22.19 percent over this period.

3. "Nearby" is defined as within 1.5 miles rather than as contiguity because quarter sections are small, thereby creating pockets of low employment in areas with high density otherwise.

4. All distances are measured from the center of the quarter section.

5. This specification follows our earlier work (McMillen and McDonald (1998a). Distance to the nearest subcenter is measured from the midpoint of the quarter section with the largest employment level among the sites included in the subcenter. Using inverses reduces multicollinearity and is more suitable than levels for variables that have localized effects. In contrast, distance to the central business district (CBD) is more appropriately entered in level form because it affects the entire urban area.

6. These variables were obtained from NIPC.

7. The complete set of land uses includes residential, manufacturing, transportation, communications, utilities, and wholesale, railroad rights of way, airports, streets,

private service, institutional service, military, cemeteries, entertainment, public buildings, parks and open space, mining, warehouses, hotels, parking lots, agriculture, and water.

8. Data presented in McMillen and McDonald (1998a) show that twelve of the twenty employment subcenters consist of at least 30 percent manufacturing employment (and several have much more).

9. The inverse Mills ratio is $\phi(\gamma_i'X_s)/\Phi(Y_i'X_s)$, where $Y_i = (\beta_i - \beta_0)/\sigma_i$. The standard errors are corrected for heteroskedasticity using a White (1980) covariance matrix estimate. The correlation between the equation [2] and [6] errors (?) and the standard error of e_i are estimated using the procedures outlined in Greene (1997, 980).

References

Anas, A. 1982. *Residential Location Markets and Urban Transportation*. New York: Academic Press.

Carlton, D. 1983. The Location and Employment Choices of New Firms: An Economic Model With Discrete and Continuous Endogenous Variables. *Review of Economics and Statistics* 65: 440–460.

Ellickson, B. 1981. An Alternative Test of the Hedonic Theory of Housing Markets. *Journal of Urban Economics* 9: 56–79.

Giuliano, G., and K. Small. 1991. Subcenters in the Los Angeles Region. *Regional Science and Urban Economics* 21: 162–182.

Gordon, P., H.W. Richardson, and H.L. Wong. 1986. The Distribution of Population and Employment in a Polycentric City: The Case of Los Angeles. *Environment and Planning A* 18: 161–173.

Greene, W.H. 1997. *Econometric Analysis*. Upper Saddle River, NJ: Prentice-Hall.

Heckman, J. 1976. The Common Structure of Statistical Models of Truncation, Sample Selection and Limited Dependent Variables and a Simple Estimator for Such Models. *Annals of Economic and Social Measurement* 5: 475–492.

Heikkila, E., P. Gordon, J.I. Kim, R.B. Peiser, H.W. Richardson, and D. Dale-Johnson. 1989. What Happened to the CBD-Distance Gradient? Land Values in a Policentric City. *Environment and Planning* A 21: 221–232.

Lee, K. 1982. A Model of Intraurban Employment Location: An Application to Bogota, Colombia. *Journal of Urban Economics* 12: 263–279.

McDonald, J.F. 1987. The Identification of Urban Employment Subcenters. *Journal of Urban Economics* 21: 242–258.

———. 1993. Local Property Tax Differences and Business Real Estate Values. *Journal of Real Estate Finance and Economics* 6: 277–287.

McDonald, J.F., and P.J. Prather. 1994. Suburban Employment Centers: The Case of Chicago. *Urban Studies* 31: 201–218.

McMillen, D.P., and J.F. McDonald. 1998a. Suburban Subcenters and Employment Density in Metropolitan Chicago. *Journal of Urban Economics* 43: 157–180.

———. 1998b. Population Density in Suburban Chicago: A Bid-Rent Approach. *Urban Studies* 35: 1119–1130.

———. 1998c. A Nonparametric Analysis of Employment Density in a Polycentric City. *Journal of Regional Science* 37: 591–612.

Munneke, H.J. 1996. Redevelopment Decisions for Commercial and Industrial Properties. *Journal of Urban Economics* 39: 229–253.

Quigley, J. 1976. Housing Demand in the Short Run: An Analysis of Polychotomous Choice. *Explorations in Economic Research* 3: 76–102.

Rosenthal, S.R., and R.W. Helsley. 1994. Redevelopment and the Urban Land Price Gradient. *Journal of Urban Economics* 35: 182–200.

Shukla, V., and P. Waddell. 1991. Firm Location and Land Use in Discrete Urban Space: A Study of the Spatial Structure of Dallas-Fort Worth. *Regional Science and Urban Economics* 21: 225–253.

Sivitanidou, R. 1996. Do Office-Commercial Firms Value Access to Service Employment Centers? A Hedonic Analysis Within Polycentric Los Angeles. *Journal of Urban Economics* 40: 125–149.

———. 1997. Are Center Access Advantages Weakening? The Case of Office-Commercial Markets. *Journal of Urban Economics* 42: 79–97.

White, H. 1980. A Heteroskedasticity-Consistent Covariance Matrix Estimator and a Direct Test for Heteroskedasticity. *Econometrica* 48: 817–838.

10

Daniel Felsenstein

High Technology Employment Concentration and Urban Sprawl in the Chicago Metropolitan Area

Introduction

High technology activity is popularly associated with the extensive use of land. Technology-based firms are often located in parklike settings in edge-city type environments. The high-income workers in these firms are likely to favor low-density, outer suburban living for their housing preferences. Their lifestyles are heavily automobile-dependent and oriented to consumption patterns that themselves are land-extensive, such as shopping malls, suburban entertainment, and leisure spaces. While this caricature may be exaggerated, it does suggest a relationship between high technology agglomeration and the process of urban expansion.

This relationship has received surprisingly little attention. Despite the fact that many high technology concentrations develop at the outer perimeter of the metropolitan area, there have been no attempts to estimate the impact of this location pattern on suburban land consumption. But these concentrations create considerable pressure on real estate markets at the urban fringe, resulting in the redesignation of land uses, the incorporation of unincorporated land, annexations, and the like. In combination with the suburban housing choices of their labor force, high technology firm clusters are likely to impact significantly on urban deconcentration.

This chapter attempts to forge the link between high technology and sprawl using the Chicago metropolitan area as context. It offers empirical estimates of how workplace concentrations of high technology activity translate into metropolitan sprawl based on the outward extension of residential communities. We examine the two existing outer suburban high technology employment concentrations that have emerged in the Chicago metropolitan area. The first is located alongside the I-88 highway in DuPage County (I-88) and encompasses some 36,000 workers in over 500 firms, while the second relates to the concentration astride the Edens Expressway in the south of Lake County (I-94) with over 10,000 employees in 120 establishments.

While measurements of the loss of open space associated with the spread of high technology employment can address only one aspect of the "costs of sprawl" debate, it is surprising that no empirical efforts have hitherto been undertaken. Possibly this state of affairs simply reflects the methodological problem of making the connection between high technology growth—a place-of-work phenomenon—and metropolitan sprawl—a place-of-residence phenomenon. The approach adopted here starts from a given location pattern of suburban high technology firms, and proceeds to investigate not only the direct land consumption of those businesses but also the additional suburban land consumed by the residential, commercial, and public activities demanded by those firms' high tech workers.

Employment Deconcentration and High Technology Location in the Chicago Metropolitan Area

The Chicago metropolitan area includes a labor market of 2.8 million places of employment located within thirty-five miles of the city center. Of these jobs, nearly 19 percent are located within a three-mile radius of the CBD, 36 percent within a ten-mile band and 63 percent outside the ten-mile cut-off. This is a level of employment deconcentration close to that of an archetypal sprawl city such as Los Angeles (Glaeser and Kahn 2001). While the Chicago metropolitan area is considered a high-density urban area by virtue of the large volume of population it contains, the population growth in the metropolitan area over the period from 1982 to 1997 fell far behind the rate at which urbanized land was added to the metropolitan area. Thus, while population grew by 9.6 percent over the above period, the change registered in urban land over that same period was 25.5 percent. In fact, metropolitan Chicago registered a reduction in density over the period from 1982 to 1997 of nearly 13 percent (Fulton et al. 2001). During the same period the Chicago metropolitan landscape has become increasingly polycentric. The classic monocentric model of the metropolitan area has become inadequate for understanding metropolitan growth as employment subcenters and edge cities become major forces for deconcentration (McMillen and McDonald 1998).

Alongside these changes in the urban morphology of the metropolitan area an additional shift has taken place relating to employment composition. Traditionally, Chicago has not been identified as a prominent high tech center. Commenting on the seeming dearth of activity in the metropolitan area in the mid-1980s, Markusen and McCurdy (1989) ostensibly claimed that Chicago had missed the high tech boat. Despite an impressive infrastructure for innovation, they attributed this lack of high tech prominence to the absence of key military installations in the Chicago area and the disinterest in military markets shown by commercial high tech firms.

Indexes of technological potential, however, reveal a different picture. In the early 1990s Chicago was ranked between fourth and sixth nationally with respect to university R&D funding, nationally ranked science and engineering programs, and bachelor's degrees in science and engineering (Beeson and Montgomery 1993). In terms of industrial research laboratories, Cook County was ranked second in the nation at the end of the 1980s with 375 laboratories, behind Los Angeles County (with 481) but ahead of Middlesex County, Massachusetts (with 367) (Appold 1991). An analysis of employment in high technology industries in all major U.S. metropolitan areas, over the period from 1989 to 1991 ranked Chicago in fourth place overall although only in twenty-third place in terms of growth rate over the same period (Acs and Ndikumwami 1998). Disaggregating the employment change over this time period shows that the metropolitan area gained employment due to a fortuitous "mix" of high technology sectors but lost high technology employment due to problems of competitiveness with respect to other metro areas. On a sectoral basis, the industries contributing to Chicago's strength were information and technology services and high tech research. Conversely, those high technology sectors in which Chicago was failing to compete were principally the biotechnology and biomedical industry and the machinery and instruments sectors.

Recent rankings of high tech centers consistently put Chicago in the top ten locations nationwide across a whole range of indicators. This reflects the resurgence of the metropolitan economy over the 1990s—a period in which high tech employment grew by nearly 9 percent. Estimates of the absolute number of high tech workers in the metropolitan area are a function of the definitions adopted and can range from 250,000 to 500,000 workers (Kotkin and DeVol 2001; Markusen et al. 2001). As a "technology pole" (a composite variable measuring high tech employment and output concentration), the Chicago metropolitan statistical area (MSA) ranks eighth in the country. In terms of output, if the Chicago economy were a national economy, it would rank twentieth worldwide, with over 11 percent of this accredited to high tech production. Using Internet-based indicators to reflect Chicago's ranking reveals a similar picture. Chicago ranks in fifth place nationally with respect to gross volume of domain names and eighth place in terms of relative Internet specialization (Table 10.1).

These indicators illustrate the developed infrastructure around which high technology agglomeration coalesced. The high tech employment concentrations near I-88 and I-94 are a development of the 1990s and heavily grounded in private sector investment in nonmilitary sectors, fueled by public sector infrastructure investment. The absence of any real defense influence is also noticeable. Even the existence of federal installations such as the Fermi National Accelerator Laboratory and the Argonne National Laboratory cannot be considered "seedbed" factors that have contributed to the growth of the I-88 cluster. Significantly, of the thirteen defense firms awarded prime contracts of over $10 million in the mid-1980s and considered as potential "seedbed" germinators by Markusen and McCurdy (1989), only one is located in Chicago's present high technology concentrations. In the final analysis, the decline in defense contracting and the ability of the Chicago economy to weather defense cuts (Hall, Persky, and Wiewel 1990) probably explain why the metropolitan area never took the military route to high technology development.

Recent development along the I-88 tollway is a result of mutually complementary public and market forces. Federal infrastructure investments in the area at the end of the 1960s (the East-West tollway, the Lake Michigan water project, and the Fermi National Accelerator Laboratory) combined with market forces such as demand for residential development (the birth of Oak Brook as a municipality occurred at the same time) to produce an initial round of residential development alongside I-88. These early events provided the impetus for a new round of office and commercial development and a surge in employment growth. DuPage County added over 77,000 jobs between 1991 and 1996. The

Table 10.1

High Technology Indicators for Metropolitan Areas

High tech concentration[1]	Technology pole[2]	GMP ($bn)[3]	World ranking[4]	High tech output ($bn)[5]	High tech output as share GMP[5]	% U.S. domain names[6]	Domain name specialization[7]
San Jose	23.69	75.4	64	43.5	57.8	2.2	3.71
Dallas	7.06	143.2	37	27.4	19.1	—	—
Los Angeles	6.91	333.9	18	43.3	13.1	7.3	2.21
Boston	6.31	215.1	27	44.4	20.6	2.5	1.77
Seattle	5.14	102.5	48	24.3	23.7	1.9	1.79
Washington, D.C.	5.08	194.6	28	39.2	20.2	3.8	2.06
Albuquerque	4.98	23.1	—	5.2	22.6	—	—
Chicago	3.75	303.5	20	34.6	11.4	3.3	1.25
New York	2.67	391.5	14	22.1	5.6	6.2	1.96
Atlanta	3.46	146.4	36	14.7	10.0	2.0	1.33

Notes:
[1] Based on MSA.
[2] Composite score based on national share and local concentration of employment and high tech output; see DeVol (1999).
[3] *Source:* U.S. Conference of Mayors (2000a). GMP = Gross metropolitan production. $bn = dollars per billion
[4] Ranking in world's top 100 economies. *Source:* U.S. Conference of Mayors (2000a).
[5] *Source:* U.S. Conference of Mayors (2000b).
[6] *Source:* Zook (2001).
[7] Concentration measure—value greater than 1.0 indicates concentration above national average. *Source:* Zook (2001).

main outcome of this history can be seen in the corridor development along I-88, comprising office, R&D, corporate head offices, and commercial land use. The conscious planning decision to develop the area as the "Illinois R&D corridor" is simply an outgrowth of these events.

Most high technology firms along the corridor have come there through corporate relocation decisions based on the strength and diversified nature of Chicago's employment pool (e.g., Amoco came from Iowa, Lucent [Bell Labs] from New Jersey), or through relocations from the central city in search of more favorable tax climates. Indigenous small-firm growth has not really been a factor. While some large firms (e.g., Lucent Technologies) have spun off new ventures, existing federal facilities have not been prominent in promoting new firms. Indeed, these facilities have engaged in only limited commercial partnering.

The present round of industrial office and commercial development along I-88 has stimulated new residential development to accommodate the growing number of high technology employees. Thus the different forms of land absorption (commercial, industrial, residential, etc.) reinforce each other with lags between phases of development. Together these developments have put considerable pressure on outer suburban land uses.

The corridor's marked radial form has been facilitated by advances in the provision of information technology (IT) infrastructure (ISDN, fiber optic cables, and digital exchanges) that are well suited to development along radial lines such as I-88 (Garcia and Yukawa 1998). While the direction of causality is not clear (IT as causing dispersal or dispersal resulting in increased demand for IT), these developments most certainly increase the pressure on suburban land uses along the corridor.

A similar picture of self-reinforcing growth has developed in the southern portion of Lake County astride Route I-94 and the Edens Expressway. While the extent of the phenomenon is more limited and the response in Lake County has been less well coordinated than in DuPage County, the basic pattern of demand for nonresidential space reinforcing the demand for residential space in a circular fashion is similar to that described for DuPage County. The demand generated by relocating firms from the city of Chicago in search of lower taxes has combined with the suburban residential preferences of the skilled labor they employ. In addition, southern Lake County is a popular bedroom area for high wage commuters who work in the central city and the inner suburbs. The county as a whole acts as a net "exporter" of workers with nearly 30,000 more employees leaving the county than entering on a daily basis. At least in this area, residential sprawl seems to have led nonresidential development.

While the development alongside I-88 and the I-94 may be the most concentrated and visible expressions of high technology development in the metropolitan area, the office and research parks astride many of the outer suburban freeways (e.g., in the Schaumburg and O'Hare areas) are representative of the growth of outer suburban employment subcenters that are home to a diffuse array of high technology companies. A recent report estimates over 340,000 employees in "technology-based companies" in metropolitan Chicago, producing 11.6 percent of gross state product (Widmayer and Greenberg 1998). Seventy-five percent of these high tech companies are located in the six-county metropolitan area and 56 percent in Cook County.

As in the past, when Chicago emerged as a hub in national rail, road, and air transportation systems, the metropolitan area seems to be playing a pivotal role with respect to emerging digital infrastructure networks. Analyses of the internet "backbone" networks and highways consistently show Chicago as occupying a strategic position. The metropolitan area acts as the major hub for routing Internet-based traffic between the East Coast (Washington, DC) and West Coast (San Francisco) nodes (Moss and Townsend 1998). These three areas are emerging as the top tier in a new metropolitan hierarchy based on bandwidth and interconnectivity, rather than population size or density. In this hierarchy, the second tier is occupied by New York and Los Angeles at the extremes of the continent with Atlanta and Dallas operating as the traffic routing hubs, akin to Chicago. Evidence so far seems to imply that while the metropolitan hierarchy may undergo some reorganization, the strong trend toward expansion in the Chicago area will continue. As in the past, the provision of infrastructure enables diffusion and dispersal as long as accessibility to major highways is unimpaired. All that seems to have changed is the nature of these highways.

Methodology

The analytic framework used in this study is presented graphically in Figure 10.1. (A more formal treatment of our methodology is provided in the chapter appendix). Essentially, we employ an accounting-type system that allocates workers in the two high tech employment concentrations to residential locations and then estimates land consumption arising from their

Figure 10.1 **Analytic Framework for Estimating the Suburban Sprawl Impacts Arising from High Technology Employment Agglomeration**

Stage 1 Estimate employment effects (place of work impacts)
         Direct and indirect
         By geographic area
         By major industries

Stage 2 Estimate population change (place of residence impacts)
         Allocate workers to place of residence on basis of census proportions
         Stratify by income group

Stage 3 Estimate land consumption in outer suburbs
         Nonresidential land consumption (based on land consumption constants for each industry)
         Residential land consumption (based on census-derived housing choice by income group)
         Associated public land uses (roads, parks)

places of work, residence, and consumption. This approach draws heavily on that used by Persky and Wiewel (2000) who looked at the sprawl-inducing consequences arising from the relocation of an individual firm. In this analysis we depart from their approach in trying to simulate the impacts of employment deconcentration at the level of the industry or cluster.

More specifically, we adopt a three-stage approach for estimating sprawl effects. Initially, we estimate the employment impacts associated with the two agglomerations of high technology activity. This involves counting not just the direct employment but also the indirect employment arising from intersectoral transactions and the induced employment arising from increased household demand (termed here collectively as the "indirect" effect). To do this we utilize a regional econometric model (the REMI model). This allows us to assess how a change in direct employment in the outer suburbs impacts both locally and in the wider metropolitan area. This REMI model (Treyz 1993) is external to the estimation method employed here. For our purposes it is used to generate indirect employment estimates that allow the continuation of the analysis. More specifically, it provides estimates of:

- the indirect employment generated by the high technology employment in the I-88 and I-94 clusters;
- the distribution of this indirect employment across industries;
- the geographic distribution of this indirect employment as between the local area and the rest of the metropolis.

The second stage involves translating the REMI-generated employment patterns into patterns of residential development. In order to do this, we need information on the commuting patterns of outer suburban workers. To this end we make extensive use of data from the public use microdata sample (PUMS) of the Census to distribute the employees of high technology firms and intermediate firms across income classes and then across residential locations. The key assumption here asserts that employees working in a subregion will pick residential locations similar to those picked by workers in the PUMS sample from the same income class and same workplace subregion. In this manner we translate employment change into population change.

The third stage is concerned with estimating land consumption in the outer suburbs. Census data are used to distribute workers of a given income class and residential area to three housing types characterized in terms of acreage (multifamily at 0.05 acres per unit, single detached at 0.25 acres per unit, and low-density single detached at 1.5 acres per unit). Nonresidential land consumption is derived from combining the industry-by-industry employment provided by the REMI simulation and estimates of acres/worker for each industry (0.05 acres per manufacturing worker, 0.2 acres per wholesale or retail worker, 0.02 acres per each worker in the finance, insurance, and real estate, services, and government sectors.) Finally, associated public land uses (road, parks etc.) are derived as a fixed proportion of the residential and nonresidential land.

High Technology Employment in the Corridors

In order to define "high technology," we adopted the core set of thirty industries identified by Acs and Ndikumwami (1998). These include the biomedical industries, information technology, aeronautics, high technology instruments, research services, and the energy and chemicals sectors. A first impression of Chicago area employment in these industries is provided by the employment service ES202 data (1997) for DuPage and Lake counties. In practice, twenty-two of them are represented in the two counties under investigation, with 48,800 employees for DuPage and 16,056 for Lake County (excluding suppressed values). These figures represent total countywide high technology employment. Our interest however is in the employment totals for the I-88 and I-94 concentrations only. In order to adjust these employment totals downward, we obtained establishment-level employment data.

Data relating to all firms located within a two-mile band north and south of Route I-88 stretching west to Aurora were obtained from the DuPage Planning Department. Using this data set allowed us to identify the size of the high tech employment concentration as 34,645 employees in close to 500 establishments. This represents 71 percent of the DuPage County total. This employment total includes the Fermi National Accelerator installation and the Argonne National Laboratory (4,200 employees) and some large establishments such as Lucent Technologies (10,200), Nicor Gas (2,696), Amoco Research Center (2,000), Nalco Chemicals (1,200), and Platinum Technology (1,000). In addition, this figure also includes various software companies such as Platinum Technology, Unisys, Computer Associates, and Hewlett Packard Research.

A similar establishment-level data source was obtained from the Lake County Economic Development Corporation. We identified the I-94 cluster as all high tech establishments located in the communities of Buffalo Grove, Deerfield, Highland Park, Lincolnshire, Highwood, Lake Forest, Lake Bluff, Riverwoods, and Woodridge. In this instance, the cluster accounts for 10,275 employees (64 percent of the Lake County total). This figure includes several large corporate entities such as Abbott Labs (4,100 employees), Baxter (3,760), Motorola, and Hewitt Associates.

Estimates of Suburban Land Consumption

Employment Effects

The estimations that follow are based on the analytical sequence outlined above (Figure 10.1). The geographic and sectoral distribution of direct and total employment are presented in Table 10.2. As noted earlier, the direct employment impact of the I-88 concentration is 34,645. Indirect and induced employment adds a further 23,558 employees locally, with total local employment attributable to the cluster totaling 58,203 and a local county employment multiplier of 1.68. The total metrowide employment impact of the initial 34,645 employees expands to 79,227.

HIGH TECH EMPLOYMENT CONCENTRATION AND URBAN SPRAWL 217

Table 10.2

Estimated Employment Effects (Direct and Indirect): I-88 and I-94 High Technology Agglomeration

	I-88	I-94
Direct employment[1]	34,645	10,275
Total employment[1]		
Construction	2,278	893
Manufacturing	14,632	8,964
Transportation, communication, and public utilities sector (TCPU)	1,213	248
Wholesale	2,126	672
Retail	5,392	1,613
Finance, insurance, and real estate (FIRE)	1,199	314
Service	30,910	4,193
Government	311	134
Other	142	92
Total	58,203	17,123
Employment created elsewhere in metropolitan area[2]	21,024	5,702

Notes:
[1] Employment created locally: for I-88 agglomeration in DuPage County, for I-94 agglomeration in Lake, McHenry, Will, and Kane counties.
[2] For I-88 agglomeration: City of Chicago, rest of Cook County, Lake, McHenry, Will, and Kane counties.
For I-94 agglomeration: city of Chicago, rest of Cook County, DuPage County.

In DuPage County the major employment impact of the I-88 agglomeration is felt in both the service and manufacturing sectors. In contrast, the I-94 employment cluster (10,275 direct jobs) expands to over 17,000 jobs locally when indirect employment is considered and to nearly 23,000 for the metrowide total. In sectoral terms, the I-94 cluster has a major impact on manufacturing in the outer suburbs (more than 8,900 direct and indirect jobs). This figure is more than twice as large as the total impact on service sector employment.

Place of Residence

Of the more than 79,000 employees generated directly and indirectly by the I-88 high technology corridor, our methodology suggests that 52,772 live in the outer suburbs, with the rest divided between the inner suburbs (16,726) and the city itself (9,725).[1] In the case of I-94, as for the I-88 cluster, the vast majority of all workers generated by the high tech-

Table 10.3

Distribution of Workers by Place of Residence and Income Group

Place of residence	I-88	I-94
Outer suburbs		
High income	12,657	3,459
Med. income	30,726	9,061
Low income	9,389	2,580
Total	52,772	15,100
Inner suburbs		
High income	4,186	1,195
Med. income	9,861	2,865
Low income	2,679	707
Total	16,726	4,767
Chicago		
High income	1,424	405
Med. income	5,062	1,557
Low income	3,239	969
Total	9,725	2,931

nology concentration reside in the outer suburbs (67 percent) with 21 percent living in the inner suburbs and the remaining 12 percent in the city of Chicago. However, due to the much smaller numbers involved, the pressures on metropolitan expansion are likely to be considerably less.

We now need to estimate the income levels of the outer suburbanites whose employment is directly or indirectly generated by the I-88 and I-94 clusters. This step is crucial if we are to accurately specify their likely housing choice. Here the focus is on outer suburbanites because only their residential choices impact land absorption. The outer suburban residents from both clusters total nearly 68,000 workers. The distributions for both clusters by income category are presented in Table 10.3. Here we find a high proportion of these outer suburban residents (82 percent) fall into the high- and middle-income categories. This group's housing choices and particularly their taste for low density development exert the greatest pressures on metropolitan expansion.

Estimating Land Consumption in the Outer Suburbs

As suggested above, the consumption of land in the outer suburbs resulting from the I-88 and I-94 employment agglomerations can be divided into three categories:

- nonresidential land, that is, the outer suburban open space directly absorbed by the construction of greenfield facilities in the outer suburbs and the indirect consumption of land in commercial and other related activities that are induced by this direct activity;
- residential land consumed through the housing choices of the workers in the I-88 and I-94 clusters;
- associated land use, which includes the ancillary land consumed through servicing the residential and nonresidential land uses (parks, roads, public facilties, etc.).

In the case of nonresidential land, the REMI-generated employment estimates (direct and indirect) are the base for estimating the amount of land absorbed. Using fixed land-to-worker values for each industry (see methodology), we arrive at estimates of land absorption by industry. These results appear in Table 10.4. Together, the I-88 and I-94 agglomerations generate nonresidential land use requiring the absorption of over 4,500 acres of open space at the metropolitan fringe. Retailing activity accounts for a much larger proportion of nonresidential land in the case of I-88 than it does in the case of I-94. This probably reflects the magnitude of the residential development spawned by the I-88 concentration.

We know that residential land absorption in the outer suburbs is related to income characteristics. In addition, land is generally consumed by household units and not by individual residents. Here we take the estimates of residents in the outer suburbs attributable to the I-88 and I-94 clusters and convert these figures into households. Using a ratio of workers to households that implies a new household formation for (roughly) every two workers, we convert total residents into total households (Table 10.4). However, as household choice is determined by income group, total households are stratified by each of these variables. The three income groups are converted into housing groups by applying fixed parameter values of acres consumed for each income group as noted above.

As can be seen from Table 10.4, the I-88 and I-94 clusters together account for a loss of about 11,000 acres of open space to residential development in the outer suburbs. The majority of this (55–56 percent) is due to the housing preferences of middle-income groups: low-density single-family residences that are assumed to consume on average 0.25 acres each. The high-income groups whose housing choice is for spacious family dwellings occupying 1.5 acres each, are expected to account for a further 32 percent of all land absorption in the outer suburbs

Table 10.4

Estimates of Residential and Nonresidential Land Consumption in the Outer Suburbs

Land consumption	I-88	I-94
Nonresidential[1]		
Construction	0	0
Manufacturing	764	456
Transportation, communication, and public utilities (TCPU)	136	30
Wholesale	467	165
Retail	1,375	374
Finance, insurance, and real estate (FIRE)	31	8
Services	647	94
Government	9	3
Other	<u>6</u>	<u>2</u>
Total	3,435	1,132
Residential		
High income	2,741	751
Med. income	4,719	1,365
Low income	<u>1,048</u>	<u>292</u>
Total	8,508	2,408

Note: [1] Based on direct and indirect employment.

(3,500 acres). Low-income groups are expected to account for the remaining 13 percent (1,300 acres) comprising multifamily housing units occupying 0.05 acres each on average. Finally, associated public land uses (roads, sidewalks, public parking, public open spaces such as parks, and other land extensive public facilities) are estimated as a fixed proportion of the residential and nonresidential land consumption estimates. They are calculated as one third of all developed land (Persky and Wiewel 2000) and these estimates appear in Table 10.5.

A Comparison with Alternative Scenarios

Any simulation exercise is not complete without some attempt at assessing what would have happened in an alternative state-of-the-world. In our context it is not simply enough to estimate suburban land consumption induced by the two high tech clusters. We really need to know what would have happened had these high tech agglomerations developed at some other (nonsuburban) location. Would this scenario have induced less sprawl and, if so, by what magnitude? To answer this question, we set up two alternative situations. Using the same method as outlined above, we estimate the suburban land consumption consequences of two hypothetical cases. The first has the I-88 and I-94 employment clusters developing in the city of Chicago and the second posits their developing in the inner suburbs.

Table 10.5 presents the results of this comparison plus a summary account of the total land consumption estimates of the real-world clusters along I-88 and I-94. Taken together, the direct employees at the two high tech concentrations (nearly 48,000 workers) expand to nearly 83,000 when indirect employment is included. Of these, some 68,000 are residents of the outer suburbs, representing over 35,000 households. The land consumption impacts of these households translate into the absorption of over 23,000 acres of outer suburban open space.

The two alternative scenarios show much more modest impacts on suburban sprawl amounting to land consumption in the vicinity of 6–8,000 acres, depending on the case. To put these magnitudes in perspective, we can note that the O'Hare International Airport complex occupies an area of 7,700 acres, the Fermi National Accelerator Laboratory spans 6,800 acres, and the Argonne National Laboratory 1,700 acres. In other words, the difference between the existing situation and a hypothetical alternative is a savings in outer suburban land equal to nearly two times the area of O'Hare Airport.

We should also note that much of the suburban sprawl impact induced under the alternative scenarios is a result of the relatively inflexible housing behavior of the middle- and high-income groups when faced with different workplace scenarios. Our scenario estimates indicate that suburban living is very attractive to these income classes irrespective of place of work. If these high technology clusters were to relocate to the city of Chicago, nearly 10,000 households would still choose to live in the outer suburbs, consuming over 6,000 acres of open space. Under the scenario of high tech in the inner suburbs, over 13,500 households would still be living in the outer suburbs and would be transforming over 8,000 acres of open land into suburban use.

The ratio of land consumption per household reflects the space requirements of the different income groups. In the present case of I-88 and I-94, open space consumption per household in the outer suburbs is 0.65 and 0.68 acres, respectively. This reflects the absolute size of the

Table 10.5

Summary of Sprawl Effects of I-88 and I-94 Agglomerations Versus Two Alternative Scenarios

Impacts on outer suburbs	I-88	I-94	Total (I-88 + I-94)	Alternative scenarios Chicago	Alternative scenarios Inner suburbs
Total employees	64,327	18,466	82,793	11,400	2,574
Total residents	52,778	15,100	67,878	18,878	6,148
Total households	27,633	7,906	35,539	9,884	3,690
Nonresidential land consumption (acres)	3,437	1,133	4,570	959	1,059
Residential land consumption (acres)	8,509	2,438	10,947	3,168	4,346
Associated public land uses (acres)	5,970	1,790	7,760	2,060	2,710
Total land consumption in outer suburbs (acres)	17,913	5,361	23,277	6,157	8,115

high- and middle-income earners amongst the labor force employed (directly and indirectly) in high technology production in the outer suburbs. Under the scenario of high tech clusters in the city of Chicago, this ratio drops to 0.63 acres per household in the outer suburbs. While the absolute number of the outer suburban households falls considerably in this case, the persistence of the high- and middle-bracket earners in choosing outer suburban residences still accounts for this relatively high ratio. The scenario of high technology in the inner suburbs results in the lowest acreage per household ratio in the outer suburbs, 0.59. This is because of the relative size of the low- and middle-income groups expected to be residing in the outer suburbs. Employment in the inner suburbs allows the lower income groups the opportunity of outer suburban residence to a greater extent than in the case of employment in the city. Their relatively larger presence in the outer suburbs combined with their less demanding space requirements, serves to moderate the size of the acreage per household ratio.

Conclusions and Implications

It should be noted that the foregoing analysis presents only a partial picture of metropolitan sprawl. We have looked at only one cost (land consumption) to the exclusion of others such as congestion, pollution, and traffic accidents generated by commuters whose choose an outer suburban residence and a workplace in the inner suburbs or city. Such factors need to be incorporated in a full-blown benefit-cost test of metropolitan sprawl, a test well beyond the scope of this study. Nevertheless, the estimates in this chapter suggest that the ongoing development of high technology agglomerations in the outer suburbs has put pressure on open space in the metropolitan area, considerably more pressure than would have been exerted by similar developments in the central city or the inner suburbs. In terms of pure acreage, this theoretical savings amounts to over two times the area of the O'Hare Airport complex.

Perhaps even more significant is the fact that the residential behavior of high-income employees in high technology industries means pressure on the outer suburban land, whatever the scenario. Even in the hypothetical scenarios of high technology clusters in the city of Chicago or inner suburbs, the estimated impact on the outer suburbs arising from the housing choices and ancillary land requirements of the highest income groups, results in land consumption equivalent in magnitude to the land area occupied by O'Hare Airport. If public policies could encourage greater development in the central city or inner suburbs, it would primarily impact the residential choices of low-income workers.

Aside from the direct impacts on open land consumption, a further implication arising from high technology-induced suburban sprawl relates to the interjurisdictional competition over high technology facilities. The competitive interjurisdictional environment and the absence of any regional strategy means that a suburban locality attracting high technology employment is likely to impose heavy costs in terms of traffic-related externalities (congestion, etc.) on all neighboring localities. This is especially the case in the I-94 area where over 10 percent of all land expansion for industrial and commercial purposes is in unincorporated areas. In many of these areas infrastructure provision is simply insufficient to deal with sprawl-related growth. The many small jurisdictions vying for high technology companies impose an efficiency loss on all neighboring localities: for example, one locality attracting a major employer disrupts access to major routeways (I-94) for all the others. This points to the need for regional cooperation to deal with some of the external effects of suburban sprawl. However, while limited regional coordination may serve to mitigate some of these excesses, it is still only a very partial approach to the distribution of the unpriced costs imposed by sprawl.

Appendix:
Method of Analysis for Estimating Outer Suburban Land Consumption Arising from Employment Deconcentration

We present a sequence of steps for converting place-of-work estimates into place-of-residence characteristics. From the REMI employment estimates we can estimate the number of workers (direct and indirect) by major industry, in the outer suburbs, as follows:

$$N_{kw} \qquad [1]$$

where, N_{kw} equals the number of workers at place of work w ($w = 1 \ldots 3$) and industry k ($k = 1 \ldots 9$).

To convert these places-of-work estimates into place-of-residence estimates, we use proportions drawn from the Census relating to place of residence of workers by industry and income group. We assume the distribution of workers resulting from our employment estimates follows that of the Census. Jobs are distributed across 27 potential categories (3 places of work multiplied by 3 places of residence multiplied by 3 income groups). Industry affiliation serves as the link in converting the place-of-work distribution into a place-of-residence distribution. This conversion is expressed as:

$$N_{kw} \times P_{kw}(ry) = N_w(ry) \qquad [2]$$

where $P_{kw}(ry)$ is the proportion of workers in industry k at place of work w, who live in place of residence r ($r = 1 \ldots 3$) and are in income group y ($y = 1 \ldots 3$). Multiplying this proportion by the number of workers in industry k and place of work w yields $N_w(ry)$, that is, the number of workers who work in w and live in r.

Nonresidential land consumption (NRES) is represented by the number of workers in each industry in the outer suburbs multiplied by the proportion of land consumption in acres, c, for each industry k (P_{kc}). This is expressed as:

$$N_{kw} \times P_{kc} = \text{NRES}_c \qquad [3]$$

In the outer suburbs, and for the purpose of land consumption, all household formation is assumed to be new: that is, place of residence in the outer suburbs requires new land consumption via new building and more sprawl or pressures on the land market through housing turnover and filtering. A new household is assumed to form for roughly every two new residents in the outer suburbs.

New household formation (NH) is derived from place of residence, such that:

$$NH = N_w(ry) \times .53 \qquad [4]$$

Residential land consumption (RES) is based on new household formation. Again taking those households residing in the outer suburbs and multiplying them by census-derived proportions for residential land consumption yields residential land consumption for each case. The residential categories used here are multifamily homes, single detached small homes (less than 1 acre), and single detached large homes (greater than 1 acre). These housing choices are estimated to consume on average 0.05, 0.25, and 1.5 acres, respectively. The proportions of the consumption of these three housing goods are taken from the Census data and applied to each outer suburban household according to income level. Thus, each outer suburban household can be assigned to one of these three groups. Residential land consumption (RES) is thus:

$$RES = NH \times P_h(y) \qquad [5]$$

where h equals proportion of average acreage consumption by income group.

Notes

This study benefited considerably from the assistance and cooperation of the following people who supplied data and information: Tim Angell, Senior Planner, Lake County Department of Planning and Development; Dalip Bammi, Director, County Community Development, DuPage County; Rita Lee, Economic Information and Analysis Division, Illinois Department of Employment Security; Bill Syverson, County Community Development, DuPage County; Bonnie Wood, East-West Corporate Corridor Association; and David Young, Director, Lake County Economic Development Corporation. Thanks also to Joe Persky for inspiration and data in the initial stages, to Wim Wiewel for instructive comments on an earlier draft, and to Kim Schaffer for assistance with materials. The usual disclaimers regarding interpretation and analysis apply here.

1. Notice that those workers living in the inner suburbs or the city may be either

reverse commuters to the corridor or employees of "indirect" firms located closer to their residences. Our estimates suggest that latter outnumber the former by a considerable margin.

References

Acs Z.J., and A. Ndikumwami. 1998. High Technology Employment Growth in Major U.S. Metropolitan Areas. *Small Business Economics* 10: 47–59.
Appold, S.J. 1991.The Location Process of Industrial Research Laboratories. *Annals of Regional Science* 25: 131–144.
Beeson, P., and E. Montgomery. 1993. The Effects of Colleges and Universities on Local Labor Markets. *Review of Economics and Statistics* 75(4): 753–761.
DeVol, R.C. 1999. *America's High Tech Economy: Growth, Development and Risks for Metropolitan Areas.* Los Angeles: Milken Institute.
Fulton W., R. Pendall, M. Nguyen, and A. Harrison. 2001. *Who Sprawls Most? How Growth Patterns Differ Across the US.* Washington, DC: Brookings Center on Urban and Metropolitan Policy, The Brookings Institution.
Garcia, V., and K. Yukawa. 1998. The Impact of Information Technology on U.S. Metropolitan Areas: Case Studies of Chicago, New York, San Francisco, and Atlanta. Paper presented at the Western Regional Science Association Annual Meeting, Monterey, CA.
Glaeser, E., and M. Kahn. 2001. Decentralized Employment and the Transformation of the American City. In *Brookings-Wharton Papers on Urban Affairs 2001*, ed. W.G. Gale and J. Rothenberg-Pack. Washington, DC: The Brookings Institution.
Hall, C., J. Persky, and W. Wiewel. 1990. *Responding to Defense Cuts: The Case of Chicago.* Chicago: Center for Urban Economic Development, University of Illinois at Chicago.
Kotkin, J, and R.C. DeVol. 2001. *Knowledge-Value Cities in the Digital Age.* Los Angeles: Milken Institute.
Markusen, A., and K. McCurdy. 1989. Chicago's Defense-Based High Technology: A Case Study of the "Seedbeds of Innovation" Hypothesis. *Economic Development Quarterly* 3(1): 15–31.
Markusen, A., K. Chapple, G. Schrock, D. Yamamoto, and P. Yu. 2001. High Tech and I-Tech: How Metros Rank and Specialize. Project on Regional and Industrial Economics, Humphrey Institute of Public Affairs, University of Minneapolis.
McMillen, D.P., and J.F. McDonald. 1998. Suburban Subcenters and Employment Density in Metropolitan Chicago. *Journal of Urban Economics* 43: 157–180.
Moss, M.L., and A.M. Townsend. 1998. Spatial Analysis of the Internet in U.S. Cities and States. Paper presented at a conference on Technological Futures—Urban Futures, Durham, England, April 23–28.
NIPC. 1998. *1990 Land Use Summary for Northeastern Illinois,* Northeastern Illinois Planning Commisssion: http://www.nipc.cog.il.us/lu-sum.htm.
Persky, J., and W. Wiewel. 2000. *When Corporations Leave Town: The Costs and Benefits of Metropolitan Job Sprawl.* Detroit: Wayne State University Press.
Treyz, G.I. 1993. *Regional Economic Modeling: A Systematic Approach to Economic Forecasting and Policy Analysis.* Boston: Kluwer.

U.S. Conference of Mayors. 2000a. *U.S. Metro Economies: The Engines of America's Growth* (U.S. Conference of Mayors and the National Association of Counties, May). Lexington, MA: McGraw Hill.

———. 2000b. *U.S. Metro Economies: Leading America's New Economy* (U.S. Conference of Mayors and the National Association of Counties, June). Lexington, MA: McGraw Hill.

Widmayer, P., and G. Greenberg. 1998. *Putting Our Minds Together: The Digital Network Infrastructure and Metropolitan Chicago.* Chicago: Metropolitan Planning Council: http://www.metroplanning.org.

Zook, M. 2001. *Domain Names in the U.S.*: http://garnet.berkeley.edu/~zook/domain_names.

11

JOSEPH J. PERSKY, HAYDAR KURBAN,
AND THOMAS W. LESTER

The Impact of Federal and State Expenditures on Residential Land Absorption: A Quantitative Case Study—Chicago

Introduction

Over the years critics of suburban expansion have accused federal and state governments of encouraging high rates of residential land absorption in suburban areas. Others have argued that public expenditures in the outer suburbs have merely followed market forces and had minimal impact on metropolitan form. This chapter considers the extent and influence on suburban land absorption of recent federal and state subsidies in one major urbanized area, Chicago.

For operational purposes we define land absorption as an increase in the physical size of an urbanized area. Residential land absorption is then an increase in the amount of land devoted to housing and closely related uses in an urbanized area. In general, we expect some land absorption to be associated with population growth. While we will not attempt a precise definition of urban sprawl, presumably sprawl involves a rate of land absorption in some sense "too large" for the rate of population growth.

Federal and state expenditures influence metropolitan land absorption in a number of ways. First, subsidies can change the relative price of peripheral land and other goods. A relative price reduction of peripheral land encourages consumers to substitute such land for other goods. Second, federal and state programs and services can reduce the need for local or private spending by outer suburban households and hence increase outer-suburban discretionary income. Increases in discretionary spending power raise outer suburban demands for all normal goods, including peripheral land.[1]

This chapter begins with a focus on the effects of federal spending on suburban expansion and then turns to the role of state policy. After a brief review of historical federal policies and the microgeography of the urbanized area, we present a method for classifying government expenditures according to their effects on residential land absorption. Though these categories were designed with federal programs and available data in mind, a parallel structure can be created for classifying state expenditures. This analysis follows the more extensive federal discussion.

Overall, we wish to determine whether federal and state subsidies have significantly reduced the cost of housing and the cost of living in Chicago's outer suburbs in such a way as to encourage land absorption. The spread of the urbanized area requires the purchase of land, construction of housing, and investment in infrastructure. These and other community building activities are supported, to a greater or lesser extent, by federal and state expenditures. In the absence of such subsidies, it would be naive to think that suburban expansion would grind to a halt. Instead, the plausible counterfactual holds that the new suburban residents would have to pay the full dollar cost of their new developments. But with these greater costs we know that they would economize on their consumption in general and on land consumption in particular.

Given the often excessive claims that have characterized much of the discussion of suburban sprawl, it may be useful to clarify what this chapter will not attempt. In particular, we cannot measure the effects of every federal and state program on land absorption in Chicago. Causal linkages between programs and the demand for residential land are multifaceted and complex. Looking at a relatively brief period of time, with no formal controls and lacking a complete model of metropolitan interactions, we cannot hope to measure every effect of federal or state activities working through indirect and sometimes circuitous channels.

Clearly, if we cannot measure all the effects of federal and state programs, we cannot hope to measure the overall benefits and costs associated with the land absorption produced by those programs. Notice that to finish such a calculation would also require an assessment of the net cost or benefit associated with the various types of land absorption. While we strongly expect from previous work (Persky and Wiewel 2000) that such net effects turn negative beyond some point, no precise estimates exist.

Our research does not consider the effects of public regulations, but only those of public subsidies. If Washington subsidizes a water treatment plant in the outer suburbs, we will pick it up. But if Washington rules that the city of Chicago must share its Lake Michigan water with outer suburbs, it will not appear on our screen.

The physical growth of the Chicago urbanized area has been dramatic over the last quarter century. In the end, we find that a substantial portion of recent residential land absorption, perhaps as high as 20 percent, can be attributed to federal subsidies and tax expenditures. The largest part of this effect is generated by the favorable federal tax treatment of owner-occupied housing. Although more difficult to measure, state level expenditures seem to have had a considerably smaller impact.

Federal Expenditures and Urban Form: A Quick Review

The role of the federal government in spurring metropolitan decentralization has been a recurring theme ever since World War II. Toward the beginning of this period attention focused on the contribution of the Federal Housing Administration (FHA) and its guaranteeing of home mortgages. These guarantees brought the possibility of home ownership to a substantial segment of the country's lower-middle-class urban population—households that had been largely excluded from traditional credit sources before the war. The FHA favored new housing construction, which in many metropolitan areas could be undertaken only in new suburbs near the periphery. It also took a conservative attitude toward risk and as a result redlined many central city neighborhoods. Most researchers have concluded that the FHA, serving populations eager to escape high urban densities, certainly facilitated considerable suburbanization, while discriminating against minorities (Gelfand 1975).

Highway construction represents a second major federal priority that has strongly influenced metropolitan form. Especially with the development of the interstate highway system in the Eisenhower administration, federal highway spending opened considerable rural and semirural land to housing development. The metropolitan expressways with their strong downtown focus encouraged automobile commuting. Some researchers have even argued that the radial pattern of these superhighways helped to preserve the centrality of traditional downtowns (Altshuler and Gomez-Ibanez 1994). In judging this claim the relevant question is: What counterfactual is most plausible? In particular, would state and local governments have designed a similar system in the absence of federal funding, or would a very different pattern of highways have emerged? Whatever the answer, there can be little doubt that, in this period, massive federal funding of highways by opening new suburban opportunities kept housing prices relatively cheap (Sen et al. 1998).

In the 1960s several researchers advanced a hypothesis of suburban exploitation of the central city. While much of this argument centered on suburban use of city public institutions, highway infrastructure was commonly mentioned as a prime example of the phenomenon. However, quantitative studies early suggested that suburban drivers bore about their fair user share of highway expenditure through their gasoline tax contributions (Bradford and Oates 1974; Meyer, Kain, and Wohl 1965).

In the 1980s attention focused on the Reagan administration's hostility to cities, with several researchers finding a decided shift in federal spending away from urban-oriented programs, suggesting perhaps a new emphasis on the suburbs. This line of argument encouraged R. Andrew Parker (1995; 1997) to use the Consolidated Federal Funds Reports (CFFR) in an effort to document as fully as possible total federal spending in city and suburbs. Parker found something of a "stealth" urban policy, as direct redistributional programs replaced those funneled through city governments.

From this synoptic review, it should be clear that federal policy toward city and suburb has engendered considerable debate over the last half century. It should also be clear that in much of this debate the precise nature of the object to be explained—suburbanization, sprawl, decentralization, urban decay, and/or urban poverty—was often left poorly defined or even undefined. Under the circumstances, conclusions have continued to be highly impressionistic in nature. By narrowing our focus, here, to subsidies of land absorption, we hope to address more sharply at least one facet of this lengthy and still poorly understood subject.

Classifying Places

To explore the hypothesis that federal expenditures have subsidized the absorption of nondeveloped land on the metropolitan periphery, we need to analyze the fine geography of federal expenditures. At the very least we need to identify the outer suburbs where the supply of land is highly elastic, and significant land absorption is taking place.

The core/periphery or inner/outer suburb dichotomy has been used by a number of researchers in considering a range of issues. However, no standardized definitions have yet emerged. Nor is it clear that one single set of definitions will be optimal for all research questions.

The simplest approach to definition is to use county boundaries. (See, e.g., Stanback 1991; Persky and Wiewel 2000). This approach has the great advantage of allowing researchers to use relatively easily accessible county data. The problem, of course, is that county boundaries have relatively little to do with the distinction at hand. While counties more distant from the central city will presumably be more newly developed, the relatively small number of counties in any metropolitan area virtually guarantees that some of them will contain both highly developed communities and actively expanding ones. In addition, outlying satellite cities in more remote counties can seriously confuse the picture. In general, counties provide just too coarse a grid.

Going below the county level, the realities of data availability in the Chicago region strongly suggest using municipalities as our basic building block. But this choice still leaves open the question of how best to aggregate these many blocks up to a level interesting from an analytical standpoint. One approach followed by Myron Orfield (1997) and Daniel Immergluck (1998) has attempted to define inner and outer suburbs in terms of the demographic characteristics of their populations and especially their income levels. While such a system of aggregation may be useful for a number of purposes, it fails to capture our interest in the distinction between old suburbs and new suburbs. The vast majority of land absorption occurs in new suburbs. Only a very modest amount occurs in old ones. By contrast, rich suburbs can be either old or new and poor suburbs can be found in any of the rings.

For the present study we have chosen to aggregate municipalities based on the date at which the U.S. Census Bureau (1992) classified them as part of the Chicago urbanized area. Roughly speaking, a municipality contiguous to the urbanized area becomes a part of that area when its density reaches 1,000 people per square mile. Grouping together municipalities by the date at which they qualified for inclusion combines a measure of age with a measure of density. Land in municipalities in older cohorts will generally be developed and little undeveloped land on such municipalities' boundaries will be available for annexation. Younger cohorts will be characterized by considerable quantities of undeveloped land both within their boundaries and nearby.

In practice we have grouped the urbanized area's municipalities into the following:

1. Chicago proper,
2. Suburbs included in the urbanized area by 1950,
3. Suburbs added to the urbanized area between 1950 and 1970,
4. Suburbs added to the urbanized area between 1970 and 1990,
5. Satellite communities.

The suburbs already defined by 1950 were virtually fully developed by 1970. These are clearly older suburbs. We make a distinction between two groups of newer suburbs. Those added to the urbanized area between 1950 and 1970 and those that only entered the area between 1970 and 1990. The suburbs in the older of these two groups, still had in 1970 considerable opportunity for expansion into unincorporated areas. However, they already possessed significant physical and social infrastructure. Generally, the suburbs added after 1970 were truly peripheral as of that date. They had little infrastructure and few constraints on their ability to absorb land.

Category 5 includes all municipalities currently in the outlying urbanized areas of Joliet, Aurora, and Elgin, as well as Waukegan and North Chicago. The central cities of these satellite areas were developed in the late nineteenth and early twentieth centuries. Thus their core land use was largely established before the post-World War II waves of suburbanization. For this reason alone we should analyze them separately from newer suburban communities. We should note that in recent years these satellite cities have experienced considerable expansion as their suburban towns have been overtaken by the outer suburbs of Chicago. We will return to this point later in the chapter.

Table 11.1 shows the population and land shares as of 1990 for each of the six rings of the urbanized area. Notice that the new suburbs entering the urbanized area since 1970 account for only 17.7 percent of the urbanized area population in 1990, but for 34.9 percent of the area's land. As a result their population densities are considerably lower than the city itself.

The borders of the urbanized area have been expanding rapidly. The 1990 census demarcated an area more than 400 square miles larger than

Table 11.1

Population and Area by Ring, 1990

Ring	City	Pre-1950	1950–1970	Post-1970	Satellites
Population 1990 in thousands	2,783.7	2,110.0	864.1	304.7	518.2
Share 1990 population	42.3%	32.1%	13.1%	4.6%	7.9%
Area 1990 in square miles	227.2	489.9	300.2	186.3	192.4
Share 1990 area	16.3%	35.1%	21.5%	13.4%	13.8%
Density, thousands per square mile	12.3	4.3	2.9	1.6	2.7

that recorded in 1970, a gain of 41 percent in twenty years (Table 11.2). Not surprisingly, the new suburbs accounted for the lion's share of this expansion.

Throughout this project we build, wherever possible, directly on municipality level data or estimates. This allows comparisons across a number of different systems of geographic aggregation. However, as suggested above, our central focus will remain the extent of per capita federal expenditures in these two new suburban rings as compared to older areas.

Classifying Federal Programs

Our strategy in approaching federal expenditures is to start as broadly as possible and then to focus on those expenditures most relevant to residential land absorption. Paying attention to the entire range of federal expenditures in the urbanized area allows us to put the spatially relevant ones in some broader social perspective. Categorization of state programs will closely follow the logic presented here.

Not all federal programs are alike, but with thousands of individual programs we can hardly treat each one individually. Serious analysis requires some system of aggregation. Here, as in the case of municipal geography, the problem becomes one of how best to aggregate. The large number of individual programs means we can find potentially an infinite number of ways to disaggregate and reaggregate federal spending. Any categorical system necessarily has an element of arbitrariness. Forswearing perfection, still, we can try to assemble one with more rather than less relevance to the question at hand, that of residential land absorption.

The most relevant previous work on differences in federal expendi-

Table 11.2

Change in Area by Ring, 1970–1990

	City	Pre-1950	1950–1970	Post-1970	Satellites	Total
Area change in square miles	4.6	35.9	106.2	186.3	73.2	406.2
Area growth percent	2.1%	7.9%	54.7%	—	1.4%	41.0%
Share of metro area change	1.1%	8.8%	26.1%	45.9%	8.0%	100.0%

tures between city and suburbs (Parker 1995) has built on the categorical system used by the Consolidated Federal Funds Report. This system emphasizes the character of the recipient and the nature of the payment. Thus it distinguishes between direct payments to individuals, grants to institutions/governments, or procurement from private businesses. While useful for a number of purposes, such categories hardly have a well-defined spatial impact. In this system a highway construction grant and one to support the study of immunology both fall into the same category, and yet the first is far more relevant to outer suburban housing costs than is the second. Clearly this system will not serve our purposes.

One way to understand the categories chosen is to explain why each differs from the one labeled in Table 11.3 as "Spatially Related Programs—Cost Reducing." Easily excluded are a range of programs, most of them grants, that have virtually no direct influence on the cost of living in one or another portion of the urbanized area.

These programs are included under category 6 in Table 11.3. Research grants for the space program or pharmacological sciences may have important benefits on a national basis, but have little direct effect on nearby residents. Admittedly, such programs may impact the intraregional distribution of workplaces. For example, they may help to anchor an urban university or stimulate the growth of a suburban high tech park. Here we take such workplaces as exogenously determined, but for a fuller discussion of such impacts see Felsenstein (chapter 10, this volume).

Similarly, federal expenditures on salaries and procurement (category 5) may have strong influence on urban form through the commuting decisions of employed workers, but they do not, in themselves, change the cost of land in the outer suburbs. Again, these would be basic data for impact estimates of basic employment growth and the stimulation of induced employment.

Table 11.3

Federal Program Groupings

1. Spatially related programs—Cost reducing
   Highways and related
   Public transit
   Other infrastructure
   Income tax subsidy for housing
   Environment and disaster
   Crime

2. Spatially related programs—Poverty relieving
   Housing and other transfers to low income
   Community development and other housing
   Education
   Community health

3. Nonspatial redistribution programs
   Earned income tax credit
   Food stamps
   Redistributional grants
   Medical assistance
   Unemployment
   Supplemental social security
   Veterans

4. Retirement
   Social Security and other
   Medicare
   Veterans and families

5. Salaries and procurement
   Salaries
   Procurement

6. All other
   Agriculture and related
   Research
   Arts
   Other health
   Other grants

On the other hand, income redistribution and retirement programs directly influence the demand for housing and land. Nevertheless, we separate these programs out (categories 3 and 4). These federal efforts represent fundamental social choices about how to distribute income. Presumably the housing choices made by the beneficiaries of these programs are irrelevant to the political debate over their scale. As such they are best taken as givens in our analysis.

More difficult than the above are a group of federal redistributional programs that have a more or less clearly defined spatial component, "Spatially Related Programs—Poverty Relieving" (category 2 in Table 11.3). Strongly concentrated in the central city and the older core satellites, these programs deal with low-income housing subsidies, educational subsidies, community development, and community health. Some have argued that the concentration of such programs in older cities has tended to keep the poor immobile and artificially concentrated. In this way they have directly reduced the demand for peripheral land. On the other hand, however, the resulting concentrations of city poverty have been cited as a spur to the flight of middle-class households toward the outer suburbs. This centrifugal indirect effect could easily outscale the centripetal direct one. We will attempt to carefully measure the differential geographic impact of these spatially related redistributional programs. However, we do separate them out so that the bulk of our analysis can focus on those programs that more directly influence the cost of new suburban locations. These programs in category 1 of Table 11.3 include highways, public transit, other infrastructure, environment, crime, and income tax subsidies for housing.

Federal Expenditures Across the Urbanized Area

Table 11.4 presents a summary of our data by ring and major program area for 1989–1996.[2] Starting with the sum of all programs, it is easy to see support for the possibility that the federal government has been engaged in a "stealth" urban policy (Parker 1997). Total federal expenditures per capita in the central city were about two-thirds higher than in the newer suburbs, those which joined the urbanized area between 1970 and 1990. But such a conclusion has a misleading quality. The vast bulk of the difference between expenditures at the core and periphery result from substantial differences in per capita expenditures on the two largest program areas, direct redistribution and retirement. The city is older and it is poorer.

Programs aimed at supporting the old and the poor we have taken as policy givens. However, we should note that such redistributions clearly increase the demand for housing and land in the city and inner suburbs relative to the newer suburbs on the periphery. Through this indirect mechanism such programs have a modest effect of reducing the land absorption in outer suburbs.

Table 11.4

Average Annual Per Capita Federal Expenditures, 1989–1996 ($)

	City	Pre-1950	1950–1970	Post-1970	Satellites
1. Spatially related programs—cost reducing	263	640	646	653	358
2. Spatially related programs—poverty relieving	409	70	48	94	155
3. Nonspatial redistribution	1,462	337	229	229	429
4. Retirement	2,233	2,517	1345	1,223	1,727
5. Salaries and procurement	817	673	944	520	1,905
6. All other	127	84	49	24	48
Total	5,310	4,322	3,261	2,744	4,621

Note: Columns may not add to totals because of rounding.

In a similar fashion the spatially related redistributional programs (category 2) favor the city strongly over the suburbs. In this case the inner suburbs are more like their peripheral neighbors than the core city. Per dollar of expenditure, these programs, in contrast to simple income subsidies, have stronger effects on the land consumption of the poor. After all, the spatially related redistributive programs are targeted directly at reducing the cost of housing or public infrastructure serving the poor. Again, however, we set aside these differential effects on core and periphery as incidental to the broad redistributional goals of the society. Put somewhat differently, our focus is not spatially related subsidies to the poor, but subsidies to the rest of us. Again this is not to judge the net benefits of category 2 programs, nor to deny that such programs may generate spatial externalities.

The spatial distribution of federal salaries and procurement are disproportionately concentrated in the satellite towns. The new highly residential suburbs of the last wave have relatively low salary and procurement. And finishing off these preliminaries, the "all other" expenditure category remains pro-city, largely driven by the concentration there of research grants.

Turn now to our chief concern, those federal programs that reduce the cost of housing, land, and related spatial infrastructure. For category 1 we find both old and new suburbs showing per capita federal expenditures far more than twice those of the central city. Somewhat surprisingly, the inner suburbs here do almost as well as those joining the

Table 11.5

Average Annual per Capita Spatially Related Programs—Cost Reducing, 1989–1996 ($)

	City	Pre-1950	1950–1970	Post-1970	Satellites
Highways and related	24	52	62	86	49
Public transit	72	36	24	18	15
Other infrastructure	23	4	1	0	1
Income tax subsidy for housing	125	546	557	545	288
Environment and disaster	4	2	1	4	4
Crime	15	0	0	0	1
Total	263	640	646	653	357

Note: Columns may not add to totals because of rounding.

urbanized area since 1970. However, the older satellites fall much closer to the central city in per capita expenditures.

Notice also the scale of these category 1 expenditures. While not insignificant, they are considerably smaller than redistribution, retirement, and salaries and procurement categories. These programs count for less than 25 percent of federal expenditures in the outer ring of municipalities and only about 5 percent of federal expenditures in the city of Chicago proper.

Spatially Related Programs—Cost Reducing

Table 11.5 gives a more detailed breakdown of the spatially related programs that reduce costs in the suburbs. As the data suggest, the federal government's role in providing infrastructure (other than for transportation), environmental assistance, and anticrime expenditures accounts for relatively modest sums on a per capita basis. Even more surprising, it is difficult to avoid noting the relatively small contribution of highway and related programs to the overall total.

In the new suburbs of urban periphery we estimate that only about $85 per capita was spent annually on this subcategory, and in the city the figure falls to about $25 per capita. Two observations should be made in connection with these statistics. First, we have tried hard to ascribe to households in each municipality their share based on use of the highway expenditures made over this period. This means that a town's allocation of highway expenditures does not depend on how many highway dollars were actually spent within its borders, but rather on the journey-to-work miles its commuters made over highways constructed, improved, or maintained with federal funds in each county.[3] Second, these estimates relate only to expenditures actually made in the eight-year period. As noted above, the Chicago area has not witnessed significant highway construction since the early 1970s. Much of the expressway system originally planned for the area was never actually built. Still, there is a sense in which current commuters and other highway users are benefiting from previous capital expenditures. One could make a case for considering the ongoing flow of services from earlier investments. However, the policies and programs that put the existing expressways in place are long gone. To give a clear picture of policy today, we had little choice but to put aside these early expenditures and focus only on current dollar flows.

Per capita public transit expenditures just about offset those going for highways. The city does much better than the rest of the urbanized area because city residents make extensive use of the Chicago Transportation Authority (CTA). Thus total transit expenses per capita are about even across the rings.

As noted above, housing subsidies through the income tax rank as by far the most important of the spatially related programs. Our approach to these subsidies starts from the longstanding view in public finance that various types of investment income should be treated similarly for tax purposes and, in particular, that implicit income from owner-occupied homes rightly should be taxed. From this point of view mortgage deductions are perfectly appropriate as a cost of engaging in a "home" business, as long as the net income generated by that business is fully taxed (Musgrave and Musgrave 1980, 359–361).[4]

To measure the tax expenditure involved in leaving these imputed incomes untaxed, we need to estimate two critical parameters: the rate of return on housing capital and the applicable income tax rate. As to the first, we make the very conservative assumption that in all communities housing capital pays a real rate of return of 5 percent per year. We put aside here issues of capital gains and inflation and in effect treat housing as an asset held in perpetuity. This 5 percent rate is applied to owner-occupied housing as reported in the 1990 census. Marginal tax rates were computed separately for each housing value category in each community.[5]

As Table 11.5 suggests, the per capita tax subsidy of housing in the suburbs is much larger than in the city. A suburban family of four receives about $2,200 a year, while a city family of four receives something over $500. The difference comes about for three reasons—higher home ownership rates in the suburbs, higher incomes in the suburbs, and higher housing values in the suburbs. Among the three rings of suburban municipalities, we find no significant differences, although more detailed data by individual municipalities show considerable variation related to income levels. Indeed the richest third of municipalities have an average subsidy of almost $4,000 per family of four.

Land Absorption

While the implicit housing subsidy remains about constant across suburban areas, this does not imply that it has no effect on land absorption at the periphery. A subsidy raises demand for housing and land. Within developed areas where supply is essentially inelastic, the increase in demand can have no significant effect on the quantity of housing and land purchased. Land and structures have higher market values, but otherwise the situation is unaffected by the subsidy. However, on the periphery, where land is highly elastic in supply, subsidies translate more or less directly into the purchase of more housing on more land.

To estimate the magnitude of this effect, we first calculate, for each type of housing in each peripheral community (e.g., homes between $100,000 and $125,000 in Grayslake), the average increase in the cost of housing that would follow on the removal of the subsidy. These increases range from 18 percent to 49 percent depending on house type and community.[6] Assuming that in these areas land and housing supply is infinitely elastic, the full price increase would be passed on to consumers. Thus their demand will be strongly affected. For every 1 percent increase in price, how much would quantity demanded fall? Research on housing demand suggests that its long-run price elasticity is about 0.6. Thus if a certain category of housing increases in price by 30 percent, the demand for this category on the periphery would fall by 0.6×30 percent = 18 percent.

Summing over all categories and places in the outer ring of suburbs, we estimate that housing tax expenditures added some 22 percent to the increase in housing and land consumption that would have occurred otherwise. A very similar effect applies to the ring of municipalities entering the urbanized area by 1970. These towns, like those on the far periphery, were faced with a highly elastic supply of land and housing. If we take this elasticity to be essentially infinite, then they too expanded some 22 percent more than they would have in the absence of the tax subsidy.

Notice that removing the subsidy on housing would bring considerable revenue into the federal treasury. Holding such a change revenue neutral implies returning to income taxpayers this newly generated surplus. This will increase their disposable incomes and to some extent increase the demand for housing. However this counter force is not all that significant. Returning taxes as an across-the-board tax reduction amounts to only a 2–5 percent increase in disposable income. The long-run income elasticity for housing is about 0.75. The corresponding elasticity for land is likely to be somewhat less, say 0.50 (Ellwood and Polinski 1979). This implies that the returned taxes would only raise land absorption by 1–2.5 percent.

What of the land absorption effects of the other spatially relevant subsidies and especially those of highways and public transit? The numbers in the last section just are not large enough to make a major impact. Given the considerable private costs, both dollar outlays and time lost, associated with automobile transit, forcing outer suburbanites to cover their share of highway construction and maintenance over this period would have increased their transportation costs by only a few percentage points.

Even with a substantial cross elasticity between transit cost and housing demand, those few percentage points could have had only a modest effect overall. The impact of public transit and the other programs considered would presumably be even smaller.

The Intrametropolitan Geography of State Expenditure

According to the theory of fiscal federalism, much of the redistributive function of government is appropriately conducted at the national level. Municipalities should undertake only those public services truly local in nature. Putting aside county governments and a host of special service districts, this leaves state government to finance and/or produce a range of intermediate level public outputs. In practice our division of public effort is not so neatly divided. Much of federal spending is funneled through and more or less shaped by state governments. In turn, a combination of federal- and state-provided funds may be further mixed with local spending before actually being realized as programmatic expenditures. Highway construction is perhaps the most notable example, but many other program areas, including education and medical assistance for the indigent, show similarly complex patterns. Wherever possible we have ascribed state-allocated but federally financed programs to the federal government, and attributed to the state only those dollars added to federal resources that were raised from state revenues.

The major problem in analyzing the geographic distribution of state expenditures stems from our lack of a basic data source comparable to the Consolidated Federal Funds Report at the national level. While various state agencies do provide information on where their funds are spent, as of this writing the state has no comprehensive record. The available data focus on state programs that distribute funding such as education and highways. The state supplies little or no data on the geography of expenditures used directly by the state to produce public services. What data there are often overlap. Moreover, we could find no comprehensive source on the geographic distribution of state procurement. (For a discussion of our data sources and their limitations, see the appendix in this chapter.)

Given the difficulties in identifying data, we have concentrated our efforts on the programmatic areas central to our primary concerns—cost-reducing spatially related programs. Chief among these are highways, public transit, income tax subsidies for housing, education, and intergovernmental aid. Our approach to estimating the first three of these categories closely follows the methodology in the federal discussion.

For the following analysis, state education expenditures are included among the cost-reducing spatially related programs, although, above, we counted federal educational expenditures as redistributional spatially related programs. This change simply recognizes the much broader role of the state in financing local primary and secondary education. Where the federal government's involvement in K-12 schools focuses on issues of poverty, the state has a more general responsibility. Even though an area's income influences its state allotment, the program has more general concerns than distribution alone. Following much the same logic, intergovernmental aid figures are also included in the cost-reducing spatially related programs.

Since our ability to present a geographic breakdown of state expenditures in the Chicago metropolitan area is limited, we have missed a num-

Table 11.6

Per Capita State Expenditures by Geography, 1989–1996

	City	Pre-1950	1950–1970	Post-1970	Satellites
1. Spatially related programs	581	486	473	720	757
2. Redistributional programs	476	62	53	51	90
3. Salaries	409	212	204	160	447
4. Other identifiable programs	5	1	0	1	0
Total (less salaries)	1,063	549	527	771	847

Notes: All figures in 1996 dollars. Columns may not add to totals because of rounding.

ber of programs, both "pro-city" and "pro-suburb." These undoubtedly deserve further scrutiny. However, the approach taken here emphasizes the largest state expenditure that directly affects the spatial prices observed by residential locators.

Table 11.6 presents our basic estimates for the period 1989 to 1996.[7] For the expenditure categories considered, the city actually obtains the highest amount per capita from the state, about $1,060. Among the suburbs of the urbanized area, those entering between 1970 and 1990 do the best with about $770 per capita.

The high value for the city reflects strong performance in each of the major categories. The most important one for our purposes, the spatially related programs, registers about $580 per capita for city residents. Although the new suburbs and satellites did somewhat better, the inner suburbs that joined the urbanized area before 1950 actually garnered a somewhat lower figure as do the suburbs entering between 1950 and 1970. Chicago proper did particularly well in redistribution programs and in salaried jobs, which are heavily concentrated in the downtown area.

The composition of spatially related expenditures is given in Table 11.7 for the 1989 to 1996 period.

Education

By a substantial amount, the largest subcategory is primary and secondary school expenditures. These numbers are influenced by the age of the population and the tax effort of the local jurisdictions. The older suburbs from the pre-1950 period and those suburbs joining the urbanized area between 1950 and 1970 have the lowest expenditures per capita. Educational expenditures are high in the youngest suburbs of the periphery of the urbanized area and even higher in the satellite towns. The city registers somewhere between the extremes.

While our approach interprets these expenditures on education as per capita subsidies by the state, it is clear that per student subsidies vary much less across these geographic areas. The state subsidy acts primarily as a transfer from older (and some younger) taxpayers to those with school-age children. This subsidy generates a modest general income effect on those families' demand for housing. Since many such families pick the new outer suburbs, this educational subsidy produces an effect on land absorption there.

Highways

Highways and related state subsidies constitute the next largest subcategory.

The amounts here are actually somewhat larger than federal per capita spending on highways, but remain modest on a per capita basis. The new suburbs do the best in the urbanized area, annually garnering $128 per capita.

Public Transit

Per capita public transit expenditures from the state level, like those from the federal level, concentrate on the central city and oldest suburbs. Adding public transit and highway expenditures together yields a fairly flat expenditure pattern across the metropolitan geography.

Intergovernmental Aid

Intergovernmental aid covers a number of different tax-sharing programs. Largest of these are income tax sharing and personal property tax replacement. The city does the best in this area, with newer suburbs receiving about 25 percent less per capita. This pattern was more progressive than we had expected.

Income Tax Subsidy for Housing

As for the federal income tax, the state's income tax subsidies for housing favor the suburbs relative to the city with its larger population of

Table 11.7

Per Capita Spatially Related State Expenditures by Geography, 1989–1996

	City	Pre-1950	1950–1970	Post-1970	Satellites
Highways and related	45	77	101	128	107
Public transit	75	41	27	21	17
Other infrastructure	2	3	0	0	6
Income tax subsidy for housing	16	61	62	62	35
Environment and disaster	0	12	7	10	5
Crime	1	0	1	1	2
Education	350	226	217	429	511
Intergovernmental aid	93	65	59	70	74
Total	581	486	473	720	757

Notes: All figures per capita, in 1996 U.S. dollars. Columns may not add to totals because of rounding.

renters. However, the estimates in Table 11.7 should be approached carefully. Since state tax laws do not allow homeowners to deduct mortgage interest against their implicit investment income, net income derived from owner-occupied homes is probably exaggerated in the table. On the other hand, it should be kept in mind that we have assumed a very modest rate of return of 5 percent on housing capital.

While somewhat crude and perhaps somewhat overstated, these estimates suggest only modest gains for the outer suburbs. The flat state tax rate is only 3 percent. A family of four in the outer suburbs gains about $250 per year from the state's treatment of implicit income. In the next section we return to the question of what overall effect this subsidy has on housing expenditures and land absorption.

State Subsidies and Peripheral Land Absorption

State tax and expenditure policies have direct impacts on land absorption. As in the case of federal tax policy, the state income tax lowers the cost of home ownership at the suburban periphery. State policies also reduce the cost of living in the outer suburbs by subsidizing highways and other public services. Of course outer suburbanites contribute to redistributive programs undertaken by the state. But if we take these as givens, the state plays a modest but significant role in encouraging the demand for suburban land.

Here, as for the federal estimates, we assume that land and structures are in highly elastic supply at the suburban periphery, but essentially inelastic in already built-up areas. The effective housing price subsidy is just equal to $t/(1 - t)$ where t is now the state's marginal income tax rate. With $t = 3$ percent this gives a subsidy of 3.1 percent. This rate is essentially constant across the entire outer suburban residential housing stock. Combining this with our maintained estimate of 0.6 for the demand price elasticity of residential land in the suburban periphery gives a total increase in quantity demanded of less than 2 percent. Again, this estimate is probably an upper bound since state law provides no income tax deduction for mortgage interest. Clearly the impact of the Illinois income tax law is much smaller than the 22 percent figure estimated for the federal income tax subsidy.

In addition to the substitution effect created by income tax breaks, state subsidies also result in income effects on peripheral land absorption. In analyzing such income effects, our maintained hypothesis holds that in the absence of state subsidies, overall public expenditure levels remain constant (i.e., any lost state subsidies must be replaced by local funds). For example, even if the state withdraws all of its subsidy from peripheral schools, households will still locate in the outer suburbs. In particular we assume they will finance the current state portion of education expenditure on their own, thus reducing their discretionary income.[8]

While the state per capita subsidy for education is substantial, its overall income effect on land absorption is probably small. Even if we interpret the entire per capita subsidy in the outer suburbs as an income windfall, the figure amounts to less than 2 percent of per capita income in that ring. With an income elasticity of land demand of about 0.5, the education subsidy increases land absorption by about 1 percent. This estimate is further reduced when we recognize that in the absence of the education subsidy, income tax bills in the outer suburbs would be somewhat lower, thus offsetting part of the subsidy loss.

The effects of state highway subsidies are even smaller. Again treating the entire highway subsidy to the outer suburbs as a windfall, discretionary incomes would rise by only 0.5 percent. With an income elasticity of 0.5, this would raise land absorption by only 0.25 percent. Even if we took into account the cross-elasticity between transportation expenditures and residential land, we could not reasonably raise this figure past

1 percent. Keep in mind that these calculations assume that local governments, combinations of municipalities and counties, would be able to work out the institutional mechanisms necessary to replace state participation in highway construction. In the absence of such cooperative mechanisms, even if residents were willing to provide finance, the highway system might have been considerably less extensive. Under such circumstances land absorption would have been substantially less.

The income effect on land absorption of other spatially related expenditures will be even smaller. The intergovernmental fiscal transfers provide only modest subsidies to outer suburbs. Even if these are considered as lump sum benefits, their impact on the demand for land cannot be great. In the absence of such transfers, much if not all of these funds could reasonably be raised locally, creating only small changes in local income and land absorption.

Summary

First we should review our most critical working assumptions. All of the preceding calculations assume that local residents can find an appropriate institutional mechanism to substitute local financing for federal funds. This has been our counterfactual throughout. In the absence of such a mechanism, overall impacts might be considerably larger. For example, if local policy prevents the substitution of local funds for federal or state highway dollars, the resulting decay of the highway system would inevitably cut off development. It is always true that in the absence of supply, quantity falls to zero.

Second, we take as given the pattern of federal and state taxation. To the extent that specific expenditures are explicitly or implicitly financed with user fees, then beneficiaries are essentially paying for their benefits and the question of a direct subsidy becomes moot. As noted above, this issue is particularly relevant to highway expenditures where gasoline taxes play a substantial role in financing.

Against this background, our major conclusions are straightforward. Yes, it is true that central city, inner suburbs, and satellite communities have experienced a considerable cash inflow, especially from the federal government, with the bulk of this inflow aimed at alleviating poverty and supporting the elderly. Despite that inflow, federal spending and tax expenditures have strongly stimulated peripheral land absorption. By consistently allowing special tax treatment to housing, the federal government has encouraged households to tilt their consumption bundles toward homes and land.

How can we be surprised that federal encouragement of home ownership leads to land absorption? Many have equated home ownership with the American dream itself. Reconciling this position with our concerns over land absorption requires a more careful crafting of federal tax and expenditure policy than common heretofore.

The state of Illinois, with its traditionally Republican governors and strong suburban representation, has often been viewed as hostile to the city of Chicago and its mayors. Nevertheless, the spatially relevant expenditures of the state are more or less evenly distributed between city and suburbs. Indeed, they are more evenly distributed than the same category of federal spending. Only in the most distant portions of the urbanized area does per capita state spending on spatially relevant programs exceed the city level.

Perhaps this outcome reflects a rather simple type of bargaining in the state legislature. Suburban communities lobby for state subsidies on major public goods (education, highways, etc.) and receive them. However, in exchange they seem willing to fund higher redistributional payments to the city. It remains unclear if this process results in either allocative efficiency or appropriate levels of redistribution. Whatever its normative qualities, this bargaining generates a flatter spatial distribution of state expenditures than we anticipated. Key, here, is the large role of the state in providing for public education, which certainly narrows the gap between city and suburbs.

Unlike the federal government, the state has not traditionally emphasized home ownership as a primary policy goal. In particular, the state's income tax subsidy for owner-occupied housing remains modest in comparison to the national tax subsidy. Primarily for this reason, we calculate the state's overall impact on residential land absorption to be small. Where the federal government spending and tax policies boost land absorption at the periphery by about 20 percent, state subsidies are directly responsible for at most 3 percent of the recent expansion of the urbanized area.

Appendix

Federal Estimates

Determining federal expenditures at the municipality level requires a good deal of perseverance and not a little hubris. The process too quickly moves from one of data assembly to one of data creation. Many key numbers can only be generated through estimation, involving models of various levels of complexity. The more gruesome details of our efforts can be found in Persky and Kurban (2001a). The purpose of this appendix is only to give an overview of the approach taken and the compromises made.

The basic data source for federal expenditures is the Consolidated Federal Funds Report (CFFR). These data themselves are drawn together from numerous sources, using sometimes conflicting geographic and program definitions. While the Census Bureau makes a yeoman effort to merge these in a meaningful manner, problems are most pronounced at the municipality level.

One of the most serious problems emerges when an agency reports an expenditure to a single municipality that represents federal dollars going to a multimunicipality or even regional activity. For example, federal contributions to the Regional Transportation Authority are recorded as an entry only for Chicago. Such entries require some alternative data source or estimating effort to allocate the federal funds among residents of all the municipalities involved. For both public transit and highways we undertook fairly substantial modeling. Our effort was motivated by a concern that for these two key programs it is critical to associate expenditures not with the physical locale in which they were made but rather with the residents of the various municipalities in proportion to their utilization of the publicly provided capital. Thus a city highway may be used heavily by suburban drivers and, in this age of reverse commuting, the opposite can also hold.

Closely related to the above problem, certain programs are not disaggregated in the CFFR below the county level. In particular, a number of major redistributional programs such as food stamps and Medicaid lack municipal detail. Here we allocated each program's county expenditures using a statistical regression equation estimated for that program across all the counties of Illinois. For example, per capita food stamp expenditure by county is regressed on proportion of the population in poverty and the proportion of households with a female head. Both variables were found to be significant. A number of these equations, including most of the major redistributional ones, fit the county data very well.[9] However, several equations have low reliability. In a few cases the results seemed so counterintuitive that we resorted to a simple allocation within counties on a per capita basis. To estimate per capita municipal expenditures, we simply used the cross-county equations along with information for each municipality on its independent variables. These data generally are taken from the 1990 Census. Estimated values for all the municipalities in a given county were then standardized to match that county's total. CFFR data on a few programs are provided only at the state level. None of these programs, with the exception of unemployment payments, is very large. For each program the state figure was allocated among municipalities based on an appropriate indicator. For example, unemployment payments were allocated in proportion to a municipality's unemployment-to-population ratio.

Unfortunately, the CFFR does not include data on tax expenditures. In terms of our purposes here, we felt it essential to attempt to estimate two of the most important—income tax subsidies for housing and the earned income tax credit. The first clearly belongs in our category 1 since it has a substantial influence on the effective price of housing and land. The second has become one of the most significant redistributional programs and our catalog in category 3 would be incomplete without it.

It should be noted that the present chapter does not include information on the spatial pattern of federal loan activity. We are planning to look at this question in more detail in the near future. However, loans are excluded here because a number of federal loan programs and, most important, the Federal Housing Administration's extremely large mortgage guarantee program actually generated surpluses over the years in question (Office of Management and Budget 1999). Under the circumstances, some care is warranted as to how best to treat federal loans in general.

State Estimates

As suggested in the main text, highway funding draws on direct spending by various levels of government as well as a range of intergovernmental grants and tax transfers. Virtually every major level of government—federal, state, county, and municipal—participates in highway planning and funding. The state's own-source contributions are well defined in aggregate. However, because both the state and lower level public entities may pool funds derived from various sources, it is difficult to ascertain the geographic distribution of the state's own-source revenues. As a result, we are forced to use various allocation algorithms to construct estimates of that distribution.

Our estimates for highway and related spending include not only state contributions to highway construction but also funds returned to local areas from the motor fuel tax. For the state contribution to highway expenditures, we begin with information obtained from the Chicago Area Transportation Study (CATS), which provided annual highway expenditures from all sources by county. From these we subtract estimates of federal highway spending by county, as derived above. This leaves state and local contributions. The funds originating from local sources are estimated by applying statewide ratios of local-to-state highway funding. Subtracting this from the state and local totals gives our estimates of state funding by county.

To these county numbers we added the state taxes returned to the counties as motor fuel tax revenues. The county totals were then distributed across all metropolitan municipalities in proportion to each municipality's commuters' miles driven in that county.

As for the federal transit contributions, the state's public transit subsidies for the three regional agencies, CTA, Pace, and Metra, were estimated by Joseph DiJohn from various agency documents. We combined these with DiJohn's estimates of the residential distribution of public transit ridership for each program.

The state income tax subsidies for housing were considerably easier to estimate than those associated with the federal income tax. Since the state income tax rate is a flat 3 percent,[10] there was no need to determine marginal tax rates for each housing type in each community. The basic data on housing values by community was sufficient to estimate the implicit subsidy. The basic per capita figures were estimated first for 1990 and then adjusted by community for average appreciation. Again, we used 5 percent as the estimated rate of return on housing capital.

The data on educational expenditures per capita were obtained from the Common Core of Data published by the National Center for Education Statistics.[11] State contributions were collected by school district and aggregated up to our five basic geographic groupings. Like all other programmatic expenditures, the final figures are presented on a per capita basis, not on a per student basis.

The intergovernmental aid figures (and a large share of our other data) are based on information generously assembled for us by the Illinois Commission on Intergovernmental Cooperation. The commission made available state intergovernmental transfers to both municipalities and counties. The county figures were spread on a per capita basis across the respective municipalities and added to municipality totals. These municipality figures were then aggregated back into our basic geographic groupings.

In addition to our work on spatially relevant programs, we were also able to make estimates for direct redistributional programs such as Medicaid and general assistance. The growth of Medicaid in the first half of the 1990s has loomed particularly large in the state budget and therefore deserves attention here.

We were also able to identify a number of smaller state grant programs concentrated in the arts and community health. These are included under other identifiable programs, even though their size is relatively small.

Finally, we make estimates of salaried state payroll by municipality. These are constructed on a where-work basis from the Census's Transportation Planning Package. This keeps the state figures at least conceptually on the same footing as federal figures from the CFFR. Unfortunately, this category still represents something of a second choice in analyzing state programs. Many of these state employees are involved in carrying out direct services to local residents. However, many others, especially those working in the state office building in downtown Chicago, carry out regional or even statewide activities. Thus their specific workplace location is only a rough guide to who benefits from their efforts. For the federal government workers this problem was less severe since, outside of the post office, most of these workers had a regionwide role. For state workers, our data can only be considered a first start.

Notes

1. In addition, federal and state production sites, contracts, and other outlays can themselves directly require land as an input. When a government agency constructs a new office building in the outer suburbs, it directly absorbs land. Many of its employees seeking nearby residential locations will eventually pick peripheral residential sites. Moreover, such increases in outer suburban economic activity can be expected to produce multiplier effects as commercial businesses expand to meet new local demands. Empirical work on the Chicago area suggests that these impacts induced by public spending are not large relative to the effects discussed here. See Persky and Kurban (2001b).

2. For a discussion of our methodology in estimating these figures see the appendix, in this chapter.

3. We use commuting miles because traditionally the capacity of a highway system is seriously challenged only during peak use. For more details on our modeling see the appendix.

4. Because of problems in implementation, taxation of imputed earnings from investments in owner-occupied dwelling has not been common among the countries of the world. However, both the Netherlands and Canada have actually implemented such taxation policies. We also note that the dollar figures we come up with using this method are quite similar to the federal tax subsidy implicit in deductibility of mortgage interest. Finally, we do not estimate the value of the property tax deduction on personal federal income taxes, since we are treating housing as a business investment and such a deduction would be appropriate before taxing business income as profits.

5. Through the Public Use Microdata Sample of the 1990 Census, we estimate for each housing value category in a municipality the income distribution of owning households in that category. For more details see the appendix.

6. The effective price increase is just equal to $t/(1-t)$, where t is the effective marginal income tax rate.

7. Some state program data are available only for 1991 to 1996. Some estimates are based on 1990 Census data.

8. Our assumption here may lead to a very modest underestimation of the impact of state subsidies if state expenditures are not fully replaced with local dollars. Such partial replacement may occur because of problems of collective action. Some households may then avoid outer-suburban residential locations. However the assumption of full replacement is far more realistic than the common assumption of zero replacement.

9. Notice that since some of these redistributional programs at the county level are themselves estimated by the CFFR, we may in these cases be just reestimating their allocation formula.

10. The Illinois income tax rate has been 3 percent throughout the period, except for the first year, 1989, when it was 2.75 percent.

11. *Common Core of Data CD-ROM 1989–96.* U.S. Department of Education, National Center for Education Statistics, 1997.

References

Altshuler, Alan, and Jose Gomez-Ibanez. 1994. *Regulation for Revenue.* Washington, DC: Brookings and Lincoln Institute for Land Policy.

Bradford, David, and Wallace Oates. 1974. Suburban Exploitation of Central Cities and Government Structure. In *Redistribution Through Public Choice*, ed. Harold Hochman and George Peterson. New York: Columbia University Press.

Ellwood, David, and Mitchell Polinski. 1979. An Empirical Reconciliation of Micro and Grouped Estimates of the Demand for Housing. *Review of Economics and Statistics* 61: 199–205.

Gelfand, Mark. 1975. *Nation of Cities: The Federal Government and Urban America, 1933–1965.* New York: Oxford University Press.

Immergluck, Daniel. 1998. *A Rising Tide . . . but Some Leaky Boats: The 1990s Economic Expansion and Job Sprawl in the Chicago Region.* Chicago: Woodstock Institute.

Meyer, John, John Kain, and Martin Wohl. 1965. *The Urban Transportation Problem.* Cambridge, MA: Harvard University Press.

Musgrave, Richard, and Peggy Musgrave. 1980. *Public Finance in Theory and Practice*. New York: McGraw-Hill.
Office of Management and Budget. 1999. *Federal Credit Supplement:* http://w3.access.gpo.gov/usbudget/fy2000/buddocs.html#budget.
Orfield, Myron. 1997. *Metropolitics*. Washington, DC: The Brookings Institution.
Parker, R. Andrew. 1995. Patterns of Federal Urban Spending: Central Cities and Their Suburbs, 1983–1992. *Urban Affairs Review* 31(2): 184–205.
———. 1997. A Stealth Urban Policy in the U.S.? Federal Spending in Five Large Metropolitan Regions, 1984–1993. *Urban Studies* 34(11): 1831–1850.
Persky, Joseph, and Haydar Kurban. 2001a. Do Federal Funds Better Support Cities or Suburbs? Discussion Paper. Washington, DC: Brookings Institution Center for Urban and Metropolitan Studies.
———. 2001b. Do Federal Expenditures Build Cities or Promote Sprawl? Mimeo.
Persky, Joseph, and Wim Wiewel. 2000. *When Corporations Leave Town*. Detroit: Wayne State University Press.
Sen, Ashish et al. 1998. Chicago: Urban Transportation Center, University of Illinois at Chicago.
Stanback, Thomas Jr. 1991. *The New Suburbanization: Challenge to the Central City*, Boulder, CO: Westview Press.
U.S. Bureau of the Census. 1992. *Census of Population and Housing, 1990: Public Use Microdata Sample U.S. Technical Documentation*. Washington, DC: U.S. Bureau of the Census.

12

WIM WIEWEL AND KIMBERLY SCHAFFER

New Federal and State Policies for Metropolitan Equity

Introduction

Sprawl: There may be as many ways to define this word as there are parking spaces at the local mega-mall. Even within this book, the working definitions of sprawl vary by researcher. Wang describes suburban sprawl as a pattern of low-density land development reinforced by a strict separation of land use. DiJohn defines decentralization as the phenomenon of increasing average distance between pairs of residents in an urbanized area, or the spread (decreasing average density) of the population over time. Dye and McGuire looked at three measures to determine the amount of sprawl in a region: the share of the population outside the urban core relative to the total population of the metropolitan area, the share of urbanized land relative to the total land area of the metropolitan area, and the annual growth in urbanized land.

Regardless of its precise definition, is sprawl something to be alarmed about? Some who argue "no" see decentralization as part of the natural, efficient evolution of cities that should be allowed, if not encouraged, to continue. In a classic article questioning the merits of the antisprawl movement, Gordon and Richardson (1997) argue that smart growth advocates have not demonstrated that compact cities are more efficient or equitable, that the United States is not nearing a land or energy shortage, and that residents overwhelmingly prefer low-density housing. Therefore, "attempting a *reversal* of existing urban development is neither feasible nor desirable."

As Lindstrom's chapter illustrates, the trend towards deconcentration and suburbanization in the Chicago region was well under way a century ago. Today the Chicago urbanized area continues to become less dense, but at a slower rate; density declined by 15.3 percent in the 1960s, by 13.9 percent in the 1970s, and by 5.3 percent in the 1980s (Cox 1999). Bruegmann (2000) points out that Chicago could be following trends seen in other U.S. regions (including Miami, Los Angeles, Portland, and Phoenix), where the rate of decentralization peaks, slows, then reaches some point at which the trend reverses and the region begins to increase in density.

Even as some measures of sprawl are declining, however, there are increasing calls for slowing or reversing the deconcentration process. We find that opposition to sprawl commonly revolves around one of five issues:

- *Environment.* This may be the most tangible of the reasons—people become concerned that open space, farmlands, and natural habitats are being paved to make room for more shopping centers and housing developments, or perceive that air quality is decreasing because there are more cars on the road.
- *Equity.* Some people are concerned with the inequity that results when the poor and unskilled become concentrated in the central cities as jobs and wealthier residents leave. In a recent book Persky and Wiewel (2000) sought to quantify the benefits and costs of metropolitan decentralization, to determine whether a decentralized region was a more efficient one, as some critics of the antisprawl movement suggest. They found that while employment deconcentration did create private benefits, it also created equivalent public costs that were distributed inequitably. So there was no net efficiency gain or loss, but substantial inequalities were created.
- *Government efficiency.* Some critics believe that having many small municipal governments is inherently inefficient and does not take advantage of economies of scale.
- *Competitiveness in a global economy.* Others believe that a dispersed, fragmented, and economically unbalanced region will be less competitive in the new, more global economy.
- *Quality of life.* Finally, other groups and people care about the ephemeral consequences of sprawl—the presumed loss of a sense of community or a general feeling that quality of life is declining in their neighborhood.

Concerns about sprawl for all of these reasons are likely to continue in the Chicago region. Population projections by the Northeastern Illinois Planning Commission indicate that the six-county region will grow by about 1.8 million people by the year 2020, a 25 percent increase since 1990 (Northeastern Planning Commission 1997). Not all of that growth can be accommodated within the current built-up area. By whatever definition we choose to use, it is likely the Chicago area will continue to sprawl. As the chapters by Orlebeke and Lindstrom discuss, it is also likely that regional leaders, community organizations, and politicians at the local, state, and federal level will continue—or begin—to recommend policies and programs intended to reverse the negative effects of past suburbanization and deal with the region's projected land use changes.

The issue has become particularly salient in the last few years because the sustained period of economic growth has generated a very high rate of new residential and commercial development. Furthermore, in the Chicago region, new growth now is beginning to occur beyond the boundaries of the metropolitan area as it has long been defined. For a long time now, the built-up area of Chicago was bounded by the ring of older industrial cities spanning from Waukegan in the north, through Elgin and Aurora in the west, to Joliet in the south. These cities were the terminal points for commuter railroads into the city and formed a circumferential arch. For the past 100 years growth essentially has consisted of infill within this arch. Now, however, growth is spilling beyond this boundary into the rural areas of Kane, McHenry, and Will counties. With no natural boundaries to constrain it, growth seems destined to keep consuming farmland endlessly. Also, in going beyond the infrastructure and geographic pattern that has long been in place, the costs and consequences of this development process may well change. Clearly, as growth proceeds all along the edge of the arch, distances across the region grow exponentially.

We have briefly described the debates over what sprawl is and why it is either good or bad for the region. There is also disagreement about why the trend toward decentralization began and has continued. Is suburbanization the result of rational choices made by households and businesses to maximize efficiency and utility? Or were these choices influenced to some degree by government policies that—directly or indirectly—favored newer suburban areas over older urban cores?

Certainly, government funding policies at all levels have had important spatial implications for American regions. At the federal level urban renewal, the initial construction of the federal highway system, and housing policies all provided many families with incentives to move to the suburbs over the past forty years. However, many of these policies that were most blatantly destructive to America's urban cores have been dismantled, and Persky, Kurban, and Lester find in their chapter that federal spending since 1989 is clearly pro-city. They estimate that this spending has little effect on slowing sprawl—about 1 percent. But, presently, the federal government is not a major villain in the story of metropolitan sprawl. Indeed, many individual federal programs like the Community Development Block Grant (CDBG) program and Empowerment Zones provide a foundation for building healthier urban cores. (The major exception to this, in the view of Persky and his colleagues, is the fiscal treatment of housing.) Because the United States still lacks any comprehensive urban policy, it continues to be the combined impact of smaller and less noticeable policies that will shape the American landscape over the next several decades.

At the state level, Persky, Kurban, and Lester find that expenditures are more skewed to benefit outer suburbs than are federal expenditures. However, state expenditures have had a much lower impact on total land consumption, since the state has not emphasized homeownership as the federal government has. In total, state spending on spatially related programs (like transportation, other infrastructure, and education) is probably responsible for about 3 percent of the expansion of the urbanized area since 1989.

This chapter proceeds from the fact that the previous chapters point to some state and federal roles in facilitating the deconcentrating patterns of land use, and that among civic leadership and public opinion there are increasing calls for some sort of change in these patterns. Furthermore, the authors accept the probability that the region's future population growth will significantly exceed recent growth and will not be accommodated within current built-up areas. Therefore, the issue of how federal and state policy can shape growth patterns in the future is very relevant, regardless of how important these policies may or may not have been in the past. In most cases the recommendations will not be new, but will draw on the experiences of other states and regions. The reforms we suggest will also take into account the efforts already being made in the Chicago region, specifically those emanating from the Chicago Commercial Club's *Chicago Metropolis 2020* report and the Campaign for Sensible Growth's *Sensible Growth in Illinois*.

Recommendations are grouped into five categories:

- Land use
- Housing
- Transportation
- Fiscal policy
- Planning/Information

Certainly there are potential policy reforms that we will not touch upon here; for each of the numerous factors that push residents and business out of the central cities or pull them to the outer regions, there are innumerable potential solutions. Because of the focus of the case study, our recommendations are based on policy reforms at the federal and state levels; we will not address the many programs that can be considered by local municipalities. Instead of attempting to be comprehensive, we will focus on identifying those policies that come most directly out of the findings in this book, and on evaluating the likely success and feasibility of these policies in the Chicago region. Like the current policies that affect sprawl, most of the options we recommend would likely have only modest effects on the region. However, taken together they do provide a framework for a new way to think about land use, equity, and the region.

Finally, we provide a more succinct listing of each suggested policy and evaluate each one on the following criteria:

- Effectiveness at slowing deconcentration or its negative effects;
- Its impact on equity;
- Its political feasibility;
- The likely effort that would be needed to implement and administer the program;
- And the secondary or unintended effects that such a program could have on the region.

Land Use Policies

As the chapter by Wang shows, the rate of change to urbanized land in the Chicago region has increased since the 1970s, with a 14.5 percent increase in urban land from 1972 to 1985 and a 30 percent increase from 1985 to 1997.

Although federal and state agencies have not traditionally dealt with land use issues directly, changes in land use policies must be at the center of any federal or state plan to deal with sprawl. However, policy changes must be implemented carefully, since the local right to determine how a municipality grows physically is guarded closely by local officials. Therefore, any federal land use policies should be designed as incentive programs that still allow local control over final land use decisions. The state can also provide financial incentives for regional land use planning and give regions legislative authority as needed to address these issues.

The recommendations:

- Impose higher regional impact fees;
- Create incentives to freeze or reduce the number of municipalities and special purpose districts;
- Encourage collaboration on annexations;
- Discourage major infrastructure investments in exurban areas;
- Preserve open space through the transfer of development rights or the purchase of development rights;
- Increase incentives for employers to locate in the central city.

Impose Higher Impact Fees at the Regional Level

Although there are many types of impact fees, the term generally describes fees paid to municipalities by developers to offset costs that are associated with new development, like new infrastructure or additional demands on schools. The fees address concerns that existing residents are often forced to subsidize new residential growth in an area. Because they attempt to make new development "pay for itself" and lessen the impact of new growth on current residents, impact fees are popular in many states.

As Templeton's chapter describes, Illinois municipalities can impose impact fees, but these regulations are stricter than those in many other states. While many states follow the "rough proportionality" test from a 1994 U.S. Supreme Court case, Illinois continues to apply a "specifically and uniquely attributable" test, meaning that localities can collect exactions from developers only to cover costs (usually infrastructure related) that are directly related to new development. For the most part, the state neither encourages nor prohibits municipalities from imposing fees.

There is one exception: State legislation does offer municipalities specific guidance on roadway fees. Counties with a population of more than 400,000[1] and home rule municipalities may in theory recover costs associated with extending roads to new developments. Even this 1989 legislation has not had much effect, however, since it applies primarily to built-up areas, since the process it allows is complicated and potentially expensive, and since developers in DuPage County managed to stall its implementation for six years through court challenges.

Therefore, while most municipalities do impose some type of impact fee on developers, many forgo monetary fees and are content to receive dedications for park and school land, which may be worth less than the public costs they are meant to offset. This is unfortunate, since impact fees are an effective—and basically equitable—tool to control sprawl. By raising the cost of building new homes, the theory is that impact fees reduce demand for larger homes on larger lots (and by extension new homes in general). While impact fees do raise questions of housing affordability, it seems fair and reasonable to impose the costs of new development on the actual users. Otherwise, when development costs are artificially low, households are able to move to new areas and impose their own negative costs on those already in the newer areas and those left behind in the older areas.

While research in this area is just beginning, a recent study concludes that imposing impact fees does have a real net effect of decreasing residential development. Analyzing a sample of municipalities in DuPage County, Skidmore and Peddle (1998) determined that the presence of fees significantly reduced the rate of new residential development. Whereas the average residential growth rate in DuPage County from 1977 to 1992 was 4.3 percent, their models showed that the adoption of impact fees by the average municipality would cause the rate of growth to fall to 3 percent. In other words, residential development would slow by 29 percent. The authors did find that this slowdown was offset somewhat by the effect of lowered property taxes, but only by about 4 percent. Therefore, the authors determined that impact fees had a net effect of decreasing the amount of residential development that would otherwise occur by 25 percent. However, they caution that several questions remain to be answered, including whether developers tend to flee to municipalities that do not have impact fees, thereby increasing the rate of development there.

Impact fees are about more than just reducing land consumption, however. By moving from older areas to new ones, residents leave behind older schools, roads, and other infrastructure, which then have less of a tax base from which to draw maintenance funds. This shift in resources is especially troublesome if these households are not paying the full costs of new infrastructure in the new communities.

For these reasons we advocate state legislation to allow for the collection of impact fees on a regional (or at least county) basis, since, as the DuPage County study suggests, impact fees set by individual municipalities are likely to shift development from areas with high impact fees to areas with low fees or none at all. Such a regional program would undoubtedly be difficult to design. However, it would have to ensure that all parts of the region charge their developers comparable fees.

While impact fees could play an important role in slowing decentralization if imposed more stringently and on a regional level, such an enlargement currently seems politically unlikely at the state level. House Bill (HB) 1881, introduced in 1999, would have repealed the Road Impact Fee statute and created the Local Government Impact Fee Act to allow exactions for roads, bridges, police, fire, school facilities, and water and sewer lines. The bill was later amended to delete these provisions in favor of simply making the Road Impact Fee statute applicable to more counties. The bill has been stalled in the legislature.

To increase the likelihood of such a program, developers would have to be on board. While this seems unlikely, several sources have documented that in many cases developers prefer to work in municipalities that have set impact fees, since it reduces uncertainty in the development process and ensures that funding for new infrastructure will exist. In addition, developers would have to be granted density bonuses in developments that they do build, since less land would be developed regionally.

Reduce or Freeze the Number of Municipalities and Special Purpose Districts

The Chicago metropolitan region today has more than 1,200 units of local government, including municipalities, townships, counties, special purpose districts, and public authorities. This proliferation occurred in part as a result of older state policies: It used to be easier to incorporate a new municipality than it was to annex land into an existing one. In addition, municipalities were limited in their powers to tax or incur debt, so numerous special districts were created that had the powers to bond and tax to provide additional services.

Dye and McGuire, in their chapter, find some evidence that regions with higher numbers of municipalities have more sprawl. Of the six regressions they ran, the number of municipalities was a highly significant variable in three regressions. To address this, the state could offer additional incentives to municipalities that merge, either entirely or of significant parts of their operations. (These incentives would also address other negatives generally associated with a governmentally fragmented region. For example, there would be fewer opportunities for municipalities to enter into bidding wars with each other for development.) Some incentives for mergers are already built into certain programs. Once a municipality has 50,000 residents, for example, it may qualify to receive Community Development Block Grant funding directly from HUD, instead of competing for pass-through funds from the state or county government (U.S. Department of Housing and Urban Development 1999).

Examples of fiscal incentives for municipal cooperation also exist in other states. In Pennsylvania, the Department of Community and Economic Development offers grants that are available only to two or more municipalities applying jointly. The Shared Municipal Services Program provides up to a few thousand dollars for municipalities to combine police record administration, purchase equipment jointly, or otherwise work together to provide services more efficiently (Pennsylvania Department of Community 1999). At the very least, the Illinois Department of Commerce and Community Affairs could institute a similar program to encourage municipal cooperation beyond the mutual aid pacts that are common now. Such economic incentives would provide immediate and tangible benefits for residents and could facilitate longer and more meaningful partnerships between municipalities in the future.

While it doesn't go so far as to recommend merging municipalities, the *Chicago Metropolis 2020* report does advocate studying the consolidation of special districts and townships, specifically to determine what costs are associated with the duplication of many efforts and what the opportunities for consolidation are. However, it recognizes that even such a step would be politically unpopular. "Because this proposal [to streamline the region's governance structure] is bound to meet stiff resistance by officeholders and staff of these districts, the Metropolis plan recommends creation of a task force that includes members having astute political sensitivities and experience with cost control and corporate simplification" (Johnson 1999, 24).

Encourage Collaboration on Annexations

In 1990 the village of Huntley covered two square miles. Having annexed huge chunks of the vacant land that surrounded it, the village now covers 11 square miles—more than five times the size it was ten years ago. Its acquisitions were done quickly, without referenda or court approval, and entirely legally. While Huntley's relative growth may be extreme, large annexations are not uncommon. In the thirty years from 1960 to 1990, Elgin, Joliet, and Waukegan all doubled in physical size, and Aurora tripled its land mass. As Templeton points out, there is really no reason for a municipality *not* to annex as much adjoining land as possible. Because developers are usually eager to have their new developments incorporated (for the fire, police, and other services the municipality then provides its buyers), they often make substantial payments to the municipality. Municipalities are usually also eager to incorporate new growth, especially if it is commercial, so they can reap the tax revenue benefits. More generally, municipalities want to be able to exert some control over new development, which they can do only if it is within their borders. In addition, annexation provides municipalities with an easy way to increase their importance regionally, literally almost overnight.

Of course, it is not the annexation itself that is the problem, since fewer large municipalities may be more desirable than many small and newly incorporated ones. However, lax annexation policies do nothing to restrict development in outlying unincorporated areas. If developers see a benefit from having their developments in incorporated areas, but municipalities are given incentives not to annex additional land, growth could shift to inside existing municipalities.

Further, benefits of annexation accrue only to municipalities that are surrounded by vacant land—those on the urban fringe. As residents and businesses leave older areas for outlying ones, these landlocked municipalities are not able to capture more growth simply by drawing themselves bigger boundaries. In this way, state policies allowing easy annexations directly favor the enlargement of outer suburban areas over established urban and suburban ones.

Currently, annexations are controlled primarily through voluntary boundary agreements, in which municipalities decide among themselves which land each will or will not annex in coming years. Since annexation procedures are set forth by the state, well-developed changes to state statutes could have important effects on the amount of land annexed and developed in outlying areas. Such changes would most likely mean creating incentives for more coordination among municipalities. For example, the state could provide funding for municipalities to engage in joint planning, either with each other or with the county or counties in which they are located. Since many annexations are driven by the provision of water and sewer lines, more state control of infrastructure funding could have important implications as well. At the regional level, the Northeastern Illinois Planning Commission could be granted authority by the state to approve or reject such annexations based on the likely effect such annexations would have on land use patterns.

The implementation of regional revenue sharing would be a further disincentive to annexation. To the extent that municipalities annex preemptively to capture the tax revenues generated by future malls and other commercial development, tax-base sharing would mean that commercial areas would not have to be located within a municipality's borders for them to reap some of the fiscal benefits. This would be facilitated through voluntary agreements among municipalities.

Discourage Major Infrastructure Investments in Outer Parts of the Region

Lindstrom's chapter illustrates that the city of Chicago would not have developed into the metropolis that is today had it not been for large amounts of federal, state, and private money spent building up the city's infrastructure (in addition to the significant funds invested by the city itself).

Persky and his colleagues show that large amounts of federal infrastructure funding still flow to the central city, but this primarily serves to maintain existing roads and public transportation. At the same time, most funds for new highways went to the newer suburbs. The city of Chicago still ranks above the suburbs that became urbanized by 1950, 1970, or 1990 in the amount of federal funding received for highway and related programs, public transit, and other infrastructure. However, the 1990 suburbs rank second, only a few dollars per capita behind the city. From 1989 to 1992 Chicago received an average of $131 per capita in these categories, while the 1990 suburbs received $118. Between 1993 and 1996 the gap narrowed even more, with the federal government contributing $107 per resident to the city and $101 to the 1990 suburbs.

The amount of federal funding is even more important than these numbers suggest, since federal dollars are often leveraged with state and/or local money. In this way, federal priorities can also dictate specifically where and how other funding sources will be spent.

Other states, noticing similar trends with state-level funding, have enacted programs to ensure that the central cores remain the focus of the state's infrastructure funding. Most notable is the state of Maryland's Smart Growth Initiatives, enacted by the state legislature in 1997. The program contains five components—including a Rural Legacies program, a Brownfields program, Job Creation Tax Credits, and Live Near Your Work—but the centerpiece of the legislation is the creation of Priority Funding Areas (PFA).

Since October 1998, state funds for projects like roads, water and sewer, and state facilities are directed to the state's priority funding areas, which include every municipality, areas inside the Baltimore and Washington beltways, and designated enterprise zones. The governor's intent was to change the state's fiscal priorities to ensure that the state did not fund sprawl-inducing development over a project that might help to revitalize an older municipality. However, faced with opposition from county planners who did not want to relinquish planning control to the state, the final legislation gives counties great leeway in establishing their area boundaries. As a concession, local governments may also designate other parts of their county as Priority Funding Areas, including in some cases areas where developments are merely proposed and do not yet exist. The legislation requires the state to accept any areas the counties designate for growth. While that proviso significantly weakened the legislation, it is not without impact, though, since state agencies are allowed to "comment" on a county's designations. Negative comments from the state planning agency could mean repercussions when dealing with other state agencies (Gurwitt 1999; Maryland Office of Planning 1999).

The Maryland PFA program holds important lessons for the state of Illinois. It is most notable because while it provides incentives for municipalities to "grow smart," it does not make direct land use restrictions on the local governments. They remain free to encourage development wherever in the county they choose, so long as no state funds are involved. Certainly, implementing a similar program in Illinois would be much harder, for a few reasons. First, Illinois counties do not have as much control over land use issues as counties in Maryland do. Second, the Persky group's analysis shows that beyond highways and public transit, the state contributes very little to other infrastructure development—less than $10 per capita to residents in each area of the region. However, a program here that would require municipalities and counties to make development plans and then channel state infrastructure funding only to designated growth areas would probably have some marginal effects on land consumption.

Preserve Open Space Through the Purchase or Transfer of Development Rights

Open space and farmland preservation efforts are one of the most popular growth control measures nationwide. Perhaps that is because for most suburban residents, one of the most immediately noticeable effects of the sprawling of urban areas is the seemingly rapid disappearance of open space. As farmland begins to be cleared to make room for new housing or commercial developments, residents may begin to feel threatened by the amount of growth in their community and work to enact land preservation measures. This phenomenon can certainly be observed in the Chicago region. As Wang's analysis of Landsat photos shows, almost 275,000 acres became urbanized in the region between 1972 and 1995, for a growth rate of almost 50 percent. Natural areas declined by 21 percent and agricultural areas by 37 percent. At the same time, residents in four of Chicago's collar counties have supported more than $200 million in bond issues to preserve farmland and open space (Bukro 1999).

There are two main ways a region can preserve open space—either through the transfer of development rights or the outright purchase of those rights (also known as conservation easements). In the latter program, farmers permanently give up the right to develop their land in exchange for a cash payment. Farmers are compensated for the difference between what the farm would sell for in agriculture use, and what it would sell for when used for development. In Pennsylvania's program, payments average about $2,000 per acre (Freese 1995). The farmer may sell the land at any time, but the easement remains with the property permanently.

A transfer of development rights program is usually more complex to administer and may take more forms. Generally, however, the local government designates certain areas within its boundaries as "sending areas" and other areas as "receiving areas." Such programs may be voluntary—developers may get density bonuses by buying the rights—or mandatory—owners are not permitted to build in sending areas, and developers may not build in receiving areas without purchasing rights.

In addition to the efforts of individual counties to preserve open space through bond issues, the state of Illinois is also beginning to take more of an interest in open space preservation. As part of the Illinois Open Land Trust initiative, passed unanimously by the House of Representatives, the state will provide $160 million over four years for state and local governments to acquire land for conservation or recreation. Although the law allows for partnerships with nongovernmental organizations, all lands acquired will have to remain under government ownership (Governor's Open Land 1999).

It is also important that, as Illinois's land conservation programs continue, policymakers distinguish between preserving farmland and preserving open space, and make sure they know which goal they are pursuing. While many U.S. programs have been farmland preservation programs, these programs may be more expensive than simply purchasing open space. In addition, it has been shown that in many cases residents want open space, and they may actually resent the secondary effects of farming in their community. If, on the other hand, a region truly does want to preserve farming, it may be necessary to ensure that a critical mass of farms is preserved near one another and that the program is bolstered with other preservation efforts such as agriculture zoning (Maynard et al. 1998).

Increase Incentives for Employers to Locate in the Central City

In 1972, 44 percent of the region's population worked in suburban Cook County or one of the collar counties. By 1995 the suburban share of the region's employment had increased to 66 percent (Illinois Department of Employment Security 2000). While many businesses have certainly benefited from the efficiency gains associated with their suburban locations, this employment shift has had important consequences for the region. First, as Felsenstein estimates in his chapter, the development of high technology employment alone in Chicago's outer regions has led to the consumption of 24,000 acres of land—18,000 acres more than would have been developed if these industries had located in the city instead. Second, the suburbanization of jobs has meant that low-income center-city residents (and suburban residents without cars) have found it increasingly difficult to find well-paying employment within their reach. This spatial jobs–housing mismatch raises transportation, housing, and general fiscal equity issues.

In deciding on a new business location, employers tend to pick for reasons of efficiency rather than equity. Therefore, government policies must work to level the field between older core areas and newer outlying areas. In past years some federal policy has had the unintended effect of making inner-city sites even less attractive to commercial and industrial firms than they otherwise would have been. For example, the Environmental Protection Agency's designation of old industrial sites as brownfields had the deleterious effect of making it cheaper to develop suburban "greenfields" than to reuse older industrial sites, since banks and other investors stayed away from brownfields, fearing they would be held liable for environmental cleanup costs.

An important example of a regional, state, and federal partnership formed to overcome this disincentive is the Chicago Brownfields Initiative, which developed a final report listing ways that various local, state, and federal agencies can work together to facilitate clean up and reuse of some of the city's contaminated industrial sites. At the county level Cook County will reduce an eligible site's property tax bill by about 55 percent for up to three years during the site's redevelopment. Statewide, Illinois also offers a brownfields tax credit worth up to $40,000 a year or $150,000 per site. And under certain conditions the federal brownfields tax incentive allows redevelopers to deduct cleanup costs in the year they occur, instead of over several years (City of Chicago 1998).

But encouraging brownfields development is just one example of how regional, state, and federal agencies can help to redirect industrial development to the inner city. Tax increment financing districts, site assembly, workforce training programs, and property tax abatements and subsidies should all be part of the city's efforts to retain and expand its employment base, as well as to create a mix of housing options. There is no doubt that in some cases these incentives are abused and offered to companies or residential developments that would have located in the city anyway. In general, however, they are critical tools for cities.

Housing Policies

In his analysis of municipalities in the region located approximately thirty miles from downtown Chicago, Zhang (2001) finds that new residential development is affected more by internal community factors than by external forces like transportation accessibility that could be affected by federal spending. Similar to Orlebeke in his chapter, he concludes that current federal policies have little direct impact on sprawl and that local policies do have an important effect on how a community grows.

Persky's group finds, however, that the current federal housing policy that pursues the expansion of private homeownership has increased land consumption by as much as 20 percent from 1970 to 1990, making homeownership subsidies the largest federal contributor to metropolitan sprawl. And McDonald and McMillen find in their chapter that it is primarily new residential development that is scattered throughout the metropolitan area (as opposed to commercial or industrial, which is more concentrated). Therefore, housing policy reform is key to addressing issues of equity and land consumption.

Federal housing policy has helped to shape residential land use patterns over the past forty years. For example, the promotion of homeownership through various subsidies and the construction of high-rise inner-city public housing units have contributed to the residential landscape. In addition, numerous federal programs from environmental regulations to immigration policies have affected residential choices indirectly.

In the future the federal actions are likely to have less direct effect on regional housing patterns as federal agencies rework some programs to give more discretion to state and local governments. In the past few decades federal grants to specific urban projects have been replaced by block grants like HOME and Community Development Block Grants. Under new HUD regulations, public housing units are being replaced by rental vouchers. As Orlebeke shows, due to failures like inner-city public housing projects and unenforceable requirements that regions prepare housing plans, the federal government has steadily disengaged itself from the housing arena.

Neither is housing activism high on the state's smart growth agenda. Although Governor George Ryan of Illinois has successfully advanced transportation and farmland preservation initiatives, his administration has made virtually no mention of housing policies. As Orlebeke writes, "Politically, action on housing is further, much further, down the list on the smart growth agenda." Few policy areas are as personal to residents as housing issues, and few issues are seen as intrinsic to a local municipality's existence as the ability to determine the residential layout of their community.

The region's changing demographics may make it easier to argue for housing policy changes. As Lindstrom points out, the region's population is expected to grow considerably browner, blacker, and grayer over the next few decades, as more minorities move into the region and as the population becomes older. In addition, Americans are generally marrying later and having fewer children. These changes in lifestyles all suggest that a typical large suburban home with a yard will become less relevant to increasing numbers of the population. Changing work roles may also lead to a change in housing demand, as more people either commute to jobs in the suburbs or skip the drive entirely in favor of telecommuting. For all of these reasons, employers and regional coalitions need to reimagine housing in the Chicago region.

The recommendations:

- Remove fiscal incentives that encourage the overconsumption of land by lowering the cap on the mortgage interest deduction or providing more incentives for higher density development;
- Continue federal programs like HOME and CDBG;
- Address affordable housing issues regionally:

    (a) Increase the availability of rental vouchers;
    (b) Provide incentives for inclusionary zoning;
    (c) Encourage transit-oriented development;
    (d) Provide incentives for employer-assisted housing.

Remove Subsidies That Encourage Overconsumption of Land

In their analysis of federal expenditures in the Chicago region from 1989 through 1996, Persky and his colleagues find that housing was one of the policy areas in which federal spending made the most difference. Their evidence suggests that aggressive federal subsidies of housing have influenced households to consume larger houses on larger lots. This suggests that changes to federal and state housing subsidies could reduce the amount of land consumed in coming decades.

Specifically, the federal government could remove income tax subsidies to homeowners. While rental property owners receive income for renting out houses that they own, they must then pay taxes on that income, after deducting the interest paid on the building's mortgage. On the other hand, individual homeowners are not taxed for the potential or imputed stream of income they could receive by renting out their home (as they are in some countries), yet they are allowed to deduct the business expense of the mortgage interest from their taxes. The federal government could either tax homeowners for their unrealized income stream and still allow the full mortgage deduction, or they could lower the deduction cap that homeowners who do not rent their property are allowed to take.

Of course, the favorable tax treatment for homeownership was originally implemented to further the national goal of increased homeownership, which it was successful in doing. Like other policies, the subsidy's effect on deconcentration has been largely unintended. While removing this subsidy would decrease land consumption considerably, changing current policies would be politically very difficult and would require a shift in public thinking. The state or federal government could choose another way to decrease deconcentration without reducing incentives for homeownership, especially by providing households with incentives to move into higher density housing. For homeowners this could mean lowering the cap on the mortgage interest deduction limit instead of removing the deduction completely. On the supply side, incentives for higher density housing could be similar to those designed to increase affordable housing in the suburbs.

Continue Existing Federal Programs That Give Metropolitan Areas Funding Flexibility

Like TEA 21 in the transportation arena, federal housing has evolved over the years into more flexible programs that are generally beneficial to cities. Each year, the city of Chicago typically receives more than $100 million in federal Community Development Block Grant funds (U.S. Department of Housing 1999). While these funds must primarily benefit low- and moderate-income households and neighborhoods, the city has wide latitude on the types of projects it may fund.

At the same time, however, suburban counties also get CDBG and HOME allocations, and with just as wide spending latitude, there's nothing to stop administrators from using these funds on projects that facilitate deconcentration. Nationally, a major use of CDBG funds is water and sewer projects, which often expand new service into more rural areas and may make these areas more attractive to new development. Similarly, a community may use HOME funds to build low-income housing, but may locate the housing in more rural areas where land is cheaper and public opposition is lower. These isolated locations may leave residents unable to access public transit or employment.

These potential problems in the federal block grant programs could be addressed with a few programmatic changes. For instance, one of the requisites to allocating funding could be that a community designate growth areas, which would be the only areas in which funds could be spent. Of course, it would be relatively easy for a community to manipulate these as it saw fit, but such a requirement would at least get suburban and rural communities thinking about the effects of their spending. Similarly, CDBG and HOME training sessions could offer information to help administrators consider the long-term effects of particular projects on their communities.

Increase the Availability of Rental Vouchers for Low-Income Residents

In recent decades the Department of Housing and Urban Development has slowly switched its emphasis from supply-side policies (providing units of public housing) to demand-side ones, offering tenants portable vouchers that they can use to subsidize their rent in a privately owned building. The Section 8 program, created in 1974, provides housing certificates and vouchers to low-income households throughout the country. In most cases, a family pays 30 percent of its income toward the monthly rent, and the government pays the landlord the difference between that amount and the cost of the apartment. In theory, residents can take their voucher to any apartment that meets HUD's minimum quality standards (and fair market rent levels, in the case of certificates), gaining more freedom and greater housing opportunities.

However, rental voucher programs have their own shortcomings. In many cases, Section 8 tenants end up resegregating themselves in high-poverty neighborhoods with no greater access to jobs. Others have indicated that they are unable to find housing because of landlord discrimination against voucher holders. In many cases tenants have never had to search for housing before and find themselves ill equipped to do so. In addition, a lack of affordable housing is in many cases only one of several barriers a family faces on its way to self-sufficiency. For example, low-income households may be affected by the job-housing mismatch and may need to travel long distances to work, often relying on public transportation. This obstacle becomes magnified when children must be delivered to day care, which may or may not be located near the parents' home or work (University of Illinois at Chicago 1999).

A new federal program begins to address some of these concerns. In October 1999 HUD allocated $280 million to fund the first 50,000 welfare-to-work vouchers (MetroLinks 1999). These vouchers provide more comprehensive assistance to low-income families in need of housing and other services. In addition to rental assistance, a household with a welfare-to-work voucher may also receive employment training, job placement, and family support services.

Of the 50,000 welfare-to-work vouchers funded nationally in 1999, 1,025 were allocated to the Chicago region as part of the MetroLinks pilot project. In what is also a notable example of burgeoning regionalism in the Chicago area, the four recipient public housing agencies (the city of Chicago and DuPage, Cook, and Lake counties) applied jointly for the allocation. In addition, these agencies received leveraged funding commitments of more than $9.9 million from other state and federal agencies as well as nonprofit organizations and foundations (MetroLinks 1999). Certainly, this allocation is evidence of some change in housing policy: Local housing authorities are thinking more regionally about housing, and state and federal officials are realizing that recipients need more comprehensive assistance. But while MetroLinks is an important pilot program for the region, the 1,025 vouchers only begin to address the unmet housing needs in the region. In the city of Chicago alone, tens of thousands of families are on the waiting list for Section 8 housing-choice vouchers, and the waiting list is often closed to new households. Once the initial welfare-to-work vouchers are used and the program is running smoothly, the federal government should increase the number of vouchers it provides and offer similar comprehensive assistance to all recipients of housing vouchers and certificates.

Provide Incentives for Inclusionary Zoning

In his book *Inside Game/Outside Game*, David Rusk (1999) advocates going beyond giving low-income residents the theoretical ability to live in more stable, economically viable neighborhoods to mandating that all communities provide low-income housing. "If I could wave a magic political wand across this country, I have no doubt which would be the most important policy: a mandatory mixed-income housing policy for all new construction," he writes (pp. 325–326). Needless to say, most regions do not immediately embrace such programs.

Montgomery County, Maryland, is one of a few regions in the country to have an ordinance requiring that developers build true mixed-income communities. Here, in each new development of more than fifty homes, the developer must allot between 12.5 and 15 percent to moderate-income families. Of these, one-third (5 percent of the total) must be offered for sale to the county's public housing authority. In return for developing a portion of the land with below-market homes, the developer is granted a density bonus of up to 22 percent (Montgomery County n.d.). As a result of this program, 10,000 moderately priced dwelling units have been built since 1974—7,200 that have been sold to moderate-income families and another 2,800 that have been rented to low-income families (Larsen 2000). In addition to increasing the number of affordable housing units in stable communities, accommodating a similar share of low-income residents in each community ensures that a few communities do not become burdened with funding services through a low tax base.

In addition, locating affordable housing units near transportation and employment options is an important part of a comprehensive affordable housing strategy. If low-income families are stranded in the suburbs without adequate transportation to jobs, they are no better off than they were in the inner cities.

In the Chicago region, counties have much less power than those in Maryland do, making transferability of this program difficult. However, incentives like reductions in impact fees, density bonuses, and state support for infrastructure could all help increase the amount of affordable housing available in the suburbs. The FHA could also give extra consideration to mixed-income projects when determining its willingness to provide financing or in setting interest rates.

Provide Incentives for Employer-Assisted Housing

As the various levels of government have become less involved in the direct provision of affordable housing, more employers are realizing that it is in their interest to offer employees housing options near their work. While government agencies may not have a direct role in this housing provision, they can offer programmatic flexibility and other incentives to employers providing housing assistance.

Perhaps no region has a more active—or more needed—Employer Assisted Housing (EAH) program than Silicon Valley, California. In a region where seven out of every ten residents cannot afford to own homes and where available rental vacancies hovered at 2 percent at the height of the economic boom (Silicon Valley Manufacturing Group 1999), employers realized that their competitiveness as a region depends in large part on the ability of their workforce to find affordable housing. Five of the region's major employers, Santa Clara County, and the city of San Jose contributed a total of $4 million in 1998 to begin building the region's Housing Trust Fund. This contribution was followed by a two-year, $20 million campaign. Initially, the trust fund will assist 5,000 families with first-time homebuyer assistance, affordable rental housing, and homeless assistance. The trust fund, which is coordinated by several organizations, including the Silicon Valley Manufacturing Group, is popular because it will not be funded by any new taxes or fees but will rely on investments from individuals, foundations, corporations, and government agencies. Employers view the trust fund as an investment in a solution, not just a charitable donation (Silicon Valley Manufacturing Group 1999).

Regions interested in affordable housing can also partner with Fannie Mae, which will work with employers to develop specific employer-assisted housing plans that take advantage of other Fannie Mae funds and incentives. As part of Fannie Mae's EAH program, employers can set up a program to provide direct financial assistance to supplement a traditional first mortgage like a grant, loan, or loan guarantee to be used for the down payment, closing costs, or monthly payments. Or employers can choose to offer more indirect assistance, like accessibility to other local assistance programs (Fannie Mae 1999). Employers who partner in Fannie Mae's EAH programs are limited to assisting employees who fall under specific income limits.

In Illinois, House Bill 4074 would create the Live Near Work Fund that would provide matching state grants to "encourage employers, counties, and municipalities to invest in employer-assisted housing." The fund would assist employees earning less than 120 percent of the area median income to acquire homes in close proximity to their jobs, thereby "expand[ing] home ownership opportunities" and "reduc[ing] traffic congestion by reducing employee commute times" (State of Illinois 2000).

Both the Metropolitan Planning Council and the *Metropolis 2020* report emphasize the importance of employer-assisted housing, both to residents and employers. While the benefits to potential homeowners may be obvious, MPC also points out that it may be cheaper for employers to assist with housing costs of existing employees than to recruit and train new employees. We recommend that the region continue its efforts to implement an employer-assisted housing program as a way of making jobs in the suburbs (and, in some cases, the city) more accessible to more of the region's residents.

Transportation Policies

In general, Americans love their cars and avoid using mass transit. As DiJohn's chapter shows, from 1973 to 1993 in the Chicago region, vehicle miles traveled increased by 57.6 percent, while transit ridership fell by 18.5 percent. While economic prosperity has certainly allowed more individuals to purchase and maintain a personal automobile, federal and state policies have also played a role in creating this shift.

Perhaps the most noticeable federal investment in the automobile culture was the building of the Interstate Highway System. From 1965 to the mid-1990s, the federal government spent $652 billion (in 1996 dollars) on highway aid. On the other hand, the federal government did not begin financing mass transit until 1961, when it made funding available under the Housing and Urban Development Act. In roughly the same time period, the federal government spent only $85 billion (in 1996 dollars), or about one-seventh the amount, in federal aid to public bus and subway systems (Rusk 1999). While these aggregated numbers do not account for the differences in numbers of users between the categories, part of the point is that transit would likely have had more users if it had been funded more equally. At the state level, it was not until the 1970 constitutional convention that Illinois designated transit as a legitimate public purpose on which state funds could be spent. Until then all transit was provided by private companies, while the state involved itself in road building.

Of course, not all road funding allocations encourage sprawl, and it could also be argued that extending transit systems in outlying areas does almost as much to draw new businesses and residents to exurban communities as a new road does. Indeed, Warner's classic *Streetcar Suburbs* makes just that point in regard to the development of Boston

(1969). In the Chicago area, most of the older suburbs were developed along the rail lines that entrepreneurial companies put in. But for proponents of both environmental and equity issues, encouraging public transportation is a key part of any comprehensive strategy to control sprawl.

In recent years the federal government has begun to pay more attention to transit through the passage of the Intermodal Surface Transportation Efficiency Act (ISTEA) and its successor, the Transportation Equity Act for the 21st Century (TEA 21). Likewise, the state of Illinois in 1999 passed Illinois FIRST (Funding for Infrastructure, Roads, Schools and Transit), a five-year, $12 billion funding program to build and repair the state's critical infrastructure. While both the federal and state programs retain substantial allocations for highways and other road projects, each has an emphasis on transit that would have been unlikely in earlier decades. As part of Illinois FIRST, highways and transit are each allocated $4.1 billion, although the transit allocation includes $2 billion in federal funds. At the federal level, $41 billion of a total $218 billion authorization over six years is earmarked for transit programs. Eighty percent of the $41 billion is guaranteed from the Highway Trust Fund, and the remaining 20 percent is expected to come from the general fund (Federal Highway Administration 2000).

TEA 21 and Illinois FIRST both provide a solid foundation for the reworking of the region's transportation policies. Each should be continued, and regional agencies should take full advantage of the flexibility the programs offer. However, more can be done. The recommendations described below offer additional ways in which state and federal transportation policies can be altered to lessen their impact on sprawl:

- Change private transportation funding:
  (a) Increasing gas taxes or implement value-pricing programs;
  (b) Consider abolishing the Highway Trust Fund.
- Address mass transit:
  (a) Increase proactive transit funding;
  (b) Fund flexible transit options.
- Address commercial transportation:
  (a) Better integrate modes of transportation and encourage railroads.

Change Private Transportation Funding

Three major changes in federal transportation funding need to be considered to level the field between private automobiles and mass transit.

First, taxes on gasoline should be significantly increased. Second, congestion, or value, pricing should be seriously considered as a funding source for regional infrastructure projects. Finally, we raise the question whether the Highway Trust Fund, a self-perpetuating source for road funding, should be abolished.

Increase Gasoline Taxes

A first important reform that should be enacted at the federal level is increasing the gasoline tax to a level that would significantly reduce the amount of vehicle miles driven. Currently, federal taxes on gasoline are about 18 cents a gallon (Federal Highway Administration 1999)—not high enough to induce drivers to drive less. By taxing the consumption of gasoline at higher rates, the government could bring the number of miles driven down to lower levels and offset the negative externalities associated with driving—like pollution, accidents, and congestion. It could also act as an incentive for more compact development, to reduce the need for driving.

An additional benefit of such a tax is that it raises revenues that can further remedy the negative effects of too much driving. The Federal Highway Administration estimates that each penny collected per gallon of fuel tax generates more than $1.4 billion in annual revenues. If taxes were raised to be comparable to those in other countries (from $1.93 per gallon in Japan to $3.54 per gallon in France), the government would still raise significant revenues even after accounting for the drop in gallons bought (Nivola 1999). The additional funding could be used for other programs discussed here, like affordable housing or open space or, more likely, the government could offer citizens an equivalent reduction in income taxes.

In a survey of Chicago, suburban, and downstate Illinois residents, a slight majority of residents said they would support a five-cent-per-gallon gasoline tax to be used toward highway and transit improvements (Sööt et al. 1998). State politicians, on the other hand, not only are wary of raising gas taxes, but are more inclined to lower them: in response to rising gasoline prices in 2000, the Illinois legislature voted to suspend a 5 percent state sales tax on gas purchases for six months (McKinney 2000). Further in the future, any increase in gas taxes at the state or federal level would likely be small and lead only to increases in fuel efficiency, rather than to a reduction in miles driven. While this would then obviate the effect on reducing sprawl, it would still have the beneficial effect of reducing pollution and congestion associated with driving.

Implement Value Pricing

Second, the Chicago region should also follow the lead of other regions and countries in implementing some form of value pricing—formerly known as congestion pricing. Under TEA 21, the federal government has authorized $51 million for fiscal years 1999–2003 for the Value Pricing Pilot Program. This funding will support the implementation of up to fifteen value pricing programs at the state or local level (Federal Highway Administration 2000). Under a value pricing program, motorists are charged tolls that are higher during peak periods of travel. Presumably, once commuters weigh their options and choose other routes, the traffic on the highway will return to the economically optimal level.

Both a gasoline tax and a value pricing program are economically efficient because they provide a way to reduce demand for highways, lower the externalities of driving, and generate revenues to further alleviate the problem or offset other taxes. However, such taxes are also regressive, having a proportionately larger effect on low-income families than on higher-income ones. Therefore, the implementation of either would raise equity concerns. TEA 21 requires that effects on low-income drivers be considered as part of any value pricing program, and funds projects to offset costs to low-income drivers. If these programs expand beyond TEA 21, it will be important, although difficult, to retain this provision.

Reconsider the Highway Trust Fund

Before 1956 revenues from motor fuel taxes went directly into the federal government's general fund. Then the Highway Revenue Act of 1956 created the Highway Trust Fund as a way to guarantee funding for the construction of the new Interstate Highway System. Today, even though the highway system is for the most part completed, all federal fuel tax funds (excluding a 4.3-cent-per-gallon tax that is sent to the General Fund for deficit reduction) and other user taxes are channeled directly into the Trust Fund, where they must be spent exclusively on transportation projects. In fiscal year 1996, $24.7 billion in tax revenues was designated for the Highway Trust Fund. Of this amount, 89 percent ($22.0

billion) was directed to the highway account and 10.5 percent was allocated to the transit account. While the percentage going to transit projects may seem low, it was not until 1983 that any HTF funding at all was directed towards transit (Federal Highway Administration 1999).

This exclusive, untouchable source of funding for road projects has skewed federal funding priorities by creating a guaranteed funding source for transportation projects. If revenue generated by fuel taxes were put into the General Fund, as is the case in most European countries, road projects would have to compete with other federal programs for funding, and fewer (presumably only the highly urgent) would be funded (Nivola 1999).

Change the Way Mass Transit Is Funded and Operated

Much of the decrease in transit ridership came during the RTA's financial crisis of the early 1980s, when funding shortfalls caused the CTA, Metra, and Pace to raise fares and cut service. In turn, riders abandoned the system rather than pay more for less value, causing even more dire funding shortfalls. During just one two-year period of 1981 to 1983 (which also coincided with a recession), the system lost 113 million rides (DiJohn, in this volume). Although ridership has been increasing since 1998, it has not been enough to offset the losses of the past twenty years. For transit to be viable, it needs to be funded proactively, and alternatives to fixed route systems need to be considered seriously.

Increase Proactive Funding

As DiJohn points out, such self-reinforcing declines in ridership can be avoided only through proactive maintenance that keeps infrastructure and service levels high. Until recently this has not often been the case in Chicago, where the small pool of transit dollars must first pay operating expenses, while larger projects are delayed. The Douglas branch of the Blue Line train, now 103 years old, is so dilapidated that trains run only a few miles per hour over parts of the track. The state has approved $315 million to rebuild the track (Dorning and Hilkevitch 1999), but presumably repairs could have been made more cheaply and without alienating riders if they had been undertaken years ago. Now that Illinois First and TEA 21 offer additional funding for transit projects, the CTA has begun to make major as well as cosmetic and service improvements. The region must continue to leverage funds to continue this new approach.

Provide Alternatives to Fixed Transit

While the region must continue to support its fixed transit system, it must also consider more innovative ways of providing transportation options for residents, especially in light of the region's jobs-housing mismatch. Again, TEA 21 allows communities to fund reverse commuting programs and other transit alternatives (such as vanpools), and the Chicago region should take advantage of this flexibility.

Address Commercial Transportation

Integrate Different Modes of Transportation and Encourage Investment in the Railroads

Chicago has historically been the freight transportation hub of the nation. While at one time that meant domination by the railroad, today Chicago leads the United States in the volume of freight moved by trucks. In fact, 41 percent of the increase in vehicle miles traveled from 1973 to 1993 can be attributed to commercial traffic. While Thakuriah in her chapter finds that the commercial trucking industry is not a major contributor to deconcentration in the region, several policy changes could shift the current emphasis on freight transportation away from trucks and back to the railroads. Doing so would improve congestion and pollution and would reduce wear on the region's roadways.

The intermodal freight industry accounted for approximately $8.7 billion—6 percent—of northeastern Illinois's gross regional product in 1996, and such activity between modes of transportation (rail to truck or air to truck) is expected to increase. According to Thakuriah, the interface between trucking and railroad facilities is a major challenge in the region. At the same time, the volume of freight moved by railroad is expected to increase by more than 75 percent between 1996 and 2020, increasing demand on the region's rail infrastructure. In order to minimize the region's dependence on trucking and to encourage freight travel by train, the federal and state government and the regional MPO (CATS) should work together to invest in the region's railways. Illinois FIRST allocates $10 million to alleviate freight congestion in the Chicago region, and TEA 21 includes provisions for up to $1 billion nationally for the "acquisition, development, improvement, or rehabilitation of intermodal or rail equipment or facilities" (Federal Highway Administration 1999). While railroads will not recapture from the trucking industry the share of goods they transport, a shift in state and federal policy to fund rail infrastructure could help reduce highway congestion in the region.

Fiscal Policies

Fiscal policies are among the least visible public policy instruments in regard to sprawl, but they can nevertheless have considerable effects on the region's development. We have already discussed the influence of the favorable treatment of home ownership in the federal tax code as a major contributor to land consumption. Other fiscal policies that we have not considered explicitly in our study are, for instance, the nature of depreciation allowances and their effect on promoting new development over rehabilitation of older buildings, thus contributing to outward expansion of the urbanized area. At the state and local level there also are taxation practices that have an effect on deconcentration. One that our study has not dealt with explicitly is the assessment system, which differs greatly between Cook County and the other counties in the region. While Dye and McGuire find little effect of property taxes on deconcentration, there is a widespread perception that the relatively unfavorable treatment of industrial and commercial property in Cook County has driven out many firms. Although there are many additional aspects of these issues, the studies that we have conducted give rise to several specific recommendations:

- Equalize school funding
- Reduce municipalities' reliance on property taxes
  (a) Increase state income taxes
  (b) Implement revenue sharing

Equalize School Funding

In their chapter Dye and McGuire theorize that policies to equalize school funding and provide more state aid could lower the level of sprawl in a region. If inner-city schools are underfunded and suburban schools are well funded, in the absence of other alternatives, families with children will move to the outer areas. On the other hand, as state aid becomes more equalizing, more families with school-age children might choose to stay in the region's core, resulting in a lower share of the region's population in the collar counties.

By examining more than 100 large metropolitan areas from 1970 to 1990, they find that sprawl may be lower in regions whose states contribute a larger share of school districts' revenues and have policies that equalize the distribution of these revenues. Compared to most other metropolitan areas that Dye and McGuire looked at, the Chicago region is losing ground in state equalization policies. In Illinois the main source of school funding is the local property tax, but each district also receives aid from the state in the form of formula grants and categorical grants.[2] Between 1980 and 1990 the state of Illinois decreased its share of school district revenues, although the state share is once again increasing (Goldstein and Njus 1999). The degree of equalization in the distribution of state revenues also decreased dramatically in the 1980s. By 1990, the amount of variation among state funding of Illinois's school districts was two times that of Wisconsin and Indiana, and three and one-half times that of Michigan. In fact, in a study of state education expenditures in 1989–1990, only Alaska had more variation. For example, Chicago, despite having a poverty rate of nearly twice the statewide average, received only about 70 percent of the mean downstate level of formula aid (McGuire and Merriman 1997). This is because the state uses assessed value in its allocation formula, instead of a more direct measure of poverty.

Dye and McGuire's findings suggest a need for a larger state role in education funding and in the equalization of that funding as a possible deterrent to residents moving out of the central city and increasing land consumption. Regardless of their effect on land use patterns, however, these fiscal disparities also need to be addressed because of the equity issues they raise within the region. Therefore, we recommend that the state of Illinois shift education funding from local property taxes to state income taxes.

Reduce Local Governments' Reliance on Property Taxes

Dye and McGuire find that differences in property taxes between the core and the collar counties had no significant effect on any of their three measures of sprawl. However, they show that 1996 aggregate effective property tax rates do vary considerably and along geographic lines throughout the six-county region. The lowest quartile of municipalities, with property tax rates ranging from 3.32 to 6.83 percent, are clustered in DuPage County and scattered throughout the five other collar counties. The highest quartile, with rates ranging from 9.76 to 17.4 percent, are almost exclusively in suburban Cook County. In addition, another preliminary study of the Chicago region suggests that higher property tax rates may discourage economic activity (Dye, McGuire, and Merriman 1999). And as described earlier, McDonald and McMillen find that a Cook County location (where industrial and commercial properties are assessed at higher rates) is a statistically significant negative determinant of industry locating in a given quarter section. Because Cook County is the core county, its higher rates would push commercial and industrial development to outer counties.

Property taxes are the most important source of revenue for local governments in Illinois, and indeed throughout most of the country. On average nationally, municipalities raise two-thirds of their own budgets, with the remainder coming from state and federal supplements (Nivola 1999). This need for funding creates an incentive for municipalities to compete with each other for commercial development because of the increased taxes that firms bring to the municipality. These additional funds then allow these communities to offer more services or reduce tax rates, further increasing their attractiveness. Through this process, a fragmented region quickly segregates into have and have-not municipalities. For reasons of equity and governmental efficiency, then, even if Dye and McGuire do not show that unequal property tax rates lead to higher deconcentration and land consumption, these fiscal disparities should be addressed. We suggest two ways in which revenue sources could be equalized—either through the sharing of sales- or property-tax revenues on a regional basis or through the reduction of property taxes in favor of increased state income taxes.

Implement Revenue Sharing

The best-known case of revenue sharing has been operating in Minneapolis-St. Paul since 1975. This program shares a portion of each municipality's tax base. Under the current plan, each city must contribute to a regional fund 40 percent of the growth in tax revenue from its commercial and industrial base. This money is then redistributed based on population and tax capacity—in other words, in inverse proportion to the amount of nonresidential assessed property in each municipality. At present about 30 percent of the regional commercial-industrial tax base is shared through this system (Rusk 1999), and it has reduced tax base disparities among municipalities from approximately 50 : 1 to approximately 12 : 1 (Orfield 1998, 87). In 1998, 137 municipalities were net recipients and 49 were net contributors (Rusk 1999).

Certainly, implementing any type of regional or statewide revenue sharing would be politically difficult. However, it is not impossible to imagine such a system. Orfield, a researcher and Minnesota state legislator, argues that in many metropolitan areas between 60 percent and 85 percent of the population lives in municipalities that would benefit from tax-base sharing. In Chicago such a coalition could be forged between the city of Chicago and the older suburbs, primarily in southern and western Cook County. Furthermore, Metropolis 2020 strongly advocates the creation of a regional coordinating mechanism that would have among its duties receiving and distributing revenues to moderate disparities in fiscal and service quality among municipalities (Johnson 1999, 22). While such a process would be difficult to design and implement, it is no longer unimaginable (Wiewel, Persky, and Schaffer 2002).

Emphasize Income Taxes, Not Property Taxes

A second option would be for the Chicago region to shift its reliance on property taxes to income taxes,[3] on a broader scale than was discussed in the section on school funding. Such a policy change would have to be made at the state level. Instead of paying any property taxes, residents and businesses would simply pay higher income taxes to the state. The state would then distribute these revenues to the individual municipalities, based on population and indicators of need. This method, too, would reduce competition among municipalities for commercial development. Because the Chicago metropolitan region is creeping toward two other states, however, such a switch could create problems along the state borders.

Planning and Information Policies

Especially with a topic as nebulously defined as sprawl, it is crucial that leaders have current, comprehensive knowledge of the changes taking place in their region and have access to planning tools to help them consider the potential uses of this information. Data are changing faster than ever; the region is faced with changing demographics and an increasing number of ways to assess these changes. The appropriate regional planning agencies must also possess the knowledge and the authority to use the data to create appropriate regional plans.

We offer the following recommendations:

- Integrate the Northeastern Illinois Planning Commission and the Chicago Area Transportation Study and provide them with secure funding;
- Develop and maintain a statewide database of land changes and program tools and continue the NASA Landsat program;
- Expand support for regional collaboration projects.

Integrate NIPC and CATS and Provide Secure Funding

As we have seen in the Chicago area, the regional planning agencies are in many ways hamstrung in their attempts to create and implement meaningful regional plans. As Lindstrom points out, the Chicago Area Transportation Study (CATS, the region's metropolitan planning organization) and the Northeastern Illinois Planning Commission (NIPC) have each created plans that have been important to the region. Ultimately, however, NIPC's plans are not enforceable and, since the agency is dependent on the donations of local governments for its funding, its actions are very much subject to local approval. Since CATS is officially a part of the Illinois Department of Transportation, its plans may be influenced significantly by that state agency. Concern over lack of an effective regional planning agency is echoed in the *Chicago Metropolis 2020* report, which advocates creating a regional coordinating mechanism that would take responsibility for regional efforts in housing, transportation, fiscal policies and general regional planning efforts, among other tasks. Because the report acknowledges that structuring and funding such a body could take several years, it advocates in the meantime consolidating CATS, NIPC, and the planning function of the Regional Transportation Authority (RTA).

Such a recommendation is also supported by the findings of Lindstrom and DiJohn. In order to become more useful to area residents, planning in the Chicago region should be more comprehensive and effective. First, the functions of CATS and NIPC should be merged and a new agency created that is responsible for both land use and transportation planning. Second, the new agency needs to be provided with a guaranteed funding stream to remove any question of local political influence. This new agency must be separated from the Illinois Department of Transportation and should draw on the experience of Portland, Oregon's Metro.

This regional planning agency was approved by the state legislature and voters and formed in 1970, at which time it lacked a steady revenue stream and was responsible only for solid waste planning for the region and, later, the Portland Zoo. Today, Metro has home rule, a seven-member council, and an executive officer and is responsible for drawing and overseeing changes to Portland's urban growth boundaries; for coordinating plans of the three counties, twenty-four cities, sixty special districts and other state and regional agencies; and for developing the region's 2040 plan (Porter 1996).

The Chicago region should push for authority from the state to create such a regional planning body. To create a body with home rule, however, would require a three-fifths majority vote in the legislature to change the state constitution—something unlikely to happen in the near future.

As the Metro example shows, the body would also need a permanent stream of funding to be successful. Other lessons include the importance of planning through consensus building, not mandates. As Porter (1996) writes: "Metro possesses wide planning powers and narrow but highly leveraged implementation responsibilities. It must and does work through other agencies at the state, regional, and local level to accomplish most of its aims." If such a body were developed in the Chicago region, it could coordinate with other agencies to implement many of the programs described here, including regional impact fees, regional affordable housing programs, a tax-base sharing program, and general planning responsibilities.

Develop Statewide Database of Land Changes and Program Tools and Continue Landsat

The urban sprawl phenomenon is just beginning to be understood quantitatively and remains to a large extent something that its challengers know when they see it. One of the important—if little known—successes in this process of knowledge building has been the Landsat Program, which has been recording land cover images of the earth's surface since 1972. Currently, as part of the NASA's Earth Science Enterprise, Landsat 7 collects 250 images of the earth each day. These images are an important record of the earth's changes over several decades.

The Landsat Program underscores the importance of a federal role in understanding land use patterns over time. Certainly, state or local agencies would not be able to continue such a program should the federal lead be cut. But there are important critical steps that the state can take to further the region's knowledge of its land use patterns. Again, Maryland provides a model for a statewide database program that could be replicated here. As part of its Smart Growth Initiatives, the state has created a "Technology Toolbox" to produce coordinated, prepackaged data in consistent formats. This toolbox contains data that include the following:

- A resource guide listing available information;
- MERLIN, Maryland's Environmental Resources and Land Information Network, an electronic atlas system to provide Department of Natural Resources employees and the public with a variety of planning data;
- Simplified property and parcel information through the MdProperty View system, that may also include watersheds, wetlands, easement areas, government boundaries, streets, historic sites, and census data among other information (Maryland State Government 1999).

Once information on land use and other changes is collected, it needs to be used by organizations that can make effective regional plans. In Maryland this information is made available to municipalities for an initial fee of a few thousand dollars, plus a yearly charge to update the information. Training is available to local officials through partnerships with universities and private data companies. As the state of Illinois begins to make more land use data available electronically, it should provide similar opportunities for regional leaders and others who might use the data to ensure the information is used and interpreted correctly.

Expand Support for Regional Collaboration Projects

In a typical federal-local relationship of the past, the federal organization would pass down an edict to a region, and the appropriate local agency would be expected to implement it. At the same time, other federal agencies would be making their own demands on localities, which in some cases were even at odds with the first federal requirements.

In late 1998 representatives of several federal agencies and national foundations met to discuss opportunities for better collaboration between federal agencies and regional initiatives and develop a way to encourage bottom-up, not top-down, answers to local problems. The approach they decided on was to choose a regional, nonpartisan project in each of four regions—Chicago, Atlanta, Denver, and the San Francisco Bay Area—that would benefit from increased federal and local cooperation. In Chicago leaders decided to expand a newly established project, the Regional Dialogue on Clean Air and Redevelopment, to benefit from a rethinking of the federal-local relationship. The Regional Dialogue has developed clean air strategies for the region and written a Memorandum of Understanding that details what assistance they will need from which federal agencies. By allowing regional leaders to determine how the federal agencies could better bolster their efforts, the partnership almost reverses the traditional federal-regional relationship.

Under leadership from the national foundations, which provide funding for overall coordination of the partnership's efforts, the partnership will continue its learning in the original regions and will likely expand to include additional projects and regions. However, current efforts also provide valuable lessons for projects without partnership designation, which could adopt its comprehensive approach to regional planning that seeks to add value to efforts already underway at the federal, state, and regional levels and provide a receptive federal audience to address these needs. Other pilot projects could further increase the "social capital" in regions, which will enhance future regional collaboration (Foster 2000).

Five Criteria for Policy Recommendations

While all of these recommendations would have an effect on slowing down the process of deconcentration, obviously some would be more effective than others. Furthermore, some are quite unlikely to be implemented any time soon. Therefore, we made an initial assessment of the value of each recommendation in regard to five criteria.

Impact on Deconcentration (Effectiveness)

How much of an impact would the policy have in reversing or slowing sprawl or the negative effects associated with decentralization?

Impact on Equity

How does this policy aid in redistributing the private gains of deconcentration to those who have typically been excluded from them, specifically the low-income minority groups and inner-city residents? Does the policy encourage participation by all segments of the population? Would the costs of implementation be borne disproportionately by the low-income population?

Political Feasibility

What is the likelihood of this policy recommendation being adopted by the appropriate level of government? How popular or unpopular is the program likely to be among the general public, involved interest groups, and affected parties?

Effort/Costs

Once adopted as policy, what resources—including time and money—would have to be dedicated to this program?

Unintended Effects

How much is known about the outcomes such a policy would bring, including unintended secondary effects? Has there been academic research on the issue? Will there be a steep learning curve, or are there real-life models that offer experience? Would any legal issues likely arise?

Table 12.1 evaluates each of the proposed policies by scoring them on each of the criteria with a simple plus sign (indicating the policy is likely to reduce sprawl or increase equity, be relatively feasible, require only modest effort or have likely beneficial secondary effects); a minus sign (for the opposite effect); or a zero, when the effects appear likely to cancel each other out. The chapter appendix provides a summary of the rationale for each of the scores.

This analysis suggests some possible priorities. Pilot projects for regional collaboration score the highest, with four pluses and no negatives. Other policies that score high include central city redevelopment,

Table 12.1

Explanations of Policy Recommendation Evaluations

	Effectiveness	Equity	Feasibility	Effort	Secondary effects
Land use					
Implement regional impact fees	+	+	−	−	−
Reduce the number of municipalities	0	+	−	−	+
Encourage collaboration on annexations	+	0	−	+	0
Discourage ex-urban infrastructure investments	+	+	−	0	0
Purchase/transfer development rights	+	−	+	0	0
Increase incentives for central city development	+	+	+	−	+
Housing					
Remove subsidies that encourage overconsumption of land	+	+	−	0	−
Continue and strengthen federal block grant programs	+	+	+	+	−
Increase the availability of rental vouchers and comprehensive assistance	0	+	0	−	+
Provide incentives for inclusionary zoning	0	+	−	−	+
Provide incentives for employer-assisted housing	0	+	+	0	+
Transportation					
Increase gas taxes	+	−	−	+	+
Implement value pricing	+	−	0	−	+
Reconsider the Highway Trust Fund	+	0	−	+	+
Increase proactive transit funding; provide alternative transit	+	+	0	−	+
Better integrate modes of transportation; encourage railroads	+	0	0	−	0
Fiscal					
Equalize school funding	0/+	+	0	0	+
Emphasize income taxes instead of property taxes	0	+	−	0	+
Implement revenue sharing	0	+	−	0	+
Planning and information					
Integrate NIPC and CATS and provide them with secure funding	0	0	−	−	+
Develop a statewide land use database	0	0	+	0	+
Expand support for regional collaborative projects	+	+	+	0	+

federal block grant programs, and incentives for employer-assisted housing, which each have three or four plus signs and one or no minus signs. Another four policies appear relatively attractive, with at least two or three plus signs and one or no minus signs. They include redirecting the Highway Trust Fund, increasing proactive transit funding, equalizing school funding, and developing a statewide land use database.

On the other side of the scale, two proposed policies appear particularly problematic, namely the implementation of regional impact fees and the integration of the regional planning agencies. In both cases the level of effort required and the political difficulties in achieving implementation appear formidable.

Conclusion

We have identified over twenty policy recommendations that would either help to reduce future deconcentration in the Chicago region directly or seek to mitigate some of the negative effects that sprawl has had on the region. These policies are aimed at federal and state agencies and fall into five categories: land use, housing, transportation, fiscal, and planning/information.

Which of these policies should have priority is largely a matter of political realities—what coalitions can be formed and which areas provide opportunities for intervention. While everyone will have his favorites, the reality is that many organizations will continue to work on any number of these policies. Policies that strengthen the urban core or permanently preserve open space are already well-accepted means of mitigating sprawl. However, policy changes that appear to receive little attention, but would also have major effects, are changes in the home mortgage deduction and increases in the gas tax.

Finally, we remind our readers what Foster (2000) has pointed out: In many cases it is not so much the policies a region has, but how the region takes advantage of the policies, that makes the difference. This makes our planning and process recommendations—the development of a regional planning body with legislated powers and the improvement of communication at all levels of government—all the more important. In this way, regional leaders have the authority to develop and implement regional programs that can best take advantage of current policies, as they work to bring about other reforms that benefit the region.

APPENDIX

Land Use

Implement Regional Impact Fees

- \+ **Effectiveness:** A study of DuPage County suggests that the adoption of impact fees could have a net effect of decreasing residential development by 25 percent.
- \+ **Equity:** The adoption of impact fees should help to ensure that the costs of development are borne by the appropriate households.
- − **Feasibility:** The Illinois legislature has not been amenable to similar bills in the past, and developers would have to be on board. Unlike most of the recommendations, impact fees would be mandated regionally as opposed to incentive-based.
- − **Effort:** Regional impact fees would have to be designed and agreed to by the many municipalities in the region; a system of collection would then have to be created and implemented.
- − **Secondary Effects:** Increased fees could raise issues of housing affordability.

Reduce the Number of Municipalities and Special Purpose Districts

- 0 **Effectiveness:** Dye and McGuire find some weak evidence that municipalities with fewer municipalities have less sprawl.
- \+ **Equity:** Fewer municipalities and special purpose districts would mean that fiscal resources were distributed over a larger base.
- − **Feasibility:** Municipal leaders and residents would undoubtedly be resistant to a change in status quo and possible reduction of power. However, any policies would be incentive-based and not mandated.
- − **Effort:** Once the decision to merge was made, the process of municipal consolidation would involve a substantial amount of work.
- \+ **Secondary Effects:** Municipalities would have fewer opportunities to enter into bidding wars for development with each other; consolidation could generally lead to residents thinking less parochially and more regionally.

Encourage Collaboration on Annexations

- \+ **Effectiveness:** Lax annexation policies do nothing to restrict development in outlying, unincorporated areas. If developers see a benefit from having their developments in incorporated areas, but municipalities are given incentives not to annex additional land, growth could shift to inside existing municipalities.
- 0 **Equity:** A change in annexation policies would have no direct impact on equity.
- − **Feasibility:** Incentives against annexations would have to be substantial.
- \+ **Effort:** Incentives would need to be developed.
- 0 **Secondary Effects:** Uncertain.

Discourage Infrastructure Investments in Outer Areas

- \+ **Effectiveness:** Although the amount of federal and state funding spent on nontransportation infrastructure is relatively low, a shift in these expenditures could be enough to create marginal land use changes.
- \+ **Equity:** Would direct infrastructure funding to older, established areas where the population is generally less wealthy.
- − **Feasibility:** Local governments would be reluctant to have to get state approval of local plans. Strict transferability of the Maryland program to Illinois would be difficult.
- 0 **Effort:** Counties and municipalities would need to make development plans, which would then be reviewed by the state and used to determine where state funds would be spent.
- 0 **Secondary Effects:** There would likely be both positive and negative secondary effects from such a program.

Preserve Open Space Through the Purchase or Transfer of Development Rights

- \+ **Effectiveness:** Programs that purchase or transfer development rights ensure that the affected land will not be developed in the foreseeable future.
- − **Equity:** These policies could increase the costs of surrounding land, while at the same time lowering land values for farmers trying to sell.

- + **Feasibility:** Residents in four of Chicago's collar counties have already supported more than $200 million in bond issues to preserve farmland and open space, and the state recently allocated $160 million for land acquisition.
- 0 **Effort:** While setting up and running a program could be time-consuming, several counties already have established regulations.
- 0 **Secondary Effects:** Residents could ultimately be disappointed if a program preserved farmland when open space would have been a more desirable and less costly goal, but this problem is avoidable with foresight.

Increase Incentives for Central City Development

- + **Effectiveness:** Felsenstein estimates that directing just high tech employment to the central city instead of outlying areas would have reduced land consumption by almost 18,000 acres.
- + **Equity:** The suburbanization of jobs has generally meant that low-income center-city residents and suburban residents without cars have found it difficult to find well-paying employment within their reach.
- + **Feasibility** Federal, state, and local programs that encourage brownfield redevelopment, workforce training, and job creation in the inner city have all been generally popular.
- − **Effort:** Creating and administering incentive programs to convince employers and developers to invest in the central city can be a momentous task.
- + **Secondary Effects:** Creating jobs and housing near population centers can help mitigate problems as varied as transportation, pollution, and day care.

Housing

Remove or Reduce Subsidies That Encourage Overconsumption of Land

- + **Effectiveness:** Persky and Kurban estimate that federal tax subsidies to housing were responsible for increasing land consumption by as much as 20 percent in areas that became urbanized between 1970 and 1990.

- **+ Equity:** Since subsidies for homeownership accrue mostly to upper-income families, removing or reducing them would be progressive rather than regressive.
- **− Feasibility:** Any changes would require congressional action.
- **0 Effort** Would require mostly one-time changes to tax forms and a reeducation of the public.
- **− Secondary Effects:** Removing such subsidies would undoubtedly lower homeownership rates, in contrast to current national goals.

Continue and Strengthen Federal Block Grant Programs

- **+ Effectiveness:** Currently these programs have a positive effect on older urban cores.
- **+ Equity:** By definition, Community Development Block Grants are spent to assist primarily low- or moderate-income residents or neighborhoods.
- **+ Feasibility:** Block grants are generally popular with municipalities and legislators.
- **+ Effort:** Since it is already established and local officials are familiar with it, minimum effort would be required to expand the CDBG program.
- **− Secondary Effects:** Block grants to outer areas could be spent on projects like water and sewer extensions that facilitate sprawl.

Increase the Availability of Rental Vouchers and Comprehensive Assistance

- **0 Effectiveness:** More vouchers could increase sprawl marginally by facilitating new moves to suburban areas.
- **+ Equity:** Vouchers provide opportunities for low-income residents who have traditionally been isolated in low-income urban areas.
- **0 Feasibility:** In 1999 HUD allocated $280 million to fund 50,000 welfare-to-work vouchers nationwide. However, this number only begins to address the unmet housing needs, and funding for a significantly higher number of vouchers seems currently unlikely.
- **− Effort:** To be most successful, programs would need to provide

clients with comprehensive, ongoing assistance ranging from child care to job skills training.

+ **Secondary Effects:** Positive effects of an increased comprehensive voucher program would likely accrue to the children of families that move.

Provide Incentives for Inclusionary Zoning

0   **Effectiveness:** This type of policy would increase sprawl by facilitating low-income household moves to suburban areas, but it would also develop densities.

+ **Equity:** Inclusionary zoning ensures more housing choice and opportunities for low-income households.

− **Feasibility:** While the program is generally well regarded in Montgomery County, Maryland, it would likely receive a much cooler response in the Chicago region. In addition, Illinois counties have much less power than do those in Maryland, making strict transferability of the program difficult.

− **Effort:** Implementing this policy would involve the creation of program guidelines, ongoing administration, and some public education.

+ **Secondary Effects:** If implemented, such a program could be an important step toward other regionalism efforts.

Provide Incentives for Employer-Assisted Housing

0   **Effectiveness:** An EAH program could increase sprawl by facilitating moves to suburban areas, but it would increase housing near employment centers.

+ **Equity:** EAH programs are usually set up to benefit employees below a certain income.

+ **Feasibility:** EAH programs have been well received in areas like Silicon Valley, where they are seen as a workforce investment, not merely a charitable donation. In the Chicago region both the Metropolitan Planning Council and the *Chicago Metropolis 2020* report emphasize the benefits of EAH.

− **Effort:** The Silicon Valley Trust Fund is being established through a two-year campaign to raise $20 million.

+ **Secondary Effects:** A well-established EAH program can be an valuable incentive to help employers retain workers.

Transportation

Increase Gas Taxes

- **+ Effectiveness:** If raised high enough, the long-term effect of such a change would be an incentive for higher-density housing.
- **− Equity:** Such a tax would be regressive—it would have a proportionately larger effect on low-income households than on higher-income ones.
- **− Feasibility:** A survey of Chicago, suburban, and downstate Illinois residents showed that a slight majority of residents would support a five-cent-per-gallon gasoline tax to be used toward highway and transit movements. State politicians, on the other hand, not only are wary of raising gas taxes, but are working on lowering them: in response to rising gasoline prices, the Illinois Senate recently voted 50–0 to suspend a 5 percent state sales tax on gas purchases for the next four years.
- **+ Effort:** Little or no effort would be required once new legislation was passed.
- **+ Secondary Effects:** Even if taxes were not increased to a level that created incentives for more compact development, it is likely that the number of vehicle miles driven would be decreased enough to lower air pollution and have some effect on congestion. On the other hand, if increased revenues were required to be spent on transportation projects (as they are now), new roads could be built that would further increase sprawl.

Implement Value Pricing

- **+ Effectiveness:** The long-term effect of such a change would be increased incentives for higher-density housing.
- **− Equity:** Such a tax would be regressive—it would have a proportionately larger effect on low-income households than on higher-income ones.
- **0 Feasibility:** Under TEA 21, the federal government has authorized $51 million to the Value Pricing Pilot Program for fiscal years 1999–2003. However, the Chicago region has not applied for any of these funds.
- **− Effort:** A system of pricing, collection, enforcement, and distribution of funds would have to be developed.

- **+ Secondary Effects:** Even if the tolls were not high enough to create incentives for more compact development, it is likely that the number of vehicle miles driven would be decreased enough to lower air pollution and affect congestion.

Reconsider the Highway Trust Fund

- **+ Effectiveness:** If revenue generated by fuel taxes were put into the federal government's general fund, as is the case in most European countries, road projects would have to compete with other federal programs for funding, and fewer—presumably only the highly urgent—would be funded. However, such a change could also decrease funding for transit projects.
- **0 Equity:** The equity impacts of such a change would largely depend on how the revenues were spent.
- **− Feasibility:** Such a change would require congressional action.
- **+ Effort** Only moderate administrative effort would be required.
- **0 Secondary Effects:** There would probably be both positive and negative secondary effects. Fewer roads could mean more congestion. Roads and public transportation infrastructure might be maintained at lower levels. However, a shift away from the current highway culture could mean lower levels of air pollution.

Increase Proactive Transit Funding; Provide Alternatives to Fixed Transit

- **+ Effectiveness:** Making transit more efficient and better maintained should lead to an increase in ridership.
- **+ Equity:** These changes would improve low-cost transportation options.
- **0 Feasibility:** Although transit upgrades and repairs in the Chicago region have historically been made retroactively, Illinois FIRST and TEA 21 offer the potential for more flexibility as well as some funding that could be used in new ways.
- **− Effort:** Transit alternatives like reverse commuting programs can be hard to design and implement.
- **+ Secondary Effects:** Better transit options that led to higher transit usage would reduce externalities associated with automobile driving, such as air pollution, congestion and accidents.

Better Integrate Modes of Transportation; Encourage Investment in the Railroads

- \+ **Effectiveness:** At the least, such policy changes should reduce congestion and wear on the region's highways and could provide an incentive for clustering around transportation hubs.
- 0 **Equity:** These changes would have no direct impact on equity in the region.
- 0 **Feasibility:** Although Illinois FIRST and TEA 21 provide some funding for railroad upgrades, and Metropolis 2020 recommends developing intermodal freight centers, a significant shift from trucking to rail seems unlikely.
- – **Effort:** Considerable effort could be involved in integrating transportation modes.
- 0 **Secondary Effects:** Uncertain. The price of goods could be affected.

Fiscal

Equalize School Funding

- 0/+ **Effectiveness**: In theory, if inner-city schools are underfunded and suburban schools are well funded, families with children will move to the outer areas. In Dye and McGuire's study, more equalization in the state aid formula had a "negative effect . . . on the share of total population residing in the collar counties and on the growth of urbanized land area, but a positive effect on the share of the total land characterized as urban."
- \+ **Equity:** In a study of state education expenditures in 1989–1990, only Alaska had more variation than did Illinois. Policies to shift the burden of education funding from the local to the state level would have important effects on equity.
- 0 **Feasibility:** While overhauling the way education is funded would not be simple, Metropolis 2020 does advocate higher levels of state "foundation" funding.
- 0 **Effort:** Such a change would probably require moderate administrative effort.
- \+ **Secondary Effects:** Presumably, more equalized education funding would provide more opportunities for children who are cur-

rently underserved, which would result in a better-prepared workforce in the future.

Emphasize Income Taxes Instead of Property Taxes

- 0 **Effectiveness:** In theory, businesses and residents should favor municipalities with lower tax rates, when all other factors are equal. However, Dye and McGuire find that differences in property taxes between the core and collar counties have no significant effect on any of their three measures of sprawl.
- \+ **Equity:** Aggregate property taxes vary considerably in the six-county region; reducing property taxes paid to the municipality and increasing income taxes paid to the state would provide an opportunity for greater equality.
- − **Feasibility:** A policy change would require changes by the state legislature.
- 0 **Effort:** This policy change would require the state to develop allocation formulas and then actually distribute the funds.
- \+ **Secondary Effects:** As a secondary effect, competition among municipalities for commercial development would be reduced.

Implement Regional Revenue Sharing

- 0 **Effectiveness:** Over time, equalization of municipalities' income could lead to an equalization of tax rates, which would in theory reduce incentives for development in outer suburban areas.
- \+ **Equity:** According to Rusk, tax-base sharing in Minneapolis-St. Paul has reduced tax-base disparities among municipalities from approximately 50 : 1 to approximately 12 : 1.
- − **Feasibility:** Metropolis 2020 supports some form of regional revenue sharing, and research by Myron Orfield suggests that a majority of residents in the region would benefit from it, but such an overhaul of the current system still remains unlikely in the near future.
- 0 **Effort:** Once a collection and distribution system was established, little ongoing effort would be required.
- \+ **Secondary Effects:** Tax-base equalization efforts would reduce competition among municipalities for commercial development.

Planning and Information

Integrate NIPC and CATS and Provide Them with Secure Funding

- 0 **Effectiveness:** This consolidation would have no direct impact on land consumption.
- 0 **Equity:** It would have no direct impact on equity.
- − **Feasibility:** Such a measure is recommended by Metropolis 2020, but even that report acknowledges that structuring and funding such a body could take several years. To create a body like Portland's Metro that has home rule would require a three-fifths majority vote in the legislature to change the state constitution.
- − **Effort:** There would be considerable effort involved in this reorganization.
- + **Secondary Effects:** Regional planning would become more comprehensive and integrated; the agency would no longer have to rely on local financial support and regional planning would therefore be less politicized.

Develop a Statewide Land Use Database

- 0 **Effectiveness:** The creation of a database might decrease land consumption only to the extent that it provided local officials with tangible evidence of land use changes.
- 0 **Equity:** The creation of a database would have no direct impact on equity.
- + **Feasibility:** Such a program would be relatively uncontroversial.
- 0 **Effort** The establishment and use of a statewide database would likely be moderate.
- + **Secondary Effects:** If put to good use, the database would increase awareness and knowledge of land use and planning issues among regional officials.

Expand Support for Regional Collaborative Projects

- + **Effectiveness:** In most cases, regional projects have as a goal a reduction in land consumption and other measures of sprawl.

- **+ Equity:** Equity is also a common concern of such projects.
- **+ Feasibility:** When the areas of collaboration remain relatively uncontroversial, there is usually wide support for collaboration.
- **0 Effort:** While regional collaborative projects may involve an initial increase in work, once under way they usually require a shift in resources as opposed to additional resources.
- **+ Secondary Effects:** Such projects should foster intergovernmental cooperation in other areas as well.

Notes

1. Only three counties, all in the Chicago region, have a population of more than 400,000.

2. Formula aid is the state's equalizing grant and targets low property value, low-income districts. It covers about two-thirds of all state aid and averages $1,453 per elementary student. Categorical aid makes up the remainder of state aid and is allocated to districts for specific programs (McGuire and Merriman 1997).

3. In his book *Laws of the Landscape*, Pietro S. Nivola (1999) argues that governments should emphasize sales/consumption taxes rather than income taxes as an alternative to property taxes. His recommendation is based on the economic principle that it is more efficient for governments to tax goods with negative externalities rather than income, which is generally considered to provide positive externalities for regions. While such a policy recommendation bears consideration, it is beyond the scope of this paper.

References

Bruegmann, Robert. 2000. E-mail correspondence with Bruegmann, professor of Art History, University of Illinois at Chicago, February 2.

Bukro, Casey. 1999. Illinois a Leader in Land Preservation. *Chicago Tribune* (October 12): www.chicagotribune.com.

City of Chicago, Department of Environment. 1998. *Chicago Brownfields Report* 3(1) (Spring): www.cityofchicago.org/Environment/Brownfields/Newsletter.97.08.html.

Cox, Wendell. 1999. *U.S. Urbanized Areas 1950–1990: Urbanized Area Data.* Belleville, IL: Wendell Cox Consultancy and the Public Purpose: www.publicpurpose.com/dm-uad.htm.

Dorning, Mike, and Jon Hilkevitch. 1999. City Gets Short End of Transit Aid Stick. *Chicago Tribune,* October 1, section 2, p. 3: www.chicagotribune.com.

Dye, Richard F., Therese J. McGuire, and David F. Merriman. 1999. The Impact of Property Taxes and Property Tax Classification on Business Locations: Evidence from the Chicago Metropolitan Area (Report), Chicago: Institute for Government and Public Affairs, University of Illinois at Chicago.

Fannie Mae. 1999. Products for Untapped Markets: Employer-Assisted Housing Plans (EAH): www.fanniemae.com/neighborhoods/products/housing/employer_assisted_housing.html.

Federal Highway Administration. 1999. Highway Trust Fund Primer: A Summary: http://fhwa.dot.gov/pubstars.html (October 2).
———. 2000. TEA-21: Moving Americans into the 21st Century: www.fhwa.dot.gov/tea21/index.htm.
Foster, Kathryn. 2000. Regional Capital. In *Urban-Suburban Interdependencies,* ed. Wim Wiewel and Rosalind Greenstein, 83–118. Cambridge, MA: Lincoln Institute of Land Policy.
Freese, Betty. 1995. Saving the Farm. *Successful Farming* (Iowa edition) 93(8) (August): 30–31.
Goldstein, Scott, and Jonathan Njus. 1999. Back to School: The State's Expanding Role in Funding Public Education (Report). Chicago: Metropolitan Planning Council.
Gordon, Peter, and Harry W. Richardson. 1997. Are Compact Cities a Desirable Planning Goal? *Journal of the American Planning Association* 63(1) (Winter): 95–106.
Governor's Open Land Trust proposal approved by General Assembly. 1999. Press release, Springfield, May 5.
Gurwitt, Rob. 1999. The State vs. Sprawl. *Governing* 12(4) (January).
Illinois Department of Employment Security. 2000. Where Workers Work in the Chicago Metro Area. Summary report, 1972–1997: http://lmi.ides.state.il.us/wwwork/intro.htm.
Johnson, Elmer W. 1999. *Chicago Metropolis 2020: Preparing Metropolitan Chicago for the 21st Century.* Chicago: The Commercial Club of Chicago.
Larsen, Eric B. 2000. E-mail correspondence with Larsen, Planner, Montgomery County, Maryland, February 23.
Maryland Office of Planning. 1999. Maryland's Smart Growth Initiatives 1997: www.op.state.md.us/smartgrowth/initiatv.html.
Maryland State Government Geographic Coordinating Committee. 1999. The Technology Toolbox from the Environmental Agenda of Governor Parris N. Glendening: www.fgdc.gov/obp/mdtool.html.
Maynard, Lehigh J., John C. Becker, Timothy W. Kelsey, and Stanford M. Lembeck. 1998. Early Experience with Pennsylvania's Agricultural Conservation Easement Program. *Journal of Soil and Water Conservation* 53(2): 106–112.
McGuire, Therese J., and David F. Merriman. 1997. *Disparities Among Illinois' School Districts* (Report). Institute of Government and Public Affairs, University of Illinois at Chicago.
McKinney, Dave. 2000. Senate Oks Gas Tax Cut. *Chicago Sun-Times* (March 9), p. 1.
MetroLinks. 1999. HUD Awards Rental Assistance Vouchers to Metrolinks: First Ever Tri-County Coordination of Housing Services. Chicago: MetroLinks
Montgomery County, Maryland, Division of Housing and Code Enforcement. The Moderately Priced Dwelling Unit Program: Montgomery County, Maryland's Inclusionary Zoning Ordinance. Program Summary and Background: www.co.mo.md.us//services/hca/Housing/MPDU/summary.htm (February 20, 2000).
Nivola, Pietro S. 1999. *Laws of the Landscape: How Policies Shape Cities in Europe and America.* Washington, DC: The Brookings Institution.
Northeastern Illinois Planning Commission. 1997. Final Forecast Results. Chicago, Northeastern Illinois Planning Commission: www.nipc.cog.il.us/2020–sum.htm.
Orfield, Myron. 1998. *Metropolitics: A Regional Agenda for Community and Sta-*

bility. Washington, DC: The Brookings Institution and the Lincoln Institute of Land Policy.

Pennsylvania Department of Community and Economic Development. 1999. Shared Municipal Services: www.dced.state.pa.us/PA_Exec/DCED/government/shared.htm.

Persky, Joseph, and Wim Wiewel. 2000. *When Corporations Leave Town: The Costs and Benefits of Metropolitan Job Sprawl.* Detroit: Wayne State University Press.

Porter, Douglas R. 1996. *Profiles in Growth Management.* Washington, DC: The Urban Land Institute.

Rusk, David. 1999. *Inside Game/Outside Game: Winning Strategies for Saving Urban America.* Washington, DC: The Brookings Institution.

Silicon Valley Manufacturing Group. 1999a. Annual Report—Housing: www.swmg.org/htm/annual_housing.htm.

Skidmore, Mark, and Michael Peddle. 1998. Do Development Impact Fees Reduce the Rate of Residential Development? *Growth and Change* 29(4): 383–400.

Sööt, Siim, Trisha Sternberg, Ashish Sen, and Joseph DiJohn. 1998. *Attitudes Towards an Increase in Gasoline Taxes: Survey Results.* Chicago: Urban Transportation Center, University of Illinois.

State of Illinois. 2000. 91st General Assembly Legislation: Status of HB4074: www.legis.state.il.us.

U.S. Department of Housing and Urban Development. 1999. Community Development Block Grant (CDBG) Entitlement Communities Program: www.hud.gov/progdesc/cdbgent.html.

University of Illinois at Chicago. 1999. For Rent . . . Housing Options in the Chicago Region. A regional rental market analysis summary report prepared for the Metropolitan Planning Council by the University of Illinois at Chicago.

Warner, Sam Bass. 1969. *Streetcar Suburbs: The Process of Growth in Boston, 1970–1900.* New York: Atheneum.

Wiewel, Wim, Joseph Persky, and Kimberly Schaffer. 2002. Less Sprawl, Greater Equity? The Potential for Revenue Sharing in the Chicago Region, In *Urban Sprawl: Causes Consequences and Policy Responses*, ed. Gregory Squires. Washington, DC: Urban Institute Press.

Zhang, Ting Wei. 2001. Community Features and Urban Sprawl: The Case of the Chicago Metropolitan Region. *Land Use Policy* 18(3): 221–232.

About the Authors and Editors

Joseph DiJohn is a research professor at the University of Illinois at Chicago's Urban Transportation Center and director of the Urban Transportation Center's Metropolitan Transportation Support Initiative. Currently, he is an advisory board member of the National Transportation Institute, a project panel member of the Transportation Cooperative Research Program, a member of Business Leaders for Transportation, a member of the Greater North Michigan Avenue Association's Traffic and Transportation Committee, and a director of the George Krambles Scholarship Foundation.

Richard F. Dye is the Ernest A. Johnson Professor of Economics at Lake Forest College. He is also an adjunct professor in the Institute of Government and Public Affairs at the University of Illinois at Chicago. Most of his recent publications have been concerned with state and local government finance, especially as it relates to economic development.

Daniel Felsenstein is director of the Institute of Urban and Regional Studies and senior lecturer in Geography at the Hebrew University of Jerusalem in Israel. His research interests include urban and regional economic development, public policy evaluation and impact evaluation methodology, high technology and regional development, and estimating measures of regional welfare. He has published widely on these topics and has edited three books in related fields.

Haydar Kurban is an assistant professor in the Department of Economics at Howard University, Washington DC. He is the coauthor of "Do Federal Funds Better Support Cities Or Suburbs? A Spatial Analysis of Federal Spending in The Chicago Metropolis" (joint with Joseph Persky), published by The Brookings Institution Center for Urban and Metropolitan Policy in November 2001.

Thomas (Bill) Lester is a researcher and planner at the Center for Urban Economic Development at the University of Illinois at Chicago. He conducts various research and technical assistance projects related to economic development for local government agencies and community organizations.

Bonnie Lindstrom is a senior research and policy analyst with Urban Innovations Analysis, Inc. Her research focuses on governance structures and metropolitan development, including regional housing, transportation, and environmental policies.

John McDonald is the Senior Associate Dean for Academic Affairs and Research and a professor of Economics and Finance at the University of Illinois at Chicago. His current research interests include urban economic development—theory and policy, congestion pricing on urban highways, land values and zoning, and urban real estate markets. He is currently the U.S. editor of *Urban Studies* and the review articles editor of the *Journal of Real Estate Literature*.

Therese McGuire is a professor of Economics and Public Affairs with a joint appointment at the Institute of Government and Public Affairs and the College of Urban Planning and Public Affairs at the University of Illinois at Chicago. Her areas of expertise are state and local government finances and economic development, and she has written about and worked with governments on state tax reform and on the impact of taxes on economic growth. McGuire is a former president of the National Tax Association and currently coeditor of the *National Tax Journal*.

Daniel McMillen is a professor of Economics and director of the Center for Urban Real Estate at the University of Illinois at Chicago. His research interests include identifying employment subcenters, housing price indices, and nonparametric methods for spatial models. His papers have appeared in such journals as *Regional Science* and *Urban Economics, Journal of Urban Economics, Review of Economics and Statistics,* and *Real Estate Economics.*

Charles J. Orlebeke is Professor Emeritus of Urban Planning and Public Affairs at the University of Illinois at Chicago. He is a former assistant secretary for Policy Development and Research at the U.S. Department of Housing and Urban Development and the author of *New Life at Ground Zero: New York, Home Ownership, and the Future of American Cities*, as well as numerous book chapters, articles, and reports on housing and urban policy.

Joseph Persky is a professor of Economics at the University of Illinois at Chicago. He is the author of *The Burden of Dependency* (John Hopkins University Press, 1992). He also coauthored *When Corporations Leave Town* (Wayne State University Press, 2000) with Wim Wiewel. He has written extensively on the logic and evaluation of state and local economic development efforts and has worked closely with several states and cities.

Kim Schaffer received her master's degree in Urban Planning and Policy from the University of Illinois at Chicago, where she coauthored several other articles on smart growth and equity issues. She currently works on social justice issues in Washington, DC.

Jean Templeton is an attorney and Ph.D. candidate at the University of Illinois at Chicago's Urban Planning and Policy Program.

Piyushimita (Vonu) Thakuriah is an associate professor in the University of Illinois at Chicago's Urban Planning and Policy Program and is the associate director of research at the University's Urban Transportation Center. She is currently working in the areas of transit impact analysis for low-income populations, Intelligent Transportation Systems, and data quality criteria issues for large-scale, integrated databases.

Y.Q. Wang is an associate professor in Terrestrial Remote Sensing at the Department of Natural Resources Science, University of Rhode Island. His research interests include observing, understanding, and modeling human-induced land use and land-cover change (LULCC) using advanced geoinformation science and technologies. His main research focus is developing modeling mechanisms to bridge driving forces (both socioeconomic and natural factors) and the consequences of land-cover changes so that human impacts on ecosystems can be effectively modeled. He was among the recipients of the prestigious Presidential Early Career Award for Scientists and Engineers in 2000.

Wim Wiewel is dean of the College of Business Administration and a professor of Urban Planning and Policy and of Managerial Studies at the University of Illinois at Chicago. He is the author or editor of five books and over fifty articles and chapters, which have appeared in *Economic Development Quarterly*, *Economic Geography*, the *Journal of the American Planning Association*, and other journals. He is also president of the Association of Collegiate Schools of Planning, a fellow of the Urban Land Institute, and vice-chair of Education for its Chicago District Council, a fellow of the Economic Policy Institute, and a faculty member at the Lincoln Institute of Land Policy.

Index

A

Acs, Z.J., 215
Adult communities, 169
Affordable Housing Plan, 162
American Community Builders, 22
Americans with Disabilities Act (ADA), 90
Amtrak, 108–109
Anas, A., 201
Annexation
  in 1830–1870 Chicago, 6–7
  in 1871–1945 years, 8, 12–13
  Aurora's growth, 76–78
  fringe area development, 75
  history of, 73–74
  Huntley's growth, 78–80
  as land use tool, 73–76, 81–84, 296
  lessons of, 80–81
  municipality boundaries changes and, 37, 74
Aurora, Illinois, 76–78

B

Blackley, Dixie, 160
Board of Water Commissioners, 6
Boundary agreements, 68–68, 78
Brownfields Initiative, 270
Bruegmann, R., 257
Burnham, Daniel, 13

Burnham's *Plan of Chicago* (1909), 13–14
Butler, Paul, 22

C

Cable cars, 9
Campaign for Sensible Growth, 174–175, 259
Carlino, G.A., 43
Carlton, D., 201
Carter administration, 165
Central business district (CBD), 92, 101, 128, 297
Charney, A., 43
Charter of 1875, 12
Chesbrough, E.S., 6
Chicago
  in 1830–1870 years, 4–7
    economic development, 5–6
    population growth and annexation, 7
    technology and public works, 6–7
  in 1871–1945 years, 7–14
    annexation, 12–13
    Burnham's *Plan of Chicago* (1909), 13–14
    drinking water, 11–12
    land use policies, 12–13
    mass transit, 9–11
    railroads, 9–11
    regional growth, 12–13
    sewage, 11–12

313

314   INDEX

Chicago
  in 1871–1945 years, 7–14 *(continued)*
    storm water management, 11–12
  in 1945–1970 years, 14–22
    drinking water, 20
    sewage, 20
    storm water management, 20
    suburban development, 20–22
    transportation infrastructure, 16–20
  city incorporation (1833), 7
  county-level urban land cover change, 28–31
  distance zones from downtown area, 31–32
  geographic location and disadvantages, 3–4
  major public projects (1910–1945), 14
  municipality boundaries change, 37–39
  post-war economic development, 14–15
  regional urban land cover change (1972–1977), 27–28, 34
Chicago Area Transportation Study (CATS), 123, 130–131, 135–138, 142, 146, 148, 152, 288–289
Chicago Board of Trade, 5
Chicago Central Area Committee (mid-1950s), 15
Chicago Comprehensive Plan of 1946, 15
Chicago Fire (1871), 7
Chicago Housing Authority, 15
Chicago River, 6
Chicago School of Architecture, 9
Chicago Transit Authority (CTA), 16–17, 90–93, 146
Cholera, 11
City Beautiful Movement, 14
Civic Committee of the Commercial Club, 150
Clean Air Act, 90, 97, 153
Clinton administration, 180
Commercial development; *see also* High technology activity

Commercial development *(continued)*
  post-1990, 191
  spatial patterns of, 193–196
Community Development Block Grant (CDBG), 259, 264, 271, 273–274
Competitiveness, 257
Comprehensive General Plan, 145
Congestion
  motor carrier industry and, 120–122
  sprawl and, 104–106
Consolidated Federal Funds Reports (CFFR), 231
Consolidated metropolitan statistical areas (CMSAs), 45, 48, 51, 54–55
Constitution (1970), 63–65
Council of Mayors, 137
Counties, 67
Cross, Tracy, 173

D

Daley, Richard J., 139
Decentralization
  policy recommendations for, 291
  of population, 122–123
  sprawl and, 101–103
  trucking and, 132–133
Department of Commerce and Community Affairs, 65
Department of Natural Resources, 65–66
Department of Transportation, 65
Development Plan for the Central Area of Chicago (1958), 15
Developmental rights, 268–269, 296
DiJohn, Joseph, 88, 256, 278, 282
Downs, A., 43
Drinking water
  in 1871–1945 years, 11–12
  in 1945–1970 years, 20
DuPage County, 83–85, 212, 215–216
Dye, Richard F., 42, 256, 264, 284–286

E

Economic development
  in 1830–1870 Chicago, 5–6
  household formation, 168–169
Ecosystem, 31, 34
Edgar, Jim, 145
Education spending, 244–245
Elevated railroads, 9
Elk Grove Village, 21–22
Ellickson, B., 201
Employer-assisted housing, 276–278, 299
Employment deconcentration
  employer incentives and, 269–270
  high technology location and, 208–213
  method of analysis for, 224–225
Employment growth, 117–118
Employment subcenters, 184–185
Empowerment Zones, 259
Environmental issues, 257
Environmental Protection Agency (EPA), 90, 270
Equity, 257, 292
Erickson, R., 43
Expressways, 16–18, 147

F

Federal-Aid Highway Act (1956), 15, 97, 128
Federal-Aid Highway Amendments Act of 1974, 128
Federal Aid Urban Systems (FAUS), 89
Federal Community Development Block Grant, 66, 298
Federal government
  classifying of programs, 234–237
  home ownership, 159–160
  housing recommendations, 273–274
  housing roles in, 157–158
  land use regulations, 66–68
  planning mandates and Chicago response, 166–168

Federal government *(continued)*
  policy in 1960s/1970s, 162–165
  rental assistance programs, 160–162
  spatially related programs, 239–241
  spending estimates, 229–231, 249–251
  urbanized area expenditures, 237–239
Federal highway legislation, 97–99
Federal Home Loan Mortgage Corporation (Freddie Mac), 159
Federal Housing Administration (FHA), 15, 159, 164, 230
Federal National Mortgage Association (Fannie Mae), 159, 277
Federal Transit Administration (FTA), 89
Federal transit legislation, 88–90
Federal urban redevelopment policies, 15–16
Felsenstein, Daniel, 207, 269
Follain, James R., 160
Ford administration, 165
Fort Dearborn, 3, 7
Foster, K., 294
Freeway revolt, 139
Freight transportation, 115
  railroads and, 108–110

G

Gasoline taxes, 280–281
Gautreaux litigation, 167
G.I. Bill, 16
Giuliano, G., 184
Global positioning system (GPS), 27
Gordon, P., 256
Government efficiency, 257
Gross domestic product (GDP), 119
Gyourko, Joseph, 160

H

Half-ring pattern, 31
Heckman, J., 204

Helsley, R.W., 201
High-tech corridor (I-88/I-94), 78, 208, 210, 212–213, 216–217, 219, 222–223
High technology activity
 alternative scenarios and, 220–222
 employment deconcentration and, 208–213
 employment effects, 215–217
 index of technological potential, 209–211
 land consumption and, 207, 218–220
 methodology of study, 213–215
 metropolitan areas, 211
 place of residence and, 217–218
Highway Trust Fund, 281–282, 301
Highways, 97–106, 112, 190, 230, 245
 completion dates of major expressways, 100
 construction projects (since 1970), 99–100
 federal legislation, 97–99
 history of, 99–100
 sprawl and, 100–101, 103–104
 TEA21 legislation, 90, 97–98, 149, 151, 153, 273, 279, 281
 travel behavior and, 106–108
Home Insurance Building, 9
HOME Investment Partnership Act (1990), 161, 271, 274
Home mortgages, 230
Home Owners Loan Corporation, 159
Home-rule provisions, 63–66
Home ownership, 159–160
Household formation, 168–169, 173
Housing
 density and land consumption, 172–173
 employer-assisted housing, 276–278
 federal government and, 159–160
  policy in 1960s/1970s, 162–165
 home builders/developers, 170–172
 policy recommendations, 271–278, 297–299

Housing *(continued)*
 region's housing patterns, 168–173
 rental assistance programs/vouchers, 160–162, 274–275
 state's role in, 165–166
 white flight and, 169–170
Housing Acts of 1949, 15
Housing Acts of 1954, 15
Housing element, 166
Housing policy, smart growth agenda, 173–179
Housing subsidy, 245–246, 274–275
Housing and Urban Development (HUD), 88, 162–164, 166, 264, 271, 274–275, 278
Huntley, Illinois, 78–80

I

I-88 (high-tech corridor), 78, 208, 210, 212–213, 216–217, 219, 222
I-94 (high-tech corridor), 208, 210, 212–213, 217, 219, 222–223
I-355 corridor, 34, 36–37, 144, 146, 152
Illinois Department of Transportation (IDOT), 137, 146, 150
Illinois FIRST (1999), 111–112, 279, 283
Illinois Housing Development Authority (IHDA), 165–166
Illinois and Michigan Canal, 4–6, 11–12
Illinois Open Land Trust Act, 65
Illinois State Toll Highway Authority (ISTHA), 17, 100, 138, 147
Immergluck, D., 232
Impact fees, 62, 81–85, 295
Inclusionary zoning, 275–276, 299
Income taxes, 245–246, 287, 303
Industrial development, 10, 183, 186, 192
 post-1990, 195
 spatial patterns of, 189–193
Industry decentralization, 117–118

Infill process, 152
Inner-ring suburbs, 21
Inner suburbs, 232
Inside Game/Outside Game (Rusk), 275
Intelligent Transportation Systems (ITS), 90
Intergovernmental aid, 245
Intergovernmental Planning Act, 148
Intergovernmental relationships, land use regulations, 66–68, 148
Intermodal Surface Transportation Efficiency Act (ISTEA), 89–90, 130, 141–142, 149, 151, 153, 279
Intermodal traffic, 129–131
Internal Improvement Act (1837), 4
Interstate Commerce Commission (ICC), 108–109
Interstate Highway System, 97, 112, 278
Interstate Transfer Funds (ITF), 89

J

Jefferson, Thomas, 3
Jenny, William LeBaron, 9
Johnson, Elmer W., 175
Joint planning, 68–69, 71–73
The Jungle (Sinclair), 11

K

Kay, M.J., 128
Klutznick, Philip M., 22
Kornhauser, A., 128
Kurban, Haydar, 228

L

Lake Michigan, 12–13, 146
Lake Shore Drive, 16
Land absorption
 defined, 228
 federal programs and, 241–242

Land absorption *(continued)*
 state subsidies and, 246–248
Land resource management, joint planning for, 68–69, 71–73
Land use policies
 in 1871–1945 years, 12–13
 collaboration on annexations, 265–266
 divided responsibilities for, 148–149
 employer-assisted housing, 276–277
 employer incentives, 269–270
 high technology industry, 216–220
 impact fees and, 261–262
 incentives for, 263–265
 inclusionary zoning, 275–276
 infrastructure investments, 266–268
 motor carrier industry and, 119, 122–124
 NIPC's plans, 145–146
 open space/development rights, 268–269
 overconsumption subsidies, 22–273
 recommendations for, 260–270, 295–297
 trucking activities and, 116–117
Land use regulations, 62
 government powers, 66–68
 home-rule provisions, 63–65
 Illinois Open Land Trust Act, 65–66
 intergovernmental relationships, 66–68
 1970 Constitution, 63–65
 state level policies, 65–66
 tools of, 62
Land use tools, 68–84
 annexation, 62, 73–76, 81–84
 boundary agreements, 68
 impact fees, 62, 81–84
 joint planning, 68–69, 71–73
 municipal boundary agreements, 62–63, 69–71
Landstat Program, 25–26, 31, 40, 289–290
Lee, K., 201–202

318 INDEX

Lester, Thomas W., 228, 259
Lindstrom, Bonnie, 3, 135, 256, 258, 266, 272
Local governments, scope of powers of, 63–65
Local Land Resource Management Planning Act, 72, 148
Loop elevated line, 9–10, 95
Low income housing, 274–275
Low Income Housing Tax Credit, 161
Luce, T.F., Jr., 43

M

McCormick, Cyrus, 5
McCurdy, K., 209–210
McDonald, John F., 182–185, 271, 296
McGuire, T.J., 42–43, 256, 264, 284–285
McMillen, Daniel P., 182–185, 271, 286
Markusen, A., 209–210
Maryland's Smart Growth Initiatives, 267
Mass transit, 16, 111–112
  in 1871–1945 years, 9–11
  development of, 9–11
  policy recommendations, 282–283
Metropolis 2020 organization, 175–178, 259, 264, 278
Metropolitan Mayors Caucus, 150
Metropolitan Planning Council (MPC), 150, 174–177
Metropolitan planning organization (MPO), 123, 135–136, 148
Metropolitan Sanitary District of Greater Chicago, 20
Metropolitan statistical areas (MSAs), 45, 51, 57, 210
Midway Airport, 19, 95, 144
Mieszkowski, P., 44
Mills, E.S., 43–44
Monocentric model, 209
Morris, A.G., 128

Motor Carrier Act (MCA) of 1980, 124–128
Motor carrier industry, 115
  conclusions and recommendations for, 132–133
  congestion levels and, 120–122
  decentralization of industry and, 117–118, 132
  deregulation of, 124–128
  general trends in, 117–119
  growth of, 122
  intermodal traffic and, 129–131
  land use and, 116–117, 119, 122–124
  less-than truckload (LTL), 125
  Motor Carrier Act of 1980, 124–128
  newer trucking operations and, 129–131
  niche carriers, 129
  policy recommendations for, 283–284
  public sector policies and, 122–124
  stakeholders of, 115–116
  truck load (TL) freight, 125
  truck size and weight policies, 128–129
Municipal boundary agreements, 69–71
Municipalities, 232
  changes in boundaries, 37–39
  land use plans, 67
Munneke, H.J., 201

N

National Association of Home Builders (NAHB), 179
National Highway System (NHS), 131
Natural communities, 31, 34
Navy Pier, 19
Ndikumwami, A., 215
1980 Transportation Study, 139–140
1995 Transportation System Plan, 140–141
1970 Constitution, 63–65
Nixon administration, 165
North Central Line, 149

Northeast Illinois Rail Corporation (NIRC), 92
Northeastern Illinois Planning Commission (NIPC), 39, 65, 135, 137–138, 142, 152, 185, 266
  financial vulnerability of, 149–150
  housing and, 166–168
  implementation authority, 146–148
  land use and water resource plans, 145–146
  managed regional development, 148
  policy recommendations for, 288–289
  proposals to change mandates, 150–151
  Regional Residential Policy Plan, 167
  smart growth agenda, 173–174

O

Oak Brook, 166–167, 210
O'Hare Airport, 19, 21–22, 95, 141, 144, 152, 183, 187, 189, 193, 196, 199–201, 221, 223
Olmsted, Frederick Law, 11
1.5-mile planning boundaries, 68–69, 74
Open communities, 164–165
Open space, 268–269, 296
Orfield, M., 43, 232
Orlebeke, Charles J., 157, 258, 271
Otis elevator, 9
Outer suburbs, 232

P

P/A ratio, 37–38
Panic of 1837, 4
Park Forest, 22
Parker, R. Andrew, 231
Peddle, M., 262
Persky, J., 228, 257, 259, 268, 271–272
Philip, James "Pate," 148
Planned communities, 11
Planning agencies, strengths and weaknesses of, 146–151

Planning agreements, 84
Polycentric development, 208
Population changes, 37
Population decentralization, sprawl and, 101–103
Population density, 51
Population growth, 6–7, 102–103
Porter, Douglas R., 289
Potawatomi Indians, 3
Preliminary Comprehensive City Plan of 1946, 16–17
Price, R., 44
Primary metropolitan statistical areas (PMSAs), 45, 48, 51, 55
Property taxes, 42–43, 189, 285–287, 303
  in 1970–1980 and 1990 analysis, 54–56
  sprawl and, 44–54
Public sector policies, motor carrier industry, 122–124
Public transit, 245
Public works, in 1830–1870 Chicago, 6–7
Pullman, George, 10

Q

Quality of life issues, 257
Quigley, J., 201

R

Railroads, 5, 108–110, 113, 129–130, 302
  in 1871–1945 years, 9–11
  intermodal policies, 131–132
Ranney, George A., Jr., 175
Real estate development
  data on, 185–186
  modeling allocation of new sites, 201–204
  spatial patterns of, 182–183
Regional econometric model (REMI model), 214, 219

Regional forecasts and plans; *see also* Northeastern Illinois Planning Commission (NIPC)
  1962–1998 overview, 138–146
  1980 Transportation Study, 139–140
  1995 Transportation Study, 140–141
  policy recommendations for, 290–291, 304–305
  2020 Regional Transportation Plan, 130–131, 135, 141–145
Regional planning agencies
  financial vulnerability of, 149–150
  in northeastern Illinois, 135–136
Regional Rail Reorganization Act of 1973, 109
Regional Transportation Authority (RTA), 92–95, 111, 146, 288
Rental assistance programs, 160–162
Rental vouchers, 274–275, 298
Residential commuter suburbs, 21
Residential development; *see also* Housing
  land absorption and, 228
  post-1990 development, 197
  spatial patterns of, 196–200
Revenue sharing, 286–287, 303
Richardson, H.W., 256
Richmond, H.R., 43
Risk, David, 275
Road capacity, 121
Road impact fees, 82
Romney, George, 162–163, 165
Rosenthal, S.R., 201
Ryan, George, 65, 176, 271

S

St. Lawrence Seaway (all-water link), 19–20
Sanitary District of Chicago (1889), 11, 13, 20
Satellite cities, 76–77
Schaffer, Kimberley, 256
Schools, 42

Schools *(continued)*
  in 1970–1980 and 1990 analysis, 54–55
  funding recommendations, 284–285, 302
  sprawl and, 44–54
  state aid, 49
Section 8 program, 274
Sewage
  in 1871–1945 years, 11–12
  in 1945–1970 years, 20
  treatment technology, 12
Shukla, V., 201
Sinclair, Upton, 11
Skidmore, M., 262
Skokie, 21
Skyscrapers, 9
Slum removal, 15
Small, K., 184
Smart growth agenda, 157, 173–179, 267
Smart Growth Task Force, 66
South Suburban Airport, 144
Sprawl; *see also* Annexation; Land use policies
  in 1970–1980 and 1990 analysis, 54–55
  competitiveness, 257
  congestion and, 104–106
  definitions of, 42–43, 256
  environment and, 257
  equity and, 257
  federal policy in 1960s/1970s, 162–165
  fiscal policy recommendations for, 284–287
  government efficiency, 257
  high technology and, 207, 214–215
  highways and highway use, 100–101, 103–104
  land use decisions and, 62
  new empirical evidence on, 44–54
  opposition to, 257
  population decentralization and, 101–103
  prosperity and, 101–103

INDEX 321

Sprawl *(continued)*
  quality of life issues and, 257
  regression analysis of, 44–54
    data appendix, 57–59
  state's role in, 165–166
  transportation policies and, 279
Staggers Rail Act, 109, 131
State aid, 49
State government
  education spending, 244–245
  highway spending, 245
  housing subsidy, 245–246
  intergovernmental aid, 245
  intrametropolitan spending, 242–244
  land use regulations, 65–66
  municipalities, 67
  peripheral land absorption, 246–248
  public transit, 245
  spending estimates, 251–253
  township governments, 66
Steel-frame skyscrapers, 9
Storm water management
  in 1871–1945 years, 11–12
  in 1945–1970 years, 20
Stratton, William, 137
Streetcar Suburbs (Warner), 278
Suburban communities, 186
  in 1870s, 10
  in 1950s, 21
  in 1960s, 21
  county boundaries, 232
  development in 1945–1970 years, 20–22
  ecosystem impact, 31, 34
  inner/outer dichotomy, 232–233
  natural communities impact, 31, 34
  planned communities, 11
  post-1990 development, 197
  spatial patterns of, 196–200
Suburban employment centers, 182, 184–185
Suburbanization
  federal spending on, 229–231

Suburbanization *(continued)*
  flight from blight, 44
  inner-ring suburbs, 21
  natural evolution theory, 44
  patterns of, 21
  residential commuter suburbs, 21
Subway system, 17
Surface transportation, 88
Surface Transportation Board, 109
Surface Transportation Program (STP), 137

T

Taxes; *see also* Property taxes
  gasoline taxes, 280–281
  income taxes, 245–246, 287, 303
Technology pole, 210
Technology and public works, in 1830–1870 Chicago, 6–7
Templeton, Jean M., 62, 261, 265
Thakuriah, Piyushimita, 115, 118, 283
Toll highway system, 17
Township governments, land use plans, 66
Tract housing, 16
Transit system, 111–112
  in 1970s, 90–93
  in 1980s, 93
  annual ridership statistics, 96
  expansion of service, 94–97
  FAST plan, 95
  federal legislation, 88–90
  government subsidies, 97
  history of, 90–94
  private funding recommendations, 279–280
Transportation Equity Act for the 21st Century (TEA21), 90, 149, 151, 153, 273, 279, 281
Transportation infrastructure, 17, 138
  in 1945–1970 years, 16–20, 152
  1980 Transportation Study, 139–140

Transportation infrastructure (*continued*)
  1995 Transportation System Plan, 140–141
  2020 Regional Transportation Plan, 141–145
  divided responsibility for, 148–149
  national regulatory environment for, 153
  policy recommendations, 278–284, 300–302
  surface transportation, 88
Travel behavior
  travel demand and, 112–113
  trip chains, 107–108, 112
  trip length and duration, 106–107
Trip chains, 107–108, 112
Trip length and duration, 106–107
Truck size and weight policies, 128–129
Trucking. *See* Motor carrier industry
Tunnel and Reservoir Plan (TARP), 20
2020 Regional Transportation Plan, 130–131, 135, 141–145, 150, 153–154
Typhoid, 11

U

U.S. Department of Commerce, 139
U.S. Department of Transportation (DOT), 89, 136, 167
U.S. General Accounting Office, 160
U.S. Geological Survey, 27
Universal Transverse Mercator (UTM) map coordinate system, 26
Urban areas, federal government expenditures, 237–239
Urban Growth and New Community Development Act (1970), 163
Urban land change, 25–27, 39–40
  county-level change, 28–31
  I-355 corridor, 34, 36–37
  methods of study, 26–27
  northeastern Illinois study (1972–1997), 25
  regional change, 27–29
  spatial pattern of urban land cover change, 31–32, 34–37
Urban Mass Transit Act, 140
Urban Mass Transit Administration (UMTA), 89, 140
Urban redevelopment policies, federal programs, 15–16
Urban sprawl. *See* Sprawl

V

Value pricing, 281, 300
Vehicle miles traveled (VMT), 103, 105, 115, 120, 122–123, 126, 129
Voith, Richard, 160

W

Waddell, P., 201
Wang, Y.Q., 25, 256, 260
Warner, S.B., 278
Wasylenko, M., 43
Water resource plans, NIPC's plans, 145–146
Welfare-to-work vouchers, 275
White flight, 169–170, 237
Wiewel, Wim, 256–257

Z

Zhang, T.W., 271
Zoning/subdivision regulations, 67, 275–276, 299

ENNIS AND NANCY HAM LIBRARY
ROCHESTER COLLEGE
800 WEST AVON ROAD
ROCHESTER HILLS, MI 48307